ROYAL HISTORICAL SOCIETY

STUDIES IN HISTORY

New Series

LOLLARDY AND ORTHODOX RELIGION IN PRE-REFORMATION ENGLAND

RECONSTRUCTING PIETY

Alabaster carving of the Resurrection from St Mildred's church, Tenterden

LOLLARDY AND ORTHODOX RELIGION
IN PRE-REFORMATION ENGLAND
RECONSTRUCTING PIETY

Robert Lutton

THE ROYAL HISTORICAL SOCIETY
THE BOYDELL PRESS

First published 2006
The Royal Historical Society, London
in association with
The Boydell Press, Woodbridge
Reprinted in paperback and transferred to digital printing 2011
The Boydell Press, Woodbridge

ISBN 97 0 86193 283 2 hardback
ISBN 978 1 84383 649 0 paperback

The Boydell Press is an imprint of Boydell & Brewer Ltd
PO Box 9, Woodbridge, Suffolk IP12 3DF, UK
and of Boydell & Brewer Inc,
668 Mt Hope Avenue, Rochester, NY 14620, USA
website: www.boydellandbrewer.com

A CIP catalogue record for this book is available
from the British Library

This publication is printed on acid-free paper

Contents

List of Figures

List of Maps

List of Plates

List of Tables

With so many possible mediations, distortions and constraints, can these massive and poor documents be anything more, finally, than the reflection of the social pressure or conventions of the moment? By the same token, will the very weakness of these serial studies of the traces not be such as to leave us on the surface of things, confined to a superficial and generalized understanding which is limited to appearances? And can we really hope, on such a basis, to approach a phenomenon as secret as faith?

M. Vovelle, *Ideologies and mentalities* (1982), Cambridge 1990, 20.

FOR SARAH, WITH LOVE

Publication of this volume was aided by a generous grant from the Scouloudi Foundation, in association with the Institute of Historical Research.

Acknowledgements

This book would never have reached completion without the many individuals and institutions that have generously offered me assistance, advice and support. To all the friends and colleagues, too numerous to mention here, who have encouraged me along the way I would like to express my most heartfelt thanks.

The personnel of The British Library, London, St Paul's Cathedral Library, London, The Public Record Office, at Chancery Lane and at Kew, the Templeman Library at the University of Kent and, in particular, the staffs of Canterbury Cathedral Archive, the Centre for Kentish Studies, Maidstone, and Lambeth Palace Library, London, have been exemplary in their generosity and efficiency in dealing with my enquiries and allowing me to inspect items from their collections.

Parts of chapters 1, 4 and 5 have been prefigured in essays published in M. Aston and C. Richmond (eds), *Lollardy and the gentry in the later Middle Ages* (Stroud–New York 1997), and in I. Davis, M. Muller and S. Rees (eds), *Love, marriage, and family ties in the later Middle Ages* (London 1959), and I acknowledge Sutton Publishing and Brepols for permitting me to use copyright material in a revised and abbreviated form here.

This book began as a PhD undertaken at the University of Kent and I am most grateful for three successive Colyer Fergusson travel grants, administered by the University. I also had the privilege of receiving a British Academy Major Award without which I would not have been able to embark on a doctorate.

The Centre for Medieval and Tudor Studies at the University of Kent provided inspiration, endless opportunities for exchange and a comforting home and continues to play a major part in my intellectual development. I can only hope that its recently threatened closure does not materialise. It would be a tragic and unjust loss if it did. I owe an enormous debt of thanks to numerous colleagues at the Centre for their encouragement and readiness to engage in discussion over the years. Sheila Sweetinburgh and Paul Lee have been particularly generous in this regard, not least by allowing me to draw on and make reference to material from their own doctoral researches here. I would also like to thank Elisabeth Salter for reminding me that this book is just one stage in a longer journey.

I spent part of the time writing my PhD teaching in the History Department at the University of Manchester and I would like to thank the staff there for their interest in my research and, in particular, Richard Davies for his rigorous comments on sections of my thesis.

I have benefited immeasurably from being able to present and discuss earlier versions of parts of this book at the Medieval and Tudor Studies Seminar and the School of History Seminar at the University of Kent, Joint Canterbury and York postgraduate conferences, the 'M6 Seminar' at Manchester, the Lollardy and Gentry Conference at Newnham College, Cambridge, the Ecclesiastical History Summer Conference, London Medieval Society colloquia and the International Medieval Congress.

My colleagues at the London College of Fashion have provided valuable assistance by allowing me to take time to bring this book to completion and I would like to thank them for showing a genuine interest in my ongoing obsession with piety and for recognising the importance of scholarly endeavour amidst the busyness of working life.

Andrew Hope has kindly offered much worthwhile advice and assistance on a whole range of subjects and Michael Zell provided helpful thoughts and information on Tenterden's economic development. I would like to thank Saul Kitchen for his generous and expert help in producing the maps, David Hardy for his enthusiastic assistance with the cover illustration, and Gill Draper for kindly supplying information on the topography of the Kentish Weald and Walland Marsh.

This book has been shaped by the judicious comments of my PhD examiners, Margaret Aston and Ken Fincham. They both encouraged me to see it published, and I am extremely grateful for their input and support.

I would also like to thank the Royal Historical Society for offering to publish this book. The months that I first predicted it would take to reach completion have become years and I would like to convey my sincerest thanks to my advisory editors Steve Gunn and Alex Walsham. They have read and re-read chapters and have never faltered in their patience, efficiency, and thoroughness. Their countless insightful suggestions have made this an immeasurably better book and the final stages of writing it an immensely stimulating and pleasurable experience. I would also like to thank Christine Linehan for her meticulous proof reading of sections of the text and for dealing with my many naïve questions regarding the technicalities of bringing a book to completion.

I owe my greatest intellectual debt to my supervisor, Andrew Butcher. His influence on this book has been profound and, despite its limitations (for which I am solely responsible), I hope it repays some of the time and effort he has invested in it. Without Andrew's prompting I would never have undertaken a research degree and his vast, but never overbearing, knowledge and unstinting commitment to intellectual life remain a constant source of inspiration. Perhaps even more important, he has never failed to realise that encouragement is the greatest spur to achievement. For all this I thank him with the deepest appreciation.

Finally, my family have patiently and lovingly shared the joys and despairs of writing this book. They have known when, and when not, to ask 'how is the book going?' and have never doubted that I would finally get there in the end. I cannot thank them enough for all their help and support, both moral and practical. My wife, Sarah, more than anyone else, has lived through the ups and downs of my endeavours. For giving me perspective, for being there and for always believing I thank her with the greatest affection.

Robert Lutton

Abbreviations

AC	*Archaeologia Cantiana*
AgHR	*Agricultural History Review*
AM	John Foxe, *Actes and monuments of these latter and perillous dayes*, London 1583
BIHR	*Bulletin of the Institute of Historical Research*
C&C	*Continuity and Change*
CCA	Canterbury Cathedral Archive
CCR	*Calendar of close rolls*
CKS	Centre for Kentish Studies
CPR	*Calendar of patent rolls*
DNB	*Dictionary of national biography*
EcHR	*Economic History Review*
ECP	*Early Chancery Proceedings*
EETS	Early English Text Society
EHR	*English Historical Review*
JEH	*Journal of Ecclesiastical History*
HMC	Royal Commission on Historical Manuscripts
HWJ	*History Workshop Journal*
KR	*Kent Archaeological Society: Kent Records*
LPL	Lambeth Palace Library
L&P	*Letters and papers, foreign and domestic, of the reign of Henry VIII*, 1509–47, ed. J. S. Brewer and others, London 1862–1932
PCC	Prerogative court of Canterbury
P&P	*Past and Present*
SCH	Studies in Church History
SH	*Southern History*
TNA, PRO	Public Record Office
TRHS	*Transactions of the Royal Historical Society*
VCH, Kent	*The Victoria history of the county of Kent*, ii, ed. W. Page, London 1926

Note on the Text

All quotations from contemporary manuscript and printed works retain original spelling except for money sums for which arabic equivalents for all roman numbers and modern symbols for pounds, shillings and pence are used. Modern spellings of place names are followed outside quotations and standard abbreviations and contractions have been silently expanded in citations from manuscript sources. Apart from in quotations, spelling of personal and family names has been standardised for the sake of clarity. All dates are based on the year beginning 1 January.

Prologue

On 26 September 1511 Archbishop William Warham's visitation to the deanery of Charing in the diocese of Canterbury received the presentments from the churchwardens and other lay officers of the parish of Tenterden on the edge of the Weald of Kent. They reported various items of concern and neglect among which were the following linked accusations: 'Johan Frank with diverse other eville disposid persones use in the tyme of divine service to be in the churcheyard comenyng & talking and many other use to sitt stille in the churche atte processione tyme'.[1] John Franke of Tenterden was examined under charges of heresy and abjured officially erroneous opinions on the eucharist, pilgrimage and images a month before this on 16 August 1511. He was one of fifty-three suspects who shared opinions that can be characterised as Wycliffite in origin investigated between April 1511 and June 1512 by Warham and a high-ranking team of officials. Almost half of those tried for heresy lived in Tenterden or one of its neighbouring parishes.[2] The record of Warham's investigation into heresy in the Kentish Weald and other parts of East Kent firmly supports the importance of Tenterden as a major Lollard centre.

In response to these freshly reported allegations John Franke admitted that he had, on occasion, walked in the churchyard during divine service as well as sometimes in the morning between masses 'but not habitually'. He was ordered to remain in church during services. It is perhaps significant that none of his perambulating accomplices were named in the presentment. The heresy trials were well under way by September 1511 and five suspects who were judged to be long-standing ringleaders and who failed to make adequate recantations had been handed over to the secular authorities and in all probability had already been burned for their heresies. The impact of these events on the parishioners of Tenterden cannot be underestimated and a reluctance to see any more of their neighbours go to the stake may have underpinned the vagueness of the phrase 'other eville disposid persones'. However, whether or not these persons also held Lollard views and were discussing such matters in the churchyard with Franke is one of a number of questions that remain unanswered by this book but which continue to provoke and inspire investigation.

---

[1] *Kentish visitations of Archbishop William Warham and his deputies, 1511–12*, ed. K. L. Wood-Legh (KR xxiv, 1984), 207–10.

[2] For a full analysis of the 1511–12 trials see pp. 154–71 below.

Another even more intriguing question concerns the equally vague but far more perplexing accusation that 'many other use to sitt stille in the churche atte processione tyme'. The inference is that these were different people from those who would gather outside the church, that they were considerable in number and that through their actions, or rather their inaction, they were making an audacious statement about the ways in which collective religious ritual and practice should or should not be conducted. Perhaps these people were Lollards or Lollard sympathisers. Then again perhaps they were neither. This last possibility has enormous implications for the nature of orthodoxy in Tenterden and provides an ideal point of departure for this book. I initially chose to write about Tenterden because of its place in a tradition of Kentish Lollard heresy dating from the early fifteenth to the early sixteenth century, but as I began to investigate the evidence I realised that in order to do justice to the rich variety of orthodox as well as heterodox piety in Tenterden it would have to be a much wider study. As a result it is principally concerned with the changing nature of orthodoxy at Tenterden as well as with the significance of Lollardy.

This book is, therefore, about the ordinary, and in some cases not-so-ordinary, people of Tenterden and their pieties, whether heterodox or orthodox. It is an unashamedly local study that contextualises piety through the detailed reconstruction of religious beliefs and practices, ways of life, family and kinship, social and political networks and material culture. In taking this approach it has something in common with one of the most influential and acclaimed studies of piety in England in the sixteenth century to emerge in recent years, Eamon Duffy's *The voices of Morebath*.[3] Like Duffy's book, this is a detailed investigation of piety in a single parish based on the close reading of local documentary evidence. However, my book differs from *Morebath* in a number of important ways and represents a new departure in the reconstruction of piety in local 'communities'.

Tenterden and Morebath were very different kinds of places. By any standards Tenterden was a large parish, with a sizeable population, scattered settlement and rapidly developing proto-industrial urban core and a handful of independently-minded satellite centres. A small-to-medium sized country town, it had its own weekly market and borough court and played an important role as a regional centre for redistributive trade in Kent and the south-east, and through its position on the river Rother and close ties to the Sussex Cinque Port of Rye, was actively engaged in seaborne trade with the continent. Tenterden lies some twenty miles from Canterbury and fifteen miles from Maidstone from where it is only another thirty miles to London. It is ten miles from the South Kent and East Sussex coast. Morebath, in contrast, was a relatively remote rural parish with a population a mere fraction of the

---

3 Eamon Duffy, *The voices of Morebath: reformation and rebellion in an English village*, New Haven–London 2001.

size of Tenterden's, little specialised industry and a marginal role in local and regional trade. Whereas Morebath was relatively socially homogeneous in the sixteenth century the gap between rich and poor in Tenterden was increasingly pronounced by 1500, and the town was home to some very rich merchant traders, craftsmen, graziers and farmers as well as a number of local and county gentry households and one important noble dynasty. Tenterden was also culturally rich with its own grammar school from around 1510 and at least one intellectually distinguished pre-Reformation humanist vicar.[4] All of these factors ensured that the religious cultures of Morebath and Tenterden were profoundly different in nature and development. They serve also as a cautionary reminder that the English parish is not necessarily a meaningfully comparable unit of analysis for the study of piety.

My book differs also from *Morebath* in evidence and method. Duffy's study is built upon his close reading and analysis of a remarkable and almost unique document: the Morebath churchwardens' accounts that were kept by the parish's extraordinary vicar, Sir Christopher Trychay, from around 1520 to 1574. Duffy draws on a range of other evidence but Trychay's manuscript is absolutely central to his book. Tenterden, on the other hand, has no surviving churchwardens' accounts. There are very few last wills and testaments for Morebath and, according to Duffy, those that do survive reveal nothing surprising about the piety of its parishioners.[5] In marked contrast, testamentary evidence survives in rich and diverse abundance for Tenterden and it is this material, in conjunction with a wide range of other evidence, including visitation presentments, proceedings against heresy, property deeds, taxation returns and municipal materials, that forms the basis of this reconstruction of the pieties of a substantial section of the parish's residents. The consequences of this evidential contrast are profound. Duffy's study not surprisingly emphasises the centrality of the parish and parochial institutions in religious life and, whilst the churchwardens' accounts reveal that the realities of everyday life fell far short of the harmonious ideal sought by Trychay, Morebath's piety is portrayed as the collective piety of the parish as a whole.[6] Partly because of differences in the nature of the surviving evidence and partly because of the very different nature of piety in Tenterden I have adopted a number of units of analysis in addition to the parish. These include locality and neighbourhood and, most importantly, family, kinship and social group.

These contrasting approaches provide starkly conflicting impressions of not only the form and substance of pre-Reformation English religious culture but of the nature of piety itself, the importance of the parish church and parish-centred institutions *vis-à-vis* other religious institutions in religious life, how piety was formed, shaped and transmitted and the relationship

---

4 For Morebath see ibid. 1–16; for Tenterden see pp. 26–37 below.
5 Duffy, *Voices of Morebath*, pp. xiii, 68.
6 Ibid. chs iii, iv.

between individual and collective pieties. Whereas Duffy asserts that through Trychay's manuscript 'all the voices of Morebath are one voice' and that 'the people of Morebath and their priest' shared a collective regional and parochial 'religion', the pious voices of Tenterden, inscribed in a wide range of evidence, became increasingly discordant in the decades before the Reformation; more a cacophony than a 'chorus'.[7] This was only partly due to the presence and influence of Lollard ideas and was largely a consequence of the increasing heterogeneity of Tenterden's orthodox piety in the late fifteenth and early sixteenth centuries before the years of dramatic religious reform under Henry VIII and Edward VI.

In this, as in many other ways, this book therefore runs against the grain of the now dominant school of thought on the nature of pre-Reformation piety in England and the impact of the Reformation. It would do a disservice to the people of Tenterden and the intellectual and emotional variety of their piety to describe their religion on the eve of the Reformation as forming part of an English 'Catholic world-view'. Duffy rightly states that the negative and hostile reactions of Morebath's priest and parishioners to reform cannot be seen as typical and admits that other centres responded very differently to the Protestant message. Nevertheless, *Morebath* supports his very influential thesis that pre-Reformation religious culture was intellectually and culturally coherent across the social spectrum, universal and largely homogeneous and that most people in most places did not welcome reform.[8]

This book is intended to challenge the grip exerted by this dominant paradigm and to contribute to the collective re-evaluation of the frameworks and approaches used in the study of late medieval and early-modern piety. For Duffy the Reformation 'inexorably dismantled the structures of Morebath's corporate life',[9] whereas for the people of Tenterden corporate life was not so all-encompassing nor their piety so enmeshed with those aspects of religious life and parochial institutions that were swept away by reform as to make the Reformation such a devastating blow. It was certainly a dramatic new turn, but only one in a series of episodes and processes by which piety was successively restructured and in which the people of Tenterden themselves played an active role.

---

[7] Ibid. 17, 46, 68–71, xv.
[8] Ibid. p. xiv. For a fuller discussion of the recent historiography see pp. 7–11 below.
[9] Ibid. ch. vi, p. xiii.

1

Method and Theory in the Reconstruction of Piety in Late Medieval England

Reconstructing the piety of the ordinary inhabitant of late medieval England has become a major historical enterprise and, in recent years, an increasingly important historiographical field in its own right. Interest in lay piety grew chiefly out of Reformation studies, as the evidence of pre-Reformation orthodoxy and heterodoxy was sifted for answers to questions concerning the series of major changes in the practice and articulation of faith in the sixteenth century.[1] Whilst research into late medieval lay piety remains closely tied to Reformation studies, due to developments over the last two decades or so it has emerged boldly from its shadow. However, the prolific growth in studies of religious belief and practice, while very welcome, has been accompanied by a considerable degree of theoretical naivety and absence of reflection on method. Perhaps it is because of the relative novelty of the field that there remains a comparative absence of attention to the theories and methods that have underpinned the reconstruction of piety. This is all the more surprising given the recent revisionist shift in approaches to orthodox religion and the considerable impact this continues to have upon interpretation of the English Reformation.[2] It is with an acute awareness of this absence that this study begins by critically examining past approaches in order to suggest ways to address more adequately the theoretical and methodological problems that beset the study of piety. Subsequent chapters will apply and test methods outlined, in abstract, in the first. In this sense, this book is not a conventional study of late medieval lay piety but is, in part, a provocation to fellow practitioners to develop more sensitive ways of working with notoriously difficult source material.

Also distinguishing what follows from the conventional model is a preoccupation with the relationships and boundaries between orthodox and heterodox pieties. It ought to be self-evident that a proper understanding of the appeal of heresy depends upon the apprehension of its relationship to the established beliefs and practices of those who adopted or were touched by it. Equally, the close contextualisation of dissent has the potential to offer illu-

---

[1] For example B. L. Manning, *The people's faith in the time of Wyclif*, Cambridge 1919; A. G. Dickens, *The English Reformation*, London–Glasgow 1964, 2nd edn, London 1989.
[2] D. Aers, 'Altars of power: reflections on Eamon Duffy's *The stripping of the altars: traditional religion in England, 1400–1580*', *Literature & History* 3rd ser. iii (1994), 90–1.

minating insights into the changing nature of orthodox religion.[3] There remains a pressing need to explain how and why heresy and dissent were attractive and survived in certain regions and centres.[4] I have, therefore, attempted to subject representations of heterodoxy and orthodoxy to close comparison in order to explore the conjunctions and discontinuities between different 'discourse communities', which formed competing but also complementary aspects of late medieval piety.[5]

The subject of this study is broader than religion or, indeed, 'religiosity'. Furthermore, although 'devotion' and 'spirituality' were important elements within piety these terms do not sufficiently describe or define it.[6] 'Piety' is a necessarily flexible and broad term and is used here to describe the range of attitudes, doctrines, emotions, identities and practices explored in the following chapters. It is not so laden with the debates, theories and judgements about the relationship between elite and popular cultural forms, or the problems of social location, which dog the term 'popular religion'.[7] It has an advantage, also, over 'traditional religion' which, despite arguments to the contrary, fails to allow room for development, change and diversity in the interpretation and appropriation of late medieval religion.[8] Piety was more than the sum of the religious mores of an individual or group. It included attitudes and sentiments, not all of which can be categorised as religious, which had a strong bearing upon religious practice. Late medieval religious life was as much influenced by convention, fashion and social expectation as by spirituality,[9] and the various and often competing motives for pious action have equal historical validity.[10] Piety encompassed attitudes and actions towards family, kin, neighbours and associates; opinions about wealth and commerce; views about the nature and functions of the Church and religious life;

---

3   Contrast with R. Rex, *The Lollards*, Basingstoke–New York 2002, 149–50.

4   Aers, 'Altars of power', 102.

5   R. N. Swanson, *Religion and devotion in Europe, c. 1215–c. 1515*, Cambridge 1995, 9, 316.

6   Idem (ed.), *Catholic England: faith, religion and observance before the Reformation*, Manchester 1993, 1–3 at p. 1.

7   N. Z. Davis, 'Some tasks and themes in the study of popular religion', in C. Trinkhaus and H. Oberman, (eds), *The pursuit of holiness*, Leiden 1974, 307–36; C. Marsh, *Popular religion in sixteenth-century England*, Basingstoke–London 1998, 6–12. For some comments on these issues, which collapse the distinctions between elite and popular see E. Duffy, *The stripping of the altars: traditional religion in England, 1400–1580*, New Haven–London 1992, 1–3 and chs ii, iii, vi, vii, viii.

8   Duffy, *Altars*, 3; Aers, 'Altars of power', passim.

9   Swanson, *Catholic England*, 25, 30.

10   For a somewhat pre-judged approach to late medieval piety see F. R. H. Du Boulay, *An age of ambition: English society in the late Middle Ages*, London 1970, 147, 157. See also L. M. A. Higgs, 'Lay piety in the borough of Colchester, 1485–1558', unpubl. PhD diss. Michigan 1983, 40–1, 45–7, and N. Z. Davis, 'The sacred and the body social in sixteenth-century Lyon', *P&P* xc (1981), 40–70.

conceptions of the family, kinship and the wider community, and the social identities which individuals and groups fashioned for themselves out of available cultural (including religious) forms.[11]

Recent historiography

The historiographical shift which has led to the 'revisionist' perspective on the nature of late medieval piety, was most famously and influentially signalled by Eamon Duffy's *The stripping of the altars*, which helped to set a new agenda for the study of lay piety prior to the reforms of the sixteenth century. Duffy's chief concern was to liberate late medieval piety from a historiography which had seen it 'diminished to the status of a set on which the real drama of the Reformation was to take place' and to persuade his readers of the 'intrinsic interest and vitality of fifteenth- and early sixteenth-century English Catholicism'.[12] This marked the ascendancy of an approach that now dominates the subject and is well illustrated by Beat Kümin's study of the English parish in the fifteenth and sixteenth centuries. Taking the parish as his unit of analysis, and churchwardens' accounts as his major source, Kümin found that Catholic religion remained buoyant up until the last years of Henry VIII's reign, and that 'religious enthusiasm' and a 'late medieval boom in traditional religious activities' typified lay piety at a time of beneficial socio-economic circumstances. Lollardy could not prevent these developments; 'Lollard ideas had very little effect on everyday communal life' and, apart from 'the possibility of significant pockets of nonconformity, at least in certain areas . . . recent scholarship leaves little doubt that evangelical beliefs did not start to take root in local communities before the mid-1530s, and that it was a long and slow process to build anything like a Protestant culture'.[13] Similarly, others have argued that 'the ordinary religion of English parishes was in a vigorous and healthy state in the early sixteenth century', and, if anything, Catholic Christianity was undergoing consolidation.[14] The domi-

---

[11] Piety encompasses *pietas*, or family duty: J. Bossy, *Christianity in the west, 1400–1700*, Oxford 1985, 27; A. P. Cohen, *The symbolic construction of community*, Chichester 1985; M. Rubin, 'Small groups: identity and solidarity in the late Middle Ages', in J. Kermode (ed.), *Enterprise and individuals in fifteenth-century England*, Stroud 1991, 134. For a recent statement on the necessity to integrate the study of piety with analysis of popular politics see E. H. Shagan, *Popular politics and the English Reformation*, Cambridge 2003, 7–11.

[12] Duffy, *Altars*, 6.

[13] B. A. Kümin, *The shaping of a community: the rise and reformation of the English parish, c. 1400–1560*, Aldershot 1996, 136–7, 196–8, 257.

[14] C. Haigh, *English reformations: religion, politics, and society under the Tudors*, Oxford 1993, 25–39 at p. 39. See also, for example, J. J. Scarisbrick, *The Reformation and the English people*, Oxford 1984, 1–39; Rex, *Lollards*, chs i, iv, vi; R. Hutton, 'The local impact of the Tudor reformations', in C. Haigh (ed.), *The English Reformation revised*, Cambridge 1987, 114–38; D. M. Palliser, 'Popular reactions to the Reformation during the years of uncertainty, 1530–1570', in F. Heal and R. O'Day (eds), *Church and society in England: Henry VIII to*

nance of 'revisionism' is demonstrated by the fact that studies of the English Reformation now appear to accept Duffy's portrayal of 'traditional religion' as authoritative, if not axiomatic.[15]

One of the problems with these conclusions and the line of inquiry upon which they are based, is that the constituency responsible for the undeniably widespread and generous enhancement of orthodox religious life in this period remains largely unidentified. Kümin's thesis, for example, that a parish elite increasingly dominated so-called 'communal' affairs, begs questions as to the genuine popularity of the institutions and practices of orthodox religion.[16] Taken at face value, the evidence appears to support the now generally accepted picture of a thriving and well supported, albeit not uncriticised, Church. What is much less certain is whether or not this portrayal is representative of the beliefs, attitudes and practices of the majority of people throughout the country, or the activities of religious institutions patronised by particular groups within local society. Equally, detailed studies grounded in a specific geographical context have to be read with the awareness that what they describe might be atypical, and that there may have been no such thing as the typical.[17]

As it becomes increasingly apparent that late medieval religion was far from homogeneous, theoretical and methodological approaches that have produced an impression of overriding homogeneity, become increasingly untenable.[18] There has, for example, been scant regard for the relationship between variations and changes in pre-Reformation orthodox religion, and the more visible and obvious divergences of Lollardy, Protestantism and favourable responses to reform, even though it is clear that there was much overlap between them, and that dissent had a definite regional character.[19] There remains a need for detailed investigations of both orthodoxy and

---

James I, London 1977, 35–56; and R. Whiting, *The blind devotion of the people: popular religion and the English Reformation*, Cambridge 1989, passim.

15 For example Shagan, *Popular politics*, 5, 164, 193, but see also p. 306; P. Collinson, *The Reformation*, London 2003, 107. For a balanced critical assessment of the dominant school of thought see Marsh, *Popular religion*, 12–16, 198–201.

16 Kümin, *Shaping of a community*, 239.

17 Norman Tanner, for example, stresses that late medieval Norwich may have been unusually religious and orthodox before the Reformation: *The Church in late medieval Norwich*, Toronto 1984, 138–40. See also his 'The Reformation and regionalism: further reflections on the Church in late medieval Norwich', in J. A. F. Thomson (ed.), *Towns and townspeople in the fifteenth century*, Gloucester 1987, 129–47.

18 Swanson, *Catholic England*, 7, 27, 32; Aers, 'Altars of power', 90–102.

19 See, for example, R. O'Day, *The debate on the English Reformation*, London–New York 1986, 133–65; A. Hudson, *The premature Reformation: Wycliffite texts and Lollard history*, Oxford 1988, 390–429; J. F. Davis, *Heresy and Reformation in the south-east of England, 1520–1559*, London 1983, passim; and W. J. Sheils and S. Sheils, 'Textiles and reform: Halifax and its hinterland', in P. Collinson and J. Craig (eds), *The Reformation in English towns, 1500–1640*, Basingstoke 1998, 130–43.

heresy within local and regional contexts.[20] Tenterden is an ideal subject for just this kind of more integrated study. Although known principally as a centre of Lollard heresy, it also knew devout orthodoxy, most visible in the overtly impressive church tower built there by parishioners in the late fifteenth century or in Small Hythe chapel. Contrasts in piety at Tenterden beg questions about discontinuities, fractures and changes in religion from below and the heterogeneity of parochial beliefs and practices.[21]

It is now a generally held view that the parish was the dominant religious community in both town and countryside in late medieval England.[22] While definitions of the parish as a religious community vary, they have common recourse to an enduring motif: the free and voluntary choice of the individual in matters of collective religion. This seems, on the one hand, to have arisen from an anxiety to present pre-Reformation piety as essentially voluntary and, therefore, vital and meaningful and, on the other, to incorporate some of the more exaggerated claims about individualism in the social and economic spheres, into notions of collective religious action.[23] So, one approach to these issues configures the impulses of the so-called free individual and the community, as two essentially harmonious elements within parochial religion. For Duffy, 'late medieval Christians identified individual spiritual welfare with that of the community as a whole, an identification in which personal initiative and corporate action in pursuit of salvation could converge without any sign of incongruity or tension'. Similarly, Kümin argues that 'the coexistence of individual and communal dimensions' was a recurring feature of all parochial religion; dimensions which he identifies with voluntary and compulsory religion respectively.[24] Others have given individual choice and voluntarism pride of place. So, for Gervase Rosser, voluntary personal commitment, and a desire for greater choice, produced both the religious gild and the subparochial chapel.[25] Similarly, in her investigations of fraternities and collective rituals, Miri Rubin is concerned to reveal choice 'in a historically powerful way' and asserts that people chose the communities to which they belonged, or negotiated 'their places within groups when less

[20] For instance A. J. Slavin, 'Upstairs, downstairs: or the roots of reformation', *Huntington Library Quarterly* xxxxix (1986), 243–60; M. Aston, 'Iconoclasm at Rickmansworth, 1522: troubles of churchwardens', *JEH* xl (1989), 524–52; L. R. Poos, *A rural society after the Black Death, Essex, 1350–1525*, Cambridge 1991, 263–79; A. D. Brown, *Popular piety in late medieval England: the diocese of Salisbury, 1250–1550*, Oxford 1995.

[21] Aers, 'Altars of power', 95.

[22] For example Kümin, *Shaping of a community*, 4–5; D. M. Palliser, 'Introduction: the parish in perspective', in S. J. Wright (ed.), *Parish, Church and people: local studies in lay religion, 1350–1750*, London 1988, 5–25; J. A. F. Thomson, *The early Tudor Church and society, 1485–1529*, London 1993, 265.

[23] See, in particular, A. MacFarlane, *The origins of English individualism*, Oxford 1978.

[24] Duffy, *Altars*, 141; Kümin, *Shaping of a community*, 181, 144.

[25] G. Rosser, 'Parochial conformity and voluntary religion in late-medieval England', *TRHS* 6th ser. i (1991), 173, 182–3, and 'Communities of parish and guild in the late Middle Ages', in Wright, *Parish, Church and people*, 44.

freedom of choice was available'. For Rubin, compared to the prescribed social arenas of the family or the village, religious practice, in particular, afforded the individual discrimination in forming bonds with others.[26] Within such a conceptual framework, it is natural that the parish and the individual parishioner have been the dominant units of analysis in the reconstruction of late medieval piety. The beliefs of the parish have tended to be reconstructed from the aggregation of what are taken to be the discrete analytical building blocks of piety, namely individual choices in religion. Where efforts have been made to explore groups within or cutting across the parish such as fraternities, these have usually taken an institutional approach, working outwards from gilds and viewing them as free associations of individuals rather than as constituent elements in personal, familial and group piety which varied in significance and use for their participants.[27]

It is in terms of assessing the relationship between collective identity and religious diversity and change that these approaches have been most stifling. Treatment of the parish as a more or less unified whole or as a force which bound competing interest groups together, presents pre-Reformation lay religious belief and practice as diverse and yet essentially harmonious, without potential for transformation from internal contradictions. The parish system, so the argument goes, provided for a range of religious tastes that were woven together into an intricate and coherent tapestry of devotion. Although there has been some acknowledgement of the social, geographical, occupational and life-cycle differentiations that characterised participants in parochial institutions, rarely have these been seen as significant in religious terms, but as indicative of the variety of orthodox piety which is taken to be one of the mainstays of its vitality.[28]

Those more sceptical about the social reality of the parish have shown less interest in the religious significance of identity, than in what religion can reveal about social relations. Bossy, for example, sees the parish as the most important among a number of collective expressions of Christian community, which had the power, through invocation in collective rituals, to alleviate tensions between hostile parties and kinship groups.[29] In a similar fashion, Rosser judges the significance of a ritualised religious event – the fraternity

---

[26] Rubin, 'Small groups', 134, 136, 148.

[27] See, for example, G. Rosser, Medieval Westminster, 1200–1540, Oxford 1989, 281–93, and C. M. Barron, 'The parish fraternities of medieval London', in C. M. Barron and C. Harper-Bill (eds), The Church in pre-Reformation society: essays in honour of F. R. H. Du Boulay, Woodbridge 1985, 13–37.

[28] See, in particular, Duffy, Altars, 131–54, and Aers's criticisms of this in his 'Altars of power', 91, 99–102.

[29] J. Bossy, 'Blood and baptism: kinship, community and Christianity in western Europe from the fourteenth to the seventeenth centuries', in D. Baker (ed.), Sanctity and secularity: the Church and the world (SCH x, 1973), 129–43; Christianity, 14–32, 57–74; and 'The mass as a social institution, 1200–1700', P&P c (1983), 29–61.

feast – in terms of its social usefulness.[30] Rather than seeking to understand piety *per se*, Rubin aims 'to appreciate the pragmatic and strategic action, the versatility in the use of current religious language' and demonstrates a greater eagerness to explore how 'religious action services identity' than how religion determines and constrains social relations.[31] Here, the primary concern is to explore how changing and emerging identities gave rise to significant shifts in religious and moral sentiment, while recognising the potential for these same beliefs to mould and constrain behaviour. The fissuring of collective religion and, in some cases, radical divergences and tensions within ortho-doxy at Tenterden had their roots in the emerging collective identities that arose from material and social developments and pressures, which intensified from the late fifteenth century. Individual choice was constrained and directed by shifting boundaries, commitments, obligations and collective rationalities, and corresponding continuities and discontinuities in cultural transmission.[32] The following chapters explore a number of significant group-ings operating between the levels of the parish and the individual, which are not identifiable by an essentially institutional approach. Family and kinship, the importance of locality and social distinction, are examined by using a range of sources. Detailed attention to place and boundary has involved using property deeds and maps, as well as testamentary materials, for topographical reconstruction. These, together with records of taxation, municipal mate-rials, accounts and the records of central government are all employed in the reconstruction of economic activity, wealth, status, office-holding and social relations. This is with the intention of rooting piety in the social and the material.

Method and theory

For more than forty years the last will and testament has been one of the most important sources for the study of late medieval piety in town and country-side.[33] By categorising and analysing the religious content of large numbers of wills some historians have attempted to reconstruct the religious preferences

---

[30] G. Rosser, 'Going to the fraternity feast: commensality and social relations in late medi-eval England', *Journal of British Studies* xxxiii (1994), 433.

[31] Rubin, 'Small groups', 147, 135, and *Corpus Christi*, Cambridge 1991, 1–11, 358–61; C. Geertz, 'Religion as a cultural system', in his *The interpretation of cultures* (1973), London 1993, 87–125.

[32] C. J. Calhoun, 'Community: toward a variable conceptualization for comparative research', *Social History* v (1980), 105–29; Geertz, 'Religion as a cultural system', passim; E. P. Thompson, *Customs in common* (1991), London 1993, 6–7; P. Bourdieu, *The logic of practice*, Cambridge 1990, 64–5.

[33] The first English study to make extensive use of wills was W. K. Jordan, *Philanthropy in England, 1480–1640: a study of the changing pattern of English social aspirations*, London 1959.

and practices of, in the words of Norman Tanner, 'the mass of Christians'.[34] More recently, however, the value of the will as a source for religious attitudes, particularly without substantial and diverse corroborative evidence, has been questioned.[35] In particular, Clive Burgess calls for 'a methodology which takes adequate account of the implications of alternative documentation', and counsels that, on their own, wills 'make very little sense'. While being warned not to risk using them in isolation, particularly without churchwardens' accounts, Burgess concedes that 'ultimately, the detail and variety of wills' content proscribes any thought of discarding them'.[36] Tenterden is one of the many places for which an abundant number of wills survive but which lack pre-Reformation churchwardens' accounts. But, like many other places, testamentary materials are supported by the records of ecclesiastical visitation and investigation of heresy, the chantry commissions of the late 1540s, physical evidence of church-building and furnishing and a wide range of documentation detailing topography and social and economic relations.[37] If churchwardens' accounts had survived for Tenterden they would no doubt have revealed a wealth of information concerning the institutional operation of the parish and its collective religious practices not found in other sources. It is very likely that this would have resulted in a greater emphasis on the communal and institutional aspects of parochial piety in this book. However, the recent privileging of churchwardens' accounts as the quintessential representation of local religious life by some writers has arguably overemphasised the importance of communal parish piety at the expense of other elements.[38] A more sensitive and integrated approach is called for which engages with

34 Tanner, *Church in Norwich*, p. xvii. See also, for example, J. A. F. Thomson, 'Piety and charity in late medieval London', *JEH* xvi (1965), 178–95; P. Heath, 'Urban piety in the later Middle Ages: the evidence of Hull wills', in R. B. Dobson (ed.), *The Church, politics and patronage in the fifteenth century*, Gloucester 1984, 209–34; and R. B. Dinn, 'Popular religion in late medieval Bury St Edmunds', unpubl. PhD diss. Manchester 1990.

35 C. Burgess, ' "By quick and by dead": wills and pious provision in late medieval Bristol', *EHR* ccccv (1987), 837–58, and 'Late medieval wills and pious convention: testamentary evidence reconsidered', in M. Hicks (ed.), *Profit, piety and the professions in later medieval England*, Gloucester 1990, 14–33. See also, for example, C. Marsh, 'In the name of God? Will-making and faith in early modern England', in G. H. Martin and P. Spufford (eds), *The records of the nation*, Woodbridge 1990, 248.

36 Burgess, 'Late medieval wills', 15, 30. In his study of religious mores in Bristol, Burgess employed unusually abundant municipal and parish records, as well as deeds, alongside some 400 wills: 'By quick and by dead', 838–40.

37 There are last wills and testaments for 261 lay people and three priests for Tenterden from 1449 to 1535 (one of the clerical wills is treated separately from the rest: John Morer, priest, 1489: TNA: PRO, PCC 20 Milles, fos 161v–162v). Occasional references are made to wills dated to after this period or those belonging to testators who lived in other parishes. The value of wills, because of their survival where many other sources are lost, is noted by G. J. Mayhew, 'The progress of the Reformation in East Sussex, 1530–1539: the evidence from wills', *SH* v (1983), 57.

38 For example Duffy, *Voices of Morebath*; K. L. French, *The people of the parish: community life in a late medieval English diocese*, Philadelphia 2001; Kümin, *Shaping of a community*.

the full range of available resources and those aspects of piety which are not so easily assimilable into models of communal parochial religion. In this case, in the absence of churchwardens' accounts, the challenge has been to develop a theoretically coherent method of testamentary analysis that makes the most of all surviving evidence germane to piety.

Although wills offer much in the way of religious content many bequests, whether outwardly religious or not, are formulaic and very similar from one will to the next. This applies, especially, to the dedicatory clauses or preambles with which testaments opened. It is now apparent that only the broadest changes in testamentary fashion and scribal convention can be identified from systematic statistical analysis of preambles and, in the pre-Reformation period, local conventions appear often to have been so uniform as to render these elements of wills meaningless. It is now taken for granted that preambles should only be studied within the context of the whole will.[39] Only a handful of the Tenterden testaments depart from the usual dedication (with its occasional slight variations) of the 'soul to almighty God, the Blessed Virgin Mary and all the saints in heaven'. The standardised structure and the formulaic language of wills have led some historians to argue that, even beyond dedicatory clauses, religious bequests provide a highly distorted impression of individual wishes.[40] It is, however, generally acknowledged that individual testators exercised real choices in the will-making process and that their wishes were respected.[41] Debate on these issues has tended to polarise around two positions. On the one hand, the formulaic and standardised character of these documents is taken as evidence of a shallowness of faith[42] and, on the other, as proof of an 'overwhelming social consensus in religious convictions and priorities'.[43] Both overemphasise the formulaic character of

[39] A number of studies have attempted to use preambles (sometimes in conjunction with the other religious contents of wills) to assess religious change during the Reformation, with varying degrees of caution. See, for example, A. G. Dickens, *Lollards and Protestants in the diocese of York, 1509–1558*, Oxford 1959, 171–2, 215–18, 220–1, 238, and C. Cross, 'The development of Protestantism in Leeds and Hull, 1520–1640: the evidence from wills', *Northern History* xviii (1982), 230–8. For influences and restrictions on the choice and construction of dedicatory clauses see, for example, M. Spufford, *Contrasting communities: English villagers in the sixteenth and seventeenth centuries*, Cambridge 1974, 319–43; M. L. Zell, 'The use of religious preambles as a measure of religious belief in the sixteenth century', *BIHR* i (1977), 246–9; E. M. Elvey, *The courts of the archdeaconry of Buckingham, 1483–1523* (Buckingham Record Society xix, 1975), pp. xxi–xxx, and J. Craig and C. Litzenberger, 'Wills as religious propaganda: the testament of William Tracy', *JEH* xliv (1993), 415–31.

[40] C. Burgess, ' "For the increase of divine service": chantries in the parish in late medieval Bristol', *JEH* xxxvi (1985), 46, and 'By quick and by dead', passim.

[41] Spufford, *Contrasting communities*, 319–44; Marsh, 'In the name of God?', passim; R. Po-chia Hsia, 'Civic wills as sources for the study of piety in Muenster, 1530–1618', *Sixteenth Century Journal* xiv (1983), 327; R. A. Houlbrooke, *Church courts and the people during the English Reformation*, Oxford 1979, 101.

[42] For example Heath, 'Urban piety', 229.

[43] Duffy, *Altars*, 355.

testamentary materials at the expense of the sometimes very marked, although more often subtle, differences in content. As with all legal documents, a degree of uniformity is to be expected and specifically religious bequests, of necessity, tend to be expressed within the boundaries of a vocabulary of traditional orthodoxy and legal convention. The unoriginality of pious gestures did not, necessarily, detract from their significance or perceived value.[44] It is what was meant by the use of certain forms and the replication of certain traditional religious bequests that is important. More than once have we been reminded that a certain type of bequest had different meanings for different people,[45] but the search for variant and changing meanings among the pious bequests in the wills of orthodox believers has, on the whole, been absent from past approaches to testamentary materials. In an indirect way this has been due to theoretical starting points and, more practically, it has to do with method.

Norman Tanner's *The Church in late medieval Norwich* remains one of the most impressive and thorough studies of late medieval orthodox belief and practice in a specific geographical setting. Based mainly on a large-scale statistical analysis of testamentary materials and founded on the assumption that the late medieval will 'in some ways . . . sums up a person's attitude to life', Tanner's study asks how movement 'came from below through the choices which ordinary Christians made about how they practised their religion' and so reveals its debt to the history of *mentalités*.[46] Following the historians of *mentalités*, Tanner adopted a method pioneered by Gabriel Le Bras in the 1950s, which marked the beginnings of a deliberate shift from study of the Church as an institution and the elites within it, to concentration upon mass attitudes and behaviour, in specific regional or local contexts.[47] Methods of quantitative social history, developed most fully by the *Annales* school, were used by the likes of Toussaert to attempt to quantify particular 'indicators' of religious sensibility over time, using large-scale sampling techniques.[48] Such indices are especially present in wills and almost all studies of pre-Reformation English lay piety that make extensive use of testamentary materials classify and count various types of religious bequests in large numbers of wills. One of the problems with this approach is that it removes

---

44 Spufford, *Contrasting communities*, 344; Marsh, 'In the name of God?', 243.

45 For example M. G. A. Vale, 'Piety, charity and literacy among the Yorkshire gentry, 1370–1480' (Borthwick Papers 1, 1976), 8; A. N. Galpern, *The religions of the people in sixteenth-century Champagne*, Cambridge, Mass.–London 1976, 31.

46 Tanner, *Church in Norwich*, pp. xv–xvi, 116. Compare this with Jordan's description of wills as 'mirrors of mens' souls': *Philanthropy in England*, 16. M. Vovelle, *Ideologies and mentalities*, Cambridge 1990, 5.

47 Vovelle, *Ideologies and mentalities*, 15–16; F. Boulard, *An introduction to religious sociology: pioneer work in France*, London 1960.

48 Tanner himself refers to Toussaert's work, among others, as an example of the new approach to the history of religion which he himself adopted: J. Toussaert, *Le Sentiment religieux en Flandre à la fin du moyen âge*, Paris 1960; Tanner, *Church in Norwich*, p. xv.

the testament and last will, as an integral text, from the methodological framework. The extraction of different categories of bequests in isolation, with very little infra-textual comparison between them, fails to respect the unity and complexity of the will as a cultural artefact, and results in the dislocation and fragmentation of the religious attitudes and aspirations of the individual testator. While the debate about the value of wills as historical evidence has hinged on whether or not they can be relied upon as expressions of individual piety,[49] in practice, individual piety has been lost among the 'anonymous traces' which are taken to represent the attitudes of the masses.[50] These perplexing contradictions have contributed to a general reluctance to address questions regarding the place of the individual in the structures and dynamics of popular piety in the later Middle Ages.

Where quantitative methods are employed in the following chapters, they are used in conjunction with complementary forms of analysis, which principally involve the close reading of testamentary and other forms of evidence. Increasing the focus of enquiry through the use of small-scale and microhistorical approaches reveals, for example, the relationships between individual and family pieties, or identities of neighbourhood and parish. Testamentary cause records reveal that family, kin, neighbours and friends often played an important role in the process of drawing up a will and that deathbed gatherings were important social occasions that drew on bonds of kinship and neighbourliness.[51] A fuller understanding of piety from testamentary evidence necessitates reconstruction (through prosopography and, where possible, record-linkage) of the familial and social connections mentioned in wills, or pertinent to them. In the words of Carlo Ginzburg, 'a close reading of a relatively small number of texts, related to a possibly circumscribed belief, can be more rewarding than the massive accumulation of evidence'.[52] In common with microhistorians, I have relied here, to a certain extent, on creative imagination or, to be more scientific, the interpretative method of abduction. Put simply, this is the suggestion of a hypothesis that explains a set of (usually) surprising facts. While every attempt has been made to prove conjectures or hypotheses, this has not always been fully possible, but there is, arguably, much value in employing what is 'the most

---

49 Marsh, 'In the name of God?', 215, and *Popular religion*, 128–34; J. D. Alsop, 'Religious preambles in early modern English wills as formulae', *JEH* xl (1989), 20.

50 A term used by Vovelle in his *Ideologies and mentalities*, 10, 16–18, 19–22. See also his *Piété baroque et déchristianisation: les attitudes devant le mort en Provence au XVIII siècle*, Paris 1973.

51 C. W. Foster, 'Introduction', to *Lincoln wills, 1271–1530*, ed. C. W. Foster (Lincoln Record Society x, 1918); Spufford, *Contrasting communities*, 322–3; Marsh, 'In the name of God?', 226–36; S. Coppel, 'Will-making and the deathbed', *Local Population Studies*, no. xl (Spring 1988), 37–45; Marsh, 'In the name of God', 217–20, 226–36, 248.

52 C. Ginzburg, 'The inquisitor as anthropologist', in his *Clues, myths and the historical method*, Baltimore 1989, 164.

fruitful', albeit sometimes 'least certain, method'. Where I have left the reader with probabilities, it is hoped that they might inspire other imaginations.[53]

Reconstructing piety from the last will and testament

Perhaps the most serious objection to the use of wills as a source for the reconstruction of piety is that they are unrepresentative of the sentiments and practices of the population as a whole. Only the better off who sought to solve problems of inheritance or settle their estates made wills and not all of these were copied into the registers of the church courts. In addition, a disproportionately small number of women made testaments or last wills.[54] Tenterden's extant wills were made by perhaps less than a tenth of all adults who died in the parish from around 1450 to 1535. However, because not all people made wills, those that survive in the probate registers comprise a much larger proportion of all will-makers and so, as a representation of testamentary piety, they are considerably more reliable.[55] Surviving wills tended to be made by enduring and stable families of moderate or high status and, as such, record the preoccupations of an important and influential, but quite particular, section of local society. These social groups may at times have set the parameters of practice and dictated the pace of change in religious tastes,[56] but their concerns were probably quite different from those of the less well-off and the more transient, about which we know comparatively little. It would, however, be perverse to ignore such a rich source of evidence because of its bias towards stable and wealthy families.[57]

Clive Burgess, in a series of influential articles, has raised a number of serious methodological problems concerning the use of wills to reconstruct

[53] E. Muir, 'Introduction: observing trifles', in E. Muir and G. Ruggiero (eds), *Microhistory and the lost peoples of Europe*, Baltimore–London 1991, p. xviii; G. Levi, 'On microhistory', in P. Burke (ed.), *New perspectives on historical writing*, Cambridge 1991, 106; C. Marsh, *The Family of Love in English society, 1550–1630*, Cambridge 1994, 10–14. On Pierce's theory of abduction see K. T. Fann, *Pierce's theory of abduction*, The Hague 1970; U. Eco and T. A. Sebeok (eds), *The sign of three: Dupin, Holmes, Pierce*, Bloomington, Indiana 1983. Much inspiration has been gained for this present study from P. Boyer and S. Nissenbaum, *Salem possessed: the social origins of witchcraft*, Cambridge, Mass. 1974.

[54] Elvey, *Archdeaconry of Buckingham*, pp. xxi–xxx; Burgess, 'Late medieval wills', 15.

[55] Tenterden's population was probably around 1,000 and growing in this period. With a likely death-rate of around 40 per 1,000, the 263 surviving wills over 85 years represent a little under a tenth of all those adults who died: M. L. Zell, *Industry in the countryside: Wealden society in the sixteenth century*, Cambridge 1994, 52–87; J. Hatcher, 'Mortality in the fifteenth century: some new evidence', *EcHR* 2nd ser. xxxix (1980), 19–38.

[56] Heath, 'Urban piety', 228; P. Spufford, 'The comparative mobility and immobility of Lollard descendants in early modern England', in M. Spufford (ed.), *The world of rural dissenters, 1520–1725*, Cambridge 1995, 309–31.

[57] Tanner, *Church in Norwich*, 115; K. Wrightson and D. Levine, *Poverty and piety in an English village: Terling, 1525–1700*, New York–San Francisco–London 1979, 96–7.

religious sensibilities. First, he claims that they tell us little about lifetime piety, that attitudes and activities in life were different from those in death, and that the will focuses disproportionately on the cult of death, and so over-emphasises the testator's religious preoccupations.[58] To some extent this is true, but testamentary piety was not wholly removed from lifetime practices.[59] When wills are compared to records of parish and gild, they more often than not reflect lifetime interests and, with the assistance of family and kin, extended these beyond the point of death.[60] Although they do not always adequately represent the extent and wealth of religious giving and other activities in life, neither do they depart wildly from them. If charted within families, wills reveal the very strong relationship between testamentary strategy and age at death, due to differing responsibilities to family and kin and, therefore, variations in the proportions of wealth available for disposal in religious acts. Also, the value of probate materials is better appreciated when the subject of study is broadened to encompass the whole range of preoccupations to which testators attended in will-making.[61]

Burgess also claims that last wills and testaments focus mainly on the funeral and its immediate aftermath, rather than longer-term services which, it is argued, were usually arranged before making a will. The predominant characteristic of late medieval pious practices, so the argument goes, was their stability; a stability that fostered well-established customs and conventions which operated without recourse to written instructions.[62] These conventions operated mainly within the family and, in particular, outlined the obligations of widows and heirs to carry out pious provisions for spouses and parents, and to sustain family commitments such as the maintenance of chantries and lights. When family wills are cross-referenced, however, even in the absence of other sources it is possible to trace bequests between spouses and generations and identify pious conventions.[63]

The evidence from Bristol used by Burgess to debunk the will as a 'blank façade disguising an intricate reality' consists largely of untypical cases made in extraordinary circumstances when normal processes would have been disrupted or foreshortened. They tend, also, to be drawn from the wealthiest members of urban society without asking whether the relationship between

---

[58] Burgess, 'Late medieval wills', 16, and 'By quick and by dead', 840.

[59] See, for example, Galpern, *Religions of the people*, 13; Dinn, 'Popular religion', 79–80; C. Peters, *Patterns of piety: women, gender and religion in late medieval and Reformation England*, Cambridge 2003, 100–1.

[60] This is true of the examples which Burgess himself employs for Bristol: 'By quick and by dead', 841–3, 845, 852, 842, 852–4.

[61] Dinn, 'Popular religion', 81; Marsh, 'In the name of God?', passim.

[62] Burgess, 'Late medieval wills', 16–17, and 'By quick and by dead', 840.

[63] Dinn asserts that 'even in Bristol . . . memorial services excluded from the wills form a minority of all memorial services. Equally, Burgess's conclusion, that a general belief in purgatory was not waning before the Reformation, can be supported by the use of testamentary evidence alone': 'Popular religion', 81.

their testamentary piety and extra-testamentary arrangements is representative of the majority of will-makers. It is probable that the wealthiest were most likely to settle their pious provisions prior to making a will, because they were in a better position to do so than most. However, even allowing for this, they still tended to make wills that were conspicuous for their diversity of giving and extravagance.[64] In addition, the importance of the will in the provision of endowments and pious arrangements varied from place to place, may have been unusually marginal at Bristol[65] and seems to have been much less limited at Tenterden.[66]

Even in those places where reliance on the will appears to have been somewhat limited, these documents remain reliable indices of priorities and interests and, sometimes, the relative intensity of religious commitments. In this respect it is unimportant that testamentary materials record intentions rather than the fulfilment of testators' last wishes.[67] None the less, the difficulty of judging the intensity of personal piety from wills remains considerable. In part, this is related to the difficulty of assessing the proportion of an individual's resources allocated to specifically religious bequests.[68] Even those conspicuously generous wills made by the wealthiest testators fail to reveal the full extent of their available resources. Payments for tithes forgotten have been used by some historians as a measure of wealth but these are far from reliable.[69] Taxation materials are a more accurate gauge, although not

---

[64] Burgess, 'Late medieval wills', 21, 25–9, and 'By quick and by dead', passim.

[65] C. Burgess and B. Kümin, 'Penitential bequests and parish regimes in late medieval England', *JEH* xliv (1993), 610–30; Kümin, *Shaping of a community*, ch. iii. Burgess himself admits that late medieval Bristol is indeed a special case and that 'findings concerning their religious aspirations are to be treated with considerable caution. So too must findings concerning parish life in Bristol': 'Divine service', 47.

[66] This is suggested by comparison of cases of unfulfilled endowments presented to the parochial visitation of 1512 with surviving wills: *Kentish visitations*, pp. xxiv, 206–11.

[67] A number of historians have drawn attention to this limitation of probate evidence, for example Thomson, 'Piety and charity', 179, and Heath, 'Urban piety', 219. See, however, Dinn, 'Popular religion', 82.

[68] Burgess, 'Late medieval wills', 25; Elvey, *Archdeaconry of Buckingham*, p. xxix.

[69] For details about the assessment of personal tithes and the voluntary element within these payments see J. A. F. Thomson, 'Tithe disputes in later medieval London', *EHR* lxxviii (1963), 2, and S. Thrupp, *The merchant class of medieval London, 1300–1500*, Chicago 1948, 185. R. S. Gottfried has used these payments as a rough index of wealth, although he provides no basis for his assertion that the amount given was fixed by legal statute as a certain proportion of the testator's liquid wealth: *Bury St Edmunds and the urban crisis: 1290–1539*, Princeton, NJ 1982, 125–9, 260, and *Epidemic disease in fifteenth century England*, Leicester 1978, 31. See also Higgs, 'Lay piety', 200–2, where Gottfried's method is followed. For criticism of this see R. H. Hilton's review of Gottfried's *Bury St Edmunds* in *Urban History Yearbook* (1983), 185. Dinn compared the high altar payments of 32 testators to their 1523–4 lay subsidy assessments and found a broad but fairly consistent correspondence, payments rising with the assessed wealth of testators: 'Popular religion', 64–8. In Norwich, the inclusion of 'for tithes forgotten' in the wording of bequests to high altars, only regularly appears from the 1490s: Tanner, *Church in Norwich*, 5–6.

without their own difficulties, and these and other pertinent sources such as property deeds are used here. A composite picture of familial wealth and status can help in assessing an individual's resources, but there were wide variations in wealth within families and changes over time. However, compared to more rural and manorialised areas there was little customary land in Tenterden and the Weald, and those who were free of the town of Tenterden were able regularly to devise freehold property in their wills, considerably aiding the assessment of individual and family wealth.[70] Moreover, individuals' testamentary strategies can be set in the contexts of familial continuities of practice or particular local traditions which lend new vigour and significance to seemingly routine bequests and help to decode conventional symbolic vocabularies. A comparative approach offers insights into the economy and logic of practice that informed will-making and the particular constraints and pressures that shaped the piety of the individual testator. As indices of the relative character of belief and practice, and contrasting patterns of piety within specific settings, last wills and testaments have scarcely begun to be exploited.

The importance of the family in the transmission of piety

The role of the family in orthodox religion in the later Middle Ages, has been given most attention in studies of the better-documented nobility and gentry.[71] In terms of work on the rest of the population, it has been most adequately addressed in the study of Lollardy and other forms of religious dissent and Nonconformity from the sixteenth century onwards. This began with W. H. Summers's work on Lollards and Nonconformists in the Chilterns. More recently, beginning with Anne Hudson among others, and culminating in the work of a group of historians working under the direction of Margaret Spufford, 'dissent as a phenomenon transmitted within the family' has been given much greater attention. This has established an awareness of the importance of the family, the wider household and kin, in the promulgation and sustenance of heresy and Nonconformity. There is now compelling evidence for regional traditions of heretical belief passed down within families over at least three generations,[72] although the full implica-

---

[70] Elvey, *Archdeaconry of Buckingham*, pp. xxiv–xxv; Burgess, 'Late medieval wills', 25–6.
[71] See, in particular, R. G. K. A. Mertes, 'The household as a religious community', in J. Rosenthal and C. Richmond (eds), *People, politics and community in the later Middle Ages*, Gloucester 1987, 123–39; C. Carpenter, 'The religion of the gentry of fifteenth century England', in D. Williams (ed.), *England in the fifteenth century*, Woodbridge 1987, 69; and J. Hughes, *Pastors and visionaries: religion and secular life in late medieval Yorkshire*, Woodbridge 1988, 5–63.
[72] See, for example, W. H. Summers, *The Lollards of the Chiltern hills: glimpses of English dissent in the Middle Ages*, London 1906, 74–142; C. Hill, 'From Lollards to Levellers', in *Collected essays of Christopher Hill, II: Religion and politics in seventeenth-century England*,

tions of this phenomenon, whether it applies to other forms of religious dissent such as post-Reformation Catholicism and recusancy and the precise connections between pre-Reformation heresy and seventeenth-century Nonconformity remain unanswered questions.[73]

The apparent reluctance among English historians to provide a larger place for the family in late medieval piety as a whole is in contrast to continental scholarship which has seen 'the family as the vital centre for the direct transmission of belief, and as the crucible in which historical continuities involving religion were shaped – or, indeed, in which traditions of rejection were perpetuated'; and as important 'both as a vital centre of acculturation and also as an area of resistance to compulsory acculturations'. This has certainly been shown to be true for early modern England, in spheres such as sexuality, marital customs and certain forms of collective behaviour.[74] In late medieval England one might reasonably expect the nuclear family to have been the most important institution for the transmission of religious belief and practice.[75] Familial solidarity arguably ensured that parents' particular preferences and commitments in spiritual matters shaped their childrens' own choices and priorities. Such evidence of religious instruction as there is reveals the perceived duty of parents to induct their children into the essentials of the faith from an early age. Before children reached their teens few departed to schools away from home and, in the development of religious sensibilities, the influence of parental control and everyday example was paramount.[76]

Brighton 1986, 89–116; P. Collinson, 'Cranbrook and the Fletchers; popular and unpopular religion in the Kentish Weald', in his *Godly people: essays in Protestantism and Puritanism*, London 1983, 399–428, esp. p. 425; Hudson, *Premature Reformation*, 121, 134–7, 456–64; M. Spufford, 'The importance of religion in the sixteenth and seventeenth centuries', 23–9; D. Plumb, 'A gathered Church? Lollards and their society', 132–63, and 'The social and economic status of the later Lollards', 103–31; and N. Evans, 'The descent of dissenters in the Chiltern Hundreds', 288–308, all in Spufford, *World of rural dissenters*; and S. McSheffrey, *Gender and heresy: women and men in Lollard communities, 1420–1530*, Philadelphia 1995, ch. iv.

[73] P. Collinson, 'Critical conclusion', in Spufford, *World of rural dissenters*, 391, 393–6; W. J. Sheils, 'Catholics and their neighbours in a rural community: Egton Chapelry, 1590–1780', *Northern History* xxxiv (1998), 109–33.

[74] Vovelle, *Ideologies and mentalities*, 167–8; Boulard, *Introduction to religious sociology*; Thompson, *Customs in common*, 6–10.

[75] R. A. Houlbrooke, *The English family, 1450–1700*, Harlow 1984, 18–20; M. Anderson, *Approaches to the history of the western family, 1500–1914*, Basingstoke–London 1980, 22–7; Z. Razi, 'The myth of the immutable English family', *P&P* cxl (1993), 3–4; K. Wrightson, 'Kinship in an English village: Terling, Essex, 1500–1700', in R. M. Smith (ed.), *Land, kinship, and life cycle*, Cambridge 1984, 323–6. See, however, M. Chaytor, 'Household and kinship: Ryton in the late sixteenth and the early seventeenth centuries', *HWJ* x (1980), 25–60, in conjunction with K. Wrightson, 'Household and kinship in sixteenth century England', *HWJ* xii (1981), 151–8; R. Wall, 'Household and kinship', *HWJ* xii (1981), 199; O. Harris, 'Households and their boundaries', *HWJ* xiii (1982), 143–52; and R. Houston and R. M. Smith, 'A new approach to family history?', *HWJ* xiv (1982), 120–31.

[76] Houlbrooke, *English family*, 147–9, 150–2; Swanson, *Catholic England*, 8–9; Wrightson

Once into their early or mid-teens, however, a substantial proportion of young people, and in some areas the majority, left home permanently or for a long period in order to enter service or apprenticeship. There were of course always those who remained at home until marriage, and it is perhaps among them that the strongest continuities of religious belief and practice are to be found.[77] But even for the rest, the strongest moral and emotional bonds usually remained those with parents. Most young people remained under the authority and influence of parents and so were still expected to conform to standards and patterns of family morality and religious observance.[78] As the evidence of Lollardy shows, while service sometimes led to a departure from parental opinions, parents could choose masters or mistresses who would compound their own views in their children.[79] The evidence for mid sixteenth-century Kent suggests that, rather than providing the young with the freedom to make their own choices in marriage and, by extension, in other spheres such as religion,[80] service and any independence of choice which came with it, operated within and was closely circumscribed by, an all-pervasive ideological and moral system of kinship.[81] This entailed values such as goodwill, family honour and respectability, dependence, reciprocity and commitment, and 'psychological, social and economic pressures which constrained a real freedom of action and within which individual behaviour was contained'. Rather than there being a culture of individualism and self-determination, those who asserted their own preferences in the face of

and Levine, *Poverty and piety*, 143–53; Spufford, *Contrasting communities*, 171–218; K. M. Davies, 'Continuity and change in literary advice on marriage', in R. B. Outhwaite (ed.), *Marriage and society: studies in the social history of marriage*, London 1981, 67.

[77] Houlbrooke, *English family*, 171–3; Anderson, *History of the western family*, 22–7. See, however, Chaytor, 'Household and kinship', 47; M. K. McIntosh, A *community transformed: the manor and liberty of Havering, 1500–1620*, Cambridge 1991, 53–64; and P. J. P. Goldberg, ' "For better, for worse": marriage and economic opportunity for women in town and country', in P. J. P. Goldberg (ed.), *Woman is a worthy wight: women in English society, c. 1200–1500*, Stroud 1992, 109–10, 122.

[78] Houlbrooke, *English family*, 171–6.

[79] Hudson, *Premature Reformation*, 131; A. Hope, 'Lollardy: the stone the builders rejected?', in P. Lake and M. Dowling (eds), *Protestantism and the national Church in sixteenth century England*, London 1987, 10–11.

[80] As argued by Goldberg in, for example, his *Women, work, and life cycle in a medieval economy: women in York and Yorkshire, c. 1300–1520*, Oxford 1992, 324–56. Goldberg himself admits that the individualism of young women and men in York and its hinterland may have been the product of an especially urbanised and particular regional culture: 'Marriage, migration, servanthood and life-cycle in Yorkshire towns of the later Middle Ages: some York cause paper evidence', *C&C* i (1986), 161.

[81] D. O'Hara, ' "Ruled by my friends": aspects of marriage in the diocese of Canterbury, c. 1540–1570', *C&C* vi (1991), 9–41, and *Courtship and constraint: rethinking the making of marriage in Tudor England*, Manchester 2000, 30–56; D. Cressy, 'Kinship and kin interaction in early modern England', *P&P* cxii (1986), 38–69.

opposition did so at personal cost and, sometimes, faced severe repercussions.[82]

Service involved a restructuring of relationships between families, households and social groups, which called upon a vocabulary of kinship.[83] Where households were unrelated, links were established and strengthened by young people moving between them. The field of influence of family and kin extended over the whole range of social relations, of which religious practice formed a part, and therefore impinged upon choices about devotional and liturgical life and concerns such as the proper use of family capital, which had a major impact on religious giving. Contrary to John Bossy's assertion that extended kinship ties operating within a supportive fraternity of contemporaries, who could be blood or 'friends', were much more important than the linear and nuclear family in religious life, the nuclear family remained the most important location of cultural transmission and the primary and most interested employer of the vocabulary of kinship.[84]

This said, in respect of the demographic scene in the fifteenth century, a family- and kin-centred analysis of religious life requires some justification. The erosion of the land–family bond, among other factors, had by the fifteenth century created highly mobile local populations and, by the sixteenth, parishes predominantly made up of nuclear households that were isolated in terms of blood or marriage.[85] These developments, however, did not apply to all social groups. For one thing, throughout the fifteenth century, in all types of community, there existed families (usually the wealthiest) which retained their continuity for a number of generations and which enjoyed increasing stability after 1500.[86] This multi-generational stability ensured that these families influenced local and regional patterns of devotion and played an active role in the transmission of practices over time. It is

---

[82] O'Hara, 'Ruled by my friends', 11–17; Chaytor, 'Household and kinship', 41–3.

[83] See, for example, Houlbrooke, *English family*, 46, and P. J. P. Goldberg, 'Female labour, service and marriage in the late medieval urban north', *Northern History* xxii (1986), 22–3, on the reliance upon kinship networks to place servants with households.

[84] Bossy, 'Blood and baptism', 129–43. For the importance of the nuclear family in godparenthood choices on the Weald of Kent see R. Lutton, 'Godparenthood, kinship and piety in Tenterden, England, 1449–1537', in I. Davis, M. Müller and S. Rees Jones (eds), *Love, marriage and family ties in the Middle Ages*, Turnhout 2003, 217–34.

[85] R. J. Faith, 'Peasant families and inheritance customs in medieval England', *AgHR* xiv (1966), 77–95; C. Dyer, 'Changes in the size of peasant holdings in some west midland villages, 1400–1540', in Smith, *Land, kinship, and life cycle*, 281; Spufford, 'Mobility and immobility', 309–31; C. Howell, *Land, family and inheritance in transition: Kibworth Harcourt, 1280–1700*, Cambridge 1983, 240–3, 249; Zell, *Industry in the countryside*, ch. iii.

[86] C. Phythian-Adams, *Desolation of a city: Coventry and the urban crisis of the late Middle Ages*, Cambridge 1979, 148–57; R. M. Smith, 'Some issues concerning families and their property in rural England, 1250–1800', in Smith, *Land, kinship, and life cycle*, 60; M. K. McIntosh, *Autonomy and community: the royal manor of Havering, 1200–1500*, Cambridge 1986, 133; Wrightson and Levine, *Poverty and piety*, 81–2; Spufford, 'Mobility and immobility', 314, 320–3, 330.

likely, also, that 'given the dispersed nature of settlement within Wealden parishes, families might be expected to have been even more important institutions of social and economic life than in regions with nucleated villages and strongly collective parochial institutions'.[87] It is also the case that demographic change varied in its intensity and consequences from one region and locality to the next. In those areas with a relatively high level of industrial activity and an abundance of small parcels of land such as the Weald of Kent, increasing availability of employment in the late fifteenth and early sixteenth centuries worked to stabilise families for more than one generation, and led to increasing immigration and the establishment of new households in centres such as Tenterden.[88] In a national context the fifty or so years from 1475 followed more than a century of demographic downturn but, in contrast, the Weald had probably seen more of a demographic restructuring than a long-term slump. By the early to mid-sixteenth century when, in some places, familial kinship ties were often less available than desired, those links that did exist by blood or marriage, were relied upon all the more heavily.[89] At the same time, in order to fill the gap left by the depletion of extended family ties, the ideology and morality of the family became an ideal metaphor for the creation of a vocabulary of kinship which moved flexibly between real, fictive and figurative kin. In this sense the family had an important structuring role in the field of social relations.[90]

Families' efforts to reproduce themselves were subject always to what has been termed the 'demographic lottery', and their influence over local affairs rose and fell accordingly.[91] The vagaries of biological replacement could, however, have the opposite effect of securing familial continuity by evening out differences in the relationship between available land and family size through the marriage market. Because sons, more than daughters, tended to remain to take up family holdings, familial continuity was largely dependent upon the survival of a son to adulthood. This was especially the case when arrangements emerged in the late fifteenth century that created a link

---

[87] Zell, *Industry in the countryside*, 75.

[88] Smith, 'Some issues concerning families', 59; I. Blanchard, 'Industrial employment and the rural land market, 1380–1520', in Smith, *Land, kinship, and life cycle*, 227–75; M. L. Zell, 'A wood-pasture agrarian regime: the Kentish Weald in the sixteenth century', *SH* vii (1985), 69–93, and *Industry in the countryside*, 61–2, chs ii, iii.

[89] Razi, 'Myth of the immutable family', 28; Smith, 'Some issues concerning families', 56–8; Cressy, 'Kinship', passim.

[90] A. Barnard and A. Good, *Research practices in the study of kinship*, London 1984, 186–9, 150–4; J. Carsten (ed.), *Cultures of relatedness: new approaches to the study of kinship*, Cambridge 2000, 1–36; P. P. Schweitzer (ed.), *Dividends of kinship: meanings and uses of social relatedness*, London–New York 2000, 1–32; M. Bloch, 'The long term and the short term: the economic and political significance of the morality of kinship', in J. Goody (ed.), *The character of kinship*, Cambridge 1973, 75–87.

[91] M. E. Mate, 'The East Sussex land market and agrarian class structure in the late Middle Ages', *P&P* cxxxix (1993), 48; Dyer, 'Size of peasant holdings', 281; Houlbrooke, *English family*, 24.

between late co-residence with parents and inheritance. This had the effect of enhancing bonds of dependence and obligation and may have helped to maintain and strengthen pious traditions within families.[92] This suggests that some of the strongest continuities in piety within localities may have been transmitted through inheriting and non-migrating sons. However, women also had an important role in tradition-formation and transmission.[93] Also, a woman's family could have a strong influence over the marital household; particularly the wife's father and brothers-in-law, with whom, at certain stages in the life-cycle, relationships could become very important and close.[94] In theory, marriage was more likely to effect profound changes in religious sentiment for women than it was for men, as women were expected to bow to their husbands' dictates,[95] but the essential dynamic was the joining and merging of traditions of practice through alliances between families. The choice of marriage partners in the forging of alliances was made according to individual and familial tastes and, arguably, because tastes included piety in their 'schemes of perception and appreciation', families of similar pious inclinations tended to be drawn together.[96]

There are at least sixteen surviving pairs of wills made by married spouses between 1449 and 1535, and a number of them, although not all, demonstrate the interplay of gendered individual choices and coherent household pieties. For example, in 1526 Thomas Mede left a total of 36s. 8d. to religious concerns, and in 1531 his widow, Helwyse, gave 40s. Thomas gave 6s. 8d. for forgotten tithes, 3s. 4d. to the Jesus Mass and 26s. 8d. for his funeral. Helwyse left only 20d. in tithes forgotten, but also gave 3s. 4d. to the Jesus Mass, 13s. 4d. to each of her funeral and month's mind, 6s. 8d. for her anniversary and 20d. for repairs to St Mildred's.[97] William and Anne Stonehouse, who both wrote their wills in 1513, apportioned exactly the same amounts to their obsequies, that is 13s. 4d. to each of their funerals and month's minds and 10s. to their anniversaries. They both gave 8d. for forgotten tithes, and whereas William left 8d. to the fabric of High Halden parish church and a bushel of wheat to poor people for the health of his soul, Anne gave 4d. to the Jesus Mass and 10d. to the light of St Mildred in Tenterden parish church.[98] These and other examples show strong continuities between the testamentary

---

92 Dyer, 'Size of peasant holdings', 290–1; Howell, *Land, family and inheritance*, ch. x. See, however, McIntosh, *Autonomy and community*, 119–22.

93 Swanson, *Religion and devotion*, 304–5. Of particular relevance to service is F. Riddy, 'Mother knows best: reading social change in a courtesy text', *Speculum* lxxi (1996), 66–86.

94 Houlbrooke, *English family*, 19, 44; Hudson, *Premature Reformation*, 460.

95 J. M. Bennett, 'The ties that bind: peasant marriages and families in late medieval England', *Journal of Interdisciplinary History* xv (1984), 111–29; R. A. Houlbrooke, 'Womens' social life and common action in England from the fifteenth century to the eve of the civil war', *C&C* i (1986), 171–89; Peters, *Patterns of piety*, 18–19, 39, 47.

96 Bourdieu, *Logic of practice*, 160; O'Hara, *Courtship and constraint*, 30–56.

97 PRO, PCC 17 Porche, fo. 131v; CKS, PRC 17/19/177.

98 PRC 17/12/227, 17/12/182.

pieties of husbands and wives as well as individual and gendered aspirations. When read together they describe shared sets of interests and concerns, which were differently focused according to gender and changes in needs and circumstances. They suggest that some widows based the structure of their testaments upon their husbands' and modified them in order to incorporate their personal choices. Some family wills may have been used as models and records of family and household tradition, scribes (who were often local clergy) performing an important function in the transmission of family pieties by helping testators to read and use them when they came to record their own last wishes.

Although complex family histories could be created by death and remarriage, active kinship bonds between families joined by marriage provided a degree of stability and continuity to family relations through crises of mortality and economic hardship.[99] Freedom of choice for widows in marriage was limited by the expectations of a wide network of people with vested interests in the match.[100] In this way, bonds of kinship may have worked to circumscribe potential discontinuities in household belief and practice. Where widows were not quick to remarry, or remained unmarried with young or adolescent children, they had an important role in promoting and sustaining household piety. Of great importance, in such circumstances, were blood and affinal relatives. In terms of the continuance of religious traditions in these households, the influence of the brothers and brothers-in-law of the widow and so uncles to her children, would have been especially significant.[101] In periods of high adult mortality and high fertility such as the early sixteenth century, one would expect wide and dense kinship networks to have existed most of all between collateral contemporary kin such as cousins.[102]

Godparenthood, for example, provided figurative kinship that was complementary to natural kinship relations between generations as well as within them.[103] The significance of godparenthood in the maintenance of traditions of piety, and its exact relationship to blood and affinal kinship, has scarcely been explored, but in Tenterden and its hinterland parishes, it was an unusually important element within testamentary piety and appears to have been a flexible relationship subject to considerable complexity and

---

[99] Chaytor, 'Household and kinship', passim; O'Hara, *Courtship and constraint*, 30–56; Houlbrooke, *English family*, 20.

[100] O'Hara, 'Ruled by my friends', 18–19, and *Courtship and constraint*, 36.

[101] Houlbrooke, *English family*, 44, 48; Wrightson, 'Kinship', 330.

[102] Although the effectiveness of these links has been called into question, this has only been from the perspective of the descent of property, which may not bear direct comparison to other spheres of social relations: Smith, 'Some issues concerning families', 56–8.

[103] J. Bestard-Camps, *What's in a relative? Household and family in Formentera*, New York–Oxford 1991, 28–42; Barnard and Good, *Study of kinship*, 150–4; Bossy, 'Blood and baptism', 132–8; R. B. Dinn, 'Baptism, spiritual kinship, and popular religion in late medieval Bury St Edmunds', *Bulletin of the John Rylands Library* lxxii (1990), 93–106.

nuance. The proportion of godchildren who were related to their godparents in these Wealden parishes was much higher than has previously been suggested for late medieval England or Europe as a whole. Contemporary collateral relations, and particularly uncles and aunts, formed the bulk of these links and probably served to reinforce marriage alliances, intensify, enrich and widen the field of effective kinship as traced from the nuclear family, and consolidate patrimony. Whilst it is impossible to judge what proportion of bonds were based on more distant kinship, it is likely that godparenthood also played a crucial role in establishing links between previously unrelated families or those only distantly related. Gifts to godchildren were closely tied to a concern that young people marry well and establish households and were motivated by pious concerns. It appears, also, that godparenthood helped to strengthen the multi-generational transmission of piety and to forge and maintain identities. This may especially have been the case when collaterals acted as godparents and would clearly have depended on the particular circumstances of relationships marked and transformed by the ritual bond and the parties involved.[104]

The comparative and collective analysis of family wills conducted in the following chapters has considerable implications for the pursuit of individual piety. It suggests that this can best be located by identifying the multi-generational transmission and reproduction of values and preoccupations, and how these were mediated by individual circumstances and choices. The interrelationship of these two elements can be seen perhaps most clearly within the context of the household. In this setting it is apparent that, whereas shifting circumstances and varying pressures were important variables in the strategy of will-making adopted, individual testators, nevertheless, acted within certain parameters. It is these psychological and moral constraints on behaviour which provide a means of identifying and describing particular household and family pieties.

Tenterden as case study for the reconstruction of late medieval piety

Tenterden was not a typical parish (if there was such a thing) and possessed a number of features that had an important bearing on piety. As a settlement it probably existed from at least the eighth century and, in common with the rest of the Weald, its parish boundary was laid down sometime before the end of the thirteenth.[105] By this time Tenterden was one of the principal market

---

104 Lutton, 'Godparenthood, kinship and piety', passim.
105 R. Furley, 'The early history of Tenterden', AC xiv (1882), 40–2, 46; K. P. Witney, *The Jutish forest: a study of the Weald of Kent from 450 to 1380 A.D.*, London 1976, 147–8; J. Roberts, 'Tenterden houses: a study of the domestic buildings of a Kent parish in their social and economic environment', unpubl. PhD diss. Nottingham 1990, 15–16; A. Everitt, *Continuity and colonization: the evolution of Kentish settlement*, Leicester 1986,

towns on the Kentish Weald, with an annual fair.[106] The parish was relatively large, comprising 8,500 acres of land, which varied markedly in quality from inflexible clays to more fertile clay and sand alluvium in the marshlands to the extreme south and east. It was also topographically diverse, the most conspicuous feature being the division created by a central ridge along which ran the town's main street and the bulk of its urban settlement by the four-teenth century. To the north-west of this is an area of round-topped hills and fast-flowing streams, typical of the High Weald and difficult to access in this period, especially in the wetter months. To the north-east, high ground slopes down to the Ingledon Valley and, subsequently, to Shirley Moor, and contained the parish's largest areas of wood. The southern half of the parish has its own distinct character, with two central large spurs, separated by Tilder Gill, descending to Small Hythe and Reading Street (see map 1).[107]

The parish's topographical variety was matched by a diffuse and diverse pattern of settlement that had significant implications for the organisation of religious life and pious sensibilities. The commercial heart of the town was concentrated around the parish church and to the north of the High Street, with less intensive development to the south. Other clusters of settlement formed at the two road junctions, West and East Cross at either end of the High Street, and along the busy road south to Small Hythe known as Broad Tenterden.[108] Around this urban core lay industrial or semi-industrial suburbs with some low density and low-status housing, namely Watermill Valley in the west of the parish and at Eastgate on the road to Woodchurch beyond East Cross. Compared to the northern half of the parish, which was either heavily wooded, steeply sloping or semi-industrial, the broad spurs to the south offered the best agricultural land and contained most of the parish's isolated rural houses.[109] In addition, there were a number of smaller settle-ments, of varying size, quite separate from Tenterden town, namely Boresisle to the north, Leigh Green on the road to Reading Street, itself an important centre, and the largest and most significant, Small Hythe, which owed its importance in the later Middle Ages to its position on the river Rother and so served as Tenterden's port and, with Reading Street, as a substantial ship-building centre.[110]

205; M. Beresford, 'Journey along boundaries', in his History on the ground: six studies in maps and landscapes, London 1957, passim; D. Bonney, 'Early boundaries in Wessex', in P. J. Fowler (ed.), Archaeology and the landscape: essays for L.V. Grinsell, London 1972, 168–9.

[106] Furley, 'Early history of Tenterden', 43; M. L. Zell, 'Population and family structure in the sixteenth-century Weald', AC c (1984), 240, and Industry in the countryside, 61–2, 116–21, 147–50.

[107] Roberts, 'Tenterden houses', 12–13.

[108] Ibid. 41–4; E. Hasted, The history and topographical survey of the county of Kent, 1797–1801, Wakefield 1972, vii. 212–13.

[109] Roberts, 'Tenterden houses', 44–50.

[110] Ibid. 48, 347–50; Furley, 'Early history of Tenterden', 56, 60.

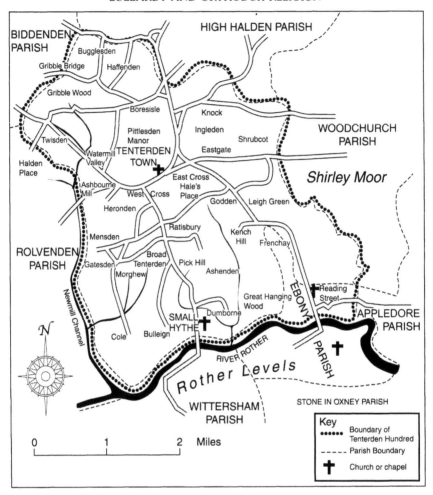

Map 1. The parish and hundred of Tenterden (adapted from H. Roberts, *Tenterden: the first thousand years*, York 1995, 71)

Fragmentation of settlement was matched by the diversity and divisions created by Tenterden's judicial and tenurial boundaries and institutions. The parish boundary was preceded by and largely coterminous with the hundred, part of the Seven Hundreds of the Weald originating from before the Conquest. This was divided into six boroughs (known as tithings in most other counties) each with elected borsholders who ensured that every holder of a tenement did regular suit and service at the hundred court and manorial courts with jurisdiction in the borough.[111] Although, like the tithing, the

111 Furley, 'Early history of Tenterden', 41–5; Witney, *Jutish forest*, 143–4; H. Roberts, *Tenterden: the first thousand years*, York 1995, 54; A. H. Taylor, 'The municipal records of Tenterden, part i', AC xxxii (1917), 289; E. B. Dewindt, *Land and people in*

borough declined in importance by the late fifteenth century, it remained the basic administrative unit of the hundred and continued to provide a focus for local identities beneath the level of the parish.[112] More ancient still, and even more intensely localised, were the dens. Common to the Weald of Kent, the dens originated as rights of pannage granted by the late Saxon kings of the county mainly to ecclesiastics and religious houses. Mostly attached to manors in East Kent belonging to Christ Church Priory and St Augustine's Abbey, Canterbury, at least thirty of Tenterden's original dens survived into the thirteenth century and many of these beyond 1500. Their boundaries were defined much like those of parishes, by crosses, trees, stones and other markers and were still beaten by residents and landholders in the early sixteenth century.[113] They remained important, primarily, because they still dictated lordship – however far removed – and so continued to provide the basic tenurial framework, and lent social and economic relations a peculiarly localised character.[114]

The Kentish Weald experienced rapid population growth from perhaps as early as the 1470s, mainly due to an influx of migrants from elsewhere in Kent and the continent.[115] Although it seems that this slowed or even came to a standstill in Tenterden in the first half of the sixteenth century there is no doubting that the parish was unusually populous by Wealden standards, its inhabitants numbering at least 1,300 in the 1560s.[116] As the Weald's population rose, large areas of remaining wood were cleared. The Rother provided

Holywell-cum-Needingworth, Toronto 1972, 206, 215, 243; C. Dyer, *Lords and peasants in a changing society: the estates of the bishopric of Worcester, 680–1540*, Cambridge 1980, 356, 358–60.

[112] See, for example, Dewindt, *Land and people*, 274; J. A. Raftis, *Warboys: two hundred years in the life of an English mediaeval village*, Toronto 1974, 219–24. Another such unit was the quarter, but the origins, locations and purposes of this division are far from clear: Furley, 'Early history of Tenterden', 41. On the division of space within the parish church and churchyard according to quarters see Rosser, 'Parochial conformity', 187–8.

[113] R. Furley, *A history of the Weald of Kent*, Ashford–London 1874, ii/2, 690–8, 701–24; Everitt, *Continuity and colonization*, 122–6; Witney, *Jutish forest*, passim; D. M. Owen, *Church and society in medieval Lincolnshire* (Society for Lincolnshire History and Archaeology, History of Lincolnshire v, 1971), 108–9. J. E. Mace, *Notes on old Tenterden*, Tenterden 1902, 9–10. There is a detailed description of the treading of the boundaries of dens in the nearby parish of Hawkhurst, dated 1507: W. J. Lightfoot (ed.), 'Notes from the records of Hawkhurst church', AC v (1863), 79–84.

[114] Furley, *History of the Weald*, 696–7.

[115] J. Cornwall, 'English population in the early sixteenth century', EcHR xxiii (1970), 32–44; B. Campbell, 'The population of early Tudor England: a re-evaluation of the 1522 muster returns and the 1524 and 1525 lay subsidies', *Journal of Historical Geography* vii (1981), 145–54; P. Clark, *English provincial society from the Reformation to the Revolution: religion, politics and society in Kent, 1500–1640*, Hassocks 1977, 7–12; Zell, 'Population and family structure', 233–8, and *Industry in the countryside*, ch. iii, esp. p. 86; Roberts, 'Tenterden houses', 23–4; O'Hara, *Courtship and constraint*, 19.

[116] Zell, 'Population and family structure', 233–5, 257, and *Industry in the countryside*, 57, 86; Roberts, 'Tenterden houses', 24, fig. i.

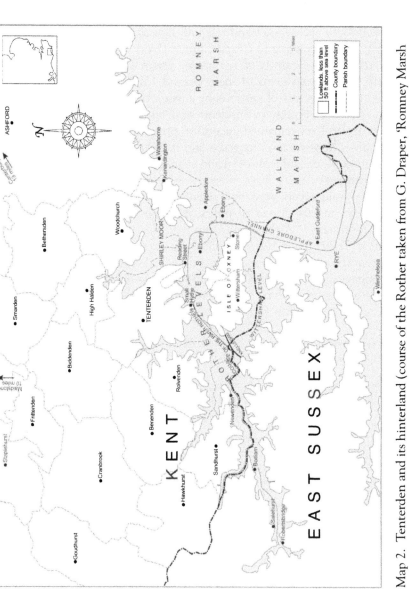

Map 2. Tenterden and its hinterland (course of the Rother taken from G. Draper, 'Romney Marsh and its towns and villages, c. 800–1500', in T. Lawson and D. Killingray [eds], *An historical atlas of Kent*, Philimore 2004, after J. Eddison, 'Drowned lands: changes in the course of the Rother and its estuary and associated drainage problems', in J. Eddison and C. Green [eds], *Romney Marsh: evolution, occupation, reclamation*, Oxford 1988, 142–61)

easy access to sea and river borne trade, allowing for the movement of felled timber and charcoal to London and the continent, whilst locally raised cattle were moved by land to feed a growing metropolitan market. Tenterden was not central to the Wealden cloth and iron industries, which mushroomed at this time, but more than likely benefited commercially.[117] Through its port of Small Hythe, Tenterden also served as a crucial link in the internal trade of Kent and Sussex, acting as a redistribution point between the interior of the Weald and centres such as Ashford, Maidstone and Canterbury as well as the coastal towns.[118] Of these, Tenterden was linked most closely to the Cinque Port of Rye which, by the 1550s, had the largest mercantile fleet on the south coast. Rye's overseas trade was mainly with the Low Countries and France, goods from which were redistributed up the Rother to Tenterden through Small Hythe and other riverside centres deeper into the Weald.[119] In the opposite direction flowed the manufactured wares of the Wealden iron industry, charcoal, leather and skins, horses, beer, tallow, cloth and, most important, timber (see map 2).[120] Tenterden's domestic and overseas trade, and role as a regional centre of some importance, meant that its inhabitants were exposed to a more diverse range of cultural and religious influences than the residents of most English market towns, not to mention more rural parishes.

As a member of the Cinque Ports confederation the town was largely exempt from central government taxation and so, for example, its inhabitants were not assessed under the lay subsidy of 1523–5. This, coupled with the fact that most of the borough's late medieval administrative records were destroyed in a seventeenth-century fire, means that Tenterden lacks some of those documentary sources most pertinent to its social and economic development.[121] There are, however, extant lay subsidy returns for the Wealden hundreds that roughly comprised Tenterden's hinterland. Containing both Low Wealden parishes such as Bethersden, Biddenden, High Halden, Woodchurch, Wittersham and Appledore and those on the High Weald, including Cranbrook, Hawkhurst and Benenden, they formed a cohesive economic region of predominantly pastoral agriculture (see map 2).[122] The distribution of assessments for these hundreds is presented in table 1 and, in table 2, the hierarchy of wealth is compared with the returns for the urbanised manor of Havering, three country towns of similar size and nature to

117 Clark, English provincial society, 7–9; Furley, 'Early history of Tenterden', 52–3.
118 Clark, English provincial society, 10–11.
119 G. J. Mayhew, Tudor Rye, Brighton 1987, 50, 236–52; Roberts, 'Tenterden houses', 347.
120 Mayhew, Tudor Rye, 6, 237–252, 308 n. 8; Roberts, 'Tenterden houses', 348–9, and Tenterden, 13, 49–51.
121 Taylor, 'Municipal records of Tenterden, part i', 285.
122 PRO, E 179, 125/324; Zell, 'Wood-pasture regime', 69–93, in revised form in his Industry in the countryside, 5–7, 88–112. The vill of Newenden, to the south of Rolvenden parish, was listed separately in the subsidy returns and is included with the Seven Hundreds.

Table 1
Numbers and percentages of individuals taxed at different levels in 1524–5 subsidy assessments in seven Wealden hundreds and the vill of Newenden

Level of assessment	East Barnfield	Barclay	Selbrittenden	Blackborne	Rolvenden	Cranbrook	Oxney	Newenden	All seven hundreds and the vill of Newenden
Up to 39s. in goods/wages; under £1 p.a. in lands	55 (36%)	99 (39%)	37 (21%)	142 (40%)	69 (36%)	179 (30%)	17 (15%)	11 (58%)	609 (32.8%)
40s.–£2 19s. in goods/wages; £1 p.a. in lands	31 (20%)	39 (15%)	39 (22%)	66 (19%)	28 (14%)	184 (31%)	22 (19%)	3 (16%)	412 (22.2%)
£3–£4 19s. in goods/wages; £1 1s.–£2 19s. p.a. in lands	32 (21%)	31 (12%)	35 (20%)	52 (15%)	34 (18%)	74 (12.5%)	26 (23%)	3 (16%)	287 (15.5.%)
£5–£9 19s. in goods; £3–£5 19s. p.a. in lands	22 (14%)	40 (16%)	34 (20%)	45 (13%)	38 (20%)	55 (9%)	18 (16%)	1 (5%)	253 (13.6%)
£10–£19 19s. in goods; £6–£9 19s. p.a. in lands	10 (7%)	27 (11%)	19 (11%)	17 (5%)	17 (9%)	48 (8%)	20 (17.5%)	1 (5%)	159 (8.6%)
£20–£39 in goods; £10–£39 p.a. in lands	3 (2%)	9 (4%)	7 (4%)	24 (7%)	5 (3%)	30 (5%)	6 (5%)	0 (0%)	84 (4.5%)
£40 or more in goods/p.a. in lands	0 (0%)	8 (3%)	3 (2%)	10 (3%)	3 (2%)	22 (4%)	5 (4%)	0 (0%)	51 (2.7%)

Source: PRO, E 179, 125/324

Tenterden, the rural parish of Terling and rural Cambridgeshire.[123] Of Wealden taxpayers 45 per cent were assessed on over £2 in goods or land which, for a largely rural area (apart from Cranbrook), is relatively high and reflects the considerable wealth of the Kentish Weald and the amounts of money to be made from pastoral agriculture in combination with the cloth industry in particular.[124] The distribution of wealth compares most closely with the exceptionally wealthy manor of Havering, dominated by the urban prosperity of Romford.[125] A proportion of 'servants' in the rolls (17 per cent), only slightly lower than in Havering, but markedly different from rural Cambridgeshire suggests a social structure characterised by a sizeable propor-tion of reasonably wealthy households reliant upon the added labour of one or more individuals.[126]

In a number of significant ways Tenterden differed from this pattern. That it had its own particular social and economic features by the second quarter of the sixteenth century is shown by Michael Zell's analysis of probate inven-tories from 1565 to1599, for a total of twelve Wealden parishes, including Tenterden, many of which either partly or wholly lay within Tenterden's hinterland hundreds. Tenterden was not a cloth parish on the scale of Cranbrook, Hawkhurst, Biddenden and Benenden, even when its production was at a peak in the late sixteenth century.[127] The probate inventories reveal farming as the main pursuit of more than 40 per cent of recorded individuals, not far off the levels for predominantly agrarian Rolvenden and High Halden. There was a broad range of trades (almost as many as Cranbrook), but only 20 per cent of the inventories indicate trade or craft activity as the main occupation, compared to 31 per cent for the twelve Wealden parishes as a whole, which suggests that the parish had 'an urban core which offered a moderately large variety of goods and services' and that 'a significant share of artisans and tradesmen were also working as farmers'.[128] The nature and scale of farming in Tenterden was peculiarly affected by the amount of marshland in the parish and access to similarly good grazing along the Rother Levels and

---

[123] For Havering see McIntosh, *Community transformed*, 167. The three country towns are Aylesbury, High Wycombe and Petworth: J. Cornwall, 'English country towns in the fifteen twenties', *EcHR* 2nd ser. xv (1962–3), 62, and his *Wealth and society in early sixteenth-century England*, London 1988, 56. For Terling see Wrightson and Levine, *Poverty and piety*, 34. For Cambridgeshire see Spufford, *Contrasting communities*, 28–36. Assessments on lands were judged to be worth roughly twice those on goods or wages and ranked accordingly.

[124] Zell, *Industry in the countryside*, 134–46.

[125] McIntosh, *Community transformed*, 165–9, and *Autonomy and community*, 233–5.

[126] Idem, *Community transformed*, 56; Spufford, *Contrasting communties*, 33; Zell, 'Popula-tion and family structure', 249–53, republished with minor revisions in his *Industry in the countryside*, 76–80. See also Cornwall, 'English country towns', 66–7. For the sake of comparison with other regions and centres, the distribution of Wealden assessments presented here includes those identified as 'servants' among the lowest strata of taxpayers: cf. McIntosh, *Autonomy and community*, 233.

[127] Zell, *Industry in the countryside*, 117, 154–5, 172, 183–4; Roberts, *Tenterden*, ch. xi.

[128] Zell, *Industry in the countryside*, 117, 119, 121, 149.

Table 2
Percentages of individuals taxed at different levels in 1524–5 subsidy assessments in Wealden hundreds and elsewhere

Level of assessment on lands, goods or wages	Seven Wealden hundreds and the vill of Newenden	Havering	Aylesbury, High Wycombe and Petworth	Rural areas	
				Terling	Cambridgeshire
£1	33%	29%	34%	28%	55%
£2	22%	23%	30%	24%	27% (£2–£4)
£3–£9	29%	29%	22%	37%	10% (£5–£9)
£10–£19	9%	9%	8%	12%	5%
£20+	7%	10%	6%		3%

Sources: PRO, E 179, 125/324; McIntosh, *Community transformed*; Cornwall, 'English country towns'; Wrightson and Levine, *Poverty and piety*; Spufford, *Contrasting communities.*

on the Walland and Romney Marshes. The pasture that this provided was used by specialist graziers who lived in Tenterden itself, or was hired as summer grazing for the herds and flocks of large-scale farmers in neighbouring parishes.[129] This seems to have ensured that, more than any of its neighbours, Tenterden was increasingly geared to relatively specialised and large-scale commercial livestock farming. As a result, the number of small family farms was relatively small, Tenterden producing the lowest proportion of inventories in the £20 to £60 range. This suggests a relatively small lower-middling social group as early as the 1520s (i.e. those householders assessed on £3–£9 in goods, or between £1 and £6 *per annum* in lands in 1524–5) akin to, or even more depleted than, Cranbrook (*see* table 1) or the small country towns of Aylesbury, High Wycombe and Petworth (*see* table 2).[130]

What marks Tenterden out more than anything else is the proportion of inventories listing personalty worth £60 and over: 43 per cent, greater even than for prosperous Cranbrook. These correspond to those medium and large-scale farmers and wealthier crafts- and trades-people assessed on £10 and upwards in goods, or £6 and over in lands in 1524–5. Comparison with Cranbrook (*see* table 1) suggests that the two wealthiest groups would have

129 Ibid. 100, 106–7, and 'Wood-pasture regime', 72–86.
130 31% of the Tenterden inventories valued goods worth from £20 to £60, compared to an average of 40% for all 12 parishes: idem, *Industry in the countryside*, 147, 101–3; Cornwall, *Wealth and society*, 60–1.

comprised at least 17 per cent of would-be taxpayers by the 1520s, a proportion typical of traditional market towns in lowland England in the early sixteenth century.[131] However, unlike most small market towns, by the second half of the century and probably earlier, Tenterden had a good number of very rich inhabitants who outnumbered the merely wealthy.[132] Forty inventories were valued at £100 or above, more than for any other parish (Cranbrook, with a larger population, produced only twenty-eight; Hawkhurst, with similar population in the 1560s, only twelve).[133] Twenty-five of these were worth £150 or more and, of these, at least eighteen detailed the possessions of large-scale graziers and farmers. The remainder listed the goods of wealthy shopkeepers (mainly woollen drapers), a clothier and a tanner (both of whom also farmed). Judging by Tenterden's outstanding prosperity later in the century, it is very likely that at least 10 per cent of would-be taxpayers in the 1520s would have been worthy of assessment on at least £20 in goods (compare with table 2). By the late sixteenth century Tenterden appears to have been dominated by a small number of substantial farmer/graziers together with some successful merchants and shopkeepers. However, even before the 1520s, although divisions of wealth were not so sharply drawn, and political power was shared by a larger section of the population, the economic foundations for accumulation and dominance by leading families were probably already in place. Tenterden's rise as an increasingly wealthy urban centre with influence over a substantial economic and demographic hinterland makes it a particularly significant subject for the investigation of piety and heterodoxy in the Kentish Weald as a whole. Equally, its status as a country town of some regional importance makes this study something of a corrective to previous geographically specific investigations of lay piety, which have tended to focus either on larger urban centres or more rural areas. This is not to suggest that piety at Tenterden was necessarily indicative for small urban centres nationally, but that it was particular to a certain type of rapidly developing economy and social structure, and cultural and political milieu.

The process of consolidation and accumulation of capital had its roots in the late fourteenth and early fifteenth centuries. Tenterden, in its original smaller pre-hundredal form, had been the possession of the manor of Minster, Tenterden literally meaning 'the den of the men of Thanet'.[134] The parish

---

131 Zell, *Industry in the countryside*, 147–50.

132 Cornwall classifies most small towns of the 1520s as having a good 'diffusion of wealth amongst a solid bloc of merchants and master craftsmen worth upwards of £10, and . . . absence of very rich people': *Wealth and society*, 60–1.

133 These wealthiest 40 inventories even outnumbered the 27 that valued goods from £60 to £100. Even so, this latter group amounts to 17% of all the Tenterden inventories, only 1 percentage point behind the largest proportions in Biddenden, Cranbrook/Frittenden and Goudhurst.

134 J. K. Wallenberg, *The place-names of Kent*, Uppsala 1934, 355, 356; Everitt, *Continuity and colonization*, 38, 123; Witney, *Jutish forest*, 45, 93.

church of St Mildred's and the manor appendant to it were appropriated to St Augustine's Abbey in 1259 which, together with Christ Church Priory, also exercised rights over the dens in the parish attached to their manors in East Kent.[135] By the fifteenth century any serious attempts by the great ecclesiastical houses to protect their timber stocks in the face of settlement had given way to a slow but inevitable process of commutation for fixed low money rents with leases of dens and manors being granted for as long as sixty to a hundred years. This fostered a land market that allowed some local families to accumulate holdings and build up estates.[136] Although St Augustine's held its manorial privileges in Tenterden until the Dissolution,[137] in 1478 Christ Church Priory effectively transferred all its jurisdictional rights within the hundred to the bailiff and commons.[138] By the late 1400s landholders were enjoying 'a climate of confidence in which' they were 'free to capitalise not only on the potential of the soil itself but on the economic value of the timber'.[139] Paradoxically, it was also precisely because distant landlords and manors retained their rights that jurisdictional control in the Weald remained weak,[140] and the history of religious dissent and heterodoxy in Tenterden and its hinterland parishes may well owe something to the area's relative isolation from major ecclesiastical or monastic centres of power.

However, the degree of independence gained from distant ecclesiastical lordship should not be overstated. Tenterden's relative autonomy also depended on its annexation to Rye in 1449, as a limb of the Cinque Ports. This was, essentially, a consequence of new-found prosperity in the fifteenth century coupled with Rye's economic difficulties, which were linked to the redirection of the Rother past Small Hythe.[141] Annexation meant that Tenterden ceased to be subject to the jurisdiction of the Seven Hundreds and became a corporation with its own bailiff and fortnightly courts.[142] The

---

135 G. Ward, 'Saxon records of Tenterden', AC xlix (1938), 241–3; Witney, Jutish forest, 116, 125–6; Furley, 'Early history of Tenterden', 45–6; Hasted, History of Kent, vii. 216; A. H. Taylor, 'The rectors and vicars of St Mildred's, Tenterden', AC xxxi (1915), 207–8.
136 Roberts, 'Tenterden houses', 16–20; Witney, Jutish forest, 85, 99–100, 163, 183; Roberts, Tenterden, chs i, viii; F. R. H. Du Boulay, 'Dens, droving and danger', AC lxxvi (1961), 75–87; Furley, 'Early history of Tenterden', 52–3, and History of the Weald, ii/1, 201–2; ii/2, 695–7.
137 Hasted, History of Kent, vii. 214–17; Furley, 'Early history of Tenterden', 46; C. Cotton, 'St Austin's Abbey, Canterbury treasurers' accounts, 1468–9, and others', AC li (1940), 74, 92, 103.
138 Indenture, copied in English in BL, MS Stowe 850, fos 111r–112v.
139 Roberts, 'Tenterden houses', 20. Similar developments have been documented for Battle in Sussex and in Havering, although in the latter case they took place over a longer period: E. Searle, Lordship and community: Battle abbey and its banlieu, 1066–1538, Toronto 1974, 324–37, 352–406; McIntosh, Autonomy and community, 136–78, 221–35.
140 Everitt, Continuity and colonization, 56.
141 Witney, Jutish forest, 146–8.
142 Copy in English of the charter of incorporation granted by Henry VI, in the Tenterden custumal: CKS, Te/C1, fos 13r–16v.

resulting exemptions from tolls and customs could only have helped nurture commercial growth, although Tenterden became locked in a protracted struggle with Rye over its precise contribution to the Cinque Ports confedera-tion.[143] Annexation to Rye had the effect of drawing Tenterden further into a network of regional and national office-holding that was exploited by powerful noble and gentry dynasties that were consolidating their estates in Wealden parishes. The activities of central government and the great reli-gious houses in Canterbury, with which some of these families were closely linked, were never far removed and ensured that Tenterden and surrounding parishes were subject to wider cultural influences.

Tenterden's religious institutions were, at first sight, relatively conven-tional. These will be examined in more detail in chapter 2 but here it suffices to draw out some of their more important, and idiosyncratic, features. The sizeable parish church of St Mildred's, extensively enhanced in the fifteenth century, has been mentioned, but its place in religious observance was complicated by the existence of a sub-parochial chapel at Small Hythe. Of ambiguous status, the chapel was peculiarly expressive of outside cultural influences, from both the Low Countries and closer to hand, as well as the relationship between Tenterden's satellite port and urban core. Small Hythe and its chapel will be examined in detail in chapter 3 in an attempt to address more general problems surrounding the nature and significance of the late medieval parish. The environmental, social and economic roots of a distinc-tive piety will also be investigated, as will the relationship between indi-vidual choice at Small Hythe and collective constraints and dispositions.

In other ways parochial religion at Tenterden was somewhat unusual. Despite a relatively high number of permanently endowed chantries in the parish, testamentary piety at Tenterden was either strikingly unengaged with traditional orthodox devotion or was peculiarly focused on particular reli-gious forms. Arrangements for temporary chantries were not nearly as popular, over the period as a whole, as giving to funerals and obits. The reli-gious orders were no more than peripheral and completely disappeared from wills in 1518, and although there was a good range of saints' cults these also failed to attract testamentary giving on a scale comparable to other places. Significantly, bequests to images were rare and stopped in 1522. Of the two fraternities of which there is a record one was dedicated to the Virgin Mary and the other, by far the more popular, to the cult of the Holy Name of Jesus, a late fifteenth-century introduction to England. The Jesus Mass was readily received by parishioners and represents a key development in Tenterden's piety, in stark contrast to the lack of impact achieved by other new devotions.

---

[143] Hasted, *History of Kent*, vii. 200–2; Te/C1, fos 13r–16v, 17r–22r; *A calendar of the white and black books of the cinque ports, 1432–1955*, ed. F. Hull (KR xix, 1966), pp. xxxvii–xxxviii, 101, 106; H. T. Riley, 'The corporation of Tenterden', in *HMC, Sixth report*, appendix (1877), 569; H. T. Riley, 'MSS of the corporation of Rye', in *HMC, Fifth report, appendix* (1876), 491, 493–4.

Quantitative and qualitative analysis of religious bequests found in wills and comparison with other centres and regions, in chapter 2, will demonstrate the distinctive character and chronology of orthodoxy at Tenterden. Coupled with reconstruction of the spectrum of piety across different families with contrasting and divergent traditions of testamentary giving, this will serve to problematise notions of homogeneous parochial religion. So as to investigate the nature and roots of heterogeneity within orthodoxy, chapter 4 will focus on families that represented one extreme in the spectrum of testamentary practice. The transmission and development over time of enduring pious dispositions will allow for discussion of how the overall tenor of piety at Tenterden shifted in a particular direction up to the early years of the Henrician Reformation. The possible roots of these developments will be assessed by exploring the relationship between shifting pieties and the dramatic economic and social changes outlined above.

Tenterden was, of course, at the centre of an enduring tradition of Wycliffite heresy on the Kentish Weald from the early fifteenth century to the early sixteenth. As such, it offers the opportunity to investigate heterodoxy closely in a particular locality and region with the benefit of a detailed reconstruction of orthodoxy. So, chapter 5 will examine the features and roots of an enduring tradition of Lollardy and the relationship of convicted heretics' beliefs and practices to changing traditions and patterns of orthodox piety. The chapter will also assesses the influence of parish clergy on lay piety as well as the important roles played by noble and gentry families in the fashioning of religious life.

It is not within the compass of this book to extend the methods applied to pre-Reformation evidence to sixteenth-century records of religious reform and upheaval. To some extent the theoretical and methodological challenges posed by the Reformation are quite different from those of the late fifteenth and early sixteenth centuries, not least in terms of the usefulness or otherwise of testamentary evidence as a barometer of responses to reform across the countryside. Whilst a proper treatment of the Reformation in Tenterden and the Weald of Kent would warrant another volume at least the size of this one, the epilogue to this book argues that the nature of orthodox and heterodox lay piety at Tenterden has significant implications for Reformation studies, particularly in terms of existing models of religious change and the growth and establishment of Protestantism.

2

Family Pieties and Urban Identity

In order to place Tenterden's religious culture in a broad comparative perspective, a considerable part of this chapter is devoted to quantitative description of the level of popularity over time of the various categories of bequests which historians of late medieval religion have tended to use in the analysis of probate materials. This is accompanied by qualitative description of the institutions and practices of parochial piety and comparison with religious belief and practice in other places. The chapter begins with an attempt to draw distinctions between different families' testamentary strategies and the ways they juxtaposed and balanced more traditional religious preoccupations with other concerns. This makes it possible to show how commitment to the forms and fashions of orthodox piety varied markedly and consistently between families. The diversity so described provides the basis for exploring, particularly in chapter 4, heterodox divergences in parochial piety and the possible roots of these shifts. A further strand within this discussion concerns the representation and construction of identity and community at Tenterden through the use of sets of symbols.[1] Elements of religious life from saints' cults to church-building were employed in the construction of identity and the shifting symbolism of devotion is interpreted in the light of social, economic and political change.

Pious priorities and testamentary strategies

Wealth, status and economic activity

Tenterden's families engaged with the institutions, structures and patterns of parochial religion to varying degrees and at a number of different levels in their wills. They did so by employing a range of testamentary strategies that were formulated in response to the interplay of competing pressures and priorities upon the disposal of available resources. These strategies were informed by shared and transmitted preconceptions and preoccupations that were not necessarily common to the whole parish. The approach to will-making adopted by the Chapman, Castelyn or Blossom families, for example, was markedly different from that taken by the Strekynbolds, who were far more similar in their sensibilities to say the Stonehouses or the Carpynters. So, whilst varying according to individual circumstances, there was a general

---

[1] Cohen, *Symbolic construction of community*.

character to any one family's testamentary practices ranging across a broad spectrum. Twenty-three families were selected for detailed examination and these can be divided into three bands at the top, middle and bottom of the pious spectrum (*see* table 4 at pp. 48–9). The criteria for their selection and for so distinguishing their particular pieties are described in more detail below but first it is necessary to say something about their relative wealth, social standing and economic activities.

The records of central government taxation that survive for Tenterden detail fifteenths or tenths on goods and chattels belonging to the freemen or 'barons of the Cinque Ports'.[2] The most complete assessments on moveables in Tenterden hundred, and in two cases pertaining also to other hundreds, fall at convenient chronological intervals in 1464, 1512–13 and 1542–3. The numerical dominance of middle-band families in the town's franchise over the period as a whole is underlined by their regular appearance in the assessments but, across all three groups, certain names appear more frequently than others. Far ahead of the rest were the Brekyndens, but the Gerveses, Prestons, Pierses, Bisshopyndens and Coupers all display a degree of long-term continuity. Bottom-band families are not well represented, suggesting that they did not share the same degree of access to the franchise, probably because of lower levels of wealth. There were exceptions to this rule. For example, Robert Bisshopynden and Stephen Castelyn were assessed on above average moveable wealth in 1464 and 1512–13 respectively. Wealth generally appears to have been concentrated toward the top of the testamentary spectrum, in families such as the Foules, Strekynbolds, Prestons and Coupers, but there were equally wealthy individuals from middle-band families such as the Brekyndens, Gerveses and Assheryndens, as well as others who appear to have been less affluent.[3]

The evidence of around 120 property transfers between 1449 and 1549 provides a complementary insight into the relative wealth of these families.[4] The middle band displays the highest levels of land market activity over the period, the Pierses and Brekyndens being outstanding in this regard. The families at the top of the spectrum were less active although the Foules, Carpynters and Davys equalled all but the Pierses and Brekyndens in their levels of engagement. The bottom band appears to have been the least active, the Blossoms alone operating at a level commensurate with the other two groups. The extent of a family's involvement in property transfers indicates as much about the pace and degree of change and reorganisation in its landed resources, as its overall landed wealth. Middle-band families and, to a lesser extent, those in the top band may have been the foremost players in the

2   *Calendar of the white and black books*, p. xxvi.
3   PRO, E 179, 230/182; 234/7; 231/228.
4   BL, Add. Charters 16319–20, 16322, 16324, 16328–31, 41799, 56976–7, 56979–85, 58708; MS Add. 48022, fos 23r, 25v–34v; CKS, U455/T84–8/T90, U410/T12/T21/ T178–9, U442/T99, U55/T414, U36/T1453–4, U1044/F1; Te/S1.

market, but land market activity can also indicate loss, and the possibility of downwards social mobility among these groups should not be ruled out. The chronology of activity is instructive in this regard. Among top-band families, only the Foules increased or maintained their level of activity after 1500, and three families which appear prior to 1500 disappear from the records after that date. In contrast, the Smyths, Pellonds, Brekyndens, Gerveses and Assheryndens all either increased their degree of involvement, or sustained it at roughly the same level, suggesting that they at least maintained or even enhanced their position in the social hierarchy in the early sixteenth century. Underlining their generally less robust economic position, the Blossoms were the only bottom-band family to appear at all in property transfers after 1500. Although some of these families, such as the Castelyns, were growing in wealth and status, generally, they do not appear to have been making the economic advances enjoyed by those in the middle and top groups.

The Tenterden borough custumal contains a list of admissions to the franchise, in rough chronological order from 1529 to c. 1558. These provide an indication not just of the composition of the leading town families by the end of the period, but those that were climbing the fastest socially. In all, the names of 124 freemen are recorded, twenty-two of whom belonged to selected families.[5] Fourteen of these were members of families from the middle of the testamentary spectrum, namely three Assheryndens, three Pellonds, four Brekyndens, two Smyths, Robert Piers and William Gerves. Represented to a much lesser extent were top-band families, by four Foules and two Coupers. The other end of the pious spectrum was present in the names of George Castelyn and William Hoke.

Eleven of the twenty-three families served at the highest level of municipal government. Six top-band families provided bailiffs who served for a total of twenty-one terms of office between 1449 and 1558, underlining the high status of this group (see table 3). Five middle-band families recorded terms of office on twenty separate occasions whereas the bottom group is entirely absent. The Foules were the only top-band family to continue to enter office after the last decade of the fifteenth century and so held or improved their position in the urban hierarchy alongside the Brekyndens and Gerveses in particular.[6]

The borough also elected annually twelve jurats, and twelve or thirteen taxors of the scott (assessors of the annual levy granted by the commonalty of the borough to the bailiff and jurats). There is a full record of their names for the years 1538 to 1542.[7] The now familiar Foules were the only top-band family to be named among the jurats, John Foule serving in 1538 and 1540–2 (he was bailiff in 1539), and only the Coupers supplied a taxor of the scott. In

[5] Te/C1, fos 116r–117v.
[6] Te/C1, fos 140r–141r. Only 37 surnames appear in the list of bailiffs, 19 of these more than once, and 12 more than 3 times.
[7] Te/S1, fos 1r, 19r, 27r, 32r, 39r.

Table 3
Selected families and their service as Tenterden bailiffs, 1449–1558

Family	Terms in office	First year in office	Last year in office	Number of years from entry into office to last year of service
Top-band families				
Davy	4	1452	1495	43
Donne	1	1455	1455	1
Preston	4	1464	1487	23
Strekynbold	3	1476	1486	10
Carpynter	3	1478	1489	11
Foule	6	1480	1540	60
Middle-band families				
Brekynden	7	1453	1549	96
Gerves	4	1465	1551	86
Pette	7	1472	1502	30
Piers	1	1474	1474	1
Assherynden	1	1522	1522	1

Source: CKS, Te/C1, fos 140r–141r.

contrast, six middle-band families are represented in either one or both of the two offices. None of the jurats over these years belonged to bottom-band families. Christopher Blossom alone, elected taxor in 1538 and 1539, represents this group. Parochial office-holding conforms to the same pattern. The names of the two annually appointed churchwardens for fourteen years within the period 1498–1523 are recorded in archiediaconal visitation returns. Only the Davys and the Foules from the top band of families supplied churchwardens, on two and three occasions respectively (the Davys in 1498 and 1499). This may be compared to the total of five terms shared by the Brekynden, Pette, Gerves and Assherynden families. The only member of a bottom-band family to be named as churchwarden was Christopher Castelyn, in 1521 and 1522.[8]

Less formal social roles included the executing, supervising and witnessing of last wills and testaments. If good social standing was not always required to witness wills it was a prerequisite to executing or supervising them, as long, that is, as these duties were not carried out by immediate family.[9] In fact, increasingly over the period, testators called upon spouses, sons, fathers, sons-in-law and other family members to execute their wills and such

8 CCA, Z.3.1–4, 37; X.8.2; CKS, U410/T179.
9 Marsh, 'In the name of God?', 231–3.

instances are excluded here. This change in practice may have been due to increasing wealth which meant that families had to rely less on well-resourced individuals from outside the immediate circle of relatives to act as executors. Affinal relationships remained important, however, and to some degree the level of a family's activity in these semi-official roles reflects the density of its affinal kinship network.[10] It also provides an impression of a family's standing in the community, the extent to which it was held in trust by neighbours, kin and associates and its financial solvency. The top group of families provided executors to wills a median of twice per family. This was matched by the middle band, whereas the bottom group acted in this capacity on only a median of one occasion per family (only four out of six were recorded in this role). Middle-band families appear to have been increasingly more likely to be entrusted with this responsibility after 1500. Only one individual from all twenty-three families is described as 'clerk', namely John Piers, in 1470.[11] Witnessing of wills is more enlightening because, increasingly, testators relied on extra-familial witnesses, which was perhaps a consequence of the greater reliance on family members as executors. Once again, the spread of activity was significantly uneven. Top-band families acted as witnesses a median of only twice each, those in the middle of the spectrum on a median of five occasions, and those at the bottom a median of only twice, underlining their comparatively lower social status, with three of these families not appearing at all in this capacity. By 1520–35 middle-band families were much more likely to act as witnesses than the rest and a similar pattern can be seen in the supervision of wills.

A number of the selected families appear to have been overwhelmingly engaged in agriculture, which in many cases seems to have been conducted on a commercial footing, coupled with involvement in industrial activities such as brewing, ship-building, ship-ownership or seaborne trade. By the late fifteenth century the Foules lived at West Cross. In 1411 one member of the family was engaged in ship ownership and William Foule devised a dyehouse with other property to his son Bartholomew in 1496. In the early 1540s John Foule either styled himself or was described as *generosus* and he and his wife Elizabeth made five sales of land and tenements comprising at least seventy-seven acres of land and pasture, two messuages and two gardens, scattered around the north-western part of the parish. The sales raised a total of £201 13s. 4d.[12] Like the Foules, most of the top-band families appear to have

10 Wrightson, 'Kinship', 313–22.

11 PRC 17/1/304.

12 PRC 17/15/64; Roberts, 'Tenterden houses', 43–4; PRC 17/6/281; CCR, Henry IV, 1409–13, 167; CKS, U455/T87; PRC 17/16/239; Te/S1, fos 35v, 36r, 40v–41r, 42r, 43v–44r; *L&P* xxi. 1280, fo. 41, 546. Titles inferring gentry status were often used by civic officials and sometimes scribes working for town governments by the fifteenth century, but they nevertheless indicate a relatively high degree of social status: R. Horrox, 'The urban gentry in the fifteenth century', in J. A. F. Thomson (ed.), *Towns and townspeople in the fifteenth century*, Gloucester 1988, 28–30.

been first and foremost involved in agriculture, supplemented with some industrial or mercantile pursuits. The Strekynbolds, Stonehouses, Prestons and Jamyns were all successful pastoral farming families. The same applies to the Carpynters who were also engaged in cloth dyeing by the end of the fifteenth century.[13] The Davys owned a large part of the lands around Small Hythe and, in the late fifteenth century, possessed a brewhouse and were supplying timber for the construction of royal navy ships at Small Hythe. One member of the family, Stephen Davy, was conducting a tailoring business in 1498.[14] The Donnes seem to have been involved in ship-building although none of their wills suggests anything other than farming as their main economic activity.[15]

The Coupers were something of an exception to this rule, and it should perhaps be remembered that they and the Foules were the only families in the top pious band to have held or advanced their position in the urban hierarchy by the end of the period. In 1486 William Couper and his 'grete bote' were hired by the Clerk of the King's Ships for the conveyance of guns and other stuff from the *Mary of the Tower*.[16] By the time of his death, in 1518, William not only held lands in various parts of the parish, but conducted a tanning business at his principal holding in the semi-industrial suburb of East Gate. This was a family concern, in which his uncle Stephen Couper (twice described as 'tanner' in wills in 1513 and 1522) was also engaged. William left leather, 'rynde' and 'tanne' to his son Stephen in 1518 who, still a minor, was entrusted into the custody of Stephen senior. Stephen junior continued the family business at East Gate, his inventory listing a 'letherd house' and a 'tannhouse' there.[17] By 1538 Stephen was being described as yeoman; along with his wife Margaret, he was able to purchase his mother-in-law's estate in Essex and, a year later, was writing to Thomas Cromwell requesting the rangership of Halden Park in Tenterden.[18] Erl of Essex – Henry VIII advisor

In contrast, seven of the eight families in the middle of the testamentary spectrum were involved, at one stage or another, in craft or industrial activity. Stephen Smyth was described as 'fuller' in 1482, and in 1512 Henry Smith supplied more than three hundred loads of elm for the fortification of Calais. Thomas Smyth died in the 1560s, one of the lesser 'parish landlords', having built up a reasonably consolidated estate in the north-west of the parish, with a principal messuage in the suburb of Boresisle, the largely industrial area

<hr>

13 PRC 17/7/48.

14 PRC 17/6/110; U455/T85; Roberts, *Tenterden*, 46; 'Naval accounts and inventories of the reign of Henry VII, 1485–8 and 1495–7', ed. M. Oppenheim (Publications of the Navy Records Society viii, 1896), 313; *L&P*, addenda i. 8; BL, MS Add. 48022, fos 32v–33r.

15 CPR, Henry V, ii. 1416–22, 165; 'Naval accounts of Henry VII', 144, 146, 149.

16 'Naval accounts of Henry VII', 15, 17–18.

17 PRC 32/12/174, 17/12/227, 17/15/242; Roberts, 'Tenterden houses', 45.

18 J. C. Jeaffreson, 'MSS of the *custos rotolorum* and justices of the peace of the county of Essex, at the Shire-Hall, Chelmsford, Essex', in HMC, *Tenth report*, appendix, pt iv (1885), 494; *L&P* xv. 542.

which contained a number of mills for the processing of both grain and cloth.[19] William Gerves, who made his will in 1525, mentioned a forge among his estate, indicating that the family's wealth, later accumulated largely through commercial agriculture was, earlier in the century, partly derived from industrial activity.[20] The Pierses were involved in butchery and shoemaking in the 1470s and owned considerable lands in and around the parish.[21] John Pette described himself as 'pannarius' (clothier/draper) in his will of 1489 and was probably one of the wealthier tradesmen of the late fifteenth century.[22] The Pellonds, described in more detail in chapter 4, operated a tailoring business by the early sixteenth century and appear to have had a hand in waterborne trade in timber. The early Assherynden wills are all entirely agricultural in content, the family being one of the larger landowners at Small Hythe, but evidence that they also engaged in craft or industrial activities by the early sixteenth century is provided by Robert Assherynden's sale of his 'tools of occupation' to his son, for 3s. 4d., in 1527.[23] The Hylles leave few clues as to their economic activities but, in 1522, Thomas Hylles devised a mill and millhouse with other realty to his heirs.[24] The Brekyndens do not appear to have engaged in industrial or craft activities to the same extent, but relied on their large landholdings and herds, interests in property and mercantile pursuits. One branch of the family, however, was famous for at least one exceptionally skilled shipwright.[25] Families in the middle of the pious spectrum also appear to have been the most likely to foster professional occupations. John Piers, clerk, appears a number of times in wills and other records from 1459 to 1473 and, in the late 1530s, Richard Piers, like Adam Pellond, was acting as attorney to property transactions.[26] The Pette family also seems to have entered this profession, namely John Pette, mentioned in 1471, and possibly Moyse Pette who, in 1489, acted as executor to the will of John Morer, vicar of Tenterden.[27]

Among bottom-band families, only the Castelyns evince any overtly commercial or industrial activities, although the Bisshopyndens appear to have had strong connections with Boresisle, one of the parish's industrial districts.[28] The Castelyns were exceptional in this group for their rise in status

---

[19] PRC 17/3/450; L&P i. 3496; Roberts, 'Tenterden houses', 196, 202–4, 214–15, and Tenterden, 99.
[20] PRC 17/16/274.
[21] PRC 17/9/245; BL, Add. Chs 56976, 16320; CCA, Dcc/C, fo. 228v; CCR, Henry VI, vi. 1454–61, 388; PRC 17/1/269, 17/3/208.
[22] PRC 17/5/152, 17/9/211.
[23] PRC 17/17/272.
[24] PRC 17/2/67, 17/14/338.
[25] L&P iii. 2992; vii. 630, 1251; BL, Add. Ch. 56981; CKS, U410/T21; Te/S1, fos 17r–v, 18r–20v, 21v, 27r, 44r–45v; 'Naval accounts of Henry VII', pp. vii–xviii, xxxvi, 28, 143–335.
[26] CCR, Henry VI, vi. 1454–61, 388; PRC 17/1/304, 17/2/148; Te/S1, fo. 23r.
[27] PRC 17/2/27; PRO, PCC 20 Milles, fos 164v–165r.
[28] PRC 17/15/258.

and influence by the early sixteenth century, which is perhaps an indication of the moderate fortunes to be made in a diverse range of crafts and trades which took advantage of expanding domestic and continental markets. On the whole, the families that had held or enhanced their social and economic position in the urban hierarchy by the end of the period tended to be engaged in crafts or trades to a greater extent than those whose activities were typified by agriculture towards the top of the pious spectrum. The Foules, and especially the Coupers, outstanding among this latter group for their continuing influence and prosperity, also appear to have been more commercially minded and involved in industry than the likes of the Prestons, Stonehouses, Carpynters and Strekynbolds. This notwithstanding, even those individuals and families whose main occupations were industrial, nearly always farmed, and some of them did so on a large scale.

Connections with local and county gentry

Long-standing parish families of relatively high social status, although locally important, were themselves influenced by powerful interest groups from both outside and inside the parish. County and local power was especially in the hands of the gentry in Kent. Those large landowners who did exist were predominantly *rentiers* with estates concentrated in the east of the county. West Kent and the Weald was characterised by relatively small gentry estates of less than a thousand acres. By the mid-sixteenth century Tenterden was typical of those large Wealden parishes that could 'contain the estates – and the pretensions – of two or three gentry of the status of knight or esquire, as well as several smaller fry known only as "gent" '. These gentry landowners leased the vast proportion of their lands to a whole range of tenants, most of whom held no more than a hundred to a hundred and fifty acres and the majority twenty, thirty or fifty.[29] There was, therefore, much potential for the creation of complex relationships between Tenterden's townsfolk and local and county gentry.

The Haleses, with whom a number of families had close connections, 'had reached county gentry status by the mid-sixteenth century'.[30] The family estate was built up over three generations from the middle of the fifteenth century, principally in Tenterden and neighbouring High Halden. Henry Hales, who died in 1464, mentioned a number of children in monastic orders in his will and the family was clearly actively engaged in orthodox religious life. John Hales, grandson of Henry and early sixteenth-century successor to the family seat, served as bailiff in Tenterden in 1504–5, established his reputation as a lawyer both in London and beyond, and was elected MP for Canterbury in 1514. He was second baron of the exchequer when he died in 1539, had served as chief steward to Christ Church Priory, as well as working

[29] Zell, 'Wood-pasture regime', 72.
[30] Roberts, 'Tenterden houses', 295; Revd R. Cox Hales, 'Brief notes on the Hales family', AC xiv (1882), 61–4.

for the powerful Guldeford family, a relationship that brought many benefits including the opportunity to add a hundred acres of the Guldeford estate to his own in the 1530s. As will be described in more detail in chapter 5, other members of the family pursued successful legal careers in the first half of the sixteenth century and were influential in the drafting and prosecuting of the Henrician and Edwardian Reformation legislation, although they were far from unified in their particular positions on reform. The family remained influential in Tenterden politics, Edward Hales, the successor to the family seat, serving as bailiff on three occasions between 1538 and 1548.[31]

The Guldefords were probably the most important family, with considerable influence in Tenterden and connections with townsfolk through landholding, the land market and local politics. One of the two leading county gentry families in central and west Kent, by the early sixteenth century, they held two manors in Tenterden which, by the late 1530s comprised more than a thousand acres.[32] The Weald was very much within the Guldeford's sphere of influence, and Tenterden perhaps the greatest power-base in their struggles with their rivals the Nevilles in the early sixteenth century, to the extent that in 1505 Sir Edward Guldeford was able to close Tenterden market as an act of retaliation against Neville aggression. Control of the Cinque Ports was a cherished prize in this simmering contest and by the early 1520s the Lord Wardenship was in Guldeford hands, adding further to their influence at Tenterden. The long-running conflict between these two families was expressed in religious terms, the Nevilles becoming identified with Catholic opposition to Henrician reform, whilst the Guldefords built up a reputation for unorthodoxy.[33] As we shall see in chapter 5, their interest in Erasmian humanism, cultural patronage and the protection which their political influence afforded more genuinely unorthodox views all had an important bearing on the development of orthodoxy and heterodoxy in Tenterden and the Weald.

The spectrum of testamentary piety

Distinguishable traditions of testamentary practice across the pious spectrum can be illustrated in a rather crude way by comparing the relative amounts left in cash bequests to, on the one hand, religious matters and, on the other, to family, kin, neighbours and associates.[34] The twenty-three selected

---

31 Te/C1, fo. 141r.

32 Clark, *English provincial society*, 6–7; Hasted, *History of Kent*, vii. 183ff., 206ff; CKS, U455/T87; Te/S1, fos 5r–15v.

33 Clark, *English provincial society*, 14–20, 51–4; *L&P* iv. 4334, 4414, 4455, 4627, 5031.

34 Charitable and civic works and payments for forgotten tithes are included among 'religious matters'. So are temporary chantries to which a specific sum is not attached in the will (usually because they were to be funded by heirs). These are evaluated on the basis of their intended duration – a year's chantry usually costing £6 13s. 4d. Payments to executors, overseers and feoffees for their 'labour' or 'expenses' are excluded. All non-religious cash bequests are included in the second category. Some gifts, particularly to unspecified

Table 4
The spectrum of testamentary piety across twenty-three selected Tenterden families, 1449–1535

1. Family	2. No. of wills	3. Median amount of all cash bequeathed in pence	4. Median % of cash bequeathed to religious concerns	5. Median of absolute amounts of cash left to religious concerns in pence	6. Indexed[1] amount to religious concerns	7. % of family testators who gave to chantries	8. % of family testators who gave to masses, prayers, etc.	9. Ranked family totals (sum of columns 4, 6, 7 & 8)
Top-band families								
Foule	4	3,296	81	2,270	79	75	75	310
Strekynbold	3	14,684	34	2,867	100	67	100	301
Stonehouse	4	4,622	71	2,176	76	25	100	272
Carpynter	3	852	67	840	29	67	100	263
Jamyn	3	488	67	488	17	67	100	251
Preston	4	3,542	52	1,174	41	50	100	243
Davy	8	472	94	432	15	37	62	208
Couper	5	604	89	424	15	20	80	204
Donne	6	596	58	354	12.3	17	100	187
Middle-band families								
Smyth	6	80	61	60	2	17	67	147
Piers	6	1,028	20	184	6.4	33	67	126
Hylles	5	12	54	12	0.4	0	60	114
Pette	5	856	25	80	3	20	60	108
Pellond	7	1,060	22	12	0.4	14	71	107

Brekynden	7	2,216	13	428	15	14	57	99
Gerves	4	1,649	10	356	12.4	25	50	97
Assherynden	5	1,644	28	132	4.6	20	40	93
Lower-band families								
Bisshopynden	5	972	1	18	0.6	20	60	82
Castelyn	7	244	35	26	1	0	43	79
Gibbon	5	44	29	20	0.7	0	40	70
Chapman	4	828	50	11	0.4	0	0	50
Blossom	5	1,000	4	80	2.8	0	40	47
Hoke	3	676	12	64	2	0	33	47

1   Where 2867d. = 100.

Sources: CKS, PRC 16/1–3,17/1–22, 32/2–16; PRO, PCC 11/4 (21 Stokton), 11/5 (25 Godyn), 11/8 (20 Milles), 11/9 (29 Dogett), 11/14 (39 Holgrave), 11/16 (14 Bennett), 11/21 (18 Bodfelde), 11/22 (17 Porche), 11/23 (20 Jankyn), 11/25 (14 Hogen).

Next page expounds upon this page/chart

families have all left at least three extant last wills and testaments that apportion cash above and beyond payments for forgotten tithes.[35] They produced a total of 114 extant wills. The families can be ranked on the basis of four criteria. These comprise, first, the median percentage of cash devoted to religious concerns by each family's testators (see the fourth column of table 4).[36] To put the distribution of resources into perspective, the second criterion is the median absolute amount of cash left in religious bequests. This has the effect of moderating the impression that families like the Smyths and Chapmans laid great stress on the religious in their wills when, in absolute terms, the sums they left were relatively small. At the other end of the spectrum, the Strekynbolds apportioned quite a small share of their cash to spiritual aspirations but actually devoted more than any other family to these ends (see table 4, comparing columns 3, 4 and 5).[37] The third criterion is the proportion of testators in any one family who made bequests or endowments for temporary or perpetual chantries (see column 7 of table 4). Chantries demanded a greater financial and familial commitment than most other forms of religious expression funded in wills, and were perhaps the most ambitious way of demonstrating traditionally orthodox piety. So as to give weight to other types of devotional bequests the final criterion is the proportion of family testators who requested masses, prayers or religious services (including funeral and commemorative ritual), or gave to lights, images, cults or fraternities (see column 8 of table 4).[38]

By adding these four proportions or figures together, comparative family totals were arrived at and these were ranked in numerical order (see column 9 of table 4). Rather than providing a hard and fast measurement of family piety they give an initial indication of each family's testamentary practices and their relationship to other strategies within a spectrum of orthodoxy. In these terms, the method is reasonably successful. It provides a firm, if largely quantitative, base from which to begin to describe and decode disparate

numbers of godchildren, have been counted as only 2 bequests where the sense is clearly plural. Cash maintenance arrangements for widows are included, but are likely to be greatly underestimated, as they have been evaluated on the basis of a single year only.

[35] 'Family' is used here and in subsequent chapters as a convenient term for a multi-generational group of interrelated households and individuals. In most cases, but not exclusively, the households discussed together in this sense were related patrilineally and so shared the same surname.

[36] That is, the median of the proportions of cash left to religious matters in each family will. The median is a more robust indication of a family's strategy than the average, when dealing with small numbers of wills.

[37] All of each of the twenty-three families' wills, including those containing no cash gifts and those leaving money for forgotten tithes only, were included in these calculations. For the sake of comparison, and so that they do not dominate the overall assessment of family strategies, the median absolute amounts are converted to indexed percentages, where 2867d., the largest amount given, is equivalent to 100 (see table 4, cf. columns 5 and 6).

[38] As with chantries, gifts and endowments of lands and goods, in addition to cash, were included when assessing these proportions.

traditions in family piety and is more rigorous and less subjective than some other approaches.[39] The twenty-three families can be divided into three groups as shown in table 4. They range from nine families which gave frequently, generously and diversely to religious concerns, through eight which were moderately preoccupied with these matters, to six which gave occasionally, sparingly and conservatively. Whilst there was some overlap at their boundaries, the groups are polythetically distinguishable; that is, each group is defined in terms of a set of characteristics, so that each of its families exhibits most of the characteristics, and each characteristic is shared by most of its families.[40]

There was no straightforward relationship between available wealth and the material value and character of religious bequests. The third column of table 4 shows the median amount of cash left in all types of bequest for each family. Across all twenty-three the median of these sums was £3 11s. 4d. Only the middle group of families – the moderately generous in their religious giving – produced a median higher than this, at £4 7s. The figures for the top and bottom groups are both slightly lower, and very similar, at £3 11s. and £3 2s. 8d. respectively. There were families with relatively little wealth at their disposal within top, middle and bottom groups and some with consider-able resources at the lower and middle range of the pious spectrum. Available wealth played an important part in setting levels of religious giving but, inde-pendently of this, individuals and families prioritised between competing concerns and responsibilities in ways that produced a distinctive character to their testamentary piety. Generous testamentary religious expression was not the preserve of the richest families, and neither was a more frugal tenor of will-making confined to those with less than moderate wealth at their disposal. This notwithstanding, the families that had the greatest resources also tended to be most unsparing in their religious giving, the four who left a median of over £12 all lying in the top group. In addition, whereas three out of the six families at the bottom of the spectrum left a median of more than £4, five out of eight in the middle group did. The best resourced family in the lowest band disposed of only 12s. more than the median for all twenty-three families.

The extent to which the individual testator had to fulfil obligations to family, kin and other individuals was dependent on a number of factors. Not least among these was the stage in the life-cycle at which an individual died. In addition, women faced different types of pressures to men, especially given the fact that most female testators were widows. Twenty-six of the 114 wills produced by these families were made by women and, of these, twenty-one can be identified as widows. They display some clear patterns in testamentary strategy which appear to have been influenced by the common circumstances in which they made their wills. For example, the general principle seems to

[39] See, for example, Higgs, 'Lay piety', 197–217.
[40] P. Burke, *History and social theory*, Cambridge 1992, 32; R. Needham, 'Polythetic classi-fication', *Man* x (1975), 349–69.

have applied that if widows had access to any more than mediocre cash resources they deployed these largely for the health of their souls. This was probably because most widows did not have to furnish dowries for daughters or inheritance parcels for sons, as these had either already been funded by husbands, or heirs had already married or left home. So, Anne Stonehouse left 4d. to the Jesus Mass, 10d. to the light of St Mildred, 13s. 4d. to each of her funeral and month's mind, and 10s. to her year's mind in 1513. To her daughters she gave household goods and put her sons in the custody of one Merton Wood until they were twelve. Her husband's will is dated two months earlier than her own and, in addition to his religious provisions, provides for their daughters' dowries which they were to receive when they reached twenty, and details additional cash bequests to kin and others.[41] In twelve out sixteen documented cases widows gave a greater proportion of their available cash resources to religious matters than their husbands. In one extreme example, Thomas Weste made no cash bequests at all but, in a very short testament, provided for his wife and daughters from his estate. In the same year, his widow Joan also undertook for her daughters but, in addition, devoted a total of 50s. to obsequies. Examples like this suggest that widows sometimes carried out a joint arrangement in their testaments on behalf of husbands once the availability of resources after provision for heirs was known. This means that only when viewed together do the wills of some married couples reflect individual, as well as household piety.[42]

Because widows were often afforded a greater freedom to express their individual interests, some gave to a much wider range of religious institutions and concerns than their husbands. Lore Blossom for example, gave to Small Hythe chapel and St Mildred's in addition to remembering daughters, sons-in-law and grandchildren. Stephen Blossom, however, was only able to make reversionary and residuary arrangements for bequests to the parish church because of the more pressing needs of family.[43] Women's testamentary strategies, on the whole, tended to be more diverse, involving a greater number of smaller bequests than men's, not just to religious concerns but to family, kin and neighbours. They had a greater propensity to look beyond the household in their giving, and women in particular often predominated as the recipients. Many of these were daughters and granddaughters, but others were more distant family or kin. These gifts frequently appear to have been of a charitable nature to young female neighbours on the threshold of marriage. Compared to their husbands, women will-makers also show a greater local emphasis to their piety, focused, in particular, on the parish church or local chapel and on particular cults. For instance, whereas Thomas Chapman apportioned 10 marks from lands to the Grey Friars of Beaulieu, Joan Chapman gave 4d. to the work of the chapel in Small Hythe. Similarly,

---

41 PRC 17/12/182; William Stonehouse, 1513: PRC 17/12/227.
42 PRC 17/14/304, 17/15/15. See also Burgess, 'By quick and by dead', passim.
43 PRC 17/19/365, 17/15/128.

William Foule left 6s. 8d. to the brothers of Lossenham, but his widow Katherine gave 3s. 4d. to the Jesus Mass in St Mildred's, a coverlet and 6s. 8d. for
the purchase of a pair of silver candlesticks for the same church.[44]

The degree to which widows had access to anything more than meagre
amounts of money when writing their wills was partly to do with family
wealth, but was also influenced by different approaches to testamentary practice and attitudes to the use of family resources. The six widows who
belonged to the most religiously active families all devoted the best part of
relatively substantial sums (upwards of £1 17s.) to spiritual aspirations and
not all of them belonged to exceptionally wealthy families. In the middle
group strategies were more diverse covering the whole spectrum of practice.
Widows in the bottom pious group were less diverse in their approaches, Lore
Blossom being the only one to leave a substantial amount, totalling £3 18s.,
and nearly all of it to religious concerns.[45] The rest left far less than this and
most only a few pence but yet belonged to families that by no means appear
to have been the least wealthy. Some widows simply did not have access to
surplus wealth or chose not to employ family resources in traditional pious
expression. Individual and familial circumstances and traditional practice in
the moral economy combined to shape their testamentary strategies.

To some extent, the family circumstances of testators can be ascertained
from references in their wills to children. It is usually possible to identify
unmarried daughters and, on occasions, sons who were minors. In the most
religiously generous group, each will-maker had a median of three children to
provide for. The middle group of families gave to a median of two, but those
with the most religiously sparse wills mentioned a median of only one child
per will. The same pattern emerges from a comparison of the proportions of
testators in families who mentioned children. In the top group a median of
every testator mentioned possible dependants, in the middle group four in
every five, and in the lowest only about three in every five family testators
provided for children. This suggests that the most religiously lavish were
more likely to mention dependants in their wills and that they tended to
remember more individual children than their counterparts.

The fact that families who apportioned the largest share of their surplus
resources to religious concerns also had the most dependent children
suggests, once again, that family circumstances and the influence of
traditional family practices combined to produce definably divergent testamentary strategies. Middle and particularly lower group families tended to
concentrate more limited cash resources upon dependent heirs. In general,
cash portions to dowries decrease in size as they move down the testamentary
spectrum, but even in the lowest group of families they could be substantial.

---

[44] 1 mark was equivalent to 13s. 4d. PRC 17/5/9, 17/5/76, 17/6/281, 17/15/64; P. H.
Cullum, ' "And hir name was charite": charitable giving by and for women in late medieval
Yorkshire', in Goldberg, Woman is a worthy wight, 185; Peters, Patterns of piety, 40–59.
[45] Lore Blossom, 1532: PRC 17/19/365.

For example, in 1460 Thomas Gibbon gave ten marks to each of his daughters and failed to make any religious bequests.[46] Families in the top group accounted for three-quarters of cash dowries of eight marks and over and in some cases this seems to be because they were wealthy enough to provide handsomely for dependent children and still make extensive religious bequests. For example, in 1498 Thomas Carpynter bequeathed twenty marks to each of two of his daughters and £20 to a third, in addition to making religious bequests totalling over ten marks.[47] However, they were also responsible for two-fifths of those dowries worth less than five marks. Among these, John Davy left his daughter only 13s. 4d. whilst employing just under £2 to fund a temporary chantry for a quarter of a year and a gift to the parish church.[48] Family circumstances certainly affected the apportionment of wealth by individual testators, but practices were constrained and guided by the character of familial piety so as to create continuities over time between related individuals and households. However, traditional practices did not remain static. Sometimes changes in testamentary strategy occurred from one generation to the next or between different branches of a family. As is shown in chapter 4, the Pellonds, Castelyns, Bisshopyndens and other families became less religiously frugal in their will-making by the second decade of the sixteenth century, although their giving remained moderate and narrow in scope.

Prolific will-making families, like those selected for detailed study here, are representative of the most stable and established core of local society beneath the level of the gentry and their pious practices should therefore be viewed as somewhat special, albeit disproportionately influential. This said, their testamentary giving is compared throughout the chapter with practices in Tenterden as a whole, as well as other studies. The range of their preoccupations does not differ markedly from that of will-makers in general, but serves to illustrate that testamentary piety was far from homogeneous and yet at the same time was characterised by traditional practices that constrained individual choice and agency.

---

[46] PRO, PCC 21 Stokton, fo. 161.

[47] PRC 17/7/48.

[48] 1492, PRC 17/5/330. A total of 60 cash dowry portions were identified in the 114 wills belonging to the 23 families with a median of £3 6s. 8d. Top group families left 28 of these with a median value of £5 6s. 8d., middle group families 14, at a median of £3 6s. 8d. and the bottom group 18 dowries worth a median of 40s. The average of those recorded in contemporaneous wills in Tenterden and across Kent before 1525, when payments began to rise significantly, was around £5: O'Hara, *Courtship and constraint*, 198–207, esp. table 13 at p. 202. Dowry payments in the Tenterden wills as a whole ranged from 20s. to £20, but most were in the order of between £1 6s. 8d. and £3 6s. 8d.

Traditional religion and the construction of identity

Chantries, funerals and commemorative ritual

The greatest expenditure upon religious aspirations at Tenterden was devoted to securing priestly intercession in the form of temporary or permanent chantries. It appears that this sort of arrangement was seen, at least by some, as the apogée of *post mortem* pious provision – an attitude observed in other centres and regions in this period.[49] The nine families at the top of the testamentary spectrum were exceptionally active in founding chantries. Probate evidence alone shows that all nine were responsible for at least one temporary or permanent foundation and that seven established two or more over the period. Seventeen of their forty extant wills (42.5 per cent) contain a total of twenty-three bequests, compared to sixty-two (24 per cent) of all 263 wills (*see* column 7 of table 4, and table 5).[50] Only eight out of forty-five willmakers in the middle band of families, and only one in the lowest group arranged chantries.

A considerably smaller share of Tenterden's testators left bequests for chantries than in most other centres that have been studied. Over similar periods in Norwich, Hull, Bury St Edmunds, Bristol and London, between just under a third and around two-fifths of lay testators made arrangements for intercessory foundations of this type.[51] To compare with non-urban centres, Tenterden also fell behind the level of endowment in the rural villages of Blackbourne deanery to the north of Bury St Edmunds.[52] Urban centres, large or small, could be less prolific in chantry endowment than some rural areas and other towns are more comparable to Tenterden. For example, in Colchester 21 per cent of testators made bequests for temporary or permanent chantries during the period 1485–1529,[53] and Sandwich on the East Kent coast, a Cinque Port and of similar size to Tenterden, sustained about the same level of provision, with about a quarter of lay testators making bequests for chantries from the mid-fifteenth century to 1539.[54]

---

[49] Duffy, *Altars*, 328; C. Burgess, 'A service for the dead: the form and function of the anniversary in late medieval Bristol', *Transactions of the Bristol and Gloucestershire Archaeological Society* cv (1987), 194–8; Tanner, *Church in Norwich*, 100–6; Burgess, 'Divine service', 49–50. See also K. L. Wood-Legh, *Perpetual chantries in Britain*, Cambridge 1965, 314.

[50] The numerous arrangements for chantries which would only come into effect in default of inheritance by beneficiaries are not included in these figures.

[51] Tanner, *Church in Norwich*, 220–1, appendix 11; Heath, 'Urban piety', 210, 220; Dinn, 'Popular religion', table 17.1a at p. 714; Burgess, 'Divine service', 47 n. 4, 52; Thomson, 'Piety and charity', 179, 191–2.

[52] Here, 39% of wills made in three selected decades contain bequests for chantries: Dinn, 'Popular religion', 86, table 17.10 at p. 753.

[53] Higgs, 'Lay piety', table 18 at pp. 231–5.

[54] This, and other information on piety at Sandwich, is based on 334 lay wills made from 1460 to 1539 and is kindly supplied by Sheila Sweetinburgh.

Table 5
Bequests for chantries and obsequies, to lights and to church fabric[*] in Tenterden wills, 1449–1535

Date range	Total number of wills	Number (and %) of wills containing bequests for temporary or perpetual chantries	Number (and %) of wills containing bequests for obsequies	Number (and %) of wills containing bequests to lights	Number (and %) of wills containing bequests to church fabric[1]
1449–79	41	15 (37%)	12 (29%)	3 (7%)	24 (59%)
1480–99	49	17 (35%)	11 (22%)	5 (10%)	23 (47%)
1500–19	84	22 (26%)	35 (42%)	18 (21%)	38 (45%)
1520–35	89	8 (10%)	64 (72%)	13 (15%)	17 (19%)
1449–1535	263	62 (24%)	112 (46%)	39 (15%)	102 (39%)

[*] To church building, repair and decoration, altars and images but excluding payments for forgotten tithes.

Sources: CKS, PRC 16/1–3,17/1–22, 32/2–16; PRO, PCC 11/4 (21 Stokton), 11/5 (25 Godyn), 11/8 (20 Milles), 11/9 (29 Dogett), 11/14 (39 Holgrave), 11/16 (14 Bennett), 11/21 (18 Bodfelde), 11/22 (17 Porche), 11/23 (20 Jankyn), 11/25 (14 Hogen).

There was a sharp sl⟨...⟩m the early 1510s in the proportion of Tenterden will-makers wh⟨...⟩gements for chantries. This was not offset by any increase in ⟨...⟩ndations and neither was it a product of a general increas⟨...⟩ testators to include less wealthy individuals who could ⟨...⟩ absolute terms, the number of will-makers establishin⟨...⟩ half from the first to the second decade of the sixteenth century, rose a little again in the early 1520s, but then in 1527 dropped to zero for the remainder of the period. Even the nine families who were distinctive for their traditionally orthodox piety did not sustain the same level of chantry foundation after around 1510. There was a similar decline in chantry foundation in other centres by the early sixteenth century but, in Tenterden, not only were they less common, but much shorter on average than elsewhere.[56] Only eight of the sixty-eight which are quantifiable were for more than a year, thirteen were annuals of masses, twenty-two were for only half this time, and the most common arrangement (twenty-five

[55] In contrast to London where both these factors have been identified: Thomson, 'Piety and charity', 191–2.

[56] The proportion of testators leaving resources for chantries in Sandwich fell from around a third in the 1470s and 1480s, to only about a tenth by the 1520s and 1530s, the most dramatic drop occurring in the 1510s. For Bury and York see Dinn, 'Popular religion', 718, and R. B. Dobson, 'The foundation of perpetual chantries by the citizens of York', in G. J. Cuming (ed.), *The province of York* (SCH iv, 1967), 35–6.

in all) was for three months. The median length of foundation was half a year, in stark contrast to other locations for which there is information.[57] The decline in the popularity of chantry arrangements in wills and the comparatively low level of testamentary investment in this form of intercession raise serious questions about attitudes to the cult of the dead and its institutions at Tenterden. At odds with revisionist assertions of the health of this central pillar of 'traditional religion', at Tenterden the chantry does not appear to have been sustainable as an option within testamentary giving beyond the late 1520s.

Perpetual, as opposed to temporary, chantries were rare in late medieval England.[58] Four are recorded in the Tenterden wills, all of them located in the chapel of St John the Baptist and endowed by residents of Small Hythe. Two augmented the chaplain's stipend rather than establish a personal or familial chantry. The other two, which took the specific form of chantries to be celebrated for the founders' souls, were inaugurated by William Davy and William Jamyn in 1501, both members of more generously religious families.[59] There were two perpetual chantries in Tenterden town, one founded in this period and another possibly already established, which do not appear in the probate evidence. The most important of these, 'Peter Marshall's chantry', was presumably established by the vicar of Tenterden of the same name who served in the parish from 1494 to 1512.[60] By 1546 this was endowed with five messuages with attached lands in Tenterden and Woodchurch including 'the Woolesack' (probably the Woolpack Inn on Tenterden High Street). Rents from these properties amounted to £17 1s. 4d. a year, of which £10 10s. provided a wage for a chaplain at St Mildred's to celebrate divine service and teach a grammar school.[61] Peter Marshall's brother, William Marshall, vicar

---

[57] At Norwich, more than half of all chantries were for two years or longer, and in Hull the average was three years: Tanner, *Church in Norwich*, appendix 11 at p. 221; Heath, 'Urban piety', 220. At Colchester, nearly all endowments were designed to secure the prayers of a priest for a year, while in Bury St Edmunds only 7% were to last for less than a year, and 42% for longer than 12 months. In the rural Blackbourne deanery, 65% of chantries mentioned in wills were intended to last for at least a year: Higgs, 'Lay piety', 232; Dinn, 'Popular religion', table 17.3, 720; table 17.12, 755.

[58] 12 out of 355 Hull wills contain arrangements for perpetual chantries, and only 1% of lay testators in Norwich sought to establish them: Heath, 'Urban piety', 219; Tanner, *Church in Norwich*, 221. Bristol was somewhat exceptional with 20 of the 140 chantries detailed in fifteenth-century wills being in perpetuity: Burgess, 'Divine service', 52.

[59] John Ingram, 1474: PRC 17/2/342; John Wayte, 1526: PRC 17/17/49; William Davy, 1501: PRC 17/8/221; William Jamyn, 1501: PRC 17/8/199.

[60] Peter Marshall died in 1518/19 having resigned the Tenterden vicarage in 1512, after the heresy trials of 1511–12: A. B. Emden, *Biographical register of the University of Oxford to A.D. 1500*, Oxford 1957–8, ii. 1229; Taylor, 'Rectors and vicars', 216. See also chapter 5 below.

[61] Furley, 'Early history of Tenterden', 52; *Kent chantries*, ed. A. Hussey (KR xii, 1932), 306. Only 7 out of 34 of the chantry or gild priests recorded in the *Valor ecclesiasticus* for the diocese of Canterbury, received a net annual income of more than £10: A. Kreider, *English chantries: the road to dissolution*, Cambridge Mass.–London 1979, table 1.4 at p. 22.

of Appledore from 1487 and rector of Warehorne from 1498 until his death in 1524, mentioned the foundation in his will. He ordained that 'two substanciall chalyses' be made and bequeathed, one of these 'to the use of the chauntry lately founded in the parishe church of Tenterden'. He also left £4 for the purchase of 'a vestment with thapparell' for the chantry priest to wear on 'the principall & festyvall daies' and two silver candlesticks to stand upon the chantry altar on the same occasions.[62] We know comparatively little about the other perpetual chantry in the parish, 'Light's Chantry', which was endowed with part of two small manors which lay between Small Hythe and Tenterden town. It was probably located in the parish church until its suppression in the late 1540s.[63]

Compared to Kent as a whole, and even in a national context, Tenterden was well provided with permanent intercessory foundations.[64] In part, this was a product of its urban status and role within an essentially rural and less affluent hinterland, but the two foundations located at St Mildred's were products of interventions by clergy and local and regional gentry. There is no evidence that either of these were further endowed and augmented by local non-gentle families.[65] Similarly, local and county gentry were responsible for the two temporary chantries of any great substance of which there is a record. Both Thomas Petlesden, in 1463, and Sir John Guldeford, in 1493, established twenty-year foundations.[66] Despite their considerable wealth by the sixteenth century, Tenterden's leading families were, on the whole, unusually inactive in establishing intercessory foundations. In relation to other places, even the most traditionally religious families only barely reached average levels of chantry provision. But, paradoxically, within their own community, they were conspicuous for their efforts to sustain such foundations.

Almost two-thirds (fifty out of seventy-eight) of all chantries mentioned

[62] In his own will, Peter Marshall made no reference to the chantry named after him: 1518, PRC 32/12/158; Taylor, 'Rectors and vicars', 216; A. H. Taylor, 'The will of a medieval Kentish parson', AC xliii (1931), 123–32.

[63] According to John Harris it was founded by one John Light but he confused it with Small Hythe chapel: The history of Kent in five parts, London 1719, 312; Hasted, History of Kent, vii. 209; Furley, 'Early history of Tenterden', 49–50.

[64] Only 56, or just over 15%, of Kent's 371 parishes possessed 'greater institutions', which included chantry foundations, in addition to gilds, free chapels, colleges, stipendiary services and hospitals, with an average of 0.2 of these institutions per parish across the county. In a total of twenty counties, including London and York, 22.7% of English parishes had 'greater institutions', of which there were, on average, 0.47 per parish: Kreider, English chantries, table 1.2. at pp. 16–18.

[65] In Bury, for example, by adding endowments to existing perpetual chantries, the benefactor's soul could be prayed for in addition to those already named: Dinn, 'Popular religion', 722–3.

[66] Petlesden belonged to the family whose eponymous seat lay at the west end of Tenterden town and served as the first bailiff in 1449–50: PRC 17/1/141; Hasted, History of Kent, vii. 208; Te/C1, fo. 140r. Sir John's family seat lay in Halden: PRO, PCC 29 Dogett, fo. 223; R. C. Jenkins, 'The family of Guldeford', AC xiv (1882), 5.

in the Tenterden wills were to be performed in the parish church of St Mildred, with seven of them specifically attached to named altars.[67] Another ten were attached to the chapel of St John the Baptist. In six cases the location of the chantry is not stated, and in five of these it is most likely that St Mildred's was intended. Only twelve bequests were to other parish churches, nine of which were in parishes either adjoining Tenterden or within a distance of ten miles. A further one was established at Tonbridge, twenty-five miles to the north-west, and another near Northhampton. Only one endowment was attached to a religious house, St Augustine's Abbey in Canterbury, and was made by Thomas Strekynbold, one of the more traditionally generous will-makers.[68] The markedly local focus was probably largely due to the fact that the vast majority of testators requested burial within St Mildred's, coupled with the belief that intercessions were most effective when made close to the body of the deceased.[69] Only two of the chantries established by the twenty-three selected families were in other parishes and both expressed family connections or origins. Chantry bequests to neighbouring or more distant parishes usually reflected testators' origins or kinship and formed a significant element of their piety. At the same time, seven out of twelve of these testators also arranged for a chantry in Tenterden, underlining their sense of belonging.[70]

Chantries were seen by some, including John Wyclif, as expressions of an essentially individualistic piety, intended principally for the spiritual benefit of the founder.[71] Some scholars have challenged this notion by stressing the practical contribution which chantry priests made to the religious and social life of the parish.[72] Also, the inclusive wording of some bequests, mentioning 'all the faithful dead' or 'all Chrysten sowlys' among the intended spiritual beneficiaries, has been taken as evidence of altruistic attitudes.[73] These

---

[67] Three to the altar of St Stephen, three to the altar and chapel of the Blessed Virgin Mary (called the 'Lady Chapel' on one occasion) and one to the cult of St Katherine.

[68] 1496: PRC 17/6/158. Very few bequests for chantries were made to regular clergy in Hull, and in Bury only 8 out of 263 for which the location is known: Heath, 'Urban piety', 220; Dinn, 'Popular religion', 738. St Augustine's had considerable influence at Tenterden through the possession of substantial property there, as well as the advowson of St Mildred's: R. Kilburne, A topographie or survey of Kent, with some chronological, historical, and other matters touching the same and the several parishes and places therein, London 1659, 262; Hasted, History of Kent, vii. 214–17; Roberts, 'Tenterden houses', 16, 323–4; Furley, 'Early history of Tenterden', 46; Cotton, 'St. Austin's Abbey', 74, 92, 103.

[69] Dinn, 'Popular religion', 736–40, ch. xv.

[70] Cf. ibid. 739.

[71] Wood-Legh, Perpetual chantries, 303–14.

[72] Kreider, English chantries, 38–70; Burgess, 'Divine service', passim; R. Hill, 'A chaunterie for soules': London chantries in the reign of Richard II', in F. R. H. Du Boulay and C. M. Barron (eds), The reign of Richard II, London 1971, 242–55; Brown, Popular piety, 100–8; Duffy, Altars, 140–1, 369–70.

[73] Dinn, 'Popular religion', 740–3. See, however, P. Marshall, Beliefs and the dead in Reformation England, Oxford 2002, 25–6, 36–7, which challenges this position.

formulaic phrases appear in a substantial proportion of the wills but there is no way of knowing the extent to which they were merely a product of scribal convention.[74] Better indications of inclusivity are the references to specific individuals or groups. As many as two-thirds to three-quarters of the Tenterden chantry endowments either failed to specify who they were to benefit, mentioned only the founder or employed the formulaic phrase, 'for my soul and all Christian souls' or variants of it. Few detail additional specific individuals or groups of people. Twelve of the seventy-eight include both or one of the testator's parents, eleven mention siblings, other possible blood or affinal kin and/or others usually referred to as 'friends', and only six include the founder's spouse. Tenterden's chantry founders give the impression of being less outward looking or altruistic than recent revisionism would suggest.[75]

The parishioners of Tenterden were much more active in making specific arrangements in their wills for religious services and activities surrounding their funerals and at subsequent commemorations than they were in instituting chantries. On the whole these were restricted to the three occasions of the funeral itself, the month's mind and the anniversary (although a number of testators extended their obit for a further number of years or for perpetuity). Over the entire period 46 per cent of testators (122 out of 263) made arrangements for one or more of these celebrations, and just over a quarter of these left some sort of instructions as to the form they should take. They were markedly more popular in Tenterden than they were in other centres.[76] This particularly applies to anniversaries or obits, which were mentioned in 28 per cent of wills.[77] The level of support for these ceremonies was a conspicuous feature of testamentary practice at Tenterden although not all testators were alike in this respect. Forty-seven of the 114 wills made by the twenty-three families mentioned funerary and commemorative celebrations. As was the case with chantry bequests, these are not evenly distributed across the testamentary spectrum, but tend to be concentrated in the top and

---

[74] Evidence for this practice is provided by the chance survival of the office copy of John Wayte of Small Hythe's will, in addition to the enregistered version: office copy: 1526, PRC 16/1/3; enregistered copy: 1526, PRC 17/17/49. See also Spufford, *Contrasting communities*, 323.

[75] Only 20% of testators establishing chantries in Bury requested masses and prayers for their own souls alone; 26% included spouses, 22% parents, and 28% friends. Benefactors, or those to whom the testator was 'bound', were mentioned in 36% of wills containing chantry bequests and 13% included 'all the faithful dead'. In Blackbourne deanery 24% mentioned spouses, 8% parents, 23% benefactors and 49% friends: Dinn, 'Popular religion', table 17.8 at p. 742; table 17.15 at p. 759.

[76] Only 18% of Bury's will-makers mentioned mortuary provisions of this type: Dinn, 'Popular religion', table 14.1 at p. 539. They were 50% more popular in the Tenterden wills than in Sandwich.

[77] In Bury only 5% of testators mentioned obits: ibid. table 14.11 at p. 574; in Hull, 16%: Heath, 'Urban piety', 218; and in Colchester 21%: Higgs, 'Lay piety', table 18 at p. 231.

middle bands. A median of one in two of the most religiously generous families' wills made such arrangements, two in five of the moderate and only one in every four among the families making the most religiously sparse wills. As table 5 shows, the popularity of funerary and commemorative ritual was not constant over the period. From the beginning of the sixteenth century, arrangements increased markedly until almost three-quarters of all wills contained them. This growth, at the same time as the decline in the popularity of the chantry, meant that these bequests began to supersede those for chantries in the first two decades of the sixteenth century, a development paralleled elsewhere, suggesting that there was a definite shift in religious tastes.[78]

it was a time of change (handwritten margin note)

By the first decade of the sixteenth century arrangements for funerals and subsequent commemorations reached a level of popularity never enjoyed by chantries. How can this apparent shift in popularity be explained? It was no doubt partly because funerary ritual was more accessible to those with comparatively limited resources, and so developed a wider social base. Some Tenterden testators left as little as between 5s. 4d. and 13s. 4d. for their funerals, month's minds and obits altogether. Although most set aside at least 20s., with the median amount being £1 13s. 4d. (the same sum as required for a quarter year's temporary chantry), only eight testators left as much as ten marks, the figure required to secure the celebration of divine service for a year.[79] Moreover, by the 1510s and 1520s, because of inflation chantries may have been becoming less secure, obsequies offering a more reliable way of gaining access to masses and prayers.[80] In such circumstances, the heavy financial burden of maintaining chantries, which fell often upon the heirs of donors, may have tipped the balance in favour of less onerous and more secure intercessory arrangements.[81]

There does not, however, seem to have been any sense in which the funeral and subsequent services were necessarily considered as an alternative to chantry provision for those who invested in the latter. More than half of all chantry founders also made bequests for celebrations to be conducted at one or more of their burial day, month's mind and obit and, after 1520, every bequest for a chantry was accompanied by such arrangements. This suggests

---

[78] By the 1530s at least four-fifths of Sandwich's testators were mentioning their funerals and/or subsequent commemorations, and only about a tenth were founding chantries; to a lesser extent this also occurred at Bury: Dinn, 'Popular religion', table 14.1 at p. 539; table 17.1 at p. 714.

[79] A total of 101 testators specified the amounts to be given for funerals, month's minds and obits. The median amount does not include calculations for perpetual obits, and so to a small extent underestimates the level of investment in commemorative ritual: Burgess, 'Service for the dead', 194–7; Marshall, *Beliefs and the dead*, 24, 44; Dinn, 'Popular religion', 718; Higgs, 'Lay piety', 228.

[80] R. B. Outhwaite, *Inflation in Tudor and early Stuart England*, London–Melbourne–Toronto 1969, 9ff; P. Heath, *The English parish clergy on the eve of the Reformation*, London 1969, 23–5.

[81] Marshall, *Beliefs and the dead*, 43–6.

Purgatory (handwritten margin note)

that, for these testators, the two different types of provision were generally seen as complementary aspects of a diverse strategy for the most effective relief from purgatorial suffering.[82] In principle, the doctrinal rationales behind chantries and anniversaries were identical, centred as they were on the Church's teachings about purgatory. Peter Marshall has recently demonstrated, however, that those teachings were far from coherent, and that the doctrine of purgatory, although absolutely fundamental to the whole complex of late medieval religion, was broadly and variously defined and vulnerable to intellectual attack. The actual existence of purgatory and the efficacy of prayers and masses for those suffering therein, were not in themselves widely questioned before the late 1520s and the visible beginnings of the influence of Lutheranism and other strands of Protestant thought in England.[83] Until then, recorded wholesale doubts about the doctrine are difficult to find, even in the records of heresy trials, and complaints tended to focus upon the 'ostentatious folly' of chantry foundations and what were seen as the avaricious motives of the clergy and religious orders that performed them.[84]

However, other indirect criticisms of the cult of the dead concerned what were seen by some as the crudely mechanistic aspects of intercession in the form of the large-scale repetition of masses, the purchase of special, particularly indulgenced, masses and the view that the chantry was often an essentially private devotion and, therefore, socially and spiritually detrimental to the wider body of the Church. Whilst the mass remained the supremely effective form of intercession for the dead, devotional writers also promoted other ways of achieving purgation for sins including charitable giving, personal devotion, giving to church fabric and fasting.[85] What might be termed reformist views were, by the mid-1520s, somewhat at odds with the arch-conservatism of the party that formed around Elizabeth Barton, the 'Nun of Kent', whose dramatic rise to prominence was initially played out at the chapel at Court at Street in 1525–6, less than thirteen miles from Tenterden. Amongst other traditionalist beliefs, including the virtues of confession and the importance of lay attendance at the mass, her prophesies buttressed the doctrine of purgatory and warned against the perils of the 'new learning'. When, in 1528, she entered the arena of high politics to speak out against the royal campaign for divorce and the looming breach with Rome, adherence to the doctrine of purgatory could be linked by her evangelical

---

[82] Wood-Legh, *Perpetual chantries*, 296–7; Burgess, 'Service for the dead', 191; Marshall, *Beliefs and the dead*, 20.

[83] Marshall, *Beliefs and the dead*, 6–32, 46–51, 310; Duffy, *Altars*, 382; Kreider, *English chantries*, 117; R. Hutton, *The rise and fall of merry England*, Oxford 1994, 80–1, 93.

[84] Kreider, *English chantries*, 95, ch. iv. Only one suspect examined in Archbishop Warham's heresy trials in Kent denied the existence of purgatory: *Kent heresy proceedings, 1511–12*, ed. N. P. Tanner (KR xxvi, 1997), 46.

[85] Marshall, *Beliefs and the dead*, 12, 27–32.

opponents to papalist treason.[86] This, of course, does not explain the decline in the popularity of chantries from around 1510 in Tenterden, but the Barton affair suggests that by 1525 conservative figures in the Church perceived a need to bolster traditional beliefs in the value of intercessory masses and prayers. Lutheranism and Protestant teachings against purgatory already had some influence in Kent as early as 1522.[87] In addition, Lollard opinions may have eroded orthodox lay beliefs. As will be described in detail in chapter 5, these were particularly anti-eucharistic and anti-sacerdotal and so may have helped to undermine the robustness of popular thinking concerning the intercessory efficacy of the mass.

[handwritten margin note: Six years before 1528]

This said, it is unlikely that Wycliffite ideas alone could have brought about such a shift in pious priorities, and Protestant thinking could only have accelerated a trend that was already marked by 1520. For a number of reasons it appears that orthodox sensibilities at Tenterden, and indeed in some other places nationally in the early sixteenth century, were shifting away from the chantry as a vehicle for post-obit intercession. Ethan Shagan has recently written of the 'remarkable willingness to put the financial needs of the living above the spiritual needs of the dead' among those who engaged, without ideological motives, in the local rationalisation and subsequent wholesale government-sponsored dissolution of chantries in the 1540s. He explains this in terms of the sense of insecurity induced in potential investors by several years of Henrician reform (particularly the dissolution of the monasteries, which were regarded as intercessory foundations *par excellence*), the appropriation of church property from the early 1530s and the paradoxical effect of attempts to protect chantry property from government dissolution by siphoning it off into private ownership. These combined forces led to the inexorable erosion of beliefs in purgatory, at least to the extent that, where local or self-interest converged with the government's evangelically-inspired programme of suppression, material gain was favoured over principled resistance. This argument, whilst offering a convincing explanation for the rapid dismantling of chantries, fails to acknowledge the very real possibility that these foundations were already going out of fashion in some parts of the country twenty or more years before there was any hint of government interest in them or public attacks on the doctrine of purgatory by the likes of Tyndale, Fish or Latimer. To write about chantries in terms of their 'ubiquity' and 'massive lay support' for them in the early sixteenth century is to over-

---

[86] Shagan, *Popular politics*, 61–88; Marshall, *Beliefs and the dead*, 70–2; A. Neame, *The holy maid of Kent: the life of Elizabeth Barton, 1506–1534*, London 1971, 35–48; Rex, *Lollards*, 122. Peter Clark uses the term 'reformist' to classify wills made in Kent in the Tudor period, which omit mention of the saints from dedicatory clauses: *English provincial society*, 58–9. It is used here in the broader sense, of those wills which in their entirety reflect reforming trends within orthodox religion. For problems with Clark's method, and others like it see Duffy, *Altars*, 504–23. See also Peters, *Patterns of piety*, 160–9.

[87] Marshall, *Beliefs and the dead*, 48; S. Wabuda, *Preaching during the English Reformation*, Cambridge 2002, 10, 116–20; Neame, *Holy maid*, 43; Clark, *English provincial society*, 30.

state the homogeneity of orthodox beliefs and opinions about the best ways in which to secure intercessions for the dead, and probably underestimates the burden of these costly institutions on individuals and families aware of orthodox and heterodox debates about purgatory.[88]

Despite the decline in chantry foundations, the fact that most of the Tenterden testators who left money for their funerals also devoted often larger sums to subsequent services (albeit on the whole no longer than for one year after death) suggests that beliefs about purgatory retained an important place in their religious mentality.[89] However, a number of important differences between commemorative rites and the chantry may have rendered the former increasingly attractive. Whereas the chantry was centred on the regular and repeated performance of the mass by a priest, the funeral and anniversary as its exact re-enactment, whilst incorporating the mass, were quintessentially public and collective rites of commemoration which encouraged a greater degree of lay participation. The Office of the Dead, consisting of *Placebo* and *Dirige* followed by the Psalms of Commendation, which preceded and accompanied the funeral, were among the best known of all the Church's prayers among the laity and, together with the requiem mass, was repeated at month's minds and anniversaries. Included in most primers in this period these prayers could be recited by the literate layperson and even for the less learned their general meaning was probably reasonably clear. Funeral doles were often paid to literate clerks and laypeople who could adequately recite the office.[90] Perhaps the appeal of services performed at the funeral and on subsequent commemorative days was partly due to the degree of lay participation they afforded in comparison to the mass, as well as the additional elements that they incorporated into the remembrance of the dead.

Indeed, the funeral and obit seem to have offered parishioners the opportunity to exercise greater control over the composition of different intercessory activities, as well as the ways funds were distributed. Whereas only two testators gave specific instructions concerning the form of temporary chantries,[91] thirty-five stipulated how funds were to be distributed at funerals and obsequies. Most of the individuals who left instructions gave alms to the poor as part of their funerary arrangements, something which was not mentioned in relation to chantry bequests. Although a customary element of mortuary provision, when testators went to the trouble of mentioning such charitable works it suggests that a conscious emphasis was being placed upon them. As an act of mercy in itself the giving of funeral doles helped to ensure the

---

[88] Shagan, *Popular politics*, 235–69 at pp. 238–9, 245; Marshall, *Beliefs and the dead*, 47–92.
[89] Practices were similar in Bury: Dinn, 'Popular religion', 560.
[90] Burgess, 'Service for the dead', 183–4, 190–1; Marshall, *Beliefs and the dead*, 18–21; Higgs, 'Lay piety', 224–5 nn. 26–7; Dinn, 'Popular religion', 560–2; Duffy, *Altars*, 210, 220–1, 369.
[91] If left to his own devices, a chantry priest would normally celebrate the mass of the day, according to the use he was following: Wood-Legh, *Perpetual chantries*, 281.

salvation of the giver, but was intended also to encourage the prayers of priests and literate clerks and, in particular, the poor for the deceased's soul. Some of these bequests read like formulaic clauses but others paid particular attention to such arrangements. In 1518 William Couper left, at both his funeral and month's mind, 6s. 8d. divided between ten priests, and 3s. 4d. to clerks and poor people. He also bequeathed 4d. 'to evry dweller and his wiffe inhabyting betwyxt the mansyon of merieyn Hood and the mansyon of Wyllam lambyn at within the seid parishe at evry of the seid dayes of my sepulture trygyntale and annyversary'. This type of discriminating charity to the local and resident (and by implication respectable) poor was a growing trend in England in this period.[92]

A number of will-makers stipulated that food and drink be provided on burial days and at obsequies. Sometimes this took the form of alms to the poor, as in the case of Thomas Syre, who in 1531 left 2s. 'to poor people in bread and vitell'.[93] More usually, such arrangements were in addition to alms and comprised a funeral or commemorative feast. Instructions for these feasts only occur from 1519, when Moyse Pellond left 13s. 4d. 'to be distrybuted to prists clerks power people and for a drynkyng to be had for the helth of my sowle in the day of my sepulture' and others left money for meat and drink to be supplied in addition to alms.[94] Such feasts served a religious and ritualistic function but also offered opportunities to display wealth, promote good-neighbourliness and strengthen ties between families. The symbolic display of wealth and status, and collective identity, afforded by the burial and its commemoration may have made it an increasingly attractive pious outlet as chantry provision declined.[95]

Evidence from elsewhere shows that bell-ringing on the evening before the funeral attracted those seeking doles and encouraged prayer for the deceased, as well as publicly announcing the departure of a significant member of the parish.[96] Likewise, the procession to the church and the gathering of priests, clerks and poor holding candles around the hearse at the funeral service, sometimes dressed in specially provided cloaks or hoods, whilst intensely religious, could also be deliberately ostentatious.[97] This said, the increasingly outstanding prosperity enjoyed by townsfolk of higher and middling status in Tenterden from the late fifteenth century does not appear, in general, to have given rise to this sort of display. There is only one reference to bell-ringing in the Tenterden wills and only two to the funeral procession in the form of bequests to hearse bearers. Neither is there any

[92] PRC 32/12/174; Duffy, Altars, 362–6, and see pp. 97–8 below.
[93] PRC 17/19/54.
[94] PRC 17/14/47. For example William Gerves, 1525: PRC 17/16/274.
[95] Dinn, 'Popular religion', 762.
[96] Duffy, Altars, 359; Higgs, 'Lay piety', 142; Dinn, 'Popular religion', 541–2.
[97] Duffy, Altars, 361; Dinn, 'Popular religion', 544–50; P. Ariès, Western attitudes toward death from the Middle Ages to the present, London 1976, 11–12; C. Gittings, Death, burial and the individual in early modern England, London 1988, 29.

mention of liveries or candles for the poor or of hearse cloths for funerals.[98] This is not to say that such rites did not regularly occur but that they were perhaps less elaborate than in other places where they have been documented. The influential Sir John Guldeford did not depart from parochial tastes when he made his conspicuously modest stipulations for mortuary provision in 1493. He wished his 'out beryng to be made not pomposely', and on his burial day, month's and year's minds willed that 4d. be given to every poor household in Tenterden to pray for his soul, and in the same manner on just his month's and year's days in four neighbouring parishes. Also, presumably in all of these parishes, on all three occasions, five masses (of the Trinity, Holy Ghost, Assumption of Our Lady, Our Lady and Requiem) were to be celebrated with prayers for Guldeford, his parents and all Christian souls. At his anniversary, he stipulated that 'a playne stone and noo tumbe' be laid over him, with epitaphs devised by himself or his executors.[99] His arrangements reflect the general tenor of piety in Tenterden and may reveal affiliation to a wider devotional tradition within orthodoxy, which sought humble burial and the denigration of the flesh. Disregard for funereal or sepulchral display has been connected with the Lollard knights, a small group of influential men, some with positions at the royal court in the late fourteenth century, who appear to have been actively sympathetic to Wycliffite heresy and heretics, as well as being open to new movements more firmly within the mainstream of orthodoxy.[100]

The most elaborate provisions were made by Thomas Wode who devoted 66s. 8d. to his burial and month mind, and arranged also for two separate obsequies in each of four neighbouring parish churches within a year after his death at 20s. for each church. These were to be performed for his own soul and those of various kinsfolk. In addition he left 6s. 8d. for obsequies at the churches where his two daughters were buried. Finally, he instituted a perpetual obit at Tenterden at 6s. 8d. a year, to be distributed

> in dirige massess and other charitable deds within fifteen days next aftre palmesunday evry yere for ever by discretyon of the curate for the tyme beyng and other discrete persones of the saide parisshe, 3s. 4d. under this manner, to the preeste that syngeth mass of requyem by noote 6d. To other three

---

98 This is similar to Colchester, which Higgs suggests may have been due to the influence of Lollardy ('Lay piety', 226) but Norwich was not very different (Tanner, *Church in Norwich*, 99). In Hull a high level of lavish funerary provision declined as the fifteenth century wore on (Heath, 'Urban piety', 217–18) and the practice was more common still in Bury (Dinn, 'Popular religion', 546–50).

99 PRO, PCC 29 Dogett, fo. 223.

100 See, for example, Heath, 'Urban piety', 213–14; Gittings, *Death, burial*, 34–7; Carpenter, 'Religion of the gentry', 61–2. On the Lollard knights see K. B. McFarlane, *Lancastrian kings and Lollard knights*, Oxford 1972, 148–76, 207–20; Rex, *Lollards*, 61–2, 79–80; M. Aston, *England's iconoclasts*, I: *Laws against images*, Oxford 1988, 125–6. Thomas Hicks of Tenterden, requested in his testament: 'my body to be buried where it pleasith god': 1522, PRC 17/15/228.

preestes synging four styll masses by evyn porcyons 16d. To the clerke 2d. To the sexton 8d., for offryng 5d., and to three children to helpe the preeste to masse 3d. Distributing also to power people of the said parishe yn evry of the dayes of the vigilis of the Byrthe of our Lord god Easter and pentycost 12d. yerely for ever. Sum therof 3s. whichis is the residue of the said 6s. 8d.[101]

By contemporary standards even Wode's obsequies were restrained and matched the economical tastes in funerary provision shared by Tenterden's leading townspeople. By the late 1520s the formulaic and almost obligatory nature of bequests for funerals and commemorative celebrations suggests that there was little room for elaboration or development beyond the compass of accepted norms. Despite these limitations, the disparities between the degree of elaboration of mortuary provision chosen by families following different pious traditions at Tenterden endured.

Obits and the money expended on them can be directly compared with other places. Although Tenterden's testators were unusually prolific at instituting obits, with 28 per cent doing so over the entire period, forty-nine of the seventy-three took the form of anniversaries for one year only.[102] Of the rest, nine were for two to seven years, three for eight to twelve years, five for sixteen to twenty years, one for forty years and five were in perpetuity.[103] Only three obits are recorded at Tenterden in the 1548 returns of obit and lamp rents for Kent, two of which were founded by parishioners in their wills and one by the vicar, Peter Marshall.[104] The other three perpetual obits were presumably never instituted or had lapsed by 1548. Despite their popularity obits did not last as long as in other places.[105] The other side of the coin is that although generally shorter than those recorded elsewhere, as well as being unusually common these commemorations were relatively well funded at Tenterden, to an extent comparable with larger and, in some cases, very wealthy urban centres.[106] These bequests are testimony to the increasing prosperity of Tenterden's leading families in this period and, for many, the strength of their orthodox, albeit peculiarly restrained, and possibly precociously reformist piety.

---

[101] 1526: PRC 17/17/158.

[102] Only roughly a third of Bury's recorded obits were for a year only as were approximately a quarter of those instituted in Hull: Dinn, 'Popular religion', table 14.7 at p. 566; Heath, 'Urban piety', 218.

[103] A further one was to last until the testator's son reached the age of 22.

[104] *Kent obit and lamp rents*, ed. A. Hussey (KR xiv, 1936), 113–14. William Preston, 1493: PRC 17/6/10; Thomas Wode, 1526: PRC 17/17/158.

[105] Dinn, 'Popular religion', table 14.7 at p. 566; Heath, 'Urban piety', 218.

[106] Whilst 14 did not specify an amount, 49 gave up to 13s. 4d., 10 from 15s. to 20s. and one 33s. 4d.; Dinn, 'Popular religion', table 14.8 at pp. 569, 568; Higgs, 'Lay piety', 228; Heath, 'Urban piety', 218; Burgess, 'By quick and by dead', 847.

Special masses and new devotions

Responses to special or new devotional forms, such as the trental, appear to have been similarly distinctive and had a similar chronology to chantry provision. In its simplest form the trental consisted of thirty masses celebrated on thirty consecutive days, usually immediately after death. By the early fifteenth century a particularly elaborate derivation of this, called the Trental of St Gregory or Pope Trental, had developed popular appeal and tacit acceptance among the English church hierarchy. The Gregorian Trental consisted of thirty masses spread out over the entire liturgical year, three masses to be said at each of the ten major feasts of Christ and Mary, together with the *Placebo*, *Dirige* and the penitential psalms, the litany of the saints, the rosary and the *De Profundis*. The priest who performed these masses and prayers was to fast on bread and water, either forego his shirt or wear a hair shirt every Friday, every vigil and on each of the ten feasts. The Pope Trental was supported by a legend which ensured 'that it contained a supernaturally authenticated scheme of intercession guaranteed to bring the torments of purgatory to a swift and certain end'. The legend tells how Pope Gregory's mother, guilty of fornication and infanticide, died unrepentant and appeared to her son in a vision whilst he was at mass. Horribly disfigured by her suffering in purgatory she confessed her sin and asked Gregory to say the Trental of masses. Gregory duly obliged and as a result his mother was so utterly transformed that he mistook her for the Virgin Mary. The Pope Trental was not, however, without its critics among theologians and more popular writers, who expressed a general disquiet about its reliance upon claims of the special efficacy of certain masses, large numbers or sequences of masses and its focus on the spiritual welfare of the individual, to the exclusion of the wider community of the faithful. Although the predominant popular mentality tended to measure the merit gained from masses in proportion to the number said, at Tenterden it seems that sentiments may have been influenced by widely held doubts about such devotional innovations.[107] Three testators requested the St Gregory's Trental and a further seven left money or arranged for non-specific trentals. These bequests only appear in the wills from 1493 and it appears that this devotion had little impact.[108] It has been

---

[107] R. W. Pfaff, 'The English devotion of St Gregory's Trental', *Speculum* xlix (1974), 75–90; Duffy, *Altars*, 43, 293–4, 369–75 at p. 373; Dinn, 'Popular religion', 576 n. 137; Tanner, *Church in Norwich*, 105; Marshall, *Beliefs and the dead*, 29–32.

[108] Only 1 testator in the bottom band of selected families, compared to 3 across the middle and top bands requested trentals. In Norwich 8% of lay testators requested Trentals of St Gregory (Tanner, *Church in Norwich*, appendix 11 at p. 221); in Bury St Edmunds, 33% of lay and clerical will-makers (1449–1530), and by the 1520s 55% made bequests for trentals (Dinn, 'Popular religion', 576–8); in Hull 11% arranged for less than an average of 3 trentals each, 24 of the total of 102 trentals being of St Gregory (Heath, 'Urban piety', 219); and, in Colchester, 10% asked for this form of celebration in the parish church, and many more requested trentals at the Grey Friars (Higgs, 'Lay piety', table 18 at pp. 231, 242).

suggested that the mendicant orders may have helped to popularise the trental and Sir John Guldeford and also possibly Thomasin Piers requested that theirs be celebrated at friaries.[109]

Another 'unequivocal manifestation of the full-blown doctrine of Purgatory', the *Scala Coeli* indulgenced mass, appears in six wills from 1516. Perhaps because it was slightly less theologically problematic, it was a little more popular than the St Gregory Trental. Another factor may have been proximity to London, with two testators actually requesting that masses 'at *Scala Coeli*' be celebrated in St Peter's, Westminster, where the indulgence was first licensed in England in 1500. The relative modesty of these masses, which cost 6d. apiece, may also have led some to acquire them. The largest number requested was nine, one for each of Thomas Wode's immediate family, costing a total of 4s. 6d. The other testators secured eight, six, three, and the remaining two, a pair each. This was frugal but, nevertheless, fashionable orthodox religion. It is possible that clerical influence played a part, as four of the wills were either witnessed by, or contain references to, clergy. Masses at *Scala Coeli* were aggressively attacked from the pulpit by Hugh Latimer from 1533, representing, as they did, one of the most popular aspects of traditional religion centred around the doctrine of purgatory and papal authority. Their marginality at Tenterden adds to the impression that such devotional forms were either viewed with some scepticism and suspicion in certain parts of the country before the 1530s or at least failed to appeal.[110]

Neither trentals nor masses at *Scala Coeli* were as popular in Tenterden as the Jesus Mass, the other new devotion in this period. The Tenterden wills only ever refer to the 'Jesus mass' in the parish church of St Mildred, but this was almost certainly the votive mass of the Holy Name of Jesus which was introduced to England in the mid-fourteenth century, but was not widely disseminated until after 1450. Its widespread popularity, including the establishment of some important gilds of Jesus, the most prominent being that of St Paul's, London, founded in 1459, led to the development of a fully established fixed Feast of the Holy Name of Jesus in 1489 sponsored by Lady Margaret Beaufort and Archbishop Rotherham. In 1494 Lady Margaret's efforts resulted in a papal grant of indulgence of several thousand years of remittance from purgatory for those who celebrated, or caused to be celebrated, the votive Mass of the Holy Name for thirty days. Even by the 1490s observance was not ubiquitous across the countryside, many centres only adopting it, like Tenterden, by the first or second decades of the sixteenth century. However, by this time it had become one of the most popular votive masses in England, and enough parishes had their own Jesus altars, gilds or brotherhoods by the turn of the

---

[109] Dinn, 'Popular religion', 578; PRO, PCC 29 Dogett, fo. 223; 1508, PRC 17/12/73.
[110] Duffy, *Altars*, 375–6, 391, 393 at p. 364; Tanner, *Church in Norwich*, appendix 11 at p. 221; Higgs, 'Lay piety', 243–5; Marshall, *Beliefs and the dead*, 51, 74–5; 1526, PRC 17/17/158.

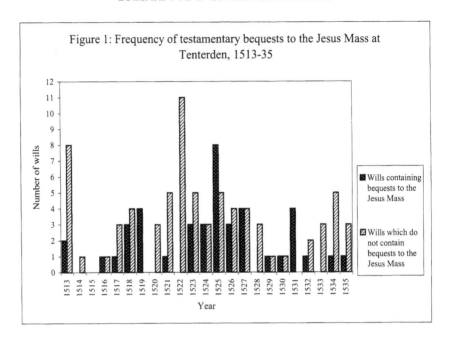

Figure 1: Frequency of testamentary bequests to the Jesus Mass at Tenterden, 1513-35

century to make the cult one of the most important devotional developments of the pre-Reformation period. One of its more enduring and pervasive elements was the adoption of Bernadino of Siena's redeveloped form of the Holy Monogram, IHS.[111]

In Kent the Jesus Mass was established in Sandwich and Lydd by the 1460s and was being celebrated in Canterbury within a decade. It appears in Cranbrook wills from 1501, a few years before it was adopted in Tenterden, and subsequently spread to neighbouring parishes.[112] The cult was much less popular in West Kent. In late fifteenth- and early sixteenth-century Dartford, for example, only three out of nearly 250 testators mentioned the Jesus Mass, and neither does it appear to have attracted bequests from will-makers in the villages around Dartford.[113] Over the border into Sussex in Rye there was a

111 R. W. Pfaff, New liturgical feasts in later medieval England, Oxford 1970, 62–83; E. G. C. F. Atchley, 'Jesus Mass and anthem', Transactions of the St Pauls Ecclesiological Society v (1905), 163–9; Wabuda, Preaching, 151–6, 163–6; Duffy, Altars, 45, 109, 113–16, 120, 224, 370; J. R. Lander, Government and community: England, 1450–1509, London 1980, 114; Barron, 'Parish fraternities', 32, 59. For evidence of the 'highly regionalised' dissemination of Christocentric piety in general see Peters, Patterns of piety, 167.
112 Testamenta cantiana: East Kent, ed. A. Hussey, London 1907, 285, 202, 48, 90, 336, 14, 19, 321, 260. For a similar urban to rural dissemination see Brown, Popular piety, 86–7. See also G. Duby, 'The diffusion of cultural patterns in feudal society', P&P xxxix (1968), 3–10.
113 Testamenta cantiana: West Kent, ed. L. L. Duncan, London 1906, 2, 40–1, 52, 67, 84. Information on Dartford and its hinterland is kindly supplied by Paul Lee: see his 'Monastic and secular religion and devotional reading in late medieval Dartford and West Kent',

Jesus altar in the parish church in the early 1540s and abrogation of the Feast of the Holy Name in 1537 caused bitter conflict between traditionalists and Protestant-inspired evangelicals.[114]

Bequests begin in the Tenterden wills in 1513, and usually consist of sums of money ranging from 4d. to 3s. 4d. These occur in forty-two of the 117, or 36 per cent of, wills made between these two dates, making the Jesus Mass overwhelmingly more popular than other cults. It was more favourably received by the people of Tenterden than in any other place for which there is comparable evidence. For example, at Bury St Edmunds the cult began in 1456 and 9 per cent of lay and clerical testators (from 1449 to 1530) mentioned the Mass or gild of Jesus, although at its most popular, in the years 1459–68 and 1479–82, it appears in just under two-fifths of wills. In Norwich the Jesus Mass was the most popular of votive and indulgenced masses from 1440 to 1532. Even so, only 11 per cent of lay and clerical will-makers mentioned it.[115] At Sandwich less than a tenth of lay testators from 1466 to 1539 gave to the Jesus Mass or Mass of the Five Wounds, or mentioned the Jesus chancel or altar in St Mary's church and, of these, only a handful did so after 1500.[116] In Tenterden the devotion retained its popularity into the early 1530s (see figure 1) having arrived there long after its heyday in Sandwich or important early centres like Bury St Edmunds.

Bequests to the Jesus Mass at Tenterden were shared by thirty-one surnames. Nine (29 per cent) of these surnames appear more than once in the list of individuals who gave to the cult. As a result, these nine surnames were responsible for twenty of the forty-two gifts; a disproportionate share of 48 per cent. In seven of these cases all the testators sharing the same surname were related, either by blood or by marriage, and in the other two instances this cannot be proven but is not unlikely. The tendency for certain families to give to the cult more times than others indicates that patronage of the Jesus Mass was, in part, like other aspects of testamentary piety, formed and sustained by bonds of family, household and kinship. Significantly, the spread of bequests across the pious spectrum represented by the twenty-three selected families is the only aspect of religious expression to defy the general pattern. Eight out of the nineteen wills made by top-band families from 1513 mention the new devotion, a similar proportion to the six out of thirteen from the most religiously sparing. Those families in the middle of the pious spectrum were responsible for seventeen wills after 1512, and six of these – about a third – mention the Jesus Mass.

Patronage of the Jesus Mass at Tenterden does not, therefore, match the

unpubl. PhD diss. Kent 1998, and *Nunneries, learning and spirituality in late medieval English society: the Dominican priory of Dartford*, Woodbridge 2001.

[114] Mayhew, 'Progress of the reformation', 54; Wabuda, *Preaching*, 172.

[115] Dinn, 'Popular religion', 195–200; Wabuda, *Preaching*, 163; Tanner, *Church in Norwich*, 94, 102–3, 220–1, appendix 11; Higgs, 'Lay piety', 236–40; Brown, *Popular piety*, 138–42.

[116] Information kindly supplied by Sheila Sweetinburgh.

overall pattern of testamentary religious expression. Families that since the mid-fifteenth century had produced often markedly sparse or moderate wills in religious terms, adhered to the new devotion to the same or even greater extent than those who had previously surpassed their contemporaries in all areas of traditional giving. The Jesus Mass was especially appealing to families that had tended to neglect other forms of institutional religious devotion. A number, including the Castelyns and Pellonds, who will be examined in more depth in chapter 4, left wills devoid of explicitly religious bequests as well as those lending support to the Jesus Mass. Nine out of eighteen, or 47 per cent, of those families who made at least one will lacking religious bequests, and for whom there is at least one other will made after 1512, also gave to the Jesus Mass. To turn this on its head, nine out of sixteen, or 56 per cent, of families who supported the new cult and for whom there are other wills, also left at least one sparse will. As parsimony gave way to a more elaborate, albeit relatively reserved, testamentary piety in the sixteenth century among these families, the cult of Jesus appears to have been both timely in its arrival and broad in its appeal.

What was it about the Jesus Mass that made it appealing to families which otherwise seem to have lacked engagement with traditional forms of orthodox religion? It cannot have been its novelty alone, as a number of other new cults attracted occasional bequests in the early sixteenth century, but none of them drew the same level and spread of support. A number of historians have sought to explain the significance of the cult of Jesus, together with other types of Christocentric devotion in England and Europe prior to the Reformation. Susan Wabuda has convincingly argued that this 'new devotional stress upon the person of Christ' was a 'product of humanism and a strong renewed evangelical current in the broad, orthodox streams of the late medieval Church' stimulated principally by the Fransiscans and strongly identified with devotions to the sacrament of the altar and its sacrificial role in aiding souls in purgatory. The cult also became associated with the growing humanist emphasis on the primacy of the Scriptures. A dynamic programme of preaching and the establishment of preaching chantries and colleges of the Holy Name was inaugurated from the 1450s. These two elements, which represented complementary (although not always entirely harmonious) aspects of evangelical Catholicism, took on fundamental importance in the doctrinal battles of the early Reformation.[117]

It is generally agreed that the Jesus Mass heralded a heightened and more personal form of Christocentric devotion, although there is less unanimity as to its precise emphases. Certainly, the use of prayers, the repetition of the name of Jesus and concentration on the passion offered an intensification of personal identification with Christ and his suffering and access to a renewed

Jesus Mass very important
Stepping stone to Reformation.

[117] Wabuda, Preaching, 8, 20–106, 148, 163–8, 173.

sense of reconciliation with God.[118] Christine Peters has argued, however, that an increasing focus on the passion of Christ and heightening of his role as chief intercessor between mankind and God had the effect of diminishing the degree of personal identification with Christ's humanity. While these different emphases are not necessarily incompatible, and may well represent the very richness of Christocentric devotion, and therefore its wide appeal, Peters's argument rests largely on an analysis of depictions of the Five Wounds and the emblems of the passion rather than the cult of the Holy Name.[119] Equally, neither does the wording of the Jesus Mass support Higgs's assertion that the 'humanity of Jesus was foremost' in the popular piety of the pre-Reformation period, and that it was only 'the Jesus of the Reformers' who 'was a Divine Saviour fulfilling a high office in the plan of salvation'.[120]

The Office of the Mass of the Holy Name, which was celebrated on Fridays in parish and cathedral churches across England, emphasised both the supremacy as well as the humanity of Christ. It began with Philippians ii.10–11: 'In nomine Jesu omne genuflectatur coelestium terrestrium et infernorum et omnis lingua confiteatur quia Dominus noster Jesu Christus in Gloria est Dei Patris' ('At the name of Jesus every knee should bow, in heaven and on earth and under the earth, and every tongue confess that Jesus Christ is Lord, to the glory of God the Father').[121] The lesson, taken from the Acts of the Apostles, contained the words of the Apostle Peter to the priests and Saducees, underlining how Christ's supremacy was central to human salvation: 'this is the stone caste asyde of you buylders whiche is sette in the chefe place of the corner, neyther is there salvacion in any other, nor yet also is there any other name gyuen to menne wherin we muste be saued'.[122] These verses, found in translation in early sixteenth-century primers containing the Jesus Mass, had the potential to inspire or reinforce indigenous orthodox but reformist ideas about Christ as sole intercessor. These biblical texts had formed part of the popular votive Mass, Office and Feast of the Holy Name from the late fifteenth century. A rudimentary lay understanding of the Latin liturgy, or at least portions of it, may have been widespread and although, due

---

[118] Duffy, *Altars*, 236; Bossy, *Christianity*, 6–10; Dinn, 'Popular religion', 195, 200, 204; Wabuda, *Preaching*, 152–4, 159–63; Lander, *Government and community*, 114.

[119] Peters, *Patterns of piety*, 3–4, 60–96, 345.

[120] Higgs, 'Lay piety', 332–3.

[121] *Missale ad usum insignis et praeclarae ecclesiae Sarum*, ed. F. H. Dickinson, Burntisland 1861–83, col. 846.

[122] Acts iv. 8–12: listed as the Epistle for the Feast of the Holy Name in St Paul's Cathedral Library, 38.D7: *The prymer in Englyshe and Latyn wyth the Epystles and Gospelles of euery sonday & holyedaye in the yere, and also the exposycion upon miserere mei deus wyth many other prayers*, London 1542 (*RSTC*, 16026), 'The Epistles and Gospels', fos xlr–v. I owe a debt of thanks to Joseph Wisdom, the Librarian at St Paul's and his assistant Maurice Sills for kindly letting me see this book. These verses are included as the lesson of the Office and votive Mass of the Holy Name in the Sarum and York Missals: *Missale ad usum Sarum*, col. 846; *Missale ad usum insignis ecclesiae Eboracensis*, ed. W. G. Henderson (Surtees Society lx, 1874), 216–20.

to their association with Lollardy, primers in English seem to have been rare by the late fifteenth century, the existence of Latin manuscript precursors to printed primers and more ephemeral common aids to devotion such as indulgence cards would have aided lay comprehension of texts used in the liturgy. Duffy interprets the popular reception of the cult of the Holy Name in England almost wholly in terms of the attraction of its magical and invocatory elements arising from notions of the virtue of reciting the name of Jesus and the various names of God as listed in the Charlemagne prayers included in the Office of the Feast. However, his interpretation arguably overplays these aspects at the expense of the scriptural elements of the Office, the function of the homily in explaining them to the laity and the pre-Reformation forms of the Jesus Anthem.[123]

Although not referred to in the Tenterden wills, the Jesus Anthem was widely adopted and sung after the Jesus Mass every Friday across England from the 1460s. Its origins and forms have yet to be conclusively established but it is perhaps best identified as the *Salve Rex*, an adaptation of the popular Breviary anthem of the Virgin, the *Salve Regina*. The *Salve Rex* Anthem can be found in Latin and English in a number of early sixteenth-century printed primers, and also presented Christ as supreme mediator and saviour whilst emphasising his humanity. It appears to have been printed for the first time in William Marshall's 1534 primer, an evangelical compilation, but went on to be included in more equivocal publications.[124] One of these, dated 1542, contains the following version, which is notable for its emphasis on Christ's unique role as saviour:

Oratio ad Christum
Salue rex Jesu Christe, rex misericorde, vita nostra, suavitas nostra ac spes nostra te salutamus. Ad te clamauimus exules filii Eve. Ad te suspiramus gementes & flentes in hac lachrimarum valle. Eia ergo aduocate noster, illos tuos misericordes oculos ad nos converte. Patremque tuum (O Jesu omni laude dignissime) post hoc nostrum exilium ostende. O clemens, o misericors, o suavis Jesu christe.

Versus. In omnibus tribulationibus & angustiis.
Respon. Jesu Christe succurre nobis.

Oratio.
Domine Jesu Christe, fili Dei ac redemptor noster, qui temetipsum in vilissimam nostram naturam transformasti, ut nos filios ire in filios gratie patri reconciliares. Concede quesumus domine, ut possimus certa fide confiteri, te esse redemptorem nostrum ac apud patrem solum mediatorem nostrum pro

---

123 Duffy, *Altars*, 210–32, 233–65, 282–5; Wabuda, *Preaching*, 24–33, 155–6, 159–63.
124 Atchley, 'Jesus Mass and anthem', 163–9. E. Hoskins, *Horae beatae Mariae virginis, or Sarum and York primers*, London 1901, 199, 217, 184. Duffy, who sees the *Salve Rex* anthem as a wholly Protestant adaptation, wrongly dates its first printing to 1538 by referencing a different version of the hymn: *Altars*, 382, 445; Hoskins, *Horae beatae*, 176.

omnibus bonis spiritualibus. Qui es deus eternus viuens & regnans cum patre & spiritu sancto: per infinita seculorum secula. Amen.

A Prayer to chryste
Hayle, Jesu Chryst, Kynge of mercy, our lyfe, our swetnes, & oure hope, we salute the : unto the we cry, which are the banyshed children of Eve : unto the we syghe sobbynge, and wepyng in thys vayle of wretchedness : hast yᵉ therfore our medyator, turne unto us those thy mercyful eyes. O Jesu, all prayse worthy, shew us the presence of thy father after thys outlawry. O gentel, O mercyfull, O swete Jesu Chryste.

The versicle. In al our trouble and heuynes.
The answer. O Jesu, oure healthe and glorye, socoure us.

The Prayer.
O Jesu Chryst, the sonne of God, our redemer, which deiectedst and humbledst thy selfe from the gloryous state and shape of thy godhed, unto the shap of our vile seruitude, because thou woldest reconcyle us the chyldren of wrathe unto the father, and so make us thy chyldren of grace, we beseech the graunte us that we mought ever fele even the by thy very self to be our present medyator before our father for all ghostly giftes, whom we knowledge with perfecte fayth to be our sauyoure : whych art the lyvely God, wyth the father and the holy ghost, lyuynge, and raygning into the world of worldes. So be it.[125]

Atchley suggests that the word *solum*, translated as 'by thy very self' and claiming Christ to be sole mediator, may have been 'an amendment due to Lutheran influence'. Luther himself took a particular dislike to the *Salve Regina* and there is some evidence that this particular version of the *Salve Rex* may have originated in German Lutheran churches in the 1520s.[126] There is not, however, any explicit emphasis upon faith as the agency of salvation, which one would expect from a Lutheran-inspired reconstruction. Rather, the stress is on Christ as the object of faith, which was arguably a peculiarly English preoccupation, with its roots in the pre-Reformation period. It may, therefore, be an amendment of one of the many English Christocentric hymns in circulation in the fifteenth and early sixteenth centuries.[127]

These questions notwithstanding, the growth in popularity of the Jesus Mass is indicative of an increasing devotional focus upon Christ which, at Tenterden, accompanied a decline in the cult of saints. Traditional Catholic orthodoxy urged the believer to trust first and foremost in Christ as saviour, as well as encouraging reliance upon a panoply of saints,[128] but the Jesus Mass may represent the most widespread and easily accessible expression of the

[125] St Paul's Cathedral Library, 38.D7, 1542: *The prymer in Englyshe and Latyn*, 60.
[126] Atchley, 'Jesus Mass and anthem', 168–9; *The Catholic encyclopedia*, ed. C. G. Herbermann, E. A. Pace and others, New York 1912, xiii. 410.
[127] Higgs, 'Lay piety', 332–3; Hoskins, *Horae beatae*, 115.
[128] Duffy, *Altars*, 507–8, 519.

intensification of Christocentric devotion and the concomitant erosion of popular perceptions of the intercessory power of saints. Christine Peters has charted this process: 'it was quite possible to call upon the help of a specialised saint . . . yet to view Christ as the only mediator in the vital question of the salvation of one's soul. However, as Christocentric devotion grew stronger, the intercession of the saints could be seen as an irrelevant distraction from true devotion, seriously reducing their role in popular piety'.[129] This may, in part, explain the appeal of the cult of Jesus to families that eschewed testamentary giving to saints' lights and images. There were also those, as will be demonstrated in chapter 5, who were familiar with heretical questioning of the value of saints' cults, and who may have viewed Christocentric devotional innovation as a welcome reform of orthodox religion.[130] By the 1530s Christocentric piety and, in particular, the cult of the Holy Name contained much common ground for Catholic and Protestant evangelicals and, for some, 'a bridge to Reformation in terms of religious understanding'.[131]

The Mass of the Holy Name encapsulated other elements that may have attracted religiously frugal families. First, its emphasis upon Jesus' human kinship and the Holy Family provided a model for pious relationships congruent with the sorts of traditional practices carried out by some of the Tenterden families described above, which invested in the family as a social and moral institution.[132] This prefigured the growing importance of the family as a metaphor for biblically-based relationships among reforming communities later in the sixteenth century.[133] Secondly, the cult of Jesus and other forms of Christocentric devotion appear to have been concentrated in urban centres. Higher levels of education and literacy in towns compared to more rural areas would have aided the dissemination of new devotional forms.[134] In addition the Mass of the Holy Name was linked nationally with preaching and towns may have been the most likely beneficiaries of a

---

[129] Peters, *Patterns of piety*, 98–9, chs iii, iv.

[130] Andrew Brown has also drawn attention to the radicalism of the cult of Jesus and its continuity with later acceptance of reform: *Popular piety*, 248. Writing on the Jesus Mass in Cranbrook church, in 1925, L. L. Duncan, remarked that 'The support of the Jesus Mass was a favourite object of devotion, and there are many bequests thereto. It had nothing to do, as Mr. Cave-Browne imagines it had, with Lollardism': 'Notes on Cranbrook church', AC xxxvii (1925), 29.

[131] Peters, *Patterns of piety*, 3, 345, chs vi, vii at p. 220; Wabuda, *Preaching*, 16–17, 83–8, 148, 168–77.

[132] Dinn, 'Popular religion', 200; Bossy, *Christianity*, 10; J. Huizinga, *The waning of the Middle Ages*, Harmondsworth 1968, 170–2.

[133] D. A. Penny, 'Family matters and Foxe's *Acts and monuments*', *Historical Journal* xxxix (1996), 599–618; Higgs, 'Lay piety', 338–40.

[134] Dinn, 'Popular religion', 203–4. See also Barron, 'Parish fraternities', 32, 59; Brown, *Popular piety*, 86–7.

humanist programme of moderate reform that aimed to disseminate the truth of Scripture, albeit through the safe mediation of the clergy.[135]

Although 'genuinely popular', Duffy argues that the Jesus Mass 'was also emphatically an observance seized on by elites in every community as a convenient expression, and perhaps an instrument, of their social dominance'. The court's patronage of the cult under Lady Margaret Beaufort, its appropriation by the Tudor dynasty and the institution of the famous Name of Jesus gild in the Crowds of St Paul's in London, all provided a powerful social incentive for involvement in Jesus gilds by leading townsfolk. In Colchester, the Jesus gild appears to have drawn its members from across the economic strata of the town, but paid considerably more attention to middling- and upper-ranking adherents.[136] The social profile of patronage of the Holy Name at Tenterden is explored in more detail in chapter 4, but for now it is worth noting that some of the families which were particularly drawn to it may have been among the most upwardly socially mobile.

The Jesus Mass was linked with the development of liturgical music and song, and it seems no coincidence that the five bequests in the Tenterden wills for the purchase of new organs were made in the years 1510–13, just before the establishment of the devotion. In his elaborate endowments in 1518, William Couper described how the Mass of Jesus was 'said and sung' every Friday.[137] For the most part, testamentary bequests were made simply 'to the Jesus mass' or 'to the maintenance of the Jesus mass'. Anne Stonehouse's gift of 4d. 'to the boxe ordenyned to dyverse gatherers in the said parishe for the masse of Jhesu ther to be contynued' was, in 1513, one of the first two references to the cult and suggests one of the ways fundraising was organised.[138] From 1516 some testators specifically stated that their gifts were intended for 'the fyndyng of the brothred priste celebratyng the masse of Jhesus every fryday in the parishe churche' suggesting that, as in other places in this period, a Jesus brotherhood was quickly established which permanently supported its own priest.[139] In 1526 Thomas Wode ordained that within four years of his death, £20 was to be given to his feoffees to buy lands and tenements, which were then to be delivered to eight or more honest persons of the parish, who in turn were to give the profits to the churchwardens to pay the salary or stipend of 'a brotherhed preest or Jhesus preeste'.[140] Tenterden appears to have been an important centre in the maintenance and

[135] Wabuda, *Preaching*, 163–8, chs i, ii.

[136] Duffy, *Altars*, 115–16; Wabuda, *Preaching*, 10; *Registrum statutorum et consuetudinum Ecclesiae Cathedralis Sancti Pauli Londensis*, ed. W. Sparrow Simpson, London 1873, 435–62, 483–4; Higgs, 'Lay piety', 239; Atchley, 'Jesus Mass and anthem', passim.

[137] Atchley, 'Jesus Mass and anthem', 164, and passim; *Registrum statutorum*, 447–50; PRC 32/12/174.

[138] PRC 17/12/182.

[139] Thomas Smyth, 1518: PRC 17/14/7; Atchley, 'Jesus Mass and anthem', passim; Duffy, *Altars*, 115–16, 120, 224.

[140] PRC 17/17/158.

development of the cult of Jesus in Kent as Jesus brotherhoods are mentioned in wills in a total of only seven or eight other parishes across the county.[141]

It appears that the papal indulgence that was granted to the votive mass was not central to the attractiveness of the devotion, there being no references to trentals of Jesus Masses in the wills. Neither was there any mention of the votive masses or feasts which focused on the suffering of Jesus, namely of the Five Wounds, the Crown of Thorns or the cult of the Transfiguration.[142] In Kent, and across the country as a whole, these did not tend to be as popular as the Mass of the Holy Name but, nevertheless, the mass of the Five Wounds in particular often accompanied it. This suggests that Christocenticism at Tenterden was largely informed by more recently fashionable and humanist-inspired forms rather than the older and more mystical associations with Christ's suffering.[143] In addition, in most other places where the cult of the Holy Name became popular, there is evidence of painted and sometimes gilded Jesus images on designated Jesus altars. In the neighbouring parish of Rolvenden in 1517, John Hubbard willed that 'the diadem which I ordered for the same image of Jesus be gilt, and set upon the same Image'.[144] Distinct from the crucifix, there is little evidence of what these images actually looked like and, most important, how they portrayed Christ, apart from clues that suggest the depiction of Jesus as a conquering king. Only two Tenterden testators made bequests to the 'Jesus light' or for lights to be set up on the Jesus altar and none mentioned an image. Whether or not one existed, bequests accord with the general profile of attitudes to images of saints over the period and their early disappearance from wills. It is of course possible that the devotion at Tenterden employed the monogram of the Holy Name as its central image, an aspect particularly malleable to Protestant reshaping.[145]

The only piece of pre-Reformation imagery that survives from Tenterden that may have originally decorated the interior of St Mildred's, is a mutilated alabaster carving depicting the Resurrection (see frontispiece). It was found at Leigh Green in the parish in the late nineteenth century. This fragment probably formed part of a multi-panelled retable, either portable or fixed, that would have stood on or behind an altar but may perhaps have been fixed to a wall in the church or have decorated the Easter sepulchre. If part of a retable it would have been accompanied by one or two panels depicting other

---

141 *Testamenta cantiana: East Kent*, 48, 55, 57, 208, 234, 235, 160, 285.
142 Duffy, *Altars*, 45–6, 238–48; Pfaff, *New feasts*, passim.
143 Dinn, 'Popular religion', 204; Atchley, 'Jesus Mass and anthem', 165–6; Peters, *Patterns of piety*, 83–6; Tanner, *Church in Norwich*, appendix 11. In Sandwich, for example, the Mass of the Wounds of Jesus appears in wills from the early 1490s to the late 1520s.
144 *Testamenta cantiana: East Kent*, 7, 44, 84, 126, 153, 217, 225, quotation at p. 260. See also *Registrum statutorum*, 460; Atchley, 'Jesus Mass and anthem', 164–7; Duffy, *Altars*, 115–16. Stephen Felip, 1523: PRC 17/16/46; William Couper, 1518: PRC 32/12/174.
145 Wabuda, *Preaching*, 156–63, 175.

episodes from the life of Christ or the Virgin, typically the Ascension, the Coronation of the Virgin, the Entombment or the Crucifixion. There are remnants of the alabaster's medieval polychrome painted and gilded finish but the top part of the carving has been entirely broken off, presumably when it was smashed from its frame during the Reformation. Consequently, the head and extended right arm of Christ are missing, in addition to the cross and banner that would have topped the staff held in his left hand. Despite this damage the depiction of Christ stepping from the tomb surrounded by armed soldiers dressed in fourteenth-century armour rousing from their slumber, is clearly identifiable as typical of Resurrection carvings of the late fourteenth or early fifteenth century. However, the portrayal of the risen Christ is particularly forceful, with an almost oversized right leg and foot stepping onto the torso of the soldier in the bottom foreground, muscular chest and massive left fist. This was perhaps an attempt to emphasise the three-dimensionality of the carving but may express a particular mentality, whether of the craftsman or patron, towards Christ. It provides some indication of the sort of visual representation of Jesus that may have existed in the church prior to and after the adoption of the Jesus Mass.[146]

One of the two will-makers who attended to lights was William Couper and his is the only will containing arrangements for the decoration of the Jesus altar. Couper ordained that his 'executors do prepare and make redye in as shorte tyme as they convenyently maye all and every suche auter clothis and torches curteynd as I of late dyd put to payntyng to one paynter of hedcrone (Headcorn) whiche I will and bequethe to the use of the seid churche and to be hanged there aboute and uppon auter where the masse of Jhesus is usyd to be celebrated'. He also gave 6s. 8d. for a pair of 'laten candylstiks continually to stand uppon the seid auter', and stipulated that 2s. from lands and tenements at farm was to be given regularly to maintain 'two tapers continually upon altar where mass of Jesus is celebrated to burn during said masses'. Once his son Stephen was twenty-four and inherited this property, he was to renew the tapers at the Feasts of the Annunciation and St Michael, and set them 'on seid auter to burn every fryday when mass of Jhesus is said and sung'. Decoration with cloths, banners and lights were common elements in the cult of Jesus up and down the country. However, Couper was one of the most lavish will-makers in this period and belonged to one of the most religiously generous families. His arrangements are not typical of the parish, and serve to remind us that the same religious observance could be interpreted and appropriated in quite different ways and for different reasons

---

[146] H. V. R., *The parish church of St Mildred Tenterden*, St Ives n.d., 10; E. S. Prior, 'The sculpture of alabaster tables', in *Illustrated catalogue of the exhibition of English medieval alabaster work*, London 1913, 16–50; W. H. St John Hope, 'On the early working of alabaster in England', *Illustrated catalogue*, 1–15.

by individuals and families following contrasting pious traditions.[147] This is reinforced by another feature of the Tenterden bequests. Whereas elsewhere (in Sandwich for example) arrangements were made for masses and prayers to be sung and said before Jesus altars specifically for the testator's and others' souls, there is nothing like this in the Tenterden wills.[148] Those who gave to the maintenance of the devotion no doubt expected to benefit spiritually along with the rest of its patrons. They may also have hoped to be prayed for by name like Robert Fraunces of Colchester, who left 5 marks to the wardens of the Jesus gild to buy four sheets of parchment 'to be set in the mass book of Jhus & in that to be set all the brethern & sisterne that hath give unto the said mass'.[149] Such aspirations are never explicitly articulated in the Tenterden bequests, however, and it is possible that the development of the Jesus Mass there was characterised by a decline in the sense of importance attached to intercessions for named individuals (also signalled by the fall-off in chantry foundation) in favour of an intensified sense of intimacy with Christ and concentration on his saving mercy.

Gifts to religious

Monastic or mendicant religious houses only rarely entered the preoccupations of Tenterden will-makers. Fifteen testators, less than 6 per cent, made bequests to religious houses, sometimes in return for masses and especially trentals but usually without specification. Strikingly, only three of these were made after 1500 and the last to do so was William Couper in 1518.[150] This is quite different from other towns. For example, in Sandwich just under a third of lay men and women gave to religious houses, with only a small decline in bequests in the sixteenth century. In other urban centres and more rural areas nationally between a quarter and a half of lay testators remembered monks, nuns or friars, and only in Colchester did gifts to all orders begin to decline by the 1520s.[151] The distribution of bequests to religious houses across families follows the same pattern as other religious elements. Four testators from the top band, two from the middle and two from the bottom group of families mentioned them, suggesting that whilst not all testators ignored monks, nuns and friars, those that gave to them were largely concentrated within more traditionally orthodox families. Secular clergy were more popular but mainly because they received numerous bequests to celebrate masses. Only nine testators left money to secular clergy (usually the vicar of Tenterden) for no

---

147 PRC 32/12/174; *Registrum statutorum*, 447–60; *Testamenta cantiana: East Kent*, 107, 127, 160, 260, 285.

148 PRC 32/9/137, 17/14/206; *Testamenta cantiana: East Kent*, 19, 127; Atchley, 'Jesus Mass and anthem', 163–6.

149 Higgs, 'Lay piety', 208.

150 PRC 32/12/174.

151 Higgs, 'Lay piety', 218; Dinn, 'Popular religion', 447–50, 460–2, 464–5; Tanner, *Church in Norwich*, 119, appendix 12 at p. 222; Heath, 'Urban piety', 220–1; Thomson, 'Piety and charity', 189–90.

specified purpose, although of course the vicar, curate or parochial chaplains sometimes acted as executors and often as witnesses to wills.

Although the testamentary evidence tells us nothing about lifetime giving, the apparent lack of popularity of the religious orders in Tenterden may in part be attributed to the fact that the nearest houses lay around ten to fifteen miles from the town at Bilsington, Winchelsea, Mottenden and Lossenham. However, this in itself does not fully explain what appears to have been general indifference to institutions that were integrated into social, educational and economic life across the Weald of Kent. It is perhaps an indication of the extent to which parochial religion was successfully providing services for the laity that at one point had been so valuably offered by monastic houses. The national trend in this period was for fewer gifts to be made to monastic houses for intercessory services and those bequests that were made tended to be to individuals rather than institutions and so are difficult to identify.[152] The religious houses were generally considered to be institutions that first and foremost prayed for the dead, and so the lack of interest in the monasteries in Tenterden's wills may have been part and parcel of the general decline in chantry endowment. That the religious orders had profited from foundations which they could not possibly support and had, on the whole, fallen short of their original ideals were opinions in common currency by the late fifteenth century, and it has recently been suggested that a conservative agenda for the reform of the monasteries, before they came under sustained attack from evangelicals, would have led to a process of secularisation had there not been a Reformation.[153]

The Carmelite Friary of Lossenham in the parish of Newenden and the Trinitarian Friary of Mottenden in the parish of Headcorn, both situated about ten miles from Tenterden, stand out for being mentioned by six and four testators respectively. Three made bequests to St Augustine's Abbey, Canterbury, and two to friaries in Winchelsea. The Observant friars in Canterbury, the Grey friars of Beaulieu in the New Forest, the Grey friars and the Charter House in London, the Benedictine nunnery of the Holy Sepulchre in Canterbury and Battle Abbey were all mentioned just once each. In other places the mendicant orders appear to have been more popular than the possessioners, and although this was also the case in Tenterden, there was not the growing support for the friars up to the Reformation as there was elsewhere.[154] There is no evidence of involvement by the friars in

[152] J. G. Clark, 'The religious orders in pre-Reformation England', and B. Thompson, 'Monasteries, society and reform in late medieval England', in J. G. Clark (ed.), The religious orders in pre-Reformation England, Woodbridge 2002, 24–33, 179–84.

[153] Marshall, Beliefs and the dead, 81; Thompson, 'Monasteries', 168, 185–95; Aston, Iconoclasts, 113. See also Dickens, English Reformation, 74–80; C. Cross, Church and people, 1450–1660: the triumph of the English Church, Hassocks 1976, 52.

[154] VCH, Kent, ii. 142–3, 203–7; Higgs, 'Lay piety', 218; Dinn, 'Popular religion', 447–50, 460–2, 464–5; Tanner, Church in Norwich, 119, appendix 12 at p. 222; Heath, 'Urban piety',

funeral rites, as has been documented elsewhere. The mendicants were, of course, famous for their preaching and role in hearing confession and were heavily involved in the devotional trends of which the cult of the Holy Name was a part and so it is somewhat surprising that gifts to the friars nearly all date to before 1500, some years before the establishment of the Jesus Mass. However, the fact that they were also associated with the performance of indulgenced masses and trentals, for which there was little demand at Tenterden, may help to explain their apparent absence. There was a long tradition of anti-fraternal polemic, by no means all of it Wycliffite in inspiration, and it should perhaps be expected that an enduring Lollard centre was relatively unengaged with the friars. Above and beyond the influence of heresy, however, the decline and then complete absence of support for the mendicants in wills in the early sixteenth century suggests that broadly orthodox sensibilities at Tenterden were increasingly disconnected from their activities.[155]

Devotion to saints *Decline in Saint worship— path to Protestantism?*
In their devotion to saints Tenterden's will-makers were also relatively sparing. Over the whole period, only thirty-nine (15 per cent) of testators made gifts to lights, and five of these gave only to lights which honoured Christ, such as the rood light or before the sacrament. In total, these types of lights were mentioned in seventeen wills, making them second only to devotions to the Virgin Mary in popularity. Bequests to all types of lights reached a peak during the years 1500–19, being found in about 20 per cent of all wills but waning by the 1520s (*see* table 5). Gifts to lights were less than half as popular in Tenterden as they were at Sandwich over a similar period, and were in stark contrast to other centres nationally in their infrequency, the only exception being Colchester where from 1518 to 1532 a mere 6.5 per cent of wills contain bequests for votive lights.[156]

Gifts for lights were, of course, intimately associated with images of saints. These are mentioned even less frequently with only fourteen testators (5 per cent) leaving money or objects for their adornment or manufacture. Significantly, the last mention of images was in 1522.[157] In Sandwich, gifts to specific altars and images were at least twice as popular as in Tenterden, and remained so into the 1530s. Bequests involving devotion to saints provide an

---

220–1; Thomson, 'Piety and charity', 189–90. Clark, 'Religious orders', 30; Thompson, 'Monasteries', 181.

[155] Clark, 'Religious orders', 30; Marshall, *Beliefs and the dead*, 81; Wabuda, *Preaching*, 107–39; R. Rex, 'The friars in the English Reformation', in P. Marshall and A. Ryrie (eds), *The beginnings of English Protestantism*, Cambridge 2002, 38–59.

[156] This is without including a number of testators who made gifts to unnamed lights in Sandwich: Tanner, *Church in Norwich*, appendix 12 at p. 222; Higgs, 'Lay piety', 222.

[157] Connected with the absence of references to images after 1522 is the lack of chantry bequests to be carried out at named saints' altars or in chapels, or any mention of saints' chapels within the parish church after 1505.

especially effective way of distinguishing between different pious traditions. Gifts to lights, in particular, were often as small as 4d. or 6d. and so were less dependent on available resources at death than other expressions of orthodox devotion. When references to saints' cults are compared across the twenty-three selected families, it emerges that devotion to saints conforms to the spectrum of testamentary piety already observed. Eight testators spread across five of the most religiously generous families gave to saints' cults, in the middle band seven testators across four families and, in the bottom group, only two individuals in two separate families made these types of bequests. In general, adherence to the cult of saints was modest and seemingly in decline at Tenterden, with no mention of pilgrimage in the wills of the most devoted for example.[158]

This may partly have been due to the tendency of Christocentric devotion to relegate humanised mediators to the role of helpers with specific powers. It is also, arguably, evidence of the circulation and growth of critical debate about the cult of saints, and their images in particular. There was a long-standing Lollard tradition of opposition to images and pilgrimage that was strongly represented by Wealden heretical networks. Lollards were particularly concerned with the social aspects of the cult of saints which they criticised for the way images and pilgrimage diverted much-needed funds to the clergy and religious orders, that ought to have been given to the poor, who were the true image of Christ.[159] Outside Lollard circles, and predating Wyclif, there was a very long tradition of debate about images and unease in some quarters about their perceived abuse. Such discussions became much more dangerous after the arrival of Lollardy but they were sustained into the sixteenth century without necessarily being connected to iconoclasm or accusations of heresy.[160] It was not until 1525 that the controversy about images took on far greater proportions. The attacks, at first, remained orthodox and do not appear to have been inspired by continental ideas or programmes of reform, although they may have been encouraged by events overseas. What is so interesting about the ideas of the likes of Thomas Bilney and Hugh Latimer is that they seem to have been part of a moderate English tradition (at least before the 1530s), only partly informed by Lollardy, and given fresh impetus by humanist and, specifically, Erasmian thought. Latimer, for example, questioned the importance and place of the adornment and veneration of images in devotional piety and sought to categorise these as secondary and voluntary works which, without proper care, could lead to superstitious abuse.[161] It is possible that these sorts of opinions, that had much in common with Lollard positions, were in circulation at a local level in the early sixteenth century. Coupled with this, continental iconoclasm

---

[158] In contrast to Norwich: Tanner, *Church in Norwich*, 85.
[159] See chapter 5 below; Aston, *Iconoclasts*, 97–110, 124–5, 156.
[160] Aston, *Iconoclasts*, 23–31, 113–58.
[161] Ibid. 160–200; Wabuda, *Preaching*, 83, 91, 120; Davis, *Heresy and reformation*, 41–2.

was being reported in England from 1522 and domestic incidents of image-breaking increased from around this time. The unusual level of iconoclasm among evangelical clergy and laypeople investigated in Kent in 1543 may be an indication not just of the legacy of Lollardy in the county, but perhaps also the long-term influence of more orthodox traditions of iconomachy.[162]

After the cult of Jesus, devotion to Mary was most popular, with twenty-five individuals mentioning her chapel, image, light or fraternity at Tenterden or in neighbouring parishes.[163] The Virgin Mary is the only saint for whom there is evidence of a fraternity at Tenterden. In 1449 William Cok left 3s. 4d. to the 'light of the fraternity of St Mary' (in addition to the separate 'light of St Mary') and bequeathed 3s. 4d. each year for six years to the finding of a chaplain for the brotherhood.[164] The altar of this brotherhood was probably situated in the chapel of St Mary (otherwise referred to as the 'Lady Chancel'), which formed the south chancel aisle of St Mildred's.[165] Marian devotion was an important element within Robert Brekynden's testamentary provisions, which included the rare request that his body be buried within St Mary's chapel. He accompanied this with the equally singular gift of a silver chain to the image of the Virgin.[166] The fraternity is not mentioned again in surviving wills until 1479 and then appears in two bequests in 1489. The second of these is in the will of Tenterden's vicar, John Morer, leaving five marks to the brotherhood, to be paid in parcels of 6s. 8d. a year for ten years. This was on the condition that an honest priest was maintained at a good standard of living to celebrate for the benefit of the brotherhood.[167] The fraternity is not mentioned again in the wills, and the chapel or chancel of St Mary appears only another two times, both in the 1490s.[168] The brotherhood survived through to the Reformation, albeit with less than adequate endowment. It was listed alongside Tenterden's obit and lamp rents in 1548 as 'The Fraternytie called our Ladyes Brotherhed founded within the parishe

---

[162] Aston, *Iconoclasts*, 35–41, 211–15; Duffy, *Altars*, 381; W. R. Jones, 'Lollards and images: the defense of religious art in later medieval England', *Journal of the History of Ideas* xxxiv (1973), 28–9, 34, 49; A. Ryrie, *The Gospel and Henry VIII: evangelicals in the early English Reformation*, Cambridge 2003, 224–32.

[163] In all the churches of East Kent, devotion to Christ and Mary superseded that to any other saints: G. Draper, G. Hornby, J. Hosking, C. Richardson and A. Wiggins, 'The fitting of the altars: gender and popular piety in East Kent', paper given at the Summer Conference of the Ecclesiastical History Society, University of Kent at Canterbury 1996.

[164] PRC 17/1/7.

[165] CCA, Z.3.2, fo. 136v, 1502 (translated in C. E. Woodruff, 'An archidiaconal visitation of 1502', AC xlvii [1935], 26); H. V. R., *Parish church*, 10.

[166] 1483, PRC 17/3/450. Only one other testator, Thomas Pette, requested burial in this chapel in 1489: PRC 17/6/108.

[167] PRO, PCC 20 Milles, fos 164/161v.

[168] PRC 17/6/10, 17/6/108.

churche of Tenterden by whom it is not known'. Attached lands worth 8s. a year provided 7s. 4d. after rent.[169]

Despite the seeming failure of St Mary's brotherhood to mobilise widespread support, devotion to the Virgin continued throughout the period. In 1507 Robert Swoffer left 16d. to 'repairs of ornaments pertaining to the altars of our lady and Saint Katherine', and numerous other individuals gave to the St Mary light, including Katherine Carpynter who, in 1510, bequeathed a candle weighing three pounds to burn before the image of 'our blyssed lady'.[170] By 1501 devotion had diversified, with some testators leaving money or wax to the light before the image of 'our lady of pity'.[171] This cult, which incorporated artistic representations of the Pietà (the dead Christ and the Virgin), became increasingly popular in the late fifteenth and early sixteenth centuries in England. The veneration of these images came under particular attack from reformers by the late 1530s and not least in Kent where, in the east of the county alone (where it first became established in Canterbury and other centres in the late 1450s and 1460s), at least sixty-two parishes fostered the cult. Bequests were being made in Cranbrook by the 1470s and the devotion seems to have spread to Tenterden and Rolvenden and then on to other neighbouring parishes.[172] It has recently been argued that by focusing on the adult Christ's suffering and saving work, this cult altered Mary's position in devotion from mother and mediator to witness of the passion. Above and beyond this shift in emphasis, however, Marianism seems to have been in decline at Tenterden by the last decade of the fifteenth century, was certainly not as popular as it was in some other urban centres and was eclipsed by other, newer cults – in particular the Jesus Mass – in the early sixteenth century.[173] Perhaps the roots of this were part and parcel of general sensibilities about saints' images. Lollard views about the irrelevance of saints in general may have had a creeping influence on orthodox piety, but whatever its causes, the decline of Marianism and the cult of saints as a whole at Tenterden was a significant aspect of a particular religious culture that does not accord with revisionist accounts of late medieval piety.

Of the other saints venerated at Tenterden, St Katherine was mentioned most in wills after Christ and Mary (see table 6).[174] St Katherine was universally popular in Kent and was widely venerated throughout late medieval England. Like Mary, she was associated with childbirth, protection from sudden and unprepared death and, beneath the level of the gentry and

[handwritten marginalia: Decline of Marianism]

---

[169] *Kent obit and lamp rents*, 113.

[170] PRC 17/13/260, 17/11/182.

[171] PRC 17/9/70, 17/14/12, 17/14/295.

[172] Duffy, *Altars*, 38, 260–2, 332, 382, 419, 436; *Testamenta cantiana: East Kent*, pp. vii, 4, 7, 14, 16, 18, 43, 72, 75, 88, 130, 154, 160–1, 166, 189, 209, 259, 288, 319, 325, 369.

[173] Peters, *Patterns of piety*, ch. iii; Dinn, 'Popular religion', 205–17.

[174] St Katherine was the most popular saint after St Mary, in the Marsh, Wealden and Chart areas of East Kent: Draper and others, 'Fitting of the altars'.

Table 6
References to saints' cults in Tenterden wills, 1449–1535

Saint/s	Number of testators mentioning
St Mary	25 (9.5%)
St Katherine	11 (4%)
St Mildred	9 (3%)
St Nicholas	6 (2%)
SS Stephen/Erasmus	3 (1%)
SS Christopher/George/ Margaret/Mark	2 (1%)
SS James/Clement/ Barbara/John the Baptist/ Crispin & Crispinianus/ Peter/Mary Magdalene	1 (0.4%)

Sources: CKS, PRC 16/1–3, 17/1–22, 32/2–16; PRO, PCC 11/4 (21 Stokton), 11/5 (25 Godyn), 11/8 (20 Milles), 11/9 (29 Dogett), 11/14 (39 Holgrave), 11/16 (14 Bennett), 11/21 (18 Bodfelde), 11/22 (17 Porche), 11/23 (20 Jankyn), 11/25 (14 Hogen).

wealthiest townsfolk, good marriage for young women.[175] In addition, St Katherine belonged to a group of virgin saints, also including St Margaret and St Barbara, who were considered especially powerful intercessors, venerated for their sexual purity and devout piety under extreme temptation and physical suffering.[176] It is then significant that despite her particular association with women, all but one of the wills making reference to her cult at Tenterden were made by men, the exception being that of a young widow made under the influence of her parents.[177]

The fifteenth-century north chancel aisle of St Mildred's was dedicated to St Katherine and it was here that, in his will of 1463, Thomas Petlesden, who had served as Tenterden's first bailiff in 1449–50, requested burial and instituted a chantry and yearly obit for the next twenty years.[178] St Katherine's

175 Duffy, *Altars*, 179–81. There is no evidence that images of either saint attracted offerings or candles in connection with the rite of churching in Tenterden as occured across the diocese of Canterbury: *L&P* xviii/2, 302.

176 Duffy, *Altars*, 171–7, 179, 182, and 'Holy maydens, holy wyfes: the cult of women saints in fifteenth and sixteenth century England', in W. J. Sheils and D. Wood (eds), *Women in the Church* (SCH xxvii, 1990), 175–96.

177 Katherine Castelyn, 1510: PRC 17/11/183, and see chapter 4 below.

178 Woodruff, 'An archidiaconal visitation', 26; H. V. R., *Parish church*, 11; PRC 17/1/141; Te/C1 fo. 140r.

attributes were detailed in *The golden legend* and provide some clues regarding the reception of her cult at Tenterden. The only daughter and heir of the pagan King Costus of Alexandria, Katherine was educated to the highest academic levels and her abilities ensured that she outstripped her teachers in knowledge and wisdom and confounded and converted the greatest pagan philosophers of her day. Described as 'marvellous in wisdom', Katherine was teacher and patron of the powerful 'for she teacheth to govern the peoples, the cities, and the commons'. Two types of men could benefit from her wisdom: those with retinues and 'governers of cities'.[179] As a member of a local gentry family and Tenterden's first bailiff, Petlesden therefore had good reason to choose Katherine as his patron. Moreover, at a time when the borough of Tenterden had only recently gained a large degree of self-government, her cult had a particular resonance for those involved in the administration and representation of the town's affairs and interests. Her image was in need of repair by 1501 and in 1505 a replacement was under construction, William Claydishe leaving 12*d.* to this end. Her re-embodiment heralded a small resurgence in devotion, with four more bequests for lights or to Katherine's image from 1507 to 1510.[180] It is perhaps significant that this coincided with the years during which Small Hythe chapel's status was officially enhanced and its relationship with St Mildred's codified. The cult of St Katherine may have been employed to reiterate Tenterden's parochial rights and borough status, with its strongly urban symbols and links with the first bailiff.

Even more intimately associated with the identity of the town was the patron saint of the parish church, St Mildred. Tenterden was the only parish in the Kentish Weald with St Mildred as patron and, together with another six churches in the county, shared a dedication peculiar to Kent.[181] Mildred belonged to the royal house of Kent and was consecrated abbess of the abbey of Minster-in-Thanet (built by her mother) at the end of the seventh century. A cult quickly grew up around her, the abbey being re-dedicated in her name and her shrine becoming a popular pilgrimage site. Tenterden's connection with St Mildred arose from its origins as the possession of the manor of Minster within which the abbey lay; in the eleventh century the manor came into the possession of St Augustine's, Canterbury.[182] Tenterden had a parish church dedicated to St Mildred by the early thirteenth century which, together with its appendant manor, was fully appropriated to St Augustine's

---

[179] 'The Life of St. Katherine', in *The golden legend or lives of the saints as Englished by William Caxton*, ed. F. S. Ellis, London 1900, vii. 28; K. J. Lewis, *The cult of St Katherine of Alexandria in late medieval England*, Woodbridge 2000, pp. xv–xvi.

[180] The final bequest was in 1523: PRC 17/16/46.

[181] Everitt, *Continuity and colonization*, 228, 235.

[182] Ward, 'Saxon records', 241–3; H. V. R., *Parish church*, 2–3; Everitt, *Continuity and colonization*, 239–40, 248; D. W. Rollason, *The Mildrith legend: a study in early medieval hagiography in England*, Leicester 1982.

in 1259.[183] For the people of Tenterden St Mildred was, therefore, a symbol of the origins and ancient allegiances of their town and parish. By the late fifteenth century the essentially beneficial relationship that tenants enjoyed with long-standing ecclesiastical landlords may have allowed St Mildred to be identified as the embodiment of freedoms gained through long-term negotiation. Her connection with a nostalgic notion of the town's past, would have been all the more heightened by incorporation and annexation to Rye as a limb of the Cinque Ports in 1449 which brought several years of 'stryves and contraversies'.[184] A temporary settlement was reached in 1492 with a composition that made a number of additions to Tenterden's original charter of incorporation in the area of the town's annual contribution to the Cinque Ports confederation.[185] Throughout these years St Mildred may have provided a potent symbol of civic identity as the borough strove to negotiate its position in an uncomfortable and largely unwelcome alliance.

Tenterden's common seal dates from the charter of 1449 and illustrates how Mildred's legend may have been appropriated. On the obverse is a large vessel with a sail bearing the arms of the Cinque Ports and a flag displaying the cross of St George. The inscription reads: 'Sigillum commune ville et hundrede de Tenterden'. On the reverse is a figure of St Mildred with a coronet on her head, a book in one hand and a staff in the other, standing under a rich canopy. Around the verge is a Latin inscription: 'Ora pro nobis, benedicta Mildreda, ut digni efficiamur promitionibus Christi' ('Pray for us blessed Mildred that we may be made worthy of the promises of Christ'). Beneath the figure is a shield that carries the arms of Thomas Petlesden the first bailiff, which were adopted as Tenterden's corporate arms.[186] Mildred's legend tells how she was tempted away from home by foreigners, persecuted and then rescued from her enemies with the help of the miraculous turning of the tide and the self-destruction of her pursuers. The people of Tenterden might well have been tempted to draw a mischievous parallel between the turning of the tide which saved St Mildred, and the redirection of the Rother past Small Hythe which brought increasing prosperity to Tenterden and economic difficulties to Rye in the mid-fifteenth century, especially since these developments were the chief reason for annexation in 1449.[187] Her cult may, therefore, have provided a focus for anxieties that the townsfolk's privileges were in danger of being eroded through its relationship with Rye.

Even in Kent Mildred was an unusual name in this period and yet more than a handful of women were named after her in Tenterden. The light or

183 Ward, 'Saxon records', 241–3; Witney, *Jutish forest*, 116, 125–6; Furley, 'Early history of Tenterden', 45–6; Hasted, *History of Kent*, vii. 216; Taylor, 'Rectors and vicars', 207–8.
184 Riley, 'The corporation of Tenterden', 569, and 'MSS of the corporation of Rye', 491, 493–4.
185 Te/C1, fos 17r–22r.
186 A. H. Taylor, 'The municipal records of Tenterden: part ii', AC xxxiii (1918), 110–11.
187 Rollason, *The Mildrith legend*, 12–13.

image of St Mildred is mentioned in nine Tenterden wills from 1449 to 1523. For example, in 1472 Sarra Daye left 5s. to the making of a candlestick to burn before her image and, in 1493, Sir John Guldeford requested that his 'body be buried in the churche of Saint Mildred of Tentirden before the Image of the same where the resurrection of our Lord is made'.[188] This has strong parallels with his kinsman Thomas Petlesden's request to be buried in the chancel of St Katherine, the other embodiment of Tenterden's corporate identity. Significantly, Guldeford's request was made only a year after the 1492 composition between Tenterden and Rye. As a member of the most important gentry family in the parish he may have been particularly concerned to maintain a measure of Tenterden's independence in its relationship with the Cinque Ports and may have marked these aspirations in his devotion to St Mildred, the embodiment of the borough's privileges.

St Nicholas, whose cult was the next most popular, was placed well within the top ten saints in Kent.[189] He was connected especially with children but was also known, among other things, for his protection of mariners, guardianship of honest business dealings and for making good marriages between the children of the poor.[190] The cult of St Stephen was also significant at Tenterden, with three testators requesting chantries before his altar.[191] A number of the more popular saints were associated with travel, especially seafaring, and offered allusions to Tenterden's commercial role and seaborne trade activities. These included SS Christopher, Peter, Nicholas and John the Baptist who was the most popular saint around the coast of Kent.[192] St Barbara, whose cult in the chapel of St John the Baptist is the only one mentioned by a testator living in Tenterden's port of Small Hythe, was known for her protection from sudden and unprepared death and, in particular, the perils of lightning, making her an attractive advocate for mariners.[193]

The decline of Marianism has been noted, and other saints such as Stephen, Nicholas and Christopher also waned in importance.[194] In their place came the new cults of Mary Magdelene, SS George, James, Mark, Clement, Erasmus, and Crispin and Crispinianus.[195] Some of these, like St George (already England's national patron) and Crispin and Crispinianus enjoyed a widespread growth in popularity in the late fifteenth and early

---

[188] PRC 17/2/93; PRO, PCC 29 Dogett, fo. 223.

[189] Draper and others, 'Fitting of the altars'.

[190] *Mirk's festial: a collection of homilies by Johannes Mirkus*, ed. T. Erbe (EETS e.s. xcvi, 1905), 11–15; *Golden legend*, ii. 106–22.

[191] 1467, PRO, PCC 25 Godyn, fo. 193v; 1471, PRC 17/2/29, 17/10/20.

[192] Draper and others, 'Fitting of the altars'; Duffy, *Altars*, 160–3.

[193] 1527, PRC 17/17/334; *Golden legend*, vi. 204.

[194] The last reference to St Stephen was in 1505, to Nicholas in 1510 and to St Christopher in 1505.

[195] First or only references to these cults were in 1523, 1505, 1528, 1513, 1525, 1517 and 1522 respectively.

sixteenth centuries. This last pair were patrons of shoemaking which, given Tenterden's involvement in the leather industries, made them attractive to local crafts- and tradespeople. In 1522 Thomas Hicks bequeathed 6s. 8d. for the purchase of two images of these saints and, in 1513, Stephen Couper left 20d. to the making of a new image of St George and 20d. 'to the giltyng of the image of St Mark if no new image is made'.[196] The cult of St Erasmus, which drew increasing national devotion, was established at Tenterden with an image in the parish church by 1517. A classic 'helper saint', otherwise known as St Elmo, like many of the other holy figures honoured by Tenterden's parishioners, his patronage was especially poignant for sailors. His cult does not, however, appear to have been popular around the coast of Kent but was concentrated in the Weald. Sometimes referred to as 'St Sunday', his legend was used by the clergy to encourage Sunday observance and the geographical spread of the cult may have been due to a deliberate campaign to reinforce churchgoing in an area known for its religious dissent, although there is no direct evidence of this.[197]

The cult of saints may have been in overall decline at Tenterden but new cults were more likely to appear first in the Weald in the sixteenth century than in any other region of the county apart from the chartlands. This suggests a greater openness to new devotions than elsewhere, although the extent to which this varied from one parish to the next is not, as yet, clear. It is possible that the relatively high turnover in cults was due to the efforts of parochial clergy in response to the overall downturn in devotion to saints. It has also been suggested that 'this may reflect a changing balance in cultural and economic vitality', from the older to the newer settled lands of Kent.[198] Related to this, demographic and economic pressures from the turn of the century brought new degrees of social fragmentation and anxiety on the Weald that may have called for a greater variety of symbols for the articulation of identity, making the adoption of innovative figures more likely, despite a general lack of engagement with the cult of saints.

Church-building
Above and beyond payments for forgotten tithes, 102 testators (just under two-fifths) left money, goods or farm stock to church building, repairs or fittings.[199] There was a considerable and steady decline in this type of giving over the period, which accelerated in the 1520s so that less than a fifth of testators made bequests to churches or chapels in the fifteen years up to 1535

---

196 Hutton, *Rise and fall*, 26–7; Duffy, *Altars*, 163; *Testamenta cantiana: East Kent*, p. xi; PRC 17/15/228, 17/12/229.

197 Duffy, *Altars*, 163–4, 170, 177–8, 180–1, 187, plate 65; Draper and others, 'Fitting of the altars'.

198 Draper and others, 'Fitting of the altars'.

199 Bequests to church building, repairs and decoration, and to altars or images are included in this category but not gifts to lights.

Plate 1. St Mildred's church, Tenterden, from the south

compared to almost three-fifths before 1479 (*see* table 5). Whereas the overall level of testamentary giving to churches was similar, and in some cases considerably higher, than that found in other towns, its marked decline is indicative of the general trend in pious giving at Tenterden.[200] Post obit gifts to church-building and upkeep represent only a proportion of the overall amounts of money left by testators to these ends but levels of lifetime giving are likely to have broadly matched testamentary trends.[201]

Most bequests were to St Mildred's or the chapel of St John the Baptist, reflecting the obligation for parishioners to maintain their parochial church buildings.[202] The median amount of cash gifts was 6s. 8d., but sums ranged

[200] In Colchester 40% of testators made this type of bequest, with the largest decline being in the period 1500–19 and a subsequent recovery after 1520: Higgs, 'Lay piety', 220–3, table 16 at p. 218. At Bury St Edmunds only 19% of lay and clerical testators left money for church repairs or furnishings, but the total amount left per decade increased markedly in the early sixteenth century: Dinn, 'Popular religion', 405, 408, table 9.2. The proportion of testators mentioning church building or repairs in Sandwich was similar to that in Tenterden and also fell over the period, but not as sharply.

[201] Burgess and Kümin, 'Penitential bequests and parish regimes', 610–30; Kümin, *Shaping of a community*, 104–27.

[202] A. H. Thompson, *The English clergy and their organization in the later Middle Ages*, Oxford 1947, 117 n. 2; S. Reynolds, *Kingdoms and communities in western Europe, 900–1300*, Oxford

Table 7
Bequests to St Mildred's church,* Tenterden, 1449–1535

Date range	Total amount bequeathed in wills
1449–69	£6 6s. 8d.
1470–79	£39 11s. 6d.
1480–9	£5 11s. 8d.
1490–9	£5 4s. 8d.
1500–9	£6 13s. 10d.
1510–19	£22 5s. 8d.
1520–35#	£26 13s. 4d.

* To church building, repair and decoration, altars and images but excluding payments for forgotten tithes.
# Only three small bequests in the 1530s totalling 16s. 8d.

Sources: CKS, PRC 16/1–3,17/1–22, 32/2–16; PRO, PCC 11/4 (21 Stokton), 11/5 (25 Godyn), 11/8 (20 Milles), 11/9 (29 Dogett), 11/14 (39 Holgrave), 11/16 (14 Bennett), 11/21 (18 Bodfelde), 11/22 (17 Porche), 11/23 (20 Jankyn), 11/25 (14 Hogen).

from 4d. up to £25 16s. To put the latter amount in perspective, about three-quarters left 20s. or less. The size of bequests, or whether a testator gave at all, seems to have been connected to his or her familial piety. Across all twenty-three selected families a median of two in every five will-makers made this type of bequest but whereas the most religiously generous families gave to churches in a median of every one out of two of their wills, among the most religiously parsimonious a little less than one in four did so. There was a similar pattern to the amounts of money left. Testators in the top group of families gave a median of 10s., those in the middle 6s. 8d. and those in the bottom group only 2s. 4d. It is difficult to see how these gifts could have been driven by the same motivations or avoided for the same reasons as other aspects of religious expression in wills such as endowments for chantries, saints' cults or new devotional forms, which had overtly doctrinal overtones.[203] However, the downturn in bequests from 1520 and their distribution across families suggests that this type of giving was affected by increasingly vociferous doctrinal and ecclesiological debates in the early sixteenth century and points to the influence of Lollard ideas about the superfluous

1984, 92; E. Mason, 'The role of the English parishioner, 1100–1500', JEH xxvii (1976), 23–5.
[203] Cf. Tanner, Church in Norwich, 126.

structures of the late medieval Church and perhaps to a general movement within lay orthodoxy towards more private family devotion.[204] Many testators may simply have been somewhat disengaged from the imperatives of parochial religion or perhaps, as will be explored in chapter 4, followed familial expectations of how resources should be most properly employed, sometimes to the exclusion of parochial institutions.

The 1470s, 1510s and 1520s stand out as times of noticeable giving (*see* table 7), but the higher amounts left in these decades were due largely to one or two exceptionally generous bequests. The construction of St Mildred's almost oversized Perpendicular bell tower in the third quarter of the fifteenth century was the most ambitious project embarked upon in this period (*see* plate 1). Visible nearly sixteen miles inland from ships at sea, it was fitted with a peal of eight bells and set of musical chimes. The crenellations along the south side of the exterior of the nave facing the High Street were also probably added in the late fifteenth century. The townspeople may have consciously copied Lydd, where a similarly impressive tower, also with a double west doorway, was built in the 1440s, and Ashford, in turn, may have followed suit.[205] Notwithstanding outside involvement, Tenterden's new bell tower was very much a collective urban effort and is evidence of growing prosperity among leading Tenterden families in the second half of the fifteenth century comparable to some other towns at this time.[206] Coupled with the display of new-found wealth, such a grandiose construction may have been another exercise in civic posturing in the context of Tenterden's uneasy alliance with Rye and the Cinque Ports. The earliest surviving will, dated 1449, the year of the borough's incorporation, contains a bequest to the building of the steeple and another eight testators contributed to the project up until 1476. Significantly, the largest bequest, totalling 100 marks, was made in 1463 by Thomas Petlesden, Tenterden's first bailiff.[207]

Other collective building programmes included work on the nave, attracting five bequests from 1492 to 1505, and the purchase of the pair of new organs, to which the same number of testators contributed from 1510 to

---

[204] For thoughts on private devotion and its possible links to Lollardy see Brown, *Popular piety*, 204–13.

[205] H. V. R., *Parish church*, 14; Hasted, *History of Kent*, vii. 214; Everitt, *Continuity and colonization*, 185.

[206] The arms of St Augustine's can be seen on the front of the tower and the project gained support from across the county: Richard Berne of Canterbury left 6s. 8d. in 1461 and John Chevening of Chatham 40s. in 1457: *Testamenta cantiana: East Kent*, 336; CKS, DRb/Pwr 2/84 (I owe this latter reference to Paul Lee). Cf. Dinn, 'Popular religion', 407; Higgs, 'Lay piety', 104–5; D. MacCulloch, *Suffolk and the Tudors: politics and religion in an English county, 1500–1600*, Oxford 1986, 139–40; J. I. Kermode, 'The merchants of three northern English towns', in C. H. Clough (ed.), *Profession, vocation and culture in later medieval England*, Liverpool 1982, 33–5; P. W. Fleming, 'Charity, faith and the gentry of Kent, 1442–1529', in A. J. Pollard (ed.), *Property and politics: essays in later medieval English history*, Gloucester 1984, 47–8.

[207] 1449, PRC 17/1/7, 17/1/141.

1513. The installation of organs reflects the adoption of an increasingly popular taste in polyphonic music rather than plainsong in the liturgy and seems to have been linked to the adoption of the Jesus Mass at St Mildred's.[208] In the late 1460s and early 1470s repairs were made to the 'great cross' (presumably the rood) and, a little later, work was carried out on the north wall of the church. Around the turn of the century a handful of testators contributed to the mending of the font.

As the sixteenth century progressed there was a growing tendency for collective giving to turn from building to church furnishings. From 1504 to 1522 nine testators left either money or decorative objects to the adornment of the high altar or the host. Six of these gifts took the form of good quality pieces of cloth, such as tablecloths or coverlets. Four of these were given by women, probably because these most domestic of objects were transmitted within the family between women and, to some extent, reflected their gendered role within the household. John Fletcher left 16s. 8d. for the purchase of a velvet cloth to hang before the high altar and Joan Easton stipulated in her will that Richard Piers was to pay the £3 that he owed to her to St Mildred's for the buying of a 'cristmatory' made of silver.[209] The increased focus upon the high altar and the host in these years may reflect the trend towards concentration upon the central Christological elements of orthodox devotion. Framed as it was by the rood screen and the depiction of the last judgement in the chancel arch, the high altar emphasised, above all else, the saving work of Christ's passion, enacted in the mass.[210]

Some major projects in this period are not mentioned in probate evidence, and in more than one case this was because the work was the responsibility of the rector, the abbot of St Augustine's. The building of the vestry onto the east end of the Lady Chapel in the south chancel aisle appears to have been undertaken at the demand of the parishioners and churchwardens, articulated in the return to the archidiaconal visitation of 1502:

> The copes, vestments, books and other goods of the church, are in bad condition through lack of a good place to keep them in; wherefore the parishioners and wardens say that a vestry should be provided for the safe custody of the said ornaments, according to the ordinal, and that such a vestry should be built and newly erected at the eastern end of the chancel of blessed Mary, which is annexed to the aforesaid church.[211]

At least two significant building projects were commissioned by individual laymen who belonged to religiously unsparing families. In his will of 1496 Thomas Strekynbold stipulated that within three years of his death, his son

---

[208] Burgess, 'Divine service', 54–9.
[209] 1510, PRC 17/17/20; 1512, 32/11/41; Peters, *Patterns of piety*, 52.
[210] Peters, *Patterns of piety*, 105–10; Duffy, *Altars*, 157–9.
[211] CCA, Z.3.2, fo. 136v (translation taken from Woodruff, 'An archidiaconal visitation', 26).

build an enclosed vice (staircase) on the exterior of the north side of the church which would enable easy inspection of the lead. This most practical of projects was duly completed in some style (*see* plate 2).[212] In 1518 William Couper ordained that his executors make, within a year of his death, a 'parclause' or screen behind the high rood, possibly to carry a depiction of the Last Judgement, and a window in the roof on the south side of the nave next to the rood.[213] There is no sign of the window today, and Couper's aspirations may not have been fulfilled. Despite considerable building work, refurbishment and ornamentation throughout the late fifteenth and early sixteenth centuries, it appears that the ongoing upkeep of the parish church was not without its crises. As will be shown in chapter 3, this seems to have been the case especially around the turn of the century, when a series of visitation returns describe, in a no doubt deliberately dramatic tone, the extent of decay. Some testators clearly attempted to alleviate these problems. For example, in 1505 John Strekynbold left 6s. 8d. for much needed repairs to books.[214]

Giving to the poor

Charitable giving secured the prayers of the poor and was of intrinsic moral and spiritual worth,[215] but it also helped to define and shape community and identity and emphasised differences in social status.[216] Thirty-six testators gave to the poor between 1449 and 1535, a similar proportion as in other towns.[217] There was no appreciable change in the level of post-obit charitable giving over time, and it was certainly not falling by the 1520s. Noticeable differences between families in the level of giving conform to the general spectrum of testamentary piety. So, whereas a median of one in four testators in religiously generous families remembered the poor, one in six of the moderate, and only one out of twenty-nine testators belonging to more religiously parsimonious families did so. This suggests that giving to the poor was largely part and parcel of a traditional religious mentality that placed a premium on acts and devotions believed directly to benefit the deceased's

[212] PRC 17/6/158.

[213] PRC 32/12/174.

[214] PRO, PCC 39 Holgrave, fo. 308.

[215] *Dives and pauper*, ed. P. H. Barnum (EETS cclxxx, 1980) 289; S. Brigden, 'Religion and social obligation in early sixteenth-century London', *P&P* ciii (1984), 102–3; M. Rubin, *Charity and community in medieval Cambridge*, Cambridge 1987, 74, 83, 264.

[216] For the argument that charity worked to maintain social difference see C. Dyer, *Standards of living in the later Middle Ages*, Cambridge 1989, 236; and Dinn, 'Popular religion', ch. xvi, esp. p. 699. For contrasting views see Galpern, *Religions of the people*, 42; and Rubin, *Charity and community*, 289.

[217] Higgs, 'Lay piety', 218; Dinn, 'Popular religion', 657; S. Sweetinburgh, *The role of the hospital in medieval England: gift-giving and the spiritual economy*, Dublin 2004, 210–13. Giving to the poor appears to have been more common in Hull and Norwich: Heath, 'Urban piety', 224; Tanner, *Church in Norwich*, appendix 12 at p. 223.

Plate 2. Thomas Strekynbold's 'vice' on the north side of
St Mildred's church, Tenterden

soul in purgatory.[218] Bequests that dispensed charity at funerals, month's days or obits, or on occasions like Good Friday, are a good indication of the perceived intercessory value of these gifts. Most will-makers who gave to the poor did so at least in part in this way, and there was a trend towards funerary charitable giving by the second decade of the sixteenth century, which was probably a result of the growing elaboration and lay control of funerary ritual as a whole.

Notwithstanding this, motives for charitable giving were by no means homogeneous and may have varied across the pious spectrum. All but one of those testators belonging to the most religiously open-handed families incorporated their charitable bequests into arrangements for funerals and obsequies. In contrast, among families in the lower two pious bands, only two out of the eight testators who gave to the poor did so wholly in this way, the rest making bequests which were more specific than funeral doles. For example, in 1471 John Piers left a 'second best' kirtle and a pair of shoes to each poor woman 'with Augustin Gilmyne' and in 1472 Agnes Hylles wished her best dish sold and the proceeds to be distributed among poor boys.[219] These gifts suggest charitable giving motivated less by traditional ideas about purgatory than by social need and the intrinsic moral value of charity. Relatively few bequests were general and unspecific in terms of whom they were to benefit. Only three testators left money simply to be given in alms or to be distributed among 'poor people', suggesting that, as in other places by the late fifteenth century, attitudes about charity were rather discriminatory with care being taken to ensure that only the 'honest' poor received help. This trend may reflect the influence of humanism and the broad current of evangelical orthodoxy that seems to have shaped other aspects of piety at Tenterden.[220] John Lilly, for example, willed that clothing be sold to buy cloth to make robes for two 'pauperibus honestis' (were his own garments considered to be too fine for these individuals?).[221] This preoccupation can be seen in those bequests which stress that the recipients of charity had to be resident in the parish, and so, presumably, housed rather than vagrant. Thomas Cok left 20s. in addition to six robes and six kirtles to twenty poor 'manentibus' (dwellers) in Tenterden.[222] Moralising attitudes can be seen most clearly in the will of William Stonehouse, a priest and member of one of the more religiously

---

[218] For a similar pattern see Higgs, 'Lay piety', 216.

[219] PRC 17/2/29, 17/2/67.

[220] W. A. Pantin, The English Church in the fourteenth century, Cambridge 1955, 259, 189ff; Vale, 'Piety, charity and literacy', 26; Fleming, 'Charity, faith and the gentry of Kent', 44–6; Thrupp, Merchant class, 179; Galpern, Religions of the people, 40; Rubin, Charity and community, 70; Dyer, Standards of living, 238–9, 244–5; M. K. McIntosh, 'Local change and community control in England, 1465–1500', Huntington Library Quarterly xlix (1986), 227–9.

[221] 1504, PRC 17/10/21.

[222] 1473, PRC 17/2/148; cf. Dinn, 'Popular religion', 690.

orthodox families. He left a house and half a garden to his niece, Katheryn Couper, and stipulated that when she died this property was to go,

> to the next of my kyn that is yn poverte and necessite. And the other house and half gardyn to an other honest pouer bodye of the next of my kyne. And they to have their dwellyng free for time of liff. And so to praye for all xyen soules. And if it shold happen the saide kateryne or any other that shall happen to dwell at Jerico be not honeste of their bodye or of tong, then I will that ether the said feoffees or executors or their assignes putt out the said evil disposed persone And sett yn an other wele disposed persone.[223]

Gifts that were geographically specific sometimes appear to have been intended to emphasise particular notions of community or identity. The most striking example is Sir John Guldeford's wish to have a large amount of money distributed in alms to 'pouer men and whemen knowen and dwelling in the vij hundreds'. These were the Wealden hundreds which made up a single administrative unit, of which Tenterden had no longer officially been a part since incorporation in 1449. Guldeford owned lands across a number of these and appears to have stressed his identification with a political community over which his family held considerable sway.[224] The young were esteemed as especially worthy of aid. John Tyler left ten marks to the maintenance of twenty poor boys and a number of individuals gave to poor maidens or their marriages.[225] Vulnerability seems to have been a strong criterion in the assessment of need, Stephen Felip, for example, leaving 3s. 4d. to the daughter of John Saunder of Smarden 'which is lame'.[226] Giving to the poor appears to have been conducted largely on an informal basis, with no mention of almshouses or hospitals in the parish and an absence of gifts to such institutions elsewhere.

Public works
Unlike charity, giving to public works involved notions about the nature of community expressed in the rhetoric of civic pride and need.[227] About the same proportion of testators (thirty-four out of 263) who gave to the poor, left money for public works in their wills, chiefly for repairs to roads or footways, with something of a decline in bequests of this type after 1520.[228] Seven out of forty testators in the top pious band of families gave to public works, five out of forty-five in the middle and one out of twenty-nine in the bottom

---

223 1528, PRC 17/18/180.
224 1493, PRO, PCC 29 Dogett, fo. 223.
225 1471, PRC 17/2/27.
226 1523, PRC 17/16/46.
227 Dinn, 'Popular religion', 683.
228 This was similar to Sandwich and London but higher than in Norwich and Bury: Thomson, 'Piety and charity', 187–8; Tanner, *Church in Norwich*, 137; Dinn, 'Popular religion', 673.

indicating that, as with gifts to the poor, civic giving was an integral element of coherent orthodox pieties. This said, none of the bequests used explicitly religious language or claimed efficacy for the testator's soul.[229] Some contributed to repairs to the crosses positioned at important points within the town and its suburbs. Both William and Katherine Foule left money for repairs to the cross near to where they lived at West Cross.[230] A number of testators left money for repairs to footways or roads between the testator's house or a named point in the parish and the parish church. It is probable that these gifts were intended to improve the approaches to the church, to aid and encourage attendance and to tie the testator symbolically to the community of regular churchgoers. Strikingly, all but one of the testators belonging to the more religiously generous families who made bequests for public works left money for repairs to crosses or mentioned the parish church, and only one testator in the other two pious bands made this type of gift. As with giving to the poor, sentiments appear to have varied between families in line with the overall character of their testamentary pieties.

Few of these bequests were very ambitious, or departed from the formulaic. John Tyler's will was exceptional in this regard. He ordained ten marks 'to the makyng of a good and sufficient way to go and to ride in the kyngs strete toward the Watermill by yond the iij leggid crosse ayenst the land of William Claydishe and the land of the heires of John Pett'. He also left 20s. 'to the makyng of a greate dike toward the watermill, a karyeng way of brede ayenst the land of the heires of John Pett so that the water rynnyth twarte the strete downward so depe that the water may ryn downe by the saide dike by the este side of the strete and no more ryn twarte the strete'.[231] These bequests were designed to ease communications between Tenterden town and the string of watermills along the valley to the north-west.[232] The only other legacy to depart from the norm was George Strekynbold's stipulation in 1524, that if a schoolhouse was being built in Tenterden within seven years of his death, then 20s. were to go to its construction. Significantly, George's father, John Strekynbold, was the only testator to leave money for repairs to books in the parish church.[233]

Only in certain respects did testamentary piety at Tenterden conform to any broad national pattern of parochial religion. As in most other urban centres in this period, a fair proportion of the townsfolk invested money, energy and creativity in extending and enhancing their church buildings and, at the same time, struggled to meet all the requirements of maintenance; giving to

---

[229] Cf. Dinn, 'Popular religion', 684–5.
[230] 1496, PRC 17/6/281; 1519, 17/15/64; Roberts, *Tenterden houses*, 44.
[231] 1503, PRC 17/9/211.
[232] Roberts, 'Tenterden houses', 45–6.
[233] PRC 17/16/269.

the poor was at a similar level in wills as in other places; gifts for public works were neither abnormally common nor unusually rare, and saints' cults that were popular regionally or nationally attracted devotion from Tenterden's testators. The cult of saints lent itself ideally to the symbolic construction of identity and community, with individual figures being adopted as symbols of Tenterden's unique origins, special status and freedoms. Most of the saints venerated were well-suited to the town's material culture, their appeal, at least in part, being derived from their everyday relevance as helpers and the imaginative and psychological resources they offered for the construction of identity. However, traditional forms and structures of religion were also received and employed in religiously significant and dramatically changing ways that suggest Tenterden does not conform to the revisionist portrayal of the vibrant and homogeneous 'traditional religion' now so widely accepted by historians.

Tenterden's religious culture was distinctive in a number of significant ways. Chantries were relatively unpopular and poorly endowed, and were generally not outward-looking in their intercessory priorities. Although arrangements for funerals and obsequies were unusually common, attracting expenditure to a level seen in larger towns, obits tended to be rather short-lived and, in general, funeral rites appear to have been restrained. The religious orders hardly featured in testators' preoccupations and although there is evidence of a good number of saints' cults in the parish, devotion to them was sparse in wills, with fewer gifts to lights and images than in most other centres.

The parish's particular orthodoxy is most clearly demonstrated by certain changes in devotional form and fashion over time. A rapid decline in testamentary chantry provision, together with a marked rise in funerary ritual in the early sixteenth century, has been found elsewhere, but not to such a noticeable degree. Belief in purgatory appears to have remained strong right up until 1535, but the change in fashion suggests that the financial burden of chantries was becoming less sustainable in the context of early sixteenth-century debates about appropriate forms of intercession for the dead and orthodox and heterodox criticisms of private masses. Obits were cheaper to secure and offered a number of incentives absent from the chantry, including a greater degree of lay control and participation and the integration of a range of good works, including charitable giving. Disquiet about certain aspects of the doctrine of purgatory may explain why new fashions in devotion that became nationally popular made little impact upon religious culture in Tenterden. The theologically controversial Pope Trental and other forms of trental failed to appeal and masses at *Scala Coeli* fared little better. In stark contrast, the Jesus Mass was a spectacular success, reaching an outstanding level of popularity in the early sixteenth century that was sustained into the 1530s. It had a broad appeal being the only religious element to feature evenly in the wills of families across the whole pious spectrum from the frugal through to the thoroughly engaged. Primarily it offered opportunities for the

100

intensification of personal identification with Christ and his saving mercy, and the different aspects of the devotion, such as its focus on the sacrificial mass as well as Scripture and preaching, lent it a polyvalency that spoke to a diverse audience. The radical potential centred around the worship of Christ as supreme, if not sole, mediator may have struck a chord with those disengaged from, or who had serious doubts about, other forms of devotion, in particular the cult of saints, whilst it also appealed to those with more traditionalist pious priorities.

A number of changes in testamentary giving in the early sixteenth century suggest that the lack of popularity of some of the more conservative aspects of devotion point to the influence of reformist and heretical ideas. The cessation of gifts to religious orders in 1518, and the absence of any ongoing loyalty to the friars found in other towns up to the Reformation; the disappearance of bequests to images from the early 1520s onwards; the decline in giving to church fabric from around 1520; and the dying out of arrangements for chantries by 1527 all signal an enormously significant shift in Tenterden's religious culture before the years of official reform. An embedded tradition of Lollard heresy no doubt had its part to play in this sea change and it is likely that Lutheran and other continentally inspired evangelical ideas were also at work from the early 1520s, but this chapter has suggested that orthodoxy itself had shifted at Tenterden and, although it remained far from homogeneous, there appears to have been a general drift towards a particularly English evangelicalism that has been identified by a number of historians – a moderate reformist strand within Catholic piety that was in part inspired by Erasmian humanism, which may also have drawn some of its inspiration from longer-standing traditions of heterodoxy.

These broad changes notwithstanding, continuities in the will-making practices of Tenterden families can convincingly be placed on a spectrum ranging from the sparse to the elaborate. There was no straightforward positive relationship between available wealth and the value or variety of religious bequests and, although strategies varied between individuals within the one family due to circumstantial differences, there was nevertheless a distinctive character to a family's testamentary piety. Whilst the overall tenor of piety in Tenterden was parsimonious, unelaborate and rather reserved, these familial continuities ensured that there were enduring contrasts in practice within the parish. There were consistent and clear differences between families in the intensity, form and substance of bequests for chantries, funerals and obsequies; in giving to the religious orders and in devotion to saints; in contributions to collective and individual church building projects; in charity to the poor and in public works. Throughout this period, some families displayed a greater motivation and commitment to traditionally orthodox devotions and structures in their wills than others. There was a good deal of overlap around the centre of the pious spectrum, but the differences between the testamentary preoccupations of, say, the Chapmans, Castelyns and the Blossoms on the one hand, and the Strekynbolds,

Stonehouses and Prestons on the other, would have been all too apparent. It is argued that these differences reflected and helped to form divergent traditions in piety which were of substantial significance in terms of the shifts in orthodoxy described above, susceptibility to Lollard heresy and evangelical reform.

3

Boundaries, Identities and Symbols: Piety at Small Hythe, Tenterden

Small Hythe lay within the parish of Tenterden and yet geographical, juris-dictional and mental boundaries defined it as a distinct area of settlement. Its significant role in the regional economy, strongly linking it to centres and influences other than Tenterden, provided scope for the development of its own cultural and political identity. The chapel at Small Hythe formed a focal point for local residents who perceived and used it in a different way to their parish church. Provision for religious services and devotion at Small Hythe was enhanced and even transformed in this period and residence there entailed heightened pressure upon the limited resources of the will-maker, resolved through a range of testamentary strategies. In will-making and in the wider compass of social relations, Small Hythe families were not only able to negotiate a position of considerable subtlety in relation to both the parish and the locality but, when necessary, were determined to defend it. For a significant number of parishioners at Tenterden, the competing demands of parochial religion entailed a considerable degree of complexity in the choices to be made about the redistribution of family resources at death, but this only appears to have been the case for residents of Small Hythe, whose particular piety was intensely localised and closely tied to distinctive environmental conditions and specialised economic development.

Origins, place and boundaries

Small Hythe enters the records relatively late, in the early thirteenth century. This is chiefly because its development was inextricably linked with the changing route of the river Rother, which before this time had mostly flowed, not north of the Isle of Oxney but south through Wittersham Level (*see* map 2). It was only as a result of a programme of drainage and embankment from 1289 to 1348, culminating in the construction of the Knelle Dam across the head of Wittersham Level, that the river was redirected past Small Hythe, Reading Street (known at the time as Reding) and Appledore. The reclama-tion of the Rother Levels allowed Small Hythe to gain a hold on the river's trade at the same time as opening up substantial new tracts of marshland which provided ideal pasture.[1] Small Hythe actually means 'small harbour'

---

[1] CPR, Henry III, 1247–1258, 169; Furley, 'Early history of Tenterden', 40–2; J. Eddison, 'Developments in the lower Rother valleys up to 1600', AC cii (1986), 95–108.

and the adoption of this place-name element may have followed Hythe and New Hythe, two other ports in Kent. By the middle of the fourteenth century there is evidence that Small Hythe's role as Tenterden's port was of considerable importance and by 1381 it was perceived as a centre in its own right.[2] From the beginning of the fifteenth century, the settlement was substantial enough to be occasionally called a town and yet it never ceased to play a subservient role in its relationship with Tenterden.[3]

Most of the medieval township of Small Hythe lay on either side of the road stretching north to Tenterden for a distance of about three-quarters of a mile from the Rother. The houses of Broad Tenterden extended south along the same road to within about three-quarters of a mile of the upper limits of Small Hythe.[4] This made the route down to Small Hythe the main artery of Tenterden's economy and the backbone of its settlement. The relative closeness of Small Hythe to the fringes of Tenterden town probably meant that it was not far enough removed to allow the establishment of its own completely distinct identity.[5] However, despite their proximity, definite boundaries existed between the two areas of settlement. Before the road was raised some time before the middle of the sixteenth century, the stream which today passes under it twice between Small Hythe and Broad Tenterden, seems periodically to have formed a barrier to the passage of all but riders and carts.[6] Other physical features divided Small Hythe from surrounding settlements. To the south lay the parish of Wittersham on the Isle of Oxney, but the Rother passed between, and in the early sixteenth century the only way across was by ferry.[7]

Jurisdictional and tenurial boundaries also defined Small Hythe as a distinct locality within the parish. Whereas Tenterden town lay within Town Borough, Small Hythe was part of the Borough of Dumborne. The householders of Dumborne Borough would have been bound to one another in law in a number of capacities, the leading men being responsible for the good behaviour of their neighbours.[8] Small Hythe Quarter, another administrative

2 Furley, 'Early history of Tenterden', 56, 60.

3 Commission de walliis et fossatis, 28 Jan. 1400: CPR, Henry IV, i. 1399–1401, 216. See also CPR, Henry V, i. 1413–16, 345; Henry V, ii. 1419–22, 222, 224, 225–6. It was described as 'Oppidum de Smalhith' in archbishop William Warham's licence for the celebration of divine service in the chapel there in 1506: LPL, Reg. Warham, i, fo. 10, transcribed and translated in A. H. Taylor, 'The chapel of St John the Baptist, Small Hythe', AC xxx (1914), 140, 143.

4 Hasted, History of Kent, vii. 212–13.

5 Beresford, 'Journey along boundaries', 38–9.

6 Everitt, Continuity and colonization, 53–4.

7 PRO, PCC 25 Godyn, fo. 193v; PRC 17/8/221. Small Hythe ferry was established by the late fourteenth century: Hasted, History of Kent, viii. 489; Roberts, Tenterden, 54–5.

8 In the Tenterden custumal, drawn up in 1557/8, 'the precept' for holding an inquest dictated that eighteen men from each borough would be summoned by the sergeant: Taylor, 'Municipal records of Tenterden, part i', 289.

unit possibly for the organisation of the parish, was also mentioned in two wills in 1490 and 1503.[9] The size and shape of Small Hythe also appears to have been defined by the primarily tenurial division of the den. At least seven lay either at Small Hythe itself or within a radius of one mile, namely, Ekre (which seems to have comprised the immediate area of the town), Dumborne, Emelisham, Hawkherst, Marsham, Queryncote and Ashenden (*see* map 1).[10] By at least the second half of the fifteenth century established Small Hythe families possessed land across several of these adjacent dens.

In 1501 yet another sense of place was impressed upon this complex geographical, legal and mental landscape when Small Hythe testators began to identify themselves not just as parishioners of Tenterden, but as inhabitants of their own township. So, in his testament, William Davy referred to himself as: 'Ego Willelmus Davy de Smalehithe in parochia de Tentreden'.[11] This does not appear to have been the result of any change in scribal convention but, rather, in local testamentary practice. Not all the extant Small Hythe wills written after 1501 contain such a description of local domicile; those that do are spaced fairly evenly from 1501 to the early 1530s and one was proved in the prerogative court of Canterbury, rather than the archdeaconry court.[12] John Brekynden senior's testament, written in 1502, reveals that the scribe making the final enregistered copy was not familiar with the new form of identification adopted by residents of Small Hythe. As a result, he made a mistake which, presumably on noticing the wording of the fair copy of the original will, he immediately corrected. The finished text reads: 'Ego Johannes Brikenden senior ~~de parochia~~ de Smalehit in parochia de Tentreden.'[13] The change in wording in the wills suggests that at least some of Small Hythe's inhabitants were voicing a more self-conscious sense of identity that was distinct from the rest of the parish.

Economic growth

Small Hythe owed its economic importance to its role as Tenterden's port and by the middle of the fourteenth century enjoyed quite substantial shipborne commerce and foreign immigrants, particularly from the Low Countries, took up residence there in order to do business.[14] Small Hythe

[9] Joan Turnor: PRC 17/5/310; John Tiler: PRC 17/9/211. Also, Haffenden Quarter: Furley, 'Early history of Tenterden', 41.

[10] With a combination of other sources, the 6in. Ordnance Survey maps, and J. K. Wallenberg, *Place-mames of Kent*, and *Kentish place-names*, Uppsala 1931, have been used to identify these dens. See also Roberts, *Tenterden*, chs i, iii, vii, viii, ix; Hasted, *History of Kent*, vii. 209.

[11] PRC 17/8/221.

[12] William Carpenter, 1530: PRO, PCC, 20 Jankyn, fo. 154.

[13] PRC 17/8/281.

[14] CPR, Edw. III, x. 1354–8, 70; xiii. 1364–7, 72–3; Hen. VI, ii. 1429–36, 561, 576.

played a crucial role in Tenterden's economic development which accelerated at the end of the fifteenth century and, particularly through its close links with Rye, was connected to trade networks with France, the Low Countries and other English ports along the south coast and further afield. Closer to home, Small Hythe was one of a series of small trading and industrial centres along the Rother, that included Appledore, Reading Street, Newenden and Robertsbridge, which served the eastern Weald (*see* map 2).

As well as being an important commercial centre Small Hythe was host to large-scale ship-building from at least the middle of the fourteenth century. Vessels were constructed for a range of customers from the Corporation of New Romney to private owners at Rye and Tenterden.[15] After 1449 Tenterden's commitment to provide ships for Rye more than likely strengthened the industry, but even before 1420 Henry V built men-of-war at Small Hythe, including *The Jesus*, a 1,000 ton ship constructed in 1416.[16] The industry drew on raw materials and expertise from as far away as Beaulieu near Southampton and large-scale ship-building continued on the Rother in the reign of Henry VIII, during which the king's smiths operated at Small Hythe.[17] These years may have marked the heyday of the industry which, because of the large amounts of capital investment and labour involved, probably had an especially collective nature. This may have helped to cement cooperative relationships between Small Hythe's major families.[18]

In addition to brewing and the manufacture of salt, it is very likely that fishing was another major occupation.[19] The increasing prosperity which produced well-built early sixteenth-century properties like Small Hythe Place and the misnamed 'Priest's House' did not stem purely from trade and industry however, but from Small Hythe's important role as an agricultural centre.[20] The township was the natural focus of the parish's most fertile lands which, on the whole, were farmed as grass for the pasture of cattle and, to a lesser extent, sheep. Stock-raising of cattle, increasingly for the London market, was the most important aspect of Tenterden's agriculture and Small

---

15 *VCH, Kent*, 268, 271; Roberts, 'Tenterden houses', 347; *CPR*, Edw. III, xiii. 1364–7, 16; Hen. IV, ii. 1401–5, 281; Riley, 'MSS of the corporation of Rye', 434, 536; *CCR*, Henry IV, 1409–13, 167.

16 *VCH, Kent*, 336.

17 'Naval accounts of Henry VII', pp. xxi–xxvii, 145–50, 218–39, 312ff; *L&P* i. 3422; iii. 2964; xx. 543; addenda, i. 68, 101, 140, 142, 1697; Roberts, *Tenterden*, 48–51; Taylor, 'Chapel of St John the Baptist', 157; *VCH, Kent*, 300.

18 G. Scammel, 'Shipowning in England, c. 1450–1550', *TRHS* 5th ser. xii (1962), 105–22.

19 CKS, U455/T85, U410/T21; Furley, *History of the Weald*, 724; PRC 17/1/99; *CPR*, Edward IV, Henry VI, 1467–77, 283.

20 Roberts, 'Tenterden houses', 99–101; S. Pearson, *The medieval houses of Kent: an historical analysis*, London 1994, 112–14, 134; A. Quiney, *English domestic architecture: Kent houses*, Woodbridge 1993, 173; J. Winnifrith, 'The 'priest' house at Smallhythe: a false identification', *AC* xcvi (1980), 363–6.

Hythe was ideally placed for this with relatively easy access to marshland grazing within and outside the parish. Industrial and professional activities were conducted alongside involvement in agriculture and it is probable that capital moved regularly between ships, goods, property, land and livestock.[21]

Small Hythe, along with the rest of the Weald, experienced in-migration and rapid population growth from perhaps as early as the last quarter of the fifteenth century. By the late 1540s there were probably around 200 more or less permanent inhabitants out of a total parochial population of around 1,300 and, at times of major ship-building, this figure may have risen substantially.[22] The lion's share of wealth created by economic and demographic growth at Small Hythe appears to have been shared among only a few families (the Brekyndens being the most prominent by far) or went to merchants, graziers and ship-owners in Rye and Tenterden town.[23] Nevertheless, the rising prosperity and aspirations of local leading families brought a new sense of confidence and importance to the township and heralded distinctive cultural developments.

The chapel of St John the Baptist:
origins, devotional piety and symbolism

The present-day chapel of St John the Baptist dates from 1514–17, the previous building having been destroyed in a fire on 31 July 1514.[24] Its origins are far from clear but dedications to St John date from the seventh to the fourteenth centuries.[25] The chapel's liminal position next to the Rother suggests the adoption of an ancient pre-Christian holy site, local knowledge of which could have endured into the thirteenth century.[26] A wayside missionary cross or saint's shrine may have given way to a chapel designed to meet the spiritual requirements of an outlying settlement and those passing through.[27] There is nothing to suggest that it was an early foundation by a lay or monastic lord, and in the late fifteenth century it belonged to the 'strete' of

---

[21] Roberts, 'Tenterden houses', 20, 350; Scammel, 'Shipowning in England', 116–19.

[22] Taylor, 'Chapel of St John the Baptist', 154, 159–62.

[23] PRO, E 179/230/182, 231/228, 234/7.

[24] Te/C1, fo. 140v; PRO, E 315/114, fo. 140, cited in Taylor, 'Chapel of St John the Baptist', 157; Riley, 'MSS of the corporation of Rye', 536.

[25] R. Morris, *Churches in the landscape*, London 1989, 91; Everitt, *Continuity and colonization*, 185–219. According to Kilburne, 'by tradition' it was 'said to have been founded by one Shepherde', but this probably stems from the fact that Robert Sheppard recovered the chapel lands and re-endowed it in the late sixteenth century: Taylor, 'Chapel of St John the Baptist', 134.

[26] Rosser, 'Parochial conformity', 183; Bonney, 'Early boundaries', 171–2; Morris, *Churches*, 91–2. A number of Kent's early baptismal churches are sited on riverbanks: Everitt, *Continuity and colonization*, 195, 295–6.

[27] Everitt, *Continuity and colonization*, 186–7.

Small Hythe – the collective of people who lived there – which more than likely explains its origins.[28]

One of the principal dedications of the late-founded churches and chapels of Kent's wilderness areas, St John the Baptist was probably considered by their inhabitants to be 'most able to protect them in a hostile environment'. As at Small Hythe, the dedication is also frequently connected with landing places or hithes.[29] The legend of St John resonated with meaning for the local inhabitants, and provided them with an imaginary landscape and narrative by which to represent their identity, which could be firmly grounded in a distinctive quotidian material base. For example, Voragine's Nativity of St John the Baptist tells how he was born 'two miles nigh to Jerusalem', offering an obvious allusion to the two-mile journey (used more than once by the inhabitants as the chief justification for the maintenance of religious services in their chapel) between the smaller settlement of Small Hythe and the larger urban centre of Tenterden town. Having left his father's house in his early teens and lived in solitude in the desert on the river Jordan, John 'drew him towards Bethany, upon the river or desert, not far from Jerusalem' where he preached to, and baptised, those who came to him. Evoking the remote and bleak landscape of Small Hythe and the Rother levels this imagery provided a religious rationale to an idea of community and an exemplar of ascetic piety. Pious austerity was fundamental to John's life-style in the wilderness summed up by his simple clothing and exotic, but basic, diet, for which he had left 'riches, honours, dignities, noblesse, and all the world'.[30]

John's most important role was as baptiser and his part in the gospel story, played out at the Jordan, made him an ideal guardian of Small Hythe's economic life dependent, as it was, on the river Rother,[31] while his role as missionary was apposite to the chapel's outlying roadside position. His distinctive dress of 'the skin of a camel . . . girded . . . with a girdle of wool, or of leather, cut out of an hide or a beast's skin', comprised commodities central to the activities of Small Hythe's graziers and tradesmen, camel skin excepted.[32] Fasting on the eve of the Nativity of John (23 June) and the lighting of fires 'yn the worschip' of the saint are described by Mirk. This is substantiated by other evidence of celebrations on St John's Eve. The fire of bones – the 'bonnefyre' – which produced a stench believed to drive disease-carrying dragons into water held considerable significance for those

---

[28] Ibid. 185–6, 205–6; Morris, *Churches*, 210, 219, 367–8; G. H. Tupling, 'The pre-Reformation parishes and chapelries of Lancashire', *Transactions of the Lancashire and Cheshire Antiquarian Society* lxvii (1957), 7; N. Orme, 'Church and chapel in medieval England', *TRHS* 6th ser. vi (1996), 82–7.

[29] Everitt, *Continuity and colonization*, 250–4, 306 at p. 253 nn. 62–3. St John the Baptist was the most popular saint in coastal areas: Draper and others, 'Fitting of the altars'. See also Morris, *Churches*, 88–92.

[30] *Golden legend*, iii. 258–9. See also *Mirk's festial*, i. 184.

[31] *Golden legend*. iii. 259–61.

[32] Ibid. iii. 253, 259; *Mirk's festial*, i. 183–5.

living in low-lying and unhealthy riverside settlements such as Small Hythe.[33] The fire of wood or 'wakefyre', intended to be seen from afar, alluded to St John's attribution as 'the lantern' and the prophetic predictions of John's ministry and his own foretelling of the messiah. This was highly pertinent to travellers who relied on the beacons lit for ships at Small Hythe. These two fires were combined in what was called 'Saynt Ionys fyre', which served as a reminder of the burning of John's bones by the emperor, Julian the Apostate.[34] Through annual re-enactment, St John's legend could be appropriated easily to the local cultural context of the everyday and provided a rich stream of imagery for the perpetuation of a distinctive ethos.

The chapel was constructed, unusually at this time, of expensive Flemish red brick and is evidence of the commercial and industrial boom enjoyed by Small Hythe in the early sixteenth century and the aspirant identity of its wealthy families.[35] For example, in his will of 1517 Robert Brekynden, member of the dominant Small Hythe family that supported the chapel over a number of generations, left 20s. for the glazing of a window in the chapel, 6s. 8d. towards the building of a house for the priest who celebrated there to live in, and 20d. to Sir Thomas Gryme, possibly the same priest, to celebrate for the health of Robert's soul.[36] The chapel's stepped east and west gables betray cultural influences from the Low Countries, arising from long-term trade links and immigration and, possibly, the employment of continental bricklayers (see plate 3).[37] It eloquently symbolised the town's commercial and cultural horizons and position in the regional urban hierarchy. Lacking a tower, porch or structural chancel, the east end is separated by a surviving oak screen of plain design which conforms to the general austerity of the interior.[38] It is probable that the chapel of East Guldeford, built by Sir Richard Guldeford around 1500 in the newly reclaimed parish of the same name, provided some inspiration. They share a similar position by the waterside and a simple red-brick design. Given the Guldefords' influence in Tenterden they may have lent their patronage to the new venture at Small Hythe.[39] William Roper, responsible for the similarly styled red-brick Roper Gateway in Canterbury, may be the best candidate for architect. Predating the Canter-

[33] See, for example, Hasted, *History of Kent*, 200; Everitt, *Continuity and colonization*, 62; *Mirk's festial*, i. 182–3; and Hutton, *Rise and fall*, 37–9.

[34] *Golden legend*, iii. 253; *Mirk's festial*, i. 182–5.

[35] Roberts, 'Tenterden houses', 48, and *Tenterden*, 52. Small numbers of Flemish bricks were imported at Rye but in 1508–9 imports temporarily rose to five times the annual average, perhaps reflecting an increasing fashion for their use: Mayhew, *Tudor Rye*, 241.

[36] PRC 17/13/263; A. H. Taylor, 'The clergy of St John the Baptist, Smallhythe', AC lv (1943), 27.

[37] E. Tyrrell-Green, *Parish church architecture*, London 1924, 70; J. C. Cox, *The English parish church*, London 1914, 243–52.

[38] J. Newman, *West Kent and the Weald: the buildings of England*, London 1980, 531; Canon S. Robertson, 'On Kentish rood-screens', AC xiv (1882), 371–3.

[39] Roberts, *Tenterden*, 68–9.

Plate 3. The west front of Small Hythe chapel, Tenterden,
from the Small Hythe to Tenterden road

bury gateway by over a decade, Small Hythe chapel's crow-steps may mark the introduction of this style into Kent, making it an altogether *avant-garde* and humanist venture. Roper's possible involvement, his divergence into Lutheranism by the early 1520s and the building's positively continental references all indicate the type of cultural milieu which had evolved in Small Hythe, Tenterden and the Kentish Weald by the early sixteenth century.[40]

The ideal, at least, was that the chapel 'be decently furnished with books, chalices, lights and other ecclesiastical ornaments necessary for divine worship'.[41] Testamentary bequests provide a fragmentary picture of provision. For example in 1503 John Jacob, a local resident, stipulated that at her inheritance his daughter was to buy 'at her owne propre charge a candellsticke of laten with iiij or v braunches, and sett it in the Chappell of Saint John baptist in Smalhed'.[42] The altar was probably decorated with fine pieces of cloth donated by townsfolk such as 'the best dyaper Table clothe' given by Lore Blossom in 1533, 'to the haultre in the Chappell of Smalithe'.[43] In 1526 John Wayte left 6s. 8d. for the purchasing of a chalice for use there, and Margaret Pellond gave two silver rings and a 'bedestone of silver', perhaps to adorn the image of St John which would have stood within the chapel.[44] In 1509 Archbishop William Warham ordered that the local inhabitants 'have the Lord's Body duly and honourably enclosed and placed suspended above the altar . . . not in a burse or small box, on account of the risk of being broken, but in a most beautiful pyx adorned with white linen within, under lock and key and faithful guardianship'.[45] In 1533 Lore Blossom willed that 'if the strete of Smalhith wyl bye a conopye for the Sacrament to hyng over the aulter there I bequethe to the bying of it 3s. 4d. more or ells not'.[46]

The fact that the cult of the head of St John the Baptist had eucharistic and Christocentric associations in the late fifteenth and early sixteenth centuries may be of significance to these developments, as well as to increasing Christocentricism in the parish as a whole, but the only reference to a saint's cult at Small Hythe is a bequest of 3s. 4d. to the light of St Barbara in the chapel in George Harryson's will of 1527.[47] This apparent lack of cults was not compensated for by devotion to saints at St Mildred's. Only twelve

---

[40] T. P. Smith, 'The Roper gateway, St Dunstan's street, Canterbury', AC cviii (1991), 171–81; N. Jones, *The English Reformation: religion and cultural adaptation*, Oxford 2002, 12–14, 128. Smith writes (p. 172) that Archbishop Warham built Small Hythe chapel but provides no evidence to support this assertion.

[41] Taylor, 'Chapel of St John the Baptist', 140–1, 143–5.

[42] PRC 17/8/271.

[43] PRC 17/19/365.

[44] PRC 17/17/49, 17/16/179.

[45] Ordinance made by Warham in 1509 which confirmed and elaborated on the licence of 1506: LPL, Reg. Warham, i, fo. 338v, transcribed and translated in Taylor, 'Chapel of St John the Baptist', 145.

[46] PRC 17/19/365.

[47] Peters, *Patterns of piety*, 87; Duffy, *Altars*, 142; PRC 17/17/334.

Sma ... fifth of those for whom there are wills – gave
to s ... es or special masses at St Mildred's or else-
whe ... is of those who lived elsewhere in the parish
did so w..... a..... ...ssed in chapter 2, was itself low in a national context.
Significantly, the Jesus Mass was only half as popular at Small Hythe as it was
in the rest of the parish. The remaining Small Hythe bequests to cults or
special masses comprise three to the Virgin Mary, one to the rood light in
St Mildred's, one to the image of St Mary at neighbouring Ebony and two for
masses at *Scala Coeli*. Devotional piety at Small Hythe seems to have been
distinctively austere compared with the rest of the parish. This corresponds
with the notion of a worldly asceticism shared by those who embraced the
rigours of an economic calling to live in a comparatively bleak and marginal
landscape, suggested from the above reading of St John's legend. Its distinctive piety might, therefore, have been shaped by particular forms of life-style,
occupation and attitudes to wealth, as well as by the austerity of the physical
environment. Alan Everitt has written of 'oddly localized forms of Nonconformity' as a feature of the marshland settlements of Kent and these sorts of
material and cultural factors may have played their part in their development. Equally, continental cultural influences may have been at work alongside indigenous reformist strands of piety also visible at Tenterden.[48]

The development and consolidation of religious provision

The emergence of a sense of separate identity at Small Hythe can be traced in
the changing role of its chapel. From the 1460s through to the 1540s the
emphasis of religious provision shifted in a definite direction, the chapel's
status was enhanced, its relationship with the parish church was formally
settled and the townsfolk ensured that it survived two major crises.

From the early 1460s to 1505 the majority of testators who remembered
the chapel were concerned with the establishment of temporary or permanent chantries. So, for example, in 1474 John Ingram willed that one of his
kinsmen 'pay to the chapel quarterly yf a preste syng there iiijd a yere so that
the preste that saith masse pray for the soules rehersyd the names iiij tymes in
the quarter of John Ingram, William Ingram, William Dolekynden and
Isabell Elyotte'.[49] Prior to 1505 five testators either established permanent
chantries in the chapel, or secured prayers by making endowments of lands
and tenements to the support of the priest. In 1501 William Jamyn stipulated
that 'viij honest men of Smalehith' be enfeoffed in four acres of marshland, to
the intent that they allow the wardens of the chapel (or other local inhabitants if there were no wardens) to take the profits 'to the use of a priest there

[48] Everitt, *Continuity and colonization*, 64–5.
[49] PRC 17/2/342.

to sing dyvine service as parcell of his salary to pray for the soules of me the said William Jamyn and Margaret my wif, Stephen Jamyn and Agnes his wif, William Eliot and Isabell his wif, and all cristen soules, and if no suche prest then therbe, to the use of the works of the same chapell for ever'.[50] These endowments not only secured masses and prayers for benefactors and their kin, but sustained the celebration of divine service by laying the basis for a permanent stipend. Not one Small Hythe or Tenterden testator made an endowment of this sort at St Mildred's. They were peculiar to Small Hythe, and were concentrated in the late fifteenth century.

The development of more permanent religious provision was manifested in other ways. From 1480 a few testators began to leave sums of money or goods, simply 'to the work' or 'to the use' of the chapel or without any such specification at all. So, for example, Richard Davy gave 3s. 4d. and from a piece of land called 'the Tod' Nicholas Assherynden established a legacy of 20d. a year for twenty years.[51] In addition, the names of successive Small Hythe chaplains start to appear in wills from the late 1480s and from 1490 chapel wardens who administered funds from endowments or 'other good men of the strete' began to be mentioned. There are glimpses of lifetime endowments in the wills of the early sixteenth century, which indicate that additions may have been made to the lands built up for the chaplain's stipend in the fifteenth. For example, William Blossom, in his will of 1527, mentioned 'the other land now perteynyng to the said chapell'.[52] When the stipend was valued in 1546 there was adequate provision from endowments, one of which can be traced back to its benefactor in the 1460s. Over fifteen acres in seven separate parcels in the tenure of a number of leading Small Hythe men were listed.[53]

With the permanent provision of divine service enhanced, in 1503 the first steps were taken towards securing the chapel's official status. Curiously enough, it was not a resident of Small Hythe who got things moving, but John Tyler of Tenterden, who may have originated from the neighbouring parish of Woodchurch. Tyler was one of only three Tenterden parishioners who gave to the chapel and did not live either at or in the immediate vicinity of Small Hythe. He stated in his will that if the quarter of Small Hythe purchased 'a perpetual lisens from the courte of Rome to have a prest singyng in the chapell of seynt John at Smalhed' within three years after his death, then seven marks were to be paid from his estate to the wardens.[54] This bequest seems to have motivated the inhabitants because, in response to their petitions, on 10 February 1506 Warham granted a licence for the cele-

---

[50] PRC 17/8/199.
[51] 1480, PRC 17/3/365; 1484, PRC 16/1/1.
[52] PRC 17/17/269.
[53] PRO, E 301/29, fo. 118, transcribed and translated in Taylor, 'Chapel of St John the Baptist', 151.
[54] PRC 17/9/211.

bration of divine service there. This document stressed the benefits of the chapel, not just to inhabitants of Small Hythe but also to sojourners (*commorantes*), underlining the significance of the transient element of the population. The archbishop provided the somewhat modest incentive of forty days indulgence to all who extended 'a helping hand to the erection, repair, maintenance, support or sustentation of the . . . chapel and . . . chaplain'.[55] This may have influenced the character of bequests from 1506, by helping to shift attention further away from the procurement of temporary chantries towards maintenance of the chapel and chaplain in the everyday administration of services, sacraments and sacramentals. The need to rebuild after the fire of 1514 would have provided added impetus. From 1506 to 1533 there were only three bequests for chantries, and two of these were only to be carried out in the event of heirs not inheriting.[56] Significantly, there were only two endowments of lands and tenements and these were made simply 'to the chapel' and 'to the onely use and mayntenance of the preest's wage that shall syng in the Chappell at Smalhithe'.[57] Fifteen of the eighteen testators who remembered the chapel in their wills after 1505 made bequests wholly of this character. The licence and need to rebuild were added incentives to a process undergirded by the intensification of local identity fuelled by economic and demographic expansion.

The material basis of Small Hythe's piety is simply but eloquently expressed by an instance early in the fifteenth century when the Cinque Port of New Romney made an offering of 3s. 4d. to the chapel at the launch of a barge which had been built for them there.[58] Just as piety was inseparable from industry and trade, the chapel served more than just a religious function. In 1528 William Brekynden of Small Hythe, who was a jurat of Tenterden, was called before the Brotherhood of the Cinque Ports on pain of £20 to answer objections made against him by the Corporation of Tenterden 'for keeping a court'. Legal bonds were often made in sacred buildings in the medieval period and an indenture of 1521 between William Brekynden of Small Hythe and John Frencham records how their transaction was to be carried out in the chapel.[59] Brekynden may well have used the building for this sort of activity on a regular basis and so attracted the attention of the

---

[55] Taylor, 'Chapel of St John the Baptist', 140–1, 143–5.

[56] In 1517 Robert Brekynden bequeathed 20d. to Sir Thomas Gryme to celebrate for the health of his soul. The others were John Hoore (1509: PRC 17/11/306) and Joan Weste, widow (1521: PRC 17/15/15).

[57] PRC 17/11/306; John Wayte, 1526: PRC 17/17/49. This also applies to two arrangements for lands to revert to the use of the chapel in the event of heirs not inheriting between 1506 and 1533: John Brekynden, 1526: PRC 17/17/207; William Blossom, 1527: PRC 17/17/269.

[58] Riley, 'MSS of the corporation of Rye', 536.

[59] *Calendar of the white and black books*, 204, 206, 208, 209–10; CKS, U410/T21; R. N. Swanson, *Church and society in late medieval England*, Oxford 1989, 257–8; Kümin, *Shaping of a community*, 53.

Tenterden borough. If a 'certain independence of mind' and 'tendency to press individual rights beyond their legal limits' sometimes lay behind the foundation of non-parochial chapels in this period, William Brekynden's unauthorised court illustrates the way in which powerful figures could capitalise on the growth of local economic and political power at the expense of long-standing privileges.[60]

The pattern of bequests

Not all the wills made by inhabitants of Small Hythe are readily distinguishable from those written by individuals who lived elsewhere in the parish. From 1501 (and in one instance before that date), if a testator were resident locally then this tended to be indicated in the opening clause of his or her testament. All told, twenty-seven wills mention 'Small Hythe in the parish of Tenterden' as domicile with some insignificant variations in wording. In addition to these, by cross-referencing the wills and systematically searching deed materials and other sources, other Small Hythe testators can be identified.[61] These amount to a further thirty-nine testators who, when added to the twenty-seven whose wills tell us that they lived at Small Hythe, produce a total of sixty-six individuals. This is not to say that none have escaped unnoticed but, judging by the number that have been identified and what is known about the size of Small Hythe's population in relation to the parish as a whole, perhaps only a handful remain hidden. This makes it possible to chart the geographical pattern of bequests to the chapel. Forty testators made such bequests between 1467 and 1535 and thirty-seven of these lived in, or near to, Small Hythe.[62] Of the three who did not, one was John Morer (or Moeer) vicar of Tenterden, whose reasons for remembering the chapel should be judged differently from those of lay testators.[63] Notwithstanding these few exceptions, the vast majority of bequests were made by individuals and families who were living within a mile of the chapel when they made their wills.

By the early fourteenth century Kent's five hundred parishes contained an estimated three hundred chapels in addition to their parish churches. Local loyalty to subparochial chapels throughout late medieval England has been

---

[60] Everitt, *Continuity and colonization*, 64–5.

[61] Deeds include regular references to the dens upon which properties lay, as well as to lands or houses 'at Small Hythe', or to individuals as being 'of Small Hythe'.

[62] All but 2 of the 37 lived at Small Hythe itself. The exceptions are Nicholas and Stephen Assherynden who dwelt at Ashenden, which lies about three-quarters of a mile north of Small Hythe chapel: 1484, PRC 16/1/1; 1491, PRC 17/5/275.

[63] PRO, PCC 20 Milles, fos 161v–162v and see chapter 5 below. The other two were Moyse Pellond (1519: PRC 17/14/47) and John Tyler as mentioned. Moyse Pellond had kinsfolk at Small Hythe: John Pellond, 1511: PRC 32/10/154; Margaret Pellond, widow, 1523: PRC 17/16/179.

well documented,[64] but what has not been investigated before now is the geographical pattern of testamentary patronage of these foundations. The pattern of bequests to Small Hythe chapel was intensely local and, whilst it is to be expected that patronage would follow use, what is remarkable is its almost complete lack of impact upon the testamentary priorities of other parishioners. It appears that it was not customary for an inhabitant of Tenterden town to interfere in, or even contribute to, the maintenance of religion at Small Hythe. Whatever its causes[65] it is difficult to reconcile this pattern with either Gervase Rosser's suggestion that the 'diversification and enrichment of opportunities to exercise a degree of choice in religious behaviour' was the driving force behind the enhancement or foundation of local chapels or, similarly, Nicholas Orme's recourse to 'deep human yearnings . . . for variety, both in devotion and companionship' to explain the proliferation of chapels both before and after the Reformation. If Small Hythe chapel was established for these reasons then, on the whole, only the local inhabitants took advantage of the opportunity for diversification in religious affiliation. As Rosser and Orme rightly state, there were other reasons for the existence of chapels to do with the practicalities of attending a relatively distant mother church, the veneration given to ancient holy sites and the need to form and express emerging local identities.[66] These factors seem to have provided the rationale for a chapel at Small Hythe, rather than aspirations for greater choice in religious observance. When seen in their proper material context, the new chapels of the later Middle Ages may speak less of 'an increasingly "natural" [and by implication inevitable] lay control over church affairs' than of the fluctuating pattern of people and wealth across the landscape.[67]

[64] Everitt, *Continuity and colonization*, 184, 205–6; Rosser 'Parochial conformity', 173–89; Orme, 'Church and chapel', 75–102. See also Tupling, 'Parishes and chapelries', 1–16; Owen, *Church and society*, 5–6, 8, 10–12, 19, 99–100, 134, 140, and 'Medieval chapels in Lincolnshire', *Lincolnshire History and Archaeology* x (1975), 15–22; and C. Kitching, 'Church and chapelry in sixteenth century England', in D. Baker (ed.), *The Church in town and countryside* (SCH xvi, 1979), 279–90.

[65] There is no evidence to suggest, for example, that Small Hythe clergy influenced local will-makers to give to the chapel.

[66] Rosser, 'Parochial conformity', 176, 182–3; Orme, 'Church and chapel', 75–102 at p. 102.

[67] Kümin, *Shaping of a community*, 182. See also Tupling, 'Parishes and chapelries', 9; Kitching, 'Church and chapelry', 279. Reading Street chapel in the adjacent parish of Ebony, but within the hundred of Tenterden, appears to have arisen out of similar economic developments as the chapel of St John the Baptist: John Winnifrith, 'The medieval church of St Mary, Ebony, and its successors', AC c (1985), 159, 162–3.

Testamentary strategies

To what degree was there a conflict of interest between the chapel and the parish church due to the enhancement of the former, as has been documented for other parishes?[68] Can any tension, arising out of a sense of obligation to both of these religious foundations, be seen in the way the inhabitants of Small Hythe made their wills and, if so, how did they attempt to resolve this? Twenty-nine of the thirty-seven Small Hythe testators who gave to their chapel, also made bequests to their parish church, so there was certainly no 'wholesale secession from the parish'. Rather than forsake their mother church the inhabitants of Small Hythe, perhaps more than any other group in the parish, reflected the diversity offered by a reasonably flexible parochial system.[69]

Comparison of the amounts of money, land and goods which individuals left to each institution reveals that the distribution of resources at death between church and chapel was rarely equal and followed an overall trend. Sixteen of the twenty-nine favoured their chapel over their parish church, two left exactly the same to both and eleven prioritised St Mildred's. Of those who gave more to the chapel, nine of them made only cash bequests. For example, in 1527 George Harryson bequeathed 3s. 4d. to Small Hythe chapel, another 3s. 4d. to the light of St Barbara within and left 8d. to the maintenance of the Jesus Mass in St Mildred's.[70] Eight testators permanently endowed their chapel with lands and property at the same time as making cash bequests. So, in 1490, Joan Turnor effectively sold a piece of land to the chapel for 5 marks and ordered that the proceeds be used to pay for a temporary chantry therein.[71] These types of endowments almost certainly expressed a greater material commitment to the chapel than to St Mildred's, but also provided a way of displaying affiliation to both institutions by leaving enough cash to give to the latter, while alienating lands in perpetuity to the former. For example, in 1501 William Jamyn, on the one hand devised four acres of marsh to the use of the chapel and, on the other left the considerable sum of 40s. to purchase a new chalice for St Mildred's.[72] Only two Small Hythe wills contain arrangements for lands to go to the use of the chapel and do not also contain cash bequests to St Mildred's, and in both cases the arrangements

---

[68] Orme, 'Church and chapel', 92–3; Kitching, 'Church and chapelry', 281; Kümin, *Shaping of a community*, 171–9.

[69] Rosser, 'Parochial conformity', passim at p. 176. Included are gifts to the upkeep and elaboration of buildings, for ornaments and lights, for masses, obits and chantries at either place and gifts simply 'to the use of' or 'to the work of' the church or chapel. All reversionary bequests are also included. Payments for tithes forgotten are not counted here as gifts to the parish church.

[70] PRC 17/17/334. Nicholas Assherynden, however, established a legacy of 20d. a year for twenty years from a piece of land: PRC 16/1/1.

[71] Joan Turnor, 1490: PRC 17/5/310.

[72] PRC 17/8/199.

were only to come into effect in the event of an heir not inheriting.[73] Eight out of a total of sixty-six Small Hythe testators gave only to their chapel, either in cash or with goods or ornaments. The Small Hythe residents who remembered St Mildred's without leaving anything to their chapel also numbered eight.

Inhabitants of the township were, it seems, faced with more choices when making their wills than most of their fellow parishioners and the availability of disposable resources was a factor in deciding which strategy to adopt. The 196 will-making parishioners who did not live at Small Hythe left an average of £3 1s. 9d. in religious bequests, which may be compared to an average of only £2 1s. 9d. (or median of 16s. 2d.) left by Small Hythe testators.[74] The twenty-nine who gave to both their chapel and their parish church, however, apportioned, on average, a much higher £3 10s. 3d. (or median of 40s.) and so were afforded greater scope to negotiate their position. This is confirmed by the relatively small amounts of money left for religious purposes by those sixteen Small Hythe testators who only remembered either their chapel or their church. On average they devoted only £1 2s. to religious concerns. Limitations on disposable wealth meant that these testators had to make hard choices, rather than having the luxury of spreading their gifts between both chapel and parish church. That these testators were not necessarily poorer than the rest is shown by William Blossom's bequests, which included 3s. 4d. for his forgotten tithes (a considerable amount for this purpose) and the same to the chapel of St John the Baptist, and yet requested burial within the parish church – a privilege enjoyed only by the relatively wealthy. His solid support for the chapel is reinforced by the stipulation that if his son failed to inherit his lands and tenements, then a parcel of land worth 6s. 8d. a year was to go to the use of the chapel 'for evermore yn suche manner and forme as the other land now perteynyng to the said chapell doth'.[75]

While prior obligations or limitations on disposable resources created a focused approach to giving, an element of choice never appears to have been absent. Choice, that is, limited by a predisposition for giving a certain amount to one religious foundation, rather than fractions of that amount to a number. This may well have been to do with the practicalities of providing enough to procure a certain number of masses and prayers, or to make a significant contribution to church fabric, but it may also have stemmed from a materialistic value system which esteemed gifts primarily for their objective

---

[73] John Brekynden, 1526: PRC 17/17/207; William Blossom,1527: PRC 17/17/269. One resident, Robert Ponte, endowed the chapel with the proceeds in perpetuity from lands and a barn and ordered that, after the death of his sister, his messuage in Small Hythe was to be sold and the profits given to St Mildred's in four parts: 1465, PRC 17/1/170.

[74] Quantifiable cash bequests for masses, prayers, chantries, to lights, images, churches, church personnel, religious houses, charitable gifts to the poor and for public works such as repairs to highways are all included. Reversionary bequests are excluded.

[75] R. B. Dinn, 'Monuments answerable to mens' worth': burial patterns, social status and gender in late medieval Bury St Edmunds', *JEH* xxxxvi (1995), 237–55; PRC 17/17/269.

monetary worth, making testators concentrate their piety into fewer more impressive gestures.[76] Whatever the causes, testamentary giving to both church and chapel appears to have been followed only by those with a relative wealth of disposable resources not over-pressed by other concerns. As a result, less than half the residents of Small Hythe took advantage of parochial diversity. What appears to have been deeply entrenched convention ensured that only a handful of people who lived outside Small Hythe did. This is an important qualification of the idea that an expanding free-market in piety was the cause and effect of the proliferation of subparochial chapels or other institutions such as the fraternity or chantry.[77]

Patronage of the chapel of St John the Baptist, in comparison to St Mildred's, fluctuated over the period. From 1463 to 1488 seven out of eighteen residents favoured the chapel and eight gave priority to St Mildred's. From then until 1509 there was a marked change, with ten out of twenty putting the chapel first, four of these giving to it alone. During these twenty or so years only one individual favoured St Mildred's. The increasing strength of affiliation to the chapel during this time is consistent with the period of consolidation of religious provision at Small Hythe which culminated in the acquisition of the licence for the celebration of divine service in 1506 and, as detailed below, the ordinance of 1509. From 1510 to 1535 there was a general reversal of priorities in the Small Hythe wills. Over these years eight out of thirty testators favoured their chapel over St Mildred's, whereas ten gave priority to the latter, despite the need to rebuild after the fire of 1514. It was only during the two decades up to 1509 that testators gave more to the chapel than to St Mildred's. Before the 1490s they left an average of 16s. to St Mildred's and while this fell to 12s. 8d. during the twenty years up to 1509, this was largely due to a sharp increase in the proportion of testators who gave to neither institution, rather than the growth in patronage of the chapel. The decline in the number of bequests to the chapel from 1490 was more than offset by a 60 per cent increase in the average gift, but the fall in material support of St Mildred's was, it seems, only to a very small extent due to this increased local patronage. Testamentary giving to St Mildred's stayed low after 1509; on average Small Hythe testators left only 13s. 8d. to their parish church from then until 1535, but giving to the chapel fell well below this to a mean of 6s. 1d., showing that the slump in patronage that was such a marked feature of Tenterden's testamentary piety as mentioned in chapter 2, also affected Small Hythe.

[76] There were outlets for small gifts at Tenterden, such as lights and the Jesus Mass but, on the whole, bequests to church fabric or for divine service had a minimum limit. The shortage of small coins in this period may also have played a part: Kümin, *Shaping of a community*, 83.
[77] Rosser, 'Parochial conformity', passim.

The threat of identity

The licence of 1506 was, in part, an attempt to clarify the duties and privileges of the inhabitants of Small Hythe in relation to their parish church. It began by acknowledging that due to the distance of Small Hythe from St Mildred's, the condition of the roads, floods, the severity of the weather and sickness and infirmity, the inhabitants and sojourners ('ipsi inhabitantes et ibidem commorantes') were 'unable, except at very great danger to themselves' to attend their parish church 'as they ought' and were 'bound by law to do'. As a result they were 'compelled to relinquish altogether those things which have respect to true religion' and, even more deplorable, many sick people living there were dying without sacraments and sacramentals ('sacramenta et sacramentalia')[78] 'to the grave peril of their souls'. Although hyperbolic language was common in such petitions and so should not be taken at face value, the ambiguous terms of the licence failed to provide a clear-cut solution to what was none the less something of a problem.[79] For instance, it ruled that in addition to divine service,[80] the sacraments and sacramentals were to be ministered to the inhabitants and sojourners there by the chaplain 'at least in times of necessity, provided, however, that nothing be done prejudicial to the rights of the rectors and vicars of the parish church or of their successors, and that there be no canonical impediment in the way'. At least there could be no misunderstanding about who was responsible for the maintenance of the chaplain and chapel: the residents of Small Hythe 'and other faithful Christians', some of whom were already 'extending a helping hand towards the maintenance' and, by implication, not the rector or vicar of Tenterden. There was, however, potential for conflict in the deceptively simple and ultimately naïve assertion that chaplains at Small Hythe were to be 'chosen by authority of the ordinary or his deputy'.[81]

At least some of the parishioners of Tenterden perceived Small Hythe chapel to be a threat to religious provision at St Mildred's in the early years of the sixteenth century. A series of presentments to archidiaconal visitations reveal that St Mildred's was in a not unfamiliar state of mild disrepair at this

[78] The sacraments referred to here were probably the eucharist and extreme unction. Sacramentals would have included holy water, holy oil and the sign of the cross and, according to the depositions of 1549, holy bread (the blessed loaf distributed after the mass to the congregation): Taylor, 'Chapel of St John the Baptist', 159; F. A. Gasquet, *Parish life in medieval England*, London 1906, 155–8.

[79] Taylor, 'Chapel of St John the Baptist', 140–1, 143–5; Kitching, 'Church and chapelry', 280.

[80] Divine service (*Divina*) included the celebration of the mass, daily matins and evensong, but the commonest practice in outlying chapels in this period was for mass to be said or sung on Sundays, all feast days and perhaps on Wednesdays and Fridays: Kitching, 'Church and chapelry', 284.

[81] Taylor, 'Chapel of St John the Baptist', 144.

time.[82] In 1502 the roof of the chancel of St Katherine was in need of urgent attention and in more than one place the perimeter of the churchyard lay open and pigs and other animals had strayed in daily to graze, sometimes entering the church and, between 1501 and 1508, other problems such as the lack of locks on the font and chrismatory were reported.[83] The presentment for 1507 touched on some of the above problems as well as others, and pointedly made reference to the people of Small Hythe. This has survived in the form of a loose fragment, presumably a rough draft of the kind which would later be copied into the court books:[84]

Tenterden. The chirche wardens there presente that the high auter chaunsell there is fawte for/
[l]ake of coveryng and also the stone of the gretewyndow is parte brokyn and leke to/
[fall] downe with owte a remedy be shortely hadde in the fawte of the parson and patron/
Also they presente that the Sonday westyment/
Also they present that the Antefoners be rente in certen levys and also be in dyverse/
[places] nygh blynde be caduke Inke/[85]
Also they presente that the body of chirche is not repeyred for lak of cavyriyng and/
[fawte] of brokyn glasse wyndey in defawte of all the parishoners there/
Also they present ~~that~~ that the chirche yarde is fawte with the high strete in the/
[defawte of] the parisshoners there/
Also they present that chirche yarde is fawte ~~for lak~~ all the west syde in defawte/
[of] the vycar there as the parisshoners sey/
~~Also they present that the more parte of the pepill dwellyng in Smaleheth/~~
~~have commyth nott duly to ther parisshe chirche as ther dute is for lak wherof/~~
~~the reparations of ther parisshe chirche is na nat~~[86] ~~maynteyned as it hath been~~
~~acustumed/~~
Also they present a woman callid Annes is Ilnamed and dempt of /

The churchwardens in 1507, William Browne and Edward Felip, both Tenterden men,[87] tried to draw a link between the problems of maintenance

---

[82] For similar cases see *Kentish visitations*, 144, 158, 160, 162, 199, 200, 218–19, 220, 272–5, 283.

[83] CCA, Z.3.2, 1501–18, fos 136v, 4r.

[84] Ibid. fo. 9r. Letters and words in square brackets are illegible but have been guessed at where possible.

[85] 'Caduke' probably means perished or corrupted, from the Latin *caducus*: *A new English dictionary on historical principles*, ed. J. A. H. Murray, Oxford 1843, ii. In 1508 the parishioners were charged with repairing the defective choir books before the next visitation on pain of a fine of 13s. 4d.: CCA, Z.3.2, fo. 82v.

[86] 'na ' and 'nat' are separately crossed out and 'the wors' is inserted above with a caret.

[87] CCA, Z.3.2, fo. 55r.

and alleged non-attendance by the residents of Small Hythe. Over the previous years, testamentary giving to St Mildred's by residents of Small Hythe had fallen by almost a half and attendance may also have declined, especially since the provision of services at Small Hythe had been enhanced. Despite being crossed through, the complaint found its way to the arch-deaconry court, fully legible but officially retracted. These thinly veiled grumblings read like a guarded reaction to a deteriorating relationship between the two communities, which may have been precipitated by the granting of the licence in 1506.

In 1509 the archbishop attempted to put the situation right through the standard procedure of issuing an ordinance intended to clarify the rights and duties of the people and chaplain of Small Hythe on the one hand, and the privileges of St Mildred's on the other. It repeated verbatim much of the licence, but revised the most important section with the insertion of a number of much more detailed and specific points which probably reveal the main areas of conflict.[88] Even greater emphasis was placed upon the responsi-bilities of the community of Small Hythe for maintaining their chapel. The procedure for appointing the chaplain was clarified: unusually, the inhabit-ants were to present their choice to the vicar of Tenterden for his approval. If he delayed or refused for more than six days, they could present their nominee to the ordinary and, with his approval, their choice would stand.[89] The only sacraments to be administered at Small Hythe were penance and the eucharist, and then only to the elderly and infirm; purification of women was allowed in cases of weakness and only the bodies of lepers, plague victims or the shipwrecked cast up at Small Hythe, could be buried there.[90] This was all on the condition that 'no prejudice accrue to the rectors and vicars of the parish church . . . nor anything to the detriment of the parishioners of Tenterden'. The inhabitants and sojourners at Small Hythe were to go to St Mildred's for the sacraments of Baptism and Matrimony, 'for all other things' and for the burial of all but those outlined above. On principal feast days, after celebrating mass in the chapel, the chaplain was to be present at high mass at St Mildred's. The inhabitants of Small Hythe, except the elderly, infirm, pregnant and servants, were to 'go as they have hitherto been wont to the parish church on all festivals', make their offerings at the four principal feasts and pay any dues such as 'le scot' for the building of the church and the fencing of its graveyard, 'just as they have been accustomed of old'. If they

---

[88] Taylor, 'Chapel of St John the Baptist', 141–3, 145–6; Kitching, 'Church and chapelry', 282.

[89] Taylor, 'Chapel of St John the Baptist', 147.

[90] An important source of revenue, right of burial was guarded closely by parish churches with subordinate chapels to contend with and was a common source of conflict as were the other pastoral services of baptism, marriage, churchings and funerals: C. Lutgens, 'The case of Waghen vs. Sutton: conflict over burial rights in late medieval England', *Medieval Studies* xxxviii (1976), 145–84; F. Johnson, 'The chapel of St Clement at Brundall', *Norfolk Archaeology* xxii (1924–5), 194–205; Orme, 'Church and chapel', 79–88.

broke or exceeded any of the premises in the ordinance, then all of the privileges granted to them would be null and void.

This appears to have quietened things down as none of the seven archidiaconal visitations of the parish of which there is a record after 1509 (including the extensive presentments to Archbishop Warham's own visitation of 1511) mention Small Hythe. Neither do any of them reveal problems of maintenance of the parish church but it is unlikely that these were solved by increased offerings from the people of Small Hythe.[91] The geographical pattern of parochial office-holding indicates a general decline in commitment to St Mildred's by the township's residents in the early sixteenth century. Until 1505 Small Hythe men appear to have served regularly as parochial officers, numbering five out of the ten churchwardens for the years 1498, 1499, 1500, 1502 and 1505, and two of the *parochiani*. After 1505 there was a marked change in the domicile of office-holders. In 1506, 1507, 1508, 1514, 1515, 1522 and 1523 not one of the churchwardens or *parochiani* came from Small Hythe. This is with the possible exception of Thomas Fordman who was sworn in as *parochianus* in 1516 and 1521. In addition, Thomas Assherynden, who lived near to the township, served as churchwarden in 1527.[92] Small Hythe men stopped serving at the same time as the licence of 1506 was granted to the chapel, which had its own wardens as early as 1490.[93] While it conferred a certain amount of prestige and offered vocational rewards, parochial office-holding could be onerous, without the added disincentive of a two-mile journey.[94] This, coupled with the impetus provided by the events of 1506–9 and the shift in identity and attitudes which they signalled, seems to have ensured that the major householders of Small Hythe resolved to concentrate on the administration of their chapel, whilst continuing to remember St Mildred's in their wills.

Identity under threat

In 1546 Small Hythe chapel was surveyed and valued by the commission appointed under the Chantries Act of 14 February of that year as having endowments which provided the chaplain with a stipend of £5 3s. 2d.[95] In

[91] CCA, Z.3.3, 1514, fo. 15v; 1515, fo. 51v; 1516, fo. 83v; Z.3.4, 1521, fos 20r, 48v; 1522, fo. 68r; 1523, fos 94v, 108r; *Kentish visitations*, 206–11.

[92] CCA, X.8.2 (2nd section), fo. 13r; Z.3.2, fo. 41r; Z.3.37, fo. 83r; Z.3.2, fo. 136v; Z.3.2 (2nd section), fos 4v, 25v, 55r, 82v; Z.3.3, fos 15v, 51v, 83v; Z.3.4, fos 20r,. 68r, 108r; CKS, U410/T179. *Parochiani* were probably sworn-in officers responsible for making presentments at archiediaconal visitations: Brown, *Popular piety*, 78; *Councils and synods with other documents relating to the English Church*, II: *A.D. 1205–1313*, ed. F. M. Powicke and C. R. Cheney, Oxford 1964, i. 261–5; Mason, 'Role of the English parishioner', 26.

[93] PRC 17/5/310; Owen, *Church and society*, 93–9, 115–20.

[94] E. Carlson, 'The origins, function, and status of the office of churchwarden, with particular reference to the diocese of Ely', in Spufford, *World of rural dissenters*, 164–207; Haigh, *Reformation and resistance*, 18, 230.

[95] Kreider, *English chantries*, 165–208; Taylor, 'Chapel of St John the Baptist', 151.

1547, shortly after the Edwardian Chantries Act, the chapel was seized by the crown, thus becoming a potential victim of what A. G. Dickens referred to as the 'stupid drafting' of the legislation.[96] There were several applicants to purchase the chapel and, shortly after March 1549, John Rowland, Page of the Robes to King Edward VI, was successful. Rowland planned to have the chapel demolished and, it seems, to lease the chaplain's house and land around it. It appears that since being alienated to the crown, there had been no chaplain at Small Hythe and so the chapel may have fallen into disuse,[97] but a number of the inhabitants, far from passively accepting the impending events, petitioned the Chancellor of the Court of Augmentations on behalf of 'all the other inhabitants of the said hamlett'.[98] Four of the petitioners belonged to long-standing Small Hythe families. Another may have been descended from an old Tenterden family, but the rest appear to have been first generation immigrants to Small Hythe, from neighbouring parishes or from further afield. One of the more entrenched Small Hythe men, John Brekynden, was bailiff of Tenterden in 1548–9, the year of the petition, and so brought considerable weight to their demands.[99] Two others were freemen of Tenterden by 1549, a further two entering the franchise in the 1550s.[100]

The petition began by stating that more than thirty years earlier the inhabitants had built 'at their cooste and charge and for their use and comoditie a certen chaple called St John Baptist Chaple wherein theye . . . did fynde a prieste to mynyster'. The distance from Tenterden, the poor state of the roads and the spiritual needs of the sick were all invoked and it was asserted that, not including strangers who stayed there from time to time, there were commonly 200 people living in the township, for whose spiritual health Archbishop Warham had granted that 'certen sacraments and sacramentals' be ministered there, a record of which could be produced if required. They tackled Rowland's plans on two bases. First, they questioned the alienation of the chapel to the crown under the Chantries Act of 1547, from which chapels of ease were excepted, by rather ambiguously asserting that 'yt . . . manyfestlie and reasonlie appere' that Small Hythe chapel 'is a chapple of ease'. Secondly, resorting to a commonly used argument in such cases, they warned that if the inhabitants were forced to worship at their parish church, Small Hythe and any vessels moored there would be vulnerable to attack in times of war.[101] The petitioners requested a commission to enquire into the chapel's status, its distance from the parish church, the condition of the

---

96 Taylor, 'Chapel of St John the Baptist', 150–1; Dickens, *English Reformation*, 230–42 at p. 237.

97 Taylor, 'Chapel of St John the Baptist', 150–3, 159–62.

98 Ibid. 153–5

99 Te/C1, fo. 141r.

100 Ibid. fos 116r–117r. The list of freemen only begins to record admissions in 1529 and so there is no record of those who may have become freemen before this date.

101 Rosser, 'Communities of parish and guild', 35.

roads, Small Hythe's situation 'upon the sea syde' and the details of the sacra-ments and sacramentals granted by the archbishop.[102]

The commission began on 4 October 1549 and was presided over by the religiously conservative Sir John Baker and Sir Walter Hendley who both had substantial estates in and around Tenterden.[103] They heard evidence from twelve witnesses aged between twenty-six and sixty, with most in their forties or fifties. Two of the original Small Hythe petitioners were present and a further four probably belonged to local families. There is no evidence to suggest that the remaining six were inhabitants of Small Hythe and, apart from two who seem to have belonged to older Tenterden families, they appear to have been first generation immigrants to Tenterden. The commis-sioners, therefore, appear to have heard evidence from six Small Hythe and six Tenterden men, which was either an attempt at even-handedness or a strategy by the Small Hythe party to broaden its campaign. George Felip, probably of Small Hythe, who gave evidence first, was bailiff of Tenterden in 1542–3 and 1546–7. Of the rest, six became freemen before 1549 and were evenly split between the two communities.[104]

The depositions concur on nearly all points, a further indication that the twelve witnesses were carefully picked to provide a solid case for the survival of the chapel. For example, they all agreed that the foundation was a chapel of ease and that it lay a distance of close to two miles from the parish church and most drew attention to Archbishop Warham's grant. Robert Rayner reported how he had been clerk of the chapel, had 'hade the booke there' and knew that divine service had been celebrated. Robert Foche declared how for some time the inhabitants of Small Hythe had attended matins and even-song. Two men confessed to never being present at the ministering of any sacraments or sacramentals, but one had heard of men being houseled and 'anheled' there, and the other knew that several people had been houseled at Easter as well as women purified, including his wife. Stephen Forde's wife had also been purified in the chapel and he claimed he had been married there. Robert Assherynden and Robert Foche gave some substance to this last claim, by reporting that several people had been married at Small Hythe. Lastly, Bartholomew Pellond said that Margaret Vyne was buried there. The first set of depositions generally reads like a credible account of the state of affairs subsequent to Warham's licence and ordinance some forty years earlier.[105]

Two weeks later a second set of witnesses was heard, as unanimous as the first, but much less favourable to the future of the chapel. Seven of the

[handwritten margin note: Fought to preserve town chapel]

---

[102] Taylor, 'Chapel of St John the Baptist', 153–5.
[103] Hasted, *History of Kent*, vii. 206–10, 186–7; Clark, *English provincial society*, 41, 55; Collinson, 'Cranbrook and the Fletchers', 401; *L&P* xx. 1336; xiv. 113, 831; xxi. 717.
[104] Te/C1, fos 141r, 116r–117r.
[105] Burials in Small Hythe are recorded from 1549 in the Tenterden parish registers: Roberts, *Tenterden*, 64.

witnesses were, or had been, from Tenterden, as opposed to Small Hythe. Three were described as yeomen, including George Castelyn, and John Foule was referred to as 'gent, now of London'. They were aged between around twenty-six and forty, most being in their thirties, so younger on the whole than the first group of deponents. The rest, significantly, were from the neighbouring parish of High Halden. These were older men, all but one in his early fifties, but none appear to have belonged to old established families, and only one seems to have originated from the Weald. Most of these deponents were of relatively high status, on the fringes of the lesser gentry. John Foule was bailiff of Tenterden in 1535–6 and 1539–40 and four others, including Castelyn, were freemen of the town.[106] A concerted effort appears to have been made to produce an impressive array of deponents who were prepared to speak against the continuing existence of the chapel.

The presence of George Castelyn among the deponents suggests that their efforts were religiously motivated. He was second cousin to Stephen Castelyn, one of the Tenterden heretics tried in 1511 and, since at least the late fifteenth century, the Castelyns had connections with the extensive and powerful Hales and Guldeford families. Although the Haleses were known for their religious conservatism in the late 1530s, a decade later they were more renowned for the activities of the radical evangelical lawyer, James Hales, who drafted the 1547 Chantries Act. The Guldefords, on the other hand, displayed a pragmatic sympathy for evangelical reform by the 1530s.[107] The act of 1547 explicitly called for an end to the superstitious activities of chantries which sustained adherence to the doctrines of purgatory, and Castelyn and others may have viewed Small Hythe chapel as little more than a glorified chantry.[108] The strict control that St Mildred's had exercised over the rights of the inhabitants had left the chapel vulnerable to just this sort of assault. It belonged to an ambiguous category of foundations which were unjustly threatened by the legislation of 1547 and the ambitions of both radical evangelicals and those less ideologically engaged but eager to gain the spoils of dissolution because, despite assertions to the contrary, it was not a chapel of ease and yet, by and large, it served as such.[109]

Whereas the first twelve depositions were in the form of answers to the questions put forward in the petition, this time a more rigorous set of interrogatories was used. No actual record of the six articles has survived but their substance can be deduced from the depositions. While remaining within the bounds of credibility, the deponents launched a unified assault on the chapel. For example, all but three agreed that it was definitely not a chapel of ease and although these three could not say for certain, two of them thought that it probably was not. They concurred, also, that the inhabitants of Small

---

106 Te/C1, fos 141r, 116r–117r.
107 See pp. 188–9 below.
108 Kitching, 'Church and chapelry', 281.
109 Dickens, *English Reformation*, 230–7; Shagan, *Popular politics*, 235–69.

Hythe had convenient access to St Mildred's at all times of the year. All agreed that, in the normal course of events, the sacraments and sacramentals that had been ministered in the chapel were limited to mass, matins, evensong and holy bread and holy water, and then only by licence of the vicar or curate of Tenterden. However, one deponent added that he remembered how licence had been given to purify one woman, christen one child and marry one couple. John Foule, on the other hand, asserted that for the twenty-five years he had lived in the parish there were to his knowledge no burials, christenings or weddings at Small Hythe and George Castelyn likewise stated that 'he never knew any there'. No mention was made of the houseling of those too sick or elderly to make the journey to Tenterden provided for by the archbishop's grant. Finally, the witnesses attempted to undermine the scale of demand for the chapel's services by claiming that there were only between sixty and one hundred communicants at Small Hythe and by playing down the township's importance in trade and ship-building, both of which were, in fact, in decline by this time but probably not as moribund as suggested.[110]

Despite this concerted attack, in the event, the inhabitants of Small Hythe succeeded in protecting their chapel and its endowments. Although not officially a chapel of ease, it was probably the fact that, to all intents and purposes, it performed that function which saved it.[111] Also, it is possible that the religiously conservative Baker and Hendley played a crucial role. Its survival notwithstanding, religious provision at Small Hythe was dealt a near fatal blow by the buffeting it received in the late 1540s. Nor could it have been helped by the religious uncertainties of the 1550s, the waning of the township's ship-building industry and the gradual decline of its riverborne trade. For the next twenty years there is no evidence of a minister serving there and after this time a reader performed very limited duties until the restoration of the chaplaincy in the early seventeenth century.[112] After around 1585 there are only two instances of gifts to the maintenance of the priest or fabric of the chapel in the Tenterden wills, in 1627 and 1628. In this latter year, William Brekynden left £6 13s. 4d. to the building and repairing of seats in the chapel, and 50s. to the poor of Small Hythe.[113] The Brekyndens gave to their chapel from the late fifteenth to the early seventeenth centuries, illustrating both the transmission of piety over the generations and the intense localisation of religious commitment at Small Hythe.

The emergence of a local identity at Small Hythe was expressed by the boundaries, real and symbolic, which lay between the two centres and appears to have been a consequence of the growth of the township as a

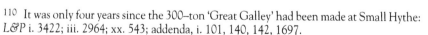

[110] It was only four years since the 300–ton 'Great Galley' had been made at Small Hythe: L&P i. 3422; iii. 2964; xx. 543; addenda, i. 101, 140, 142, 1697.
[111] Dickens, English Reformation, 237.
[112] Taylor, 'Chapel of St John the Baptist', 162–3, 178–9.
[113] Roberts, Tenterden, 64.

commercial, industrial and agricultural centre of some regional and even national importance from the late fifteenth century rather than any conscious programme for the diversification of religious provision on the part of Tenterden's parishioners. This represents an important corrective to some of the more influential thinking on the underlying causes of the rise of the subparochial chapel in late medieval England. In particular, Rosser, who acknowledges 'territorial localism within the parish' and 'the impulse within the parish community to splinter into fragments', remains persuaded that there was 'a transcendent parochial unity' and that if diversity was 'manifested overtly' it was in 'ways which aspired to harmony but could be contentious'.[114] Rather, just as it cannot be assumed that there was an inherent desire for diversity and greater choice in religious options, it is not at all clear that there was a commonly shared abstract ideal of the parish community to which individuals collectively aspired. Instead of seeing the parish as a universally understood concept, an overwhelmingly homogeneous experience and the apogée of social and religious solidarity as Duffy has done, for example,[115] it would perhaps be more fruitful to consider how the experiences of belonging to particular parish communities meant different things to different individuals and groups who found themselves somehow having to reconcile competing loyalties. Such decisions would have been difficult, uncomfortable even, and it is all too easy to romanticise the ways in which choices, diversity and conflict were resolved or to ignore instances when processes of resolution broke down.

Close and comparative analysis of testamentary material in conjunction with other types of evidence, as advocated in this study, reveals the complexity of devotional loyalty to Tenterden's competing parochial institutions and the intensely local nature of testamentary practice and piety at Small Hythe. The local inhabitants were almost wholly alone in supporting their foundation, whilst continuing to patronise their parish church, and the choices they made and strategies they adopted were bounded by finite disposable resources at death and the pressures of familial responsibility. Within these strictures, and the ongoing negotiation and codification of rights and responsibilities between the two institutions, their bequests were integral to the development and changing nature of the chapel. Many, but not all, testators exercised subtlety and pragmatism in negotiating their position in relation to competing and overlapping identities and held potentially conflicting priorities in tension. The only period when Small Hythe testators on the whole favoured their local foundation over St Mildred's was from the late 1480s to around 1509, although levels of giving to the chapel held up for longer than those to the parish church, before declining by the 1530s.

The tenor of piety at Small Hythe was eloquently expressed by the choice

---

114 Rosser, 'Parochial conformity', 184, 187.
115 Duffy, *Altars*, and *Voices of Morebath*, passim.

of St John as dedicatee. His legend provided a pool of images and motifs upon which the inhabitants could draw in the recreation of identity over the generations. The surviving building was symbolic of economic success and long-standing commercial and cultural links with the Low Countries and, as such, represented an element of Small Hythe's otherness from Tenterden town. Compared to the rest of the parish, piety at Small Hythe was austere, even in the wills of its most wealthy inhabitants such as the Brekynden and Assherynden families, its most striking feature being the almost complete absence of saints' cults from the testamentary preoccupations of the port's inhabitants. This is all the more significant given the general character of Tenterden's religious culture with all its moderation, frugality and increasing disengagement from some of the more traditional elements of pre-Reformation devotional life. Lollardy does not appear to have been particularly strong at Small Hythe and so cannot be singled out as the cause. Continental influences should not be ruled out, nor should the role of evangelical humanist figures like William Roper or powerful families like the Guldefords, but Small Hythe's pared down devotional and pious aesthetic almost seems to have grown out of the landscape in which the chapel of St John the Baptist sat, and was closely related to the commercial and specialised industrial activities of its patron families. It was the pious articulation of a peculiarly distinctive culture and of a proud sense of independence bolstered by economic success.

4

The Social Origins of Parsimonious Piety

Because of their relative lack of engagement with parochial religion, the most religiously frugal will-makers have, so far, largely escaped analysis but, in order to do justice to the heterorogeneity of piety at Tenterden, they are examined here in detail. This chapter represents an innovative attempt to redress the balance within the historiography of late medieval piety and the Reformation which has largely ignored the pieties of those who contributed relatively little to the institutions and collective practices of orthodox religion and yet constituted a significant section of the will-making population.

Parsimonious piety was marked, in particular, by a tradition conspicuous for its lack of explicitly religious acts and propensity to prioritise the demands of family and kin in testamentary giving. Certain families in the middle and especially the bottom band of the pious spectrum made wills predominantly of this character. The nature and tenor of their pious traditions and the possible roots from which they sprang are investigated here through detailed examination of two families: the Castelyns and the Pellonds. Apart from frugality in religious giving, their wills indicate preferences weighted against more traditional orthodox devotions and institutions and, by the sixteenth century, a propensity to patronise the Jesus Mass. They are, therefore, expecially representative of the trajectory of orthodox piety in general at Tenterden and so deserve closer attention.

The characteristics of parsimonious piety

Parsimonious testamentary piety was characterised by unelaborate religious bequests of relatively low monetary value, a narrowness in the range of traditional elements to which the testator gave and, at its most extreme, wills devoid of any explicitly religious provisions whatsoever apart, that is, from those obligatory elements such as the preamble and payment for tithes forgotten. Although all testaments began, almost without exception, with a religious preamble, this employed the formulaic dedication of the testator's soul to almighty God, the Virgin Mary and the holy company of saints and does not, generally, appear to have been considered optional or to admit alteration. The same applies to payments for 'forgotten tithes', although of course the size of these gifts varied greatly and they are considered in some detail below. Other, more voluntary, types of giving are also not classified here as explicitly religious gestures. These include bequests to the poor or for public works that do not employ openly religious language; formulaic and vague requests for the disposal of residue and reversionary bequests, which were only to come into effect in default of inheritance.[1] The incidence of wills lacking non-obligatory religious bequests across the twenty-three selected families is markedly uneven. Not surprisingly, their greatest concentration was among the lowest band of families, eleven in all at a median of just over two in five of their wills. Middle-band families produced twelve but at a lower concentration of two in every seven. Only one was made by a more generously religious family. In contrast, the testamentary traditions of parsimonious families were almost typified by this approach to will-making.

Across all the surviving Tenterden wills a total of fifty-two out of 263, or 20 per cent, lack explicitly religious elements, a similar proportion to Colchester but much higher than in some of the other centres or regions studied.[2] The fifty-two testators represent forty different surnames and a total of ten surnames appear more than once as makers of these wills. The familial concentration and continuity of this type of testamentary strategy can be shown in two ways. Firstly, the ten surname groups or families represent only a quarter of the forty surnames mentioned above, and yet together they made twenty-two, or 42 per cent, of the wills of this type. Secondly, although they only produced under a fifth of all wills (fifty out of 263), they made more than two-fifths of those lacking religious provisions. Although a testamentary strategy which excluded religious concerns might be employed from time to time by individual testators for a variety of reasons, certain families tended to return to such an approach, perhaps out of a common motive and within a shared tradition.

What factors might have given rise to these wills? In many cases, limitations on available resources, especially cash, appear to have played their part. Five testators bequeathed no money at all, and a further nineteen seem to have had access to only enough to make relatively small payments for tithes forgotten. Because religious gifts were more likely than other types of bequests to take the form of cash legacies, they may have been the first elements in testamentary arrangements to be curtailed by financial strictures. None the less, this does not fully explain the spread of sparse wills. For one thing, there are numerous other examples among the Tenterden wills that make sometimes extensive cash bequests, either wholly or in part on the strength of goods, lands or stock to be sold by executors, leased to feoffees or

---

[1] For some thoughts on preambles see p. 13 above. There are only 9 wills which lack explicitly religious provisions and contain reversionary arrangements: 4 for chantries and the rest for such things as gifts to church fabric, the poor or for unspecified distribution.

[2] Of Colchester's wills between 1485 and 1529 24% left nothing for religious or charitable purposes: Higgs, 'Lay piety', 219. In contrast Scarisbrick estimates that only 3–4% of the 2,500 early sixteenth-century wills he examined contain no religious bequests: *Reformation and the English people*, 3, 6. See also Tanner, *Church in Norwich*, 104, which suggests that wills of this type are rare among those surviving for Norwich.

held by heirs. William Stonehouse stipulated that his ploughs, wains and harrows be sold to perform his testament, which included cash bequests for his funeral, month's mind and year's mind, to church fabric, and to family, kin and friends. Thomas Hicks arranged for lands in the neighbouring parish of Rolvenden to be sold for £23 in order to fulfil his extensive bequests. Such arrangements allowed for the conversion of household and family resources into disposable wealth, to be passed outside the family.[3] Others gave items of household goods, stock and sometimes even lands to the parish church or Small Hythe chapel, sometimes in return for priestly intercessions. A particularly popular way of doing this was to bequeath one or two cows to the use or fabric of St Mildred's, or one of the parish fraternities. The making of religious bequests was not always dependent upon the possession of money – there were numerous ways of utilising moveables and realty to fulfil spiritual aspirations.

Twelve testators who did not attend to religious provisions left minimal amounts of cash for forgotten tithes (or none at all) in very short wills. Most were probably less well-off than average, belonging to families which do not appear to have endured in Tenterden, as only one or two wills survive for them. In contrast, ten others devised lands and tenements, bequeathed more substantial amounts of household goods, and occasionally, livestock. These were clearly wealthier individuals, some of whom belonged to enduring Tenterden families. That they made no efforts at all in their wills to fund religious bequests from moveables or realty suggests that such concerns were not as important to them as they were to many of their fellow parishioners.

Twenty-eight of the fifty-two testators who did not attend to religious provisions, nevertheless, made cash bequests. In nine cases these amounted to only 10s. or less, but twelve left at least £6 6s. 8d. with most belonging to families which produced at least three wills. For example, in 1466 William Blossom left 20d. to the high altar of St Mildred's, 6s. 8d. to each of his godchildren and £12 13s. 4d. to his brother Richard. To Richard's daughter, Thomasina, he bequeathed 40s. on the condition that she remain with William's wife until her marriage. Philip Blossom, in 1471, gave 3s. 4d. for his forgotten tithes, and entrusted the residue of his goods to his wife Roberta. To his sons he devised all his lands and tenements, to be divided equally between them at the age of twenty. After making arrangements for his wife in her old age, he stipulated that his sons give 40s. to each of his five daughters for their dowries. Religious concerns were only to be met in the event of all Philip's daughters dying before marrying or inheriting at the age of twenty. Isak Chapman made a similar will in 1522, leaving 40s. to each of four of his daughters and 10s. to a fifth, as well as lands and tenements to his two sons.[4]

Given that wills were religious as well as legal documents, those which

3   1513, PRC 17/12/227; 1522, 17/15/228.
4   PRC 17/1/218, 17/2/54, 17/19/145.

omit religious concerns altogether are most conspicuous when the testator had access to adequate resources to make, if they so chose, at least some gesture toward the conventions of traditional piety.[5] Clive Burgess, however, takes a more sceptical view, asserting that, 'a meagre will may be indicative more of the fact that the testator died with his wishes and estate well in order and with widow and parish prepared for what was to be done, rather than suggesting lack of funds or apathy toward religion'.[6] Even the most cursory testament, however, was intended to solve problems of inheritance and achieve the desired distribution of the testator's resources. Moreover, it is unlikely that wills which mention moderate or large amounts of cash and property were produced by individuals who went to the trouble to arrange all their religious bequests in advance and waited until close to death to provide for family and kin. As argued in chapter 1, the last will and testament appears to have been more central to the enactment of post-obit piety at Tenterden than it was at Bristol, whence Burgess draws his evidence, although its importance may have varied over time. The continuity of conspicuously sparse wills within certain families, and the fact that other family testators who did attend to religious concerns rarely did so in a generous or elaborate fashion, strongly suggests that they were the product of shared attitudes and traditions passed from one generation to the next, as opposed to a consistent disregard for the will as a vehicle for post-obit piety. In addition, although wills rarely directly reveal anything about lifetime giving, on the whole they do tend to reflect lifetime affiliations and commitments, and collective comparative analysis across the spectrum of familial testamentary piety affords insights into patterns of belief and practice that are suggestive of the relative character of lifetime pieties. One of the criticisms of wills is that they overemphasise the intensity of religious sensibilities due to their concentration on the cult of death, but this was certainly not a characteristic of this type of will-making.

The incidence of wills lacking traditionally orthodox religious bequests was not constant over time. They fell from over a quarter of all those made in the late fifteenth century to just over a tenth by 1520–35, beginning to decline in frequency around 1500 (see table 8).[7] To some extent testamentary piety became more detailed and elaborate. In part, this change was the result of increasing prosperity and social status among those families who tended to parsimony in their testamentary giving.

The Castelyns were one such family. They have left seven wills dating between 1473 and 1532 and representing four generations, beginning with the last will and testament of Robert Castelyn senior, dated 21 September

---

[5] Marsh, 'In the name of God?', passim; Spufford, *Contrasting communities*, 319–43; P. Ariès, *The hour of our death*, London 1981, 188–92. Tanner notes how 'in a few cases the absence or paucity of such bequests is conspicuous': *Church in Norwich*, 116–18.

[6] Burgess, 'Late medieval wills', 21 and passim.

[7] Cf. Dinn, 'Popular religion', 538.

Table 8
Religiously parsimonious wills* at Tenterden, 1449–1535

Date range	All wills	Number (and %) of parsimonious wills[1]
1449–79	41	11 (27%)
1480–99	49	14 (29%)
1500–19	84	16 (19%)
1520–35	89	11 (12%)
1449–1535	263	52 (20%)

* Lacking explicitly religious provisions apart from payments for forgotten tithes and reversionary religious bequests.

Sources: CKS, PRC 16/1–3,17/1–22, 32/2–16; PRO, PCC 11/4 (21 Stokton), 11/5 (25 Godyn), 11/8 (20 Milles), 11/9 (29 Dogett), 11/14 (39 Holgrave), 11/16 (14 Bennett), 11/21 (18 Bodfelde), 11/22 (17 Porche), 11/23 (20 Jankyn), 11/25 (14 Hogen).

1473 (*see* figure 2).[8] The preamble is entirely orthodox and Robert senior left a relatively small sum of 4*d.* for tithes forgotten to the high altar of Tenterden parish church, which in itself does not necessarily reflect low social status or lack of wealth.[9] His occupation and status is hinted at by the mention of 'omnia instrumenta artificioli mei' left to his son Robert. He devised the residue of his estate to his wife Alice, whom he appointed executor. Alice also received his messuage and garden for life, as long as she remained a widow. Otherwise it was to pass to his son Robert, once he was twenty-one, and if he died it was to revert to Robert senior's other two sons Thomas and John, providing they pay 5 marks to their sister, Margaret. With this, his bequests finish.

In 1463 Robert Castelyn senior acted as a witness, along with four other men, to a grant of two acres of land in Tenterden by Thomas Petlesdon esquire, Thomas Carpynter and Thomas Jan junior to Robert Donne.[10] The Petlesdons were an important gentry family in Tenterden, Thomas Petlesden serving as the borough's first bailiff in 1449–50 and again in 1450–1 and 1458–9.[11] Thomas Carpynter served as bailiff three times between 1478 and 1496.[12] The Jans held not insubstantial lands in Tenterden

8 PRC 17/2/347.
9 See pp. 18–19 above. Out of 263 testators 33, or 13%, left 4*d.* or less for forgotten tithes, 13 of these omitting to make any payment.
10 CKS, U410/T21.
11 Hasted, *History of Kent*, vii. 206; Te/C1, fos 13r–16v, 140r.
12 Te/C1, fos 140r–v.

and High Halden and Robert Donne, to whom the grant was made, served as bailiff in 1455–6.[13] Robert Castelyn's name appears last in the list of witnesses to the grant, which includes William Harynden and William Wygge. Harynden was bailiff in 1457–8 and he and Wygge acted in tandem as *rentiers*, recorded as leasing the whole or half of a parcel of property totalling fifteen acres between 1449 and 1450.[14] These glimpses of political and economic activity suggest that Harynden and Wygge belonged to leading middling families in Tenterden; the sort of men of good reputation and sufficient status to witness such a grant. That Robert Castelyn senior acted alongside and on behalf of such leading local figures, suggests that he was of similar social standing.[15] It appears that from at least the 1460s the Castelyns were one of the more established families in Tenterden, and yet their testamentary piety has the appearance of self-conscious frugality, with family being the only preoccupation.

Fourteen years later, in 1487, Robert Castelyn junior made a will which closely adhered to the tenor of testamentary piety followed by his father.[16] An orthodox preamble and payment for tithes forgotten, once again of 4d., is accompanied by bequests to family. Robert junior left his messuage and gardens to his wife Joan, and ensured that Alice, his mother, could remain for life in the house and gardens left to her by her husband. On their deaths all this was to go to his sons (who are most likely to have been Richard and Stephen Castelyn) and 20s. to his daughter Juliana. If Robert's heirs died before his wife, then she was to pay his sister Margaret or her heirs 40s., but if his wife then died his messuages and gardens were to be sold and 5 marks were to go to his sister or her heirs. Only then, if there was any residue, was family wealth to be distributed for his soul, his parents' souls and all the Christian faithful. John Castelyn, one of Robert senior's other sons, made his will in 1507, with an orthodox preamble, and in which he left 2s. 2d. to the high altar of St Mildred's for forgotten tithes, further confirmation of the family's wealth and status.[17] John had rented a shop on the north side of Tenterden High Street from which he had probably traded and his heirs took up the lease until the 1530s. He may also have invested in other spheres: the *John Castelyn*, an armed merchantman, was one of the ships listed in the Teller's rolls as being hired by the crown in 1497.[18] He appears to have had greater access to cash than his father and brother, the majority of which, 66s. 8d., he devoted to his daughter Joan's dowry. He also bequeathed goods to his wife

---

13 Stephen Jan, 1471: PRC 17/2/131; Richard Jan, 1495: PRC 17/6/133; Te/C1, fo. 140r.
14 Te/C1, fo. 140r; BL, Add. Chs, 16319, 56976, 56977, 16322, 16326.
15 C. Dyer, 'The rising of 1381 in Suffolk: its origins and participants', *Proceedings of the Suffolk Institute of Archaeology and History* xxxvi (1985), appendix xi, at p. 285.
16 PRC 17/5/5.
17 PRC 32/9/65. Out of 263, 68 or 26% of Tenterden wills contain payments of 2s or more to high altars.
18 Roberts, 'Tenterden houses', fig. 43 at p. 335; 'Naval accounts of Henry VII', p. xlv.

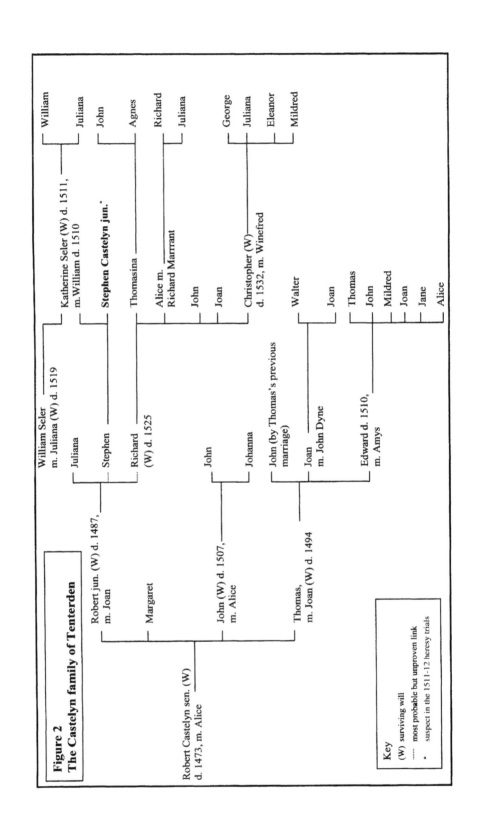

Figure 2
The Castelyn family of Tenterden

William Seler
m. Juliana (W) d. 1519

- William
- Katherine Seler (W) d. 1511, ⎯ Juliana
  m. William d. 1510
- Stephen Castelyn jun.* ⎯⎯ John
                          ⎯ Agnes
- Thomasina ⎯⎯ Richard
           ⎯ Juliana
- Alice m.
  Richard Marrrant
- John
- Joan
- Christopher (W) ⎯⎯ George
  d. 1532, m. Winefred ⎯ Juliana
                       ⎯ Eleanor
                       ⎯ Mildred
- Walter
- Joan
- Thomas
- John
- Mildred
- Joan
- Jane
- Alice

Juliana

Stephen

Richard
(W) d. 1525

Margaret

Robert jun. (W) d. 1487,
m. Joan

John (W) d. 1507,
m. Alice

John

Johanna

Thomas,
m. Joan (W) d. 1494

John (by Thomas's previous
marriage)

Joan
m. John Dyne

Edward d. 1510,
m. Amys

Robert Castelyn sen. (W)
d. 1473, m. Alice

Key

(W)   surviving will
......   most probable but unproven link
*   suspect in the 1511-12 heresy trials

Alice and son John. In his last will, John made provision – but only in the event of his daughter not marrying – for 20s. to go toward repairs of Tenterden parish church, 20s. to be left to Thomas Weldysh and the residue to poor maidens and for other works of charity. Despite the greater presence of cash in his will, like his father and brother, John concentrated almost wholly upon providing for his immediate family.

The will of Joan Castelyn, widow of Thomas Castelyn, the third of Robert senior's sons, written in 1494, shares the character of the other Castelyn wills, but reflects Joan's own particular social network and sense of obligation and responsibility.[19] She left 4d. in tithes forgotten and gave 4d. to repairs of the parish church – the first definite religious gift in the surviving Castelyn wills. The rest of her testament lists bequests of household goods to a total of eighteen individuals. Eleven of these gifts were to close relatives: her daughter and her daughter's family, grandchildren, a nephew's children (Stephen Castelyn senior's daughters) and 'filio mariti mei'. She also made bequests to the daughters of Robert Eastlyng, and six gifts to women. Joan included a wider circle of people within the compass of her giving than her father-in-law or brothers-in-law, mediating her family piety through a particular set of social relationships, in part to do with her being a woman, a mother and a widow.[20]

Katherine Castelyn, on the other hand, who died in 1511, departed markedly from family tradition in her will-making. The widow of William, great-grandson of Robert Castelyn senior who died late in 1510, she appears to have lived only to her late twenties or early thirties as two children are mentioned in Katherine's testament and her parents, William and Juliana Seler of the neighbouring parish of Ebony, were beneficiaries, her father an executor and her mother a witness. Parental influence and the transmission of family piety provides the best explanation for the divergence of Katherine's testamentary piety from the pattern of earlier Castelyn wills. She left 2d. to each of the lights of the rood, the Blessed Virgin Mary, St Mildred and St Katherine. In 1519 her mother Juliana made a much more impressively orthodox testament in which she gave to a total of seven lights, three of which were of the rood, St Mary and St Katherine. Katherine's testamentary piety was closer to her mother's than to her Castelyn kinsfolk's, perhaps because of a combination of her widowhood and early death.[21] Her testament also provides further hints of Castelyn economic activity. Katherine left her husband's brother Stephen Castelyn, 'half of my husband's remaining steel and a hundred weight of iron'. Stephen may have practised the same craft as his brother, being himself described as 'cutler' in the 1511 heresy trials, in

[19] PRC 17/6/96.
[20] Cullum, 'And hir name was charite', 185.
[21] PRC 17/11/183, 3/3/77, 16/1/100; Marsh, 'In the name of God?', 230–3; Duffy, Altars, 315–23; Spufford, Contrasting communities, 319–43.

which he was involved as a suspect.[22] This type of craft activity is further evidence of the Castelyns' middle-to-upper social status.[23]

The 1520s and 1530s saw what appears to have been the ongoing consolidation of Castelyn wealth and influence, together with something of a shift in testamentary piety. Katherine's uncle, Richard Castelyn, died in 1525, probably in his early fifties. Richard left 3s. 4d. in tithes forgotten, followed by a gift of 8d. every quarter for three years after his death to the Jesus Mass. He apportioned 20s. to his funeral, 20s. to his month's mind, and arranged for a yearly obit for seven years at 6s. 8d. a year. He left 4d. to each of his godchildren, and 6s. 8d. to each of four of his grandchildren. He held lands and tenements in Tenterden and Rolvenden, most of which were situated in a more or less consolidated bloc further augmented by his son and grandson. Compared to earlier family wills, Richard's is conspicuous for its numerous cash bequests, and orthodox religious arrangements.[24] Richard's son Christopher Castelyn, who acted as his father's executor, died only seven years later in 1532. In terms of religious bequests, his will closely resembles his father's. He left 2s. in tithes forgotten, 6s. 8d. in wax to the light before the sacrament in St Mildred's, 4d. every quarter for six years to the Jesus Mass, 26s. 8d. divided equally between his funeral and month's mind and 10s. to his year's mind. His wealth is attested to not only by these bequests but, in addition, by a dowry of £10 for his daughter Juliana. In his last will he made an arrangement for 6s. 8d. a year to be paid for 'masses and diriges' at his obit in St Mildred's for seven years. As well as cash gifts, he bequeathed portions of his estate to his wife, son, two other daughters and three individuals who were possibly kinsmen.[25] Like the earlier Castelyn wills, a strong continuity between the generations is evinced in Richard and Christopher's testamentary strategies. Both gave 8s. to the Jesus Mass, and both left similar amounts for obsequies, including an exactly duplicated arrangement for a seven-year obit. Christopher was executor of his father's will, and so may have been carrying out his father's wishes by including the obit in his own, or alternatively he was following family tradition by renewing an endowment which, since it was seven years after Richard's death, would only just have lapsed, the latter possibility being a common phenomenon of late medieval wills.[26]

The wills of Richard and Christopher represent something of a departure from earlier family tradition. Significantly, their religious arrangements were focused on the Jesus Mass, the sacrament of the altar, the funeral and subsequent commemorations, and so were particularly representative of the major trends in parochial piety by the 1520s, namely growing Christocentricism

[22] LPL, Reg. Warham, i, fos 161v–162r, 168r, and see also pp. 178–9 below.
[23] Zell, Industry in the countryside, 132–4, 138; McIntosh, Community transformed, 130, 167.
[24] PRC 17/16/293; Roberts, Tenterden, 73–4.
[25] PRC 17/21/58.
[26] Burgess, 'By quick and by dead', 837–58.

and concentration on funerary and commemorative ritual. Their engagement with these developments was probably partly the result of the
Castelyns' increasing status and wealth. Richard's standing is illustrated by
his involvement in the making of other families' wills, as a witness or executor, on five recorded occasions between 1498 and 1519.[27] He served as one
of the two or four named *parochiani* in Tenterden in 1505, 1506 and 1515 and
was listed among the wealthier townsfolk in taxation returns.[28] Christopher
may have surpassed his father in prestige and status, serving as churchwarden
for two consecutive years in 1521 and 1522 and acting as feoffee to wills in
1513, 1518 and 1524.[29] His son, George Castelyn, lived in considerable prosperity until 1592, the goods in his inventory being valued at £184 7s. 8d.,
while Christopher's daughter Mildred married Peter Shorte, tying the
Castelyns to one of Tenterden's wealthiest yeoman families.[30]

It would be a mistake, however, to over-emphasise the apparent rise in
fortune of Richard and Christopher. To begin with, in the late fifteenth and
early sixteenth centuries, only a minority of richer families were likely to
succeed in one parish for over four generations as the Castelyns did. Richard
and Christopher's wealth probably owed much to the economic achievements of their forebears. Moreover, their apparent rise in prosperity and
status should be seen in the context of industrial and agricultural developments which took place across the Kentish Weald from the end of the
fifteenth century and benefited Tenterden as a whole.[31] In relative terms,
when compared to their contemporaries, Richard and Christopher may have
been no wealthier than Robert Castelyn senior. Nevertheless, the growing
diversification of Castelyn economic interests which could be legitimately
transformed into symbolic gifts, and the family's developing role within the
institutions of parish, town and region, appear to have brought a change in
testamentary practice. This accords with what is known about lay piety in
larger urban centres in this period. That is, the religion of leading townsfolk
was of a peculiarly civic character; they were expected and aspired to set a
good pious example in their actions and devotions, and the higher their
social and political aspirations, the more obvious was their piety.[32] This said,
at Tenterden, leading families like the Castelyns were more conspicuous for
their reserved pious expression than for traditionally orthodox generosity,
and as their testamentary piety became more elaborate they displayed adher-

---

[27] PRC 17/8/41, 17/7/250, 17/10/19, 17/12/312, 17/15/64.
[28] CCA, Z.3.2, 1501–8, 2nd section, fos 4v, 25v; Z.3.3, 1514–16, fo. 51v; Brown, *Popular piety*, 78; PRC 17/16/293; PRO, E 179, 231/228.
[29] CCA, Z.3.4, 1520–3, fos 20r, 68r. Service as churchwarden usually indicates that an individual fell within 'broad middling status': Kümin, *Shaping of a community*, 37–40; Carlson, 'Office of churchwarden', 193–9; PRC 17/12/312, 32/12/174, 17/16/269.
[30] Roberts, 'Tenterden houses', 169–70, 205, 217, 248–51.
[31] Clark, *English provincial society*, 7–8, 14; Zell, *Industry in the countryside*, 147–50.
[32] Higgs, 'Lay piety', 266–74, esp. p. 273, and Phythian-Adams, *Desolation of a city*, 138.

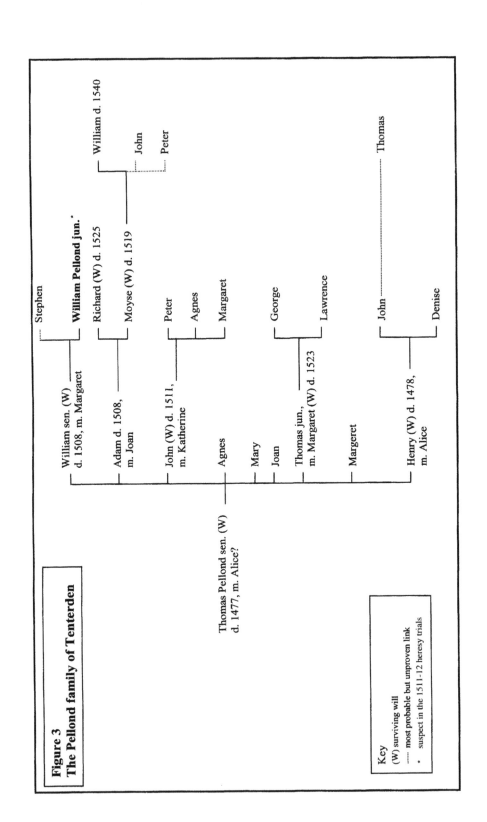

Figure 3
The Pellond family of Tenterden

Key
(W) surviving will
------ most probable but unproven link
* suspect in the 1511-12 heresy trials

ence to the recently established Jesus Mass and increasingly popular forms of commemoration but made no arrangements for chantries and, apart from one exception, showed no concern for the cult of saints.

In terms of their parsimony and the way they developed over time, the Pellond family's testamentary practices were very similar. The Pellonds were established landholders in and around Tenterden from the late fourteenth century, were engaged in brewing by the 1470s, were involved in tailoring or drapery by the sixteenth century and, like many other families, had a hand in the waterborne trade of Wealden goods.[33] They were perhaps of higher status and older pedigree in Tenterden than the Castelyns.[34] By the early 1530s the Pellonds were among the freemen of Tenterden and Adam Pellond served as the Common Mace Bearer of the Corporation from 1538 to 1542, as well as acting as attorney to parties in numerous common recoveries of lands and tenements in these years.[35]

Thomas Pellond senior's will of 1477 is dominated by at least five sons, four daughters and ten or more grandchildren (*see* figure 3). Thomas left a total of 20s., various household and industrial goods to family and kin, as well as 5 marks in cash and moveables to his daughter Margaret's dowry; 3s. 4d. to each of his executors who were his sons John and Adam; and 4d. to each of his godchildren. In addition, he devised lands to his wife and one of his sons, and six acres to another son, from which his bequests were to be funded. He paid 12d. in tithes forgotten and made no bequests for masses or prayers. In his last will however, he made a detailed arrangement for the paving of a footway in the parish.[36] Thomas's son, William Pellond senior, also made a will which lacked explicitly religious bequests. A brief testament which, like Thomas's, left 12d. for forgotten tithes, bequeathed the residue of his estate to his wife Margaret to dispose for the health of his soul. How this was to be done is not specified.

The other early Pellond wills contain more in the way of religious provisions, but retain a reserved tone. Henry Pellond, another of Thomas senior's sons, made his in 1478, in which he distributed his estate to his wife and two children. He also stipulated that a parcel of wood be sold to pay for his funeral, month's mind and anniversary 'for my soule and all cristens'. Only if his son failed to inherit were additional sums to be employed to procure further masses, to fund a gift to the parish church and in 'almesse giving'.

---

[33] 1477, PRC 17/3/156, 17/3/217, 17/14/47, 17/9/70; Roberts, *Tenterden*, 97; CKS, U55/T414, U36/T1454, U442/T99, U410/T21; BL, Add. Ch. 56982; MS Add. 48022, fos 26r, 27r, 34r; 'Naval accounts of Henry VII', 313; Roberts, 'Tenterden houses', 349, appendix b.

[34] PRO, E 179, 230/182.

[35] *L&P* iv. 459; Te/C1, fos 116r, 141r; PRC 3/8/47; Te/S1, fos 1r, 2r–v, 3r, 21v, 23r, 27r, 28r, 32r, 39r, 42v, 43v–r.

[36] PRC 17/3/156.

John Pellond, the third of Thomas senior's sons for whom there is a will, was a little more attentive to religious concerns. He left 40*d*. for repairs to St Mildred's as well as 16*d*. towards the purchase of a new pair of organs, possibly in preparation for the establishment of the Jesus Mass. He apportioned 13*s*. 4*d*. to his funeral, 16*s*. 8*d*. to his month's mind and 6*s*. 8*d*. to his anniversary; gave 10*s*. for 'an honest prest to syng for my soule by the space of a month' and 6*s*. 8*d*. to the 'emendyng of the foote way betwix Tenterden and Smalhith'. John Pellond's not insubstantial wealth is attested to by dowries of 33*s*. 4*d*. for his daughters and £20 to buy lands which would pass to his son at the age of twenty.[37]

As the sixteenth century wore on, in a similar fashion to the Castelyns, the Pellonds became more unsparing in their testamentary piety. In 1519 and 1525, respectively, the brothers Moyse and Richard Pellond made wills of matching character, which in terms of their place in the tenor of Pellond family piety, are best compared to those of Richard and Christopher Castelyn. Both left only 12*d*. for 'forgotten tithes' but Moyse Pellond's religious provisions comprised a gift of 6*s*. 8*d*. to the chapel of St John the Baptist at Small Hythe; 13*s*. 4*d*. to be distributed to priests, clerks and poor people, and for a drinking for the health of his soul on his burial day; 6*s*. 8*d*. at his month's mind and, unique among the Tenterden wills for its position beneath the witness list at the end of the text, a bequest of 12*d*. to the maintenance of the Jesus Mass within the parish church. Among a series of bequests of cloth to a number of individuals, is a gift of a portion of russet 'to one power mayden of Tenterden called Iden'. Until all his children reached the age of twenty, Moyse, who appears to have died a widower, left his lands under the charge of Stephen Aace of Wittersham, one of his executors.[38]

Richard Pellond began his testament where, six years earlier, his brother's had left off by giving 20*d*. a year for sixteen years to the Jesus Mass. For the same length of time he willed that 40*d*. be given to poor people in the parish every Good Friday, and stipulated that a yearly obit be conducted for his soul in St Mildred's within 'the twelve days', at 3*s*. 4*d*. a year. These arrangements were to be funded by the farm from lands in Wittersham and Heronden for sixteen years. To each of his burial and month's mind Richard apportioned 20*s*. to priests, clerks and in meat and drink, and 10*s*. to poor people and, at his anniversary, 20*s*. were to be given to priests, clerks and poor folk. He also left 20*s*. to the mending of each of a footway and a 'streetway' between Tenterden and Small Hythe. Lastly, a house and garden at Eastgate was to be sold, 10 marks of the proceeds to be used to pay for a year's temporary chantry in St Mildred's and the residue to be distributed to poor people. Richard Pellond does not appear to have been married or to have had any children but left at least £1 17*s*. 4*d*. in seven separate bequests to kin, including

---

37 1508, PRC 17/11/36, 17/3/217, 32/10/154.
38 PRC 17/14/47.

godchildren.[39] His will throws some light on the wealth of the Pellond family by the 1520s which, like other leading families, was growing at this time.[40] The arrangements that were to be funded by lands at farm indicate the growing complexity of a moral and religious economy within which a wider range of strategies was being employed for the conversion of resources into pious gestures. Elsewhere in England, at this time, the transmission of such endowments between family members seems to have involved an awareness of the symbolic value of specific parcels of property.[41] These later Pellond wills share an unusual emphasis upon charity and public works, the latter also being found in two of the earlier family wills. Like the Castleyns they also tended to provide for commemorative arrangements rather than to found chantries. The other continuity within Pellond testamentary piety by the second and third decades of the sixteenth century, shared by the later Castelyn wills, was patronage of the Jesus Mass coupled with an absence of gifts to saints' cults. These socially mobile and increasingly important families were particularly representative of the general shift in orthodoxy, by the 1520s, towards an indigenous and possibly evangelically-inspired orthodox reformism. Their lack of commitment to more traditionalist orthodox devotions and institutions in the late fifteenth century, appears to have given them a propensity to adopt new developments within piety, namely, Christocentricism, more fashionable but at the same time less controversial forms of intercession and commemoration, and focused charitable and civic giving.

The social origins of parsimonious piety

The evidence assembled in chapter 2 cumulatively and consistently points to a link between wealth and social status, and the character of family piety. Religiously frugal families were not as well-off, as involved in town and parochial government, or held in the same esteem as their more religiously moderate or lavish contemporaries. However, this was not simply to do with differences in the availability of resources in the process of will-making. In addition, there appears to have been no straightforward causal link between status and piety further up the religious spectrum. This is shown by those very wealthy and influential families who were not nearly as open-handed as other high-status families. The most religiously generous did tend to be the most consistently wealthy, but there were equally wealthy and high status families in the centre of the spectrum, together with others of lower standing. Just as apparent is the connection between upward social mobility and moderate, parsimonious and reformist piety. Most of the selected families that

---

[39] PRC 17/16/244.
[40] Both Moyse and Richard Pellond left only 12d. for their tithes forgotten.
[41] Burgess, 'By quick and by dead', 841–5.

succeeded in economic and social life over the period tended to be reserved in their testamentary religious giving. The predominant tenor to the piety of Tenterden's most upwardly mobile families by the 1530s was towards moderation and reformism. There were some exceptions to this rule, most obviously the Foules and Coupers, which stand as a reminder that increasing family resources and political responsibility could lead to greater generosity in piety that remained traditionalist. There was, then, no crude economic or social determinism in the relationship between pious sensibilities and wealth and status. Moderate or parsimonious families, which rose to the top of the urban hierarchy by the early sixteenth century, symbolised their success in less traditionally orthodox ways than some of the leading families of the late fifteenth. Moderation or economy in will-making formed part of an ethic shaped by the imperatives of material and social advancement for families like the Brekyndens, Pierses, Pellonds and Castelyns. Their social mobility and entry into urban government were matched and supported by strategies which involved resources being fed back into the family and household, rather than being expended in traditionally orthodox giving. I will return to the apparent connection between social mobility and moderate or parsimonious piety at the end of this chapter.

The relatively large numbers of wills which have survived for the selected families provide a limited insight into their kinship links. A total of eleven affinal (marital) connections between the twenty-three selected families can be identified. However, on the whole, only endogamous marriage within Tenterden is examined here, and around fifty per cent of individuals probably married outside the parish.[42] For this reason, differences in the density of affinal kinship networks between selected families are, in part, due to variations in the resort to exogamous marriage. On the whole, top-band families were less interconnected by kinship with other leading Tenterden lineages than their more religiously moderate fellows. They either had comparatively more links with families outside the parish, or tended to marry into families that had recently arrived in Tenterden, and so do not have such a presence in the records. Both of these possibilities are reinforced once all references to affinal links with the twenty-three families are examined. These include connections with families not selected for special study here. Top-band families had a total of fourteen affinal links, of which only about a fifth were with other selected families. Middle-band families had fourteen, half of which were with other families among the twenty-three, and bottom-band families had sixteen, of which six were within the selected group. With the exception of the Foules, the most religiously generous families were not inter-marrying with other leading Tenterden families by the late fifteenth and early sixteenth centuries to the same extent as their contemporaries.

Families which devoted the largest proportion of their disposable wealth at

42 O'Hara, *Courtship and constraint*, 122–57.

death to traditional religious concerns, and also appear to have been the most consistently wealthy, with one or two exceptions, were by no means at the centre of the emerging group of leading lineages by the early sixteenth century. They were more isolated in terms of kinship within the parish, were becoming less involved in municipal and parochial government, less active in witnessing, executing and overseeing their neighbours' wills and not so involved in the commercial land market as families which were more moderate in their testamentary strategies. They do not seem to have shared the ethos which characterised wills made by families like the Brekyndens, Smyths, Pierses, Pellonds and Castelyns, their piety being rather different from that which underlay the social and cultural identity of the town's ruling group by the 1520s or, for that matter, those most frugal families which, due to their comparatively lower status, had little share in local power structures. It is probable that this was because they were, to some extent, socially distinct. That is, short of qualifying for gentry status (and indeed at least one of these families was styling itself in this mould by the end of the period), they were among the most substantial landholders among will-makers; what have been termed very large farmers or more substantial yeomen. House-holders within this social group have been found to have been less active in parish or town affairs in the sixteenth and seventeenth centuries in English communities than their more middling counterparts. In the Liberty of Havering in the late sixteenth century, for example, individuals who can be identified as landholders and rural yeomen made far fewer testamentary bequests to kin beyond the immediate family and to friends than the urban yeomen, those individuals who arose out of the commercial world of the 1520s and 1530s, acted as middlemen in local markets and dominated politi-cally.[43]

Tenterden's religiously moderate families have all the appearance of middling-to-upper status householders described elsewhere, who formed the core of leading burgesses, were relatively closely interrelated by marriage and who relied upon mutual assistance to sustain their position in what were, generally, increasingly polarised local societies by the mid-sixteenth century. As suggested in chapter 1, Tenterden may have been becoming more socially divided than most small towns by the 1530s.[44] Finding it more difficult to hold their own, were the religiously frugal families, most of whom do not appear to have had much of a say in urban or parochial affairs, and who prob-ably spanned the ranks from middling husbandmen, lesser tradesmen and craftsmen to more prosperous farmer-tradesmen.[45] The higher density of affinal kinship among moderate and parsimonious families was, in part, a strategy of both social climbing and survival, an attempt to move up in the

[43] Wrightson and Levine, *Poverty and piety*, 34, 103–9; McIntosh, *Community transformed*, 167, 86, 139–41.
[44] Ibid. 86, 107–20, 139–41, 167; Wrightson and Levine, *Poverty and piety*, 34, 103–9.
[45] Ibid. 34, 103–9; McIntosh, *Community transformed*, 120, 167.

scheme of things or to prevent downward mobility.[46] It points, also, to the possible influence of like-minded piety upon the formation of kinship bonds, and of kinship upon piety, which runs against received opinion on the relationship between religious affiliation and kinship. Nonconformists in seventeenth-century Terling, for example, do not appear to have formed their own distinct kinship group and recusants in the sixteenth, seventeenth and eighteenth centuries in the diocese of York formed bonds of kinship with those both inside and outside Catholic networks.[47] The evidence is not conclusive on this point but it remains a question worthy of further study.

The occupational profiles and comparative wealth and status of these families invite some tentative suggestions concerning the roots of heterogeneity in orthodoxy at Tenterden. They suggest that identified differences in piety may have been due, at least in part, to social differentiations between craftsmen and tradesmen who inhabited the upper and middling social bands, and larger farmers who tended to form an established subgentry. The fluidity of such social groups and the porosity of their boundaries is demonstrated, however, by the fact that by the late sixteenth century 'manufacturers – of cloth, leather and metalwares – were at the top of the hierarchy of wealth' alongside 'wealthier farmers and landowners'.[48] It is suggested, therefore, that parsimonious piety was forged partly, but certainly not in any rigidly deterministic way, from the efforts of middling individuals and families to consolidate and expand their fortunes in a time of increasing social stratification. A family's occupational profile was important in this regard because upward social mobility of craftsmen and tradesmen was fuelled by intensive capital investment, particularly in the more industrial pursuits. With estates composed of agricultural, industrial and commercial resources pooled together in family networks, increasing capital investment in specialised activities like butchery, tanning, fulling, metal-working and trades such as tailoring and drapery demanded that a larger share of an individual's resources be redistributed within the family at various points in the life-cycle. This had a marked influence on inheritance practices, with a propensity to expend available funds on family and kin, and a subsequently diminished attention to religious bequests in last wills and testaments.[49] This may also

46 R. M. Smith, 'Kin and neighbours in a thirteenth century Suffolk community', *Journal of Family History* iv (1979), 219–56.
47 Lutton, 'Godparenthood, kinship, and piety', 230–4; Wrightson and Levine, *Poverty and piety*, 169–70; Sheils, 'Catholics and their neighbours', passim, and 'Household, age and gender among Jacobean Yorkshire recusants', in M. B. Rowlands (ed.), *English Catholics of parish and town, 1558–1778*, London 1999, 137–9.
48 Zell, *Industry in the countryside*, ch. v at p. 138; McIntosh, *Autonomy and community*, 152–6, 233, and *Community transformed*, 130, 167, 174; Cornwall, 'English country towns', 63.
49 McIntosh, *Autonomy and community*, 228–9, 235; Searle, *Lordship and community*,

have been an inevitable feature of the wills of large and successful established families whose kinship links, and the moral and social obligations they entailed, multiplied as the population began to grow at the end of the fifteenth century. The tendency to keep resources within the family reversed the detrimental effects of late medieval piety on long-term familial social mobility and estate-building as described by Higgs writing on Colchester:

> Economically, piety spread money around the community; rather than keeping it within the family, the pious gave money to the church, to the poor, and to the community as a whole. Furthermore, the wide distribution of money had political implications for the community, since each generation in Colchester had to prove itself. Very few families in Colchester were wealthy enough to perform pious works and still leave enough money for their sons to become leaders without having to work for it themselves. Political power was therefore less concentrated and was dispersed among a larger number of families. The diffusion of the family's money meant, too, that each generation had to develop its own confidence and self-reliance; each generation had to remain viable, or the family quickly declined.[50]

It is also possible that the desire to further family fortunes may have manifested itself in a switch from legacies in kind to those in cash, as occurred elsewhere in the sixteenth century; a development which may have especially encroached upon religious giving.[51] In one sense, parsimonious and moderate pieties were less ceremonial and communal than the sensibilities of more generous will-makers, perhaps because the inducements of traditional religious giving were perceived as insufficient to warrant investment compared to the benefits of individual and familial profit and advancement.[52]

Religiously moderate and sparing families, in general, appear to have lived and operated in Tenterden town itself, in its more industrial suburbs of Boresisle and East Gate or in Small Hythe. Probably because they were predominantly farmers, the religiously generous tended to dwell in the more rural and isolated farmsteads in the southern half of the parish among the best pasture and arable. The subtle cultural differences which could result from such settlement patterns have been illustrated in relation to Small Hythe. Suburbs and settlements, boroughs, quarters and even dens could be employed in the creation of identity. Startling in this regard is Robert

365–6, 432–3; Roberts, 'Tenterden houses', 204–8, 229–30, 304–5; Zell, *Industry in the countryside*, ch. vii.

[50] Higgs, 'Lay piety', 273.

[51] Howell, *Land, family and inheritance*, 264–9.

[52] McIntosh, *Autonomy and community*, 176–8; cf. Charles Phythian-Adams, 'Ceremony and the citizen: the communal year at Coventry, 1450–1550', in P. Clark and P. Slack (eds), *Crisis and order in English towns, 1500–1700*, London 1972, 57–85, and Calhoun, 'Community', 105–29.

Bisshopynden's bequest of a penny 'to every child in the parish of Borsile' in 1523 when no such parish actually existed.[53]

Hand-in-hand with these factors went the need for a distinctive piety to match an emerging political identity. The families that had dominated in the late fifteenth century generally attended to traditional religious arrangements and gave more than their counterparts. Those that rose to prominence or sustained their position into the sixteenth, may have sought to express their piety in new ways. Tenterden was, after all, becoming more urbanised by the sixteenth century, and it was in crafts, trade and commerce that some of the largest gains in wealth could be made.[54] With their economic success bringing political advancement, those who followed more urban occupations did engage with the religious life of the parish to a greater extent than their forebears but retained a relatively narrow focus to their testamentary piety. Their religiosity was informed by particular social, ethical and cultural assumptions that meant that they continued to invest as much if not more of their resources in the family and in the welfare of kin, as they did in arrangements for funerals and obits, charitable and civic giving and in the only devotional development of the early sixteenth century to which they were drawn, the Jesus Mass.

---

[53] PRC 17/15/258.
[54] Searle, *Lordship and community*, 432–3.

5

Religious Dissent and Heterodox Pieties

Why Tenterden?

Of all the places in Kent associated with Lollardy, Tenterden is deservedly the most famous. Wycliffite heresy was embedded in the Tenterden area by the 1420s, seems to have disappeared without trace from around 1450, but then re-emerged in the records in 1511 in the activities of a burgeoning network. Lack of evidence makes it very difficult to demonstrate the existence of an unbroken tradition of dissent, but it is very unlikely that its reappearance was accidental. One of the concerns here, therefore, is to chart the geographical, familial and doctrinal continuities and differences between the earlier and later traditions of Lollardy in Tenterden and neighbouring parishes. Examination of how early sixteenth-century Wealden Lollards organised and conducted themselves, and practised and passed on their beliefs, addresses the roles played by family, household and kinship, as well as leading literate figures who transmitted and taught new and controversial ideas. Most of the heretical groups and households across Kent formed a loose network within which Tenterden retained a central role. The place of so-called heretics in local society, the degree to which they were open about their religious views, and involved in the practices of orthodox religion, must all have had great bearing upon the perception and reception of heresy by the more orthodox. That Tenterden was a centre of dissent for so long suggests that sympathy or at least tolerance rather than hostility typified reactions to heresy.

Detailed reconstruction (as far as is possible) of the social and economic profile of earlier and later Lollardy, including involvement in town and parish life and government, is here set against old and new theories as to whether there was a social dimension to late medieval English heresy. In particular, the identification of two individuals who abjured heresies in 1511 and who belonged to the Castelyn and Pellond families investigated in chapter 4, allows for some rare insights into the social background of Lollardy, and the relationship between heresy and heterogeneous orthodox pieties. This paves the way for an assessment of the various explanations for the ongoing appeal and survival of Lollardy in the Weald of Kent and other regions. Some new suggestions are put forward as to why Tenterden remained an increasingly important heretical centre over a number of generations. Lollardy needs to be set in the context of the dramatic social, economic and religious changes that were taking place in Tenterden and its hinterland from the early fifteenth century and which accelerated in the early sixteenth. In addition, local and county gentry helped to create and sustain the right conditions for unorthodoxy, as well as acting as channels for the introduction

149

of new ideas that may have caused some people in Tenterden to be drawn towards Protestantism by the 1520s. Finally, the role of parish clergy in the development of local religious culture is examined.

Early Lollardy

The first signs of the Wycliffite teachers who laid down a local tradition of Lollardy can be dated to 1422 when Thomas Drayton, a Wycliffite from the Chilterns and then Bristol (where he had been associated with the academic heretic William Taylor), became rector of Snave on Romney Marsh, some eight miles from Tenterden. Already a twice-tried Lollard when called before convocation in 1425, the charges that he had approved of heretical books and supported heretics since his last abjuration could not be made to stick. Shortly afterwards he exchanged Snave for the benefice of Herne, north of Canterbury and, in 1428, renounced his Lollardy.[1] The more obvious and better-known heresiarch of Tenterden was William White, priest and probably academic, who wrote one or more Wycliffite texts.[2] Chaplain in Tenterden when caught preaching without a licence in the parish church in July 1422, he admitted teaching in Gillingham and Tenterden against the eucharist, the mendicants and temporal goods of the Church among other points, along lines very similar to Wycliffe, but by no means halted his evangelising efforts in the locality.[3] That is until around the summer of 1425, when action against Drayton may have caused White to move to the diocese of Norwich, where he continued with great success to win converts to Lollardy.[4] Almost three years after White's departure Bartholomew Cornmonger, a Lollard teacher also from the Tenterden area, was apprehended. Cornmonger informed on his accomplices and sparked off Archbishop Chichele's 1428 anti-heresy drive in the south-east of England.[5]

---

[1] Hudson, *Premature Reformation*, 125; M. Aston, 'Lollardy and sedition, 1381–1431', *P&P* xvii (1960), 1–44, repr. in *Lollards and reformers: images and literacy in late medieval religion*, London 1984, 1–47 at p. 30; J. A. F. Thomson, *The later Lollards, 1414–1520*, Oxford 1965, 173–5; J. F. Davis, 'Lollard survival and the textile industry in the south-east of England', in G. J. Cuming (ed.), (SCH iii, 1966), 197; *Register of Henry Chichele*, ed. E. F. Jacob (Canterbury and York Society xlii, xlv–xlvii, 1938–47), iii. 107–9.

[2] McSheffrey, *Gender and heresy*, 17; M. Aston, 'William White's Lollard followers', *Catholic Historical Review* lxviii (1982), 469–97, repr. in *Lollards and reformers*, 71–100; Davis, 'Lollard survival', 197.

[3] Davis, 'Lollard survival', 197; *Fasciculi zizaniorum Magistri Johannis Wyclif cum tritico*, ed. W. W. Shirley (Rolls Series, 1858), 418–20; cf. AM, 662; Thomson, *Later Lollards*, 173.

[4] *Fasciculi zizaniorum*, 420–1; Aston, *Lollards and reformers*, 87.

[5] Aston, *Lollards and reformers*, 29, 78–80; *Reg. Chichele*, iii. 199; iv. 297–301. For references to Cornmonger's activities in the diocese of Norwich see *Heresy trials in the diocese of Norwich, 1428–31*, ed. N. P. Tanner (Camden 4th ser. xx, 1977), index. Foxe misdates Cornmonger's and William Henry/Harry's first encounters with the authorities to 1416:

The archbishop did not move quickly enough to prevent the dispersal of a Wycliffite group that had probably been built up by White. Nineteen of the twenty-three named individuals who were summoned on suspicion of heresy in May 1428 had not been found by 31 July when all, excluding Cornmonger, were excommunicated. Of the twenty men and three women who were named, Cornmonger, William White 'parochial chaplain', Thomas Grenestede 'alleged chaplain', John Waddon and his wife Joan, Thomas and William Everden, Stephen Robyn, William Chyvelyng and John Tame were all from Tenterden. Of the rest, most lived in the immediate vicinity: three individuals were said to come from Woodchurch, there was one from each of Wittersham, Benenden and Stapleherst and three were of Romney. Not named among the initial group, four individuals were apprehended in their parishes on 23 May 1428. Two of these men, namely Henry Esteghe and Peter Attewyde, were from Tenterden, the other two being from nearby High Halden and Rolvenden.[6] From the beginning Lollardy in the Weald of Kent was centred on Tenterden.

Cornmonger's confession pointed to a planned Lollard rising, but there is only the slightest hint of corroborative evidence of anything so ambitious.[7] Nevertheless, the rumour gave Chichele a greater sense of urgency and, after capturing a number of Lollards in the summer of 1428, some of whom were hanged and others imprisoned, he proceeded in the following year to arrest and imprison at least thirty. Even so, some of those first named in 1428 were never found.[8] A few may have gone to ground in Kent, and others in East Anglia, after fleeing there with or after William White.[9] Six or seven of the suspects summoned by Chichele in Kent in 1428, were already, or went on to become, leaders of the East Anglian movement uncovered in Bishop Alnwick's trials of 1428–31, namely William White, John Waddon, John Fowlyn, Thomas and William Everden, Bartholomew Cornmonger and, possibly, John Abraham. It is likely that at least some of them had visited the Norwich diocese before, that Lollardy in East Anglia pre-dated their arrival between 1425 and 1428 and that their teaching added considerable impetus to the heretical conventicles meeting there. Presumably Lollardy in the Weald also benefited from these links.[10] The foundations of early Lollardy in

---

AM, 642–3, 658–65. I would like to thank Margaret Aston for bringing this last point to my attention.

[6] *Reg. Chichele*, iv. 297–301; Thomson, *Later Lollards*, 175; Aston, *Lollards and reformers*, 78–80; AM, 642–3.

[7] Aston, *Lollards and reformers*, 79–80; Thomson, *Later Lollards*, 175; *Heresy trials*, 47.

[8] Thomson, *Later Lollards*, 175; Aston, *Lollards and reformers*, 29; *Reg. Chichele*, i, p. cxxxvii.

[9] At least one individual, who was not among the original 23, William Harry of Tenterden, fled to London: *Reg. Chichele*, i, p. cxxxix; Thomson, *Later Lollards*, 176; Hudson, *Premature Reformation*, 124; Aston, *Lollards and reformers*, 79.

[10] *Heresy trials*, 29–30, 45, 152; Aston, *Lollards and reformers*, 81, 86–7; Thomson, *Later Lollards*, 121–2, 175–6; Hudson, *Premature Reformation*, 121, 139–40.

Tenterden were, it seems, reasonably solid. White was both extremely active and successful until his capture, being one of two men cited most often in the Norwich trials as a teacher of heresy; many of the suspects who mentioned him also named Thomas and William Everden, Fowlyn and Cornmonger as teachers;[11] on a number of occasions heretical books are mentioned in relation to White and some of these other men; most, if not all of them, were probably literate, a possibility which applies also to the 'alleged chaplain' Thomas Grenestede;[12] and William Everden and John Fowlyn were among those who took part in the infamous 'Lollard mass' allegedly conducted by White at Bergh Apton in April 1428. The fact that they were sought a month later in Kent, not only underlines the possibility of active links between the two heretical groups, but that some of those who had fled Kent may have returned there once things had calmed down, to build on their earlier work.[13]

The heretical beliefs attributed to and allegedly taught by White and his Kentish accomplices in East Anglia, albeit stereotyped and filtered by the questions put to suspects, should indicate the general character of Lollard ideas disseminated in Tenterden and its environs.[14] Views about the sacraments were the most important and most generally held. Denial of transubstantiation, rejection of prayers to saints, veneration of images and pilgrimage all featured strongly. Other important beliefs concerned the rejection of fasting,[15] observance of Sundays and feast-days and payment of tithes, offerings and mortuary fees. Underpinning all of these ideas was a strong element of anticlericalism and a desire for reform of the clergy. Most of these opinions can be traced to Wycliffe.[16]

Whilst there is no evidence that Kent played any part in the Lollard rising of 1431, prosecutions of suspected heretics in the Tenterden area continued after 1428. John and Thomas Glover of Wittersham abjured erroneous opinions in 1431 and had been present at the reading of heretical books. Just over the county border at Salehurst, John Boreham was accused in 1438 of teaching heresies in the parish church for twenty years. Although he denied all Wycliffite charges and some of the accusations against him concerned magic, he admitted to owning Wycliffite books, including four vernacular Gospels.[17] In the same year, heretical ideas appear to have played some part

---

11 McSheffrey, *Gender and heresy*, 78. See, for example, *Heresy trials*, 71, 73, 81, 85–6, 93–6, 138–42, 146–8, 164–6, 175–80, 209.

12 *Heresy trials*, 29, 30, 39, 41, 47–8, 60; *Reg. Chichele*, iv. 297.

13 *Fasciculi zizaniorum*, 423–4; *Heresy trials*, 33 n.14; Aston, *Lollards and reformers*, 81, 86–7.

14 *Heresy trials*, 10–22; A. Hudson, 'The examination of Lollards', *BIHR* xlvi (1973), 145–59; Thomson, *Later Lollards*, 239.

15 Objection to fasting, which is not found in Wyclif, may have originated with William White: Aston, *Lollards and reformers*, 93; McSheffrey, *Gender and heresy*, 220 n. 40.

16 *Heresy trials*, 10–22.

17 Thomson, *Later Lollards*, 177, 176, 179–80.

in a revolt at Tenterden. A royal writ of 5 June, found in the register of Abbot Curteys of Bury St Edmunds, addresses an uprising of 'mysgoverned men' especially of Kent, 'aswel lollardes as other robbers and pillers of oure peple' led by Sir Nicholas Conway, knight. A commission of 'oyer and terminer' of 1 June refers to 'Lollardies and insurrections, rebellions and felonies', and one continuation of the *Brut* records that five men 'of the cuntre of Tynderden' were 'founden and taken for heresyes and destroyers of the Kinges peple' and hanged, drawn and quartered at Maidstone on 13 June.[18] A number of others were imprisoned in London on suspicion of heresy and treason, including Thomas Denys, John Pette, John Elnoth, William Brewer and Thomas Harry 'laborer' of Tenterden; Thomas Harry, of High Halden; another three men from High Halden, one from Frittenden and four from Biddenden. By November they had been released to attend the Kent sessions and the rising appears to have been crushed.[19] Even so, sometime shortly before May 1440, Alan Elys of Tenterden had been executed for treason, his head placed on a pike in the town and quarters displayed at Cranbrook and Appledore. Sir Nicholas Conway was more fortunate, receiving a grant of pardon in May of the same year.[20]

In 1450 a Tenterden woman was accused of holding that offerings should not be made in churches or at saints' shrines and of eating meat at Lent and, in the years immediately following Cade's Rebellion, charges of heresy were raised against some of those involved in the disturbances who lived in Wealden parishes. John Glover of Wittersham, who had abjured in 1431, and Thomas Harry of High Halden, who had been imprisoned in 1438, both received royal pardons in 1450 following their part in the revolt.[21] In the disorders of April 1456 many of those involved came from parishes around Tenterden, and some of them were described as Lollards, but this may only have been a convenient label for anticlerical statements. The last extant piece of direct evidence of investigations into heresy in the Tenterden area before the sixteenth century concerns a man of Wittersham, summoned in 1455 to give account for alleged errors.[22] Over twenty-five years after William White and his disciples were scattered by Chichele, Lollardy was by no means extinguished in the Tenterden area. Heresy appears to have gone hand in hand with rebellion in these early years, even after the failure of the

---

[18] J. A. F. Thomson, 'A Lollard rising in Kent: 1431 or 1438?', *BIHR* xxxvii (1964), 100–2; *The Brut*, ed. F. W. Brie (EETS, 1906–8), ii. 472.

[19] Thomson, *Later Lollards*, 178; CCR, Hen VI, iii. 1435–41, 117–18.

[20] CCR, Hen. VI, iii. 1435–41, 313; CPR, Hen. VI, 1436–41, 398.

[21] I. M. W. Harvey, *Jack Cade's rebellion of 1450*, Oxford 1991, 30.

[22] Thomson, *Later Lollards*, 180–2. Elsewhere in the county, particularly around Maidstone, convictions of heresy began to re-emerge in the 1490s, and Foxe records that in 1498 a priest was burned for heretical beliefs which he only recanted after persuasion from the king. His execution suggests he was a relapsed heretic: AM, 731; Hudson, *Premature Reformation*, 157, 168; Thomson, *Later Lollards*, 184.

1431 revolt, perhaps precisely because it had not involved Kent and probably, to some extent, because Lollardy was seen as the natural accompaniment of the unrest which came to a head in the county under Cade.[23]

Later Lollardy

Not until the investigations into heresy led by Archbishop William Warham from 28 April 1511 until 28 June 1512 is it possible to gain any further insights into heretical beliefs and activities in the Weald of Kent.[24] The records of Warham's visitation to the deanery of Charing on 26 September 1511 also provide a handful of references to reported heretical individuals.[25] Fifty-three suspects were involved in the trials, although one or possibly two of these was cleared of any charges or escaped prosecution, and a number were found guilty only of assisting and concealing heretics rather than holding to errors themselves.[26] Another five individuals (two of them being deceased) were presented to the parochial visitations of 1511–12 as suspected or known heretics.[27]

The continuing importance of Tenterden as a centre of heretical activity is emphasised by the fact that twenty-three of these suspects lived either in Tenterden itself or in the adjacent parishes of Benenden, High Halden, Rolvenden and Wittersham (see map 3).[28] The strikingly similar spread across these parishes in 1511 compared to 1428 suggests the likelihood of an unbroken tradition of heresy in the district. Not far away, seven individuals came from Cranbrook. Another group of eight dwelt at Staplehurst, lying on the Cranbrook to Maidstone road on the northern edge of the Weald, about eight miles from Tenterden. About the same distance away, on the route from Tenterden to Canterbury, was a cluster of five suspects: one from Ashford, one from neighbouring Great Chart and three from Godmersham, further up the road to Canterbury. Five suspects were named who had lived, or still did live, in the city itself. Out on a limb, one came from Waldershare near Dover and Deal.[29] Finally, there was an important cluster of heretics living in the

---

[23] Thomson, 'A Lollard rising', 102; Harvey, *Jack Cade's rebellion*, 23–30.

[24] LPL, Reg. Warham, i, fos 159r–167v, 168r–175v. All references to the 1511–12 proceedings are hereafter from the *Kent heresy proceedings*.

[25] *Kentish visitations*, p. xxiv.

[26] James Buckherst, and possibly William Buckherst for whom there is no indication of the outcome of his trial: *Kent heresy proceedings*, 123–4. John Dodde and Joan Bukherst were both found merely to have concealed their spouses' beliefs: ibid. 121–2.

[27] Alice Raynold, Kateryne Cardar and Anges (*sic*) Roche, deceased, all of Tenterden; John Baylis of Rolvenden, who successfully purged himself on 20 April 1512; and John Ive, deceased, of the parish of St George, Canterbury: *Kentish visitations*, 207–11, 72.

[28] Fourteen were from Tenterden.

[29] Simon Piers of Waldershare appears to have had no connection with the other groups, and his belief that Christ was incarnate from the beginning of the world suggests conti-

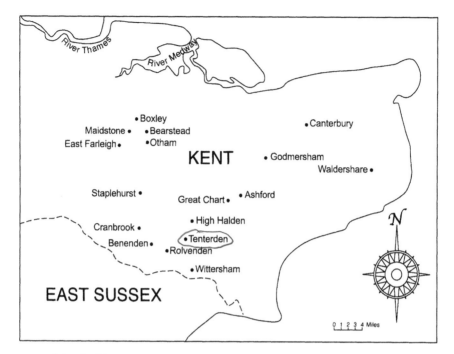

Map 3. Places in Kent associated with heresy in the 1511–12 trials

Maidstone district: two at Maidstone itself, three in Boxley, two at Bearsted and one in East Farleigh. All the indications are that these groups had been established for some considerable time, in some cases from at least as early as the 1470s or 1480s. Robert Hilles of Tenterden, John Grebill senior and Agnes Grebill his wife of Benenden, Agnes Ive of Canterbury, William Olberde senior of Godmersham, Robert Bright of Maidstone and Robert Harryson of Canterbury were all at least sixty years old at the time of the trials, and Thomas Harwode of Rolvenden was seventy-four.[30]

A hint of the deep roots upon which the heretical groups could draw in and around Tenterden is provided by John Grebill senior's deposition against William Carder. Grebill told how 'the said William Cardar aboute xx[ti] yeres past in the house of this deponent at Tenterden werkyng in his lome the said William Carder began first to rede in a booke of ij evangelists and teche this deponent of the said belyves'. Carder may have been employed as Grebill's servant. Grebill went on to relate 'that he thynketh that the said (Carder)

---

nental, rather than Lollard influences. Also possibly isolated from the rest was the Staplehurst group, among whom John Bukhurst shared seemingly Lollard opinions with three other individuals, but also denied the incarnation, that Christ suffered to redeem mankind and the resurrection: *Kent heresy proceedings*, 59–60, 116–17; Thomson, *Later Lollards*, 189–90.

[30] *Kent heresy proceedings*, 10–12, 6, 5, 54, 1, 46.

was borne in Lincolnshyre, and that the said Carder shewed to this deponent that his fader and moder were of the same secte. And he saith that the moder of the said Carder fled from Tenterden about xl yeres past for fere of the saide heresies but whether he knoweth not'.[31] J. A. F. Thomson suggested that this story is evidence of an anti-heresy drive in the late fifteenth century by Arch-bishop Bourchier, and it is an indication of the continuing Lollard presence in the area during these years.[32] Grebill also told how his wife 'Agnes hath holden and belived sithe thesaid terme aboute thende of kyng Edward the iiij[th] dayes till this tyme of deteccion', that is since the early 1480s.[33] John Lynche of Tenterden admitted to holding heretical opinions for more than twenty years, Robert Hilles for more than twelve and his wife Juliana for more than six years.[34] John Browne of Ashford's confession that, twelve years before, he had abjured before Archbishop Morton at Maidstone opinions learnt from John Rich, who was buried at High Halden, resulted in his execu-tion as a relapsed heretic.[35] John Bans of Boxley and Robert Bright of Maidstone admitted to holding heresies for sixteen and fourteen years respec-tively; William Olberde junior of Godmersham and Robert Reignold of Cranbrook confessed to believing in heresies for more than seven years, and William Riche of Benenden admitted that he had met and talked with Carder on numerous occasions over a period of some eight years.[36] The Wealden groups appear to have been part of a tradition of heresy dating from the 1480s or perhaps earlier, which had been gathering momentum by winning new converts from around the turn of the century.

It is probable, but as yet unproved, that some of the Lollards of the late fifteenth century were descended, or at least received their heresies, from the groups of the 1420s and 1430s.[37] There are two possible family continuities. Robert Herward of Rolvenden was arrested in 1428 on suspicion of heresy and Thomas and Joan Harwode and their son Philip, all of Rolvenden, confessed to heretical opinions in 1511. Thomas Harwode was seventy-four in 1511, old enough to make him a direct descendant of Robert Herward's generation, and claims of only recent conversion should probably be treated with suspicion.[38] Secondly, John Bukherst of Frittenden was among those arrested and imprisoned in London after the 1438 Tenterden rising and, in

---

31 Ibid. 11; Hudson, *Premature Reformation*, 136.
32 Thomson, *Later Lollards*, 187. Hudson suggests that the seeming lull in Lollardy in these years is probably due to less documentation, the inability of the church authorities to sustain their investigations and the civil struggles which embroiled the likes of Archbishop Bourchier: *Premature Reformation*, 447–8.
33 *Kent heresy proceedings*, 20.
34 Ibid. 87, 41, 108.
35 Thomson, *Later Lollards*, 184–5.
36 *Kent heresy proceedings*, 100, 95, 66, 12.
37 Ibid. p. xxi; On this question Hudson comments, 'Though reinfestation remains a possi-bility, it seems less likely than survival': *Premature Reformation*, 121.
38 *Reg. Chichele*, iv. 298–9.

1512, a John Bukherst of Stapleherst (only two miles from Frittenden) abjured heretical opinions. His wife, although apparently not a heretic herself, was also examined, as were James and William Bukherst who were probably also of Staplehurst and may have been related to them.[39] It is also clear that a number of fresh converts had been made in the area. Some of these were the children of established heretics, such as Christopher Grebill, who was finally convinced by the teaching of John Ive only three years before the trials, and his brother, John Grebill junior who, not for want of any effort by his parents, claimed to have been won over only a year before his arrest. Others had been brought into heretical circles recently through other means. Stephen Castelyn of Tenterden, twenty-three years of age in 1511, said 'that William Carder of Tenterden taught hym first to belive ayenst the sacrament of thaulter that it was not godds body flesshe and bloode but oonly brede in maydestone aboute a iiij yeres agoo'. Robert Bright, a cordwainer of Maidstone, who was sixty years old, had moved to the district more than twenty years earlier from the Ipswich area, and claimed that he first believed against the sacrament of the altar after being taught by John Bampton in the latter's house in Bearsted, about midsummer 1510. Bright also mentioned a seventeen-year-old youth who had come with William Riche of Benenden to John Bampton's house for a heretical meeting at Christmas 1509. Riche said that the young man came with Bampton, and agreed with all those present against the orthodox doctrine of the eucharist.[40] Whichever account is correct, it adds to the impression that, whether or not any of the early sixteenth-century suspects was directly descended from Lollard families of the early fifteenth, Wycliffite heresy was enjoying something of a small revival.

The heretical beliefs abjured in 1511–12 were less wide-ranging and sophisticated than those purportedly taught by William White and his followers. Compared to Bishop Alnwick's trials, Warham's involved a shorter list of charges and perhaps less freedom for the expression of idiosyncratic personal opinion by suspects. Warham's list of questions may well have been selected from Alnwick's or another similar model, thus narrowing the suspects' answers. Alternatively, the greater simplicity of the later abjurations may reflect a process of distillation over time of a fairly complex spread of heresies into a few key beliefs. It is impossible to answer this question but, broadly speaking, the most generally held views recorded in 1511 accord with the main themes of White's reported teachings in the 1420s.[41] A standard list of ten charges concerning doctrine and further accusations of meeting and talking with others about heresies, and the possession of heretical books, seems to have been put to all the defendants. Each individual abjured her/his own particular errors from among this list of charges, many only confessing to

---

[39] CCR, Henry VI, iii. 1435–41, 117–18; Kent heresy proceedings, 116–22, 123, 124.
[40] Kent heresy proceedings, 20–1, 12, 54, 55.
[41] Hudson, Premature Reformation, 468–72, and 'Examination of Lollards', 145–59.

Table 9
Beliefs abjured by thirty suspects in the 1511–12 Kentish heresy trials

Charges concerning	Number of suspects
Eucharist	29
Pilgrimage	29
Saints' images	29
Confession/absolution/penance	14
Baptism and confirmation	9
Priesthood	8
Matrimony	8
Holy water and bread	8
Extreme unction	7
Prayers to saints	7
All sacraments	2
Indulgence and pardons	2
All teachings of the Church	1
Ownership of suspect books	2

Source: *Kent heresy proceedings*.

as few as three, others admitting to more. In a number of cases 'other damnable opinions' are mentioned but are not recorded.

On the basis of the trials of thirty individuals predominantly from the Tenterden and Maidstone areas, it is clear that beliefs about the sacraments, especially the eucharist, formed a major component of the abjurations (*see* table 9).[42] All but one of the thirty suspects confessed to holding that the sacrament of the altar was not truly the body of Christ but material bread.[43] William Baker of Cranbrook added the traditional Lollard justification 'that god made man but man coude not make gode'.[44] There is nothing to suggest belief in a Wycliffite real presence, but, rather, a sacramentarian view of the eucharist as a memorial only.[45] Depositions against Edward Walker of Maidstone reveal the thinking of a group of heretics from the Maidstone and Tenterden areas who met together on a number of occasions in 1509 and 1510. Justification for a reformed doctrine of the eucharist is found in the conception 'a thing made in mynde and for the remembraunce of criste for

[42] For a full summary of all 46 abjurations which survive see *Kent heresy proceedings*, pp. xii–xv, xxv.
[43] The exception was Joan Colyn of Tenterden: ibid. 38–9.
[44] Ibid. 65.
[45] Hudson, *Premature Reformation*, 282–4.

the people, for crists owne body was in heven and his worde was in erthe'. The biblical inspiration for these ideas, pitched against the teachings of the Church, can be seen in the opinion

> that the sacrament of thaulter was not the body of god flesshe and bloode as preests said it was but it was oonly brede and geven from god, for criste hymself in his owne body gave brede to his disciples and not his owne body, and so do preests in lykewise geve brede that commeth from god in rembraunce of the brede geven by criste in his maundy.[46]

This extreme sacramentarianism was continuous with White's teachings in East Anglia, and most probably the Tenterden region in the early fifteenth century.[47]

A much smaller number of suspects abjured the common Lollard opinion that the sacraments of baptism and confirmation were unnecessary for the profit of a person's soul.[48] According to her son Christopher, Agnes Grebill believed 'that baptisme was nothing worth for a childe putt into the founte was nomore better then if he had be putt into other water, and that confirmacion ys avayn thing and of noon effecte'.[49] Wycliffite opinions about confession, absolution and, in one case, penance, were relatively common among the suspects. The general article was that confession ought not to be made to a priest, but occasionally this was expanded upon. So, Stephen Castelyn of Tenterden abjured the opinion 'that a prest was not sufficient to here a mannys confession and absoile hym of his synnes for suche absolucion of a prest was nothing profitable for a mannys soule, but that confession was to be made oonly to god by mynde'.[50] The Grebills held to a fundamentally Wycliffite view that 'confession made to a preest beying the folowar of peter and beyng pure and clene in life was good & profitable, and no confession was good that was made to a preest not beyng clene life for he had no power to assoyle any manne of his synnes'.[51] A smaller number again considered solemnisation to be an unnecessary part of the marriage contract. At one meeting John Bampton, William Riche, Edward Walker and an unnamed young man read St Matthew's Gospel together in English and 'were wele contentid and pleasid saying that it was pitie that it might not be knowen openly the whiche redyng in the said booke, as they understood it was agenst the sacraments of thaulter, baptisme, matrymony and presthode'. These men

---

[46] *Kent heresy proceedings*, 50–6.

[47] For sacramentarianism among Lollards and Protestants in Kent see Davis, *Heresy and Reformation*, 2, 4, 70–101.

[48] Hudson, *Premature Reformation*, 291–2. Foxe omitted this article from the two lists of charges which he included in his account of the trials, perhaps because it did not fit with his portrayal of the Kent heretics as precursors to Lutheranism: AM, 1276, 1278.

[49] *Kent heresy proceedings*, 20.

[50] Ibid. 62, 63.

[51] Ibid. 19; Hudson, *Premature Reformation*, 294–7.

appear to have looked to Scripture for confirmation of Wycliffite opinions.[52] About the same number rejected extreme unction and holy orders, also common Lollard positions found in Wyclif. In the case of the latter doctrine, they were charged with the belief that God gave no more power to a priest than to a layman; essentially the idea of the priesthood of all believers, developed within some Lollard circles, including White's followers in East Anglia.[53] Anti-sacerdotalism probably informed the view that holy water and blessed bread remained the same after the priest's benediction as before it. Putting this belief into action, John Grebill senior and his family 'brought home holy brede deverse tymes to his house and ete it and had noone other regard unto it but as to other brede'.[54] Only Robert Harryson of Canterbury was said to have held the opinion that indulgences and pardons 'have no effect nor profit'.[55]

Beliefs about pilgrimage, images and saints were, alongside views on the eucharist, the most generally held and fully articulated. In this respect, Warham's investigations fit the pattern of most other trials of Lollards.[56] Nearly all abjurations included the beliefs that pilgrimages 'to holy and devoute places bee not profitable nother meritorious for mannys soule', and 'that images of seynts be not to be worchipped'. A number of suspects added 'that labor and money spent therabout (in pilgrimage) ys but lost and doon in vayne', and one had reportedly said it was 'but a lost labour'. An alternative to expenditure upon pilgrimage was enacted by William Baker after meeting and agreeing with other heretics on May Day 1509 in Edward Walker's house at Maidstone, against pilgrimage and the worship and giving of offerings to saints. Baker told how, 'aftir the said communicacion this deponent whiche was mynded to goo and offer to the Roode of grace outdrewe his mynde and went not thider but gave his offeryng to A poore man'.[57] This was an idea commonly found in Wycliffite texts, as well as cropping up in other trials.[58] Hostility to images, including the crucifix as well as representations of the Virgin and other saints, was articulated by Joan Riche of Wittersham who stated that they 'ought not to be worshipped bicause they were made with mannys hands and that they were but stokks and stonys'. The five suspects who refused to abjure were charged with holding that those who went on pilgrimage to holy and devout places and venerated relics committed idolatry. Robert Harryson had apparently said to Christopher Grebill that candles before images in church were not profitable to man's soul.[59] Far fewer

---

[52] *Kent heresy proceedings*, 53; *Heresy trials*, 11; Hudson, *Premature Reformation*, 292.

[53] *Heresy trials*, 11–12; Hudson, *Premature Reformation*, 325–7.

[54] This, incidentally, reveals that the Grebills continued to attend their parish church: *Kent heresy proceedings*, 19–20.

[55] Ibid. 4.

[56] Hudson, *Premature Reformation*, 302; *Heresy trials*, 12–14.

[57] *Kent heresy proceedings*, 27, 65, 67, 87, 90, 4, 53.

[58] Hudson, *Premature Reformation*, 307; *Heresy trials*, 14.

[59] *Kent heresy proceedings*, 85, 2, 9, 17, 44, 46, 51, 4.

suspects admitted to holding to the allied opinion, but distinct article, that prayers should not be made to saints but only to God, a view propounded by Wyclif and present among the heretics of East Anglia in the early fifteenth century. John Browne of Ashford was the only suspect alleged to have denied the existence of purgatory, William Baker deposing that 'Browne said that there was no purgatory but oonly in this world, and aftir that a man was decessid he shulde goo straight to heven or to hell'.[60]

Although the recorded trials in Warham's register never mention Lollards or Lollardy, but refer only to 'heresy' or 'heretics', the abjurations and depositions leave little doubt as to the origins of the beliefs.[61] There is not a single point among them that cannot be found in Lollard literature or other trials and many were wholly Wycliffite. The dominant opinions, concerning the eucharist, pilgrimage and images, accord with some of the more central teachings of William White and his circle, who may well have laid the basis for later Lollardy in Kent. All the recorded beliefs of the thirty heretics examined in detail here can be found in Alnwick's register.[62] No outright attacks on the Church appear to have been recorded in the course of the trials. Nor, apparently, was an aggressive position adopted toward the sacraments, images and cult of saints. Apart from the views that confession should not be made to a priest but privately to God and that prayers should not be addressed to saints, the general position appears to have been that these things were unnecessary and unprofitable, rather than harmful. In this sense, in their articulation of what were, nevertheless, serious heresies, the Kent Lollards were relatively moderate.[63]

The story of a conversation between John Bayly and his wife, of Rolvenden, reported by Bayly's servant and recorded in the visitation presentments of 1511, serves to illustrate how close in their opinions convinced Lollards may have been to those who considered themselves to be religiously orthodox, but who were not beyond questioning certain traditional aspects of religion. Bayly's wife had made a pilgrimage (presumably to Canterbury) on Relics Sunday (the feast of St Thomas the Martyr, next after 7 July) and on returning home, when he asked her where she had been, she answered, 'At pilgrymage at the reliques for the parson declarid and said for every foote that a man or a woman sett to the reliques ward he shal have great pardone.' John reportedly responded, 'he said soo bicause he wille have folks money', to which his wife replied, 'Nay, for the parson said that when the churche was brennyd the silke with the reliks closid and the fyre had noo

---

[60] Hudson, *Premature Reformation*, 302; *Heresy trials*, 11–12; *Kent heresy proceedings*, 46.

[61] *Kent heresy proceedings*, p. xv.

[62] See the more general comments in Hudson, *Premature Reformation*, 468–72, but also comments at p. 156 n. 37 above.

[63] An exception to this is perhaps found in William Riche's deposition against Agnes Grebill, that she and her husband believed that the sacraments, in addition to pilgrimage etc, 'were not to be allowed but to be damned as nothing worth': *Kent heresy proceedings*, 22.

power on theym.' John, cast as a doubting Thomas, allegedly declared, 'Whan I shalle see theym bifore me putt betwene ij faggots brennyng & they not perysshed, then wille I believe that they bene holy relics.' Bayly denied he had ever said this, and successfully purged himself on 20 April 1511. From this it appears he was no heretic but, whatever his exact words, it seems he was sceptical of the power imputed by the Church to saints' relics.[64]

Families, households and heretical networks

The importance of the family for the survival, sustenance and organisation of Lollardy has been argued by Anne Hudson and, in terms of the continuity of dissent in general in late medieval and early modern England, by Margaret Spufford and others following in her footsteps.[65] The family and the social arena of the household seem to have played particularly important roles in Lollard survival and activity in the Tenterden area and elsewhere in Kent. From the trials alone it is apparent that no fewer than twenty-six individuals were related to at least one other suspect, and eighteen to two or more.[66] A further fifteen shared the same surname with at least one other suspect but cannot be conclusively linked by family from the heresy trial materials in isolation. However, testamentary evidence shows that of these fifteen John Lynche of Tenterden and Vincent Lynche of Halden were brothers.[67] The same may apply to John Franke and Robert Franke of Tenterden.[68] Overall, as many as two-thirds of the suspected heretics may have been related to others who were investigated at the same time, making the density of family relationships exceptionally high and comparable to the very stable networks in the Chilterns.[69] This might, in part, have been due to relatively low levels of out-migration from the Kentish Weald and the other areas from which the

---

64 *Kentish visitations*, 211. Although McSheffrey does not include Bayly among suspects investigated in 1511–12 by Warham she nevertheless assumes that he was a Lollard: *Gender and heresy*, 163, cf. p. 94. Compare Bayly's wife's story of the relic surviving the flames, with the indulgence published by Cardinal Wolsey after the arson at Rickmansworth: Aston, 'Iconoclasm at Rickmansworth', 524, 552.

65 Hudson, *Premature Reformation*, 121, 134–7, 456–64; Spufford, *World of rural dissenters*, esp. pp. 23–9 and articles therein by Plumb and Evans. See also pp. 19–20 above.

66 Of these, John and Joan Bukherst and John and Joan Dodde of Staplehurst may not represent confirmed Lollard couples as Joan Bukherst and John Dodde were both found guilty only of concealing their spouses' opinions: see above and McSheffrey, *Gender and heresy*, 94–5.

67 PRC 17/16/152, 17/17/294. Vincent bequeathed 13s. 4d. to the marriage of Wylmyne Lynche, the daughter of John Lynche, and John referred to his daughter Wylmyne in his own will.

68 PRC 17/1/99, 3/5/33.

69 McSheffrey, *Gender and heresy*, 156–60; Plumb, 'A gathered Church?', 132–63; R. G. Davies, 'Lollardy and locality', *TRHS* 6th ser. i (1991), 193–7; Evans, 'Descent of dissenters', 288–308.

groups came, as was also the case in the Chiltern Hundreds.[70] It is, perhaps, also evidence of the more widely observed tendency for convinced Lollards to remain close to their heretical groups, which often comprised or contained their natal households, and to marry other Lollards.[71]

The relatively large number of two-generation Lollard families in Kent is another indication of the maturity and longevity of the heretical groups there.[72] A number of known family relationships stretched across parish boundaries and sometimes much greater distances. John and Christopher Grebill are good examples of children who had left their natal home and yet remained in close contact with their parents, calling at the family house in Benenden from time to time, while living in Tenterden and Cranbrook respectively. These visits may have been motivated partly by the opportunity they afforded for discussion of heresies with their parents and others who met at the house.[73] Agnes Ive appears to have kept in touch with her brother, Robert Hilles of Tenterden, when she lived at Canterbury.[74] It should be remembered that in early modern England kinship bonds, however latent due to distance of blood, marriage, geography or social status, could be reactivated when required.[75] Other adult sons and daughters were either still living with their parents or had established their own households in their home parishes. Alice Hilles, the daughter of Robert and Juliana Hilles of Tenterden, was only around twenty at the time of the trials and so not surprisingly does not seem to have left home. Philip Harwode was twenty-nine, and is recorded as living in Rolvenden, the same parish as his parents. He and his parents made a joint abjuration, suggesting that they were treated as a single family unit by the authorities.[76]

The importance of the family and household for the transmission of dissent within the Kentish groups, is no better illustrated than by the Grebill family, although, paradoxically, it seems to have been the betrayal of close family bonds which led the elderly Agnes Grebill to take such an uncompromising and, ultimately, tragic stand. John Grebill, with the help of one of his own teachers, the literate John Ive, had first taught and convinced his wife Agnes of errors concerning the eucharist, pilgrimage and worshipping and the giving of offerings to saints, some time in the early 1480s. William Carder, who had taught Ive and Grebill, also appears to have been influential in her instruction. On many occasions since then Agnes had affirmed that

---

[70] Zell, *Industry in the countryside*, 52–60, 85; Spufford, 'Mobility and immobility', 309–31.
[71] Spufford, 'Mobility and immobility', 330–1; Collinson, 'Critical conclusion', 393; McSheffrey, *Gender and heresy*, 95–7, 103–6; Hudson, *Premature Reformation*, 169; Plumb, 'A gathered church?', 132–63.
[72] McSheffrey, *Gender and heresy*, 100.
[73] *Kent heresy proceedings*, 13, 21.
[74] Ibid. 12.
[75] Cressy, 'Kinship', 38–69.
[76] *Kent heresy proceedings*, 79, 61–4.

these opinions were good and 'comyned and defended' them in the presence of her husband and two sons in their house in Benenden.[77] According to John Grebill senior, he had taught his two sons, Christopher and John, that the sacrament of the altar was not the fleshly body of Christ but only bread, from when they were only about seven years old. Agnes had not only been in agreement with this teaching, but was 'well contentid that hir children aforsaid were of the said opynyons'.[78] Christopher and John junior presented a somewhat different account. According to the former, who was twenty-two in 1511, his parents had first taught him his errors, discussing them many times with him at his father's house in Benenden, 'but he saith he hath no felyng in that maters of errors tyll he herd John Ive teche hym and till he sawe in John Ives bookes' about three years before the trials. Since then he had had many discussions about these ideas with his parents, who had been 'comfortyng hym in the same'. According to his father, Christopher had also met and talked with William Carder in the family house. Twenty-one at the time of the trials, John Grebill junior at first claimed that his parents had initially taught and counselled him against the sacrament of the altar, pilgrimage, offering to and worshipping of saints' images, with the affirmation of his brother, only twelve months before. However, he went on to reveal that his parents had taught heresies and discussed them with him many times when he was fourteen or fifteen years old, and many times since 'but he never coude perceyve their teching nor geve any hert ther unto tyll this yere last past'.[79]

It is difficult to construe the story of Christopher and John's eventual assent to heresy as a clear 'case of rebellion against Lollard parents', as one writer has done.[80] There is no suggestion in the depositions that they actively resisted their parents' teachings, but rather that they only grasped them at a certain point of conversion, expressed by them in the terms, 'felyng' and 'hert'. The apprehension of ideas that they had heard since their youth may well have come with adulthood, together with, in Christopher's case, exposure to the written word and a literate expositor. John Grebill senior stated that all four of them 'were agreed to gider by all the said tymes in his house never to make confession of these aforsaid errors', a pact also mentioned by Christopher.[81] In the event of her family's testimony against her, Agnes

---

[77] Ibid. 11–12, 18–22; McSheffrey, *Gender and heresy*, 92, 110–12, 114, 207 nn. 7, 14.

[78] *Kent heresy proceedings*, 21. William Riche mentioned a third child, a 'distrawght yong woman, doughter to the said John and Agnes Grebill' who was present when he went there to discuss heresy (ibid. 22). She was perhaps mentally ill, rather than emotionally distressed by her family's heretical activities: McSheffrey, *Gender and heresy*, 203 n. 115.

[79] *Kent heresy proceedings*, 13, 18–21.

[80] McSheffrey, *Gender and heresy*, 99.

[81] *Kent heresy proceedings*, 18–21; Davies, 'Lollardy and locality', 195. On the Lollard advocacy of a personal inward conversion see Jones, 'Lollards and images', 34, and also P. Collinson, 'Night schools, conventicles and churches', in Marshall and Ryrie, *Beginnings of English Protestantism*, 219–20.

denied the veracity of their claims and, according to the record of her trial, in an outburst of bitter emotion, declared that she regretted ever bearing her sons.[82]

A number of households appear to have been key meeting places for the heretical groups, where connections were made, hospitality was given, discussion, teaching and communal reading of the Scriptures took place. The Grebills' house in Benenden was one such place, as was Edward Walker's in Maidstone, John Bampton's in Bearsted/Otham, John and Agnes Ive's in Canterbury, Robert Harryson's home beside St John's Hospital in Canterbury, John Browne's in Ashford and, perhaps to a lesser extent, the Hilles's in Tenterden, William Riche's home in Benenden and William Carder's in Tenterden. For obvious reasons these were the safest and most natural places to meet, discuss and teach dangerous doctrines. Whilst women did not have a leading role among the Kentish groups, it was here, in the domestic sphere, within normal socialised boundaries, that they appear to have played their most important part.[83]

In addition to family connections, the trials reveal the importance of a small number of teachers who moved between heretical households and groups and established new clusters in fresh areas. William Carder is the best example of one such literate, book-owning teacher, but there were others such as John Ive and Robert Harryson.[84] The depositions allege that, all in all, William Carder converted, or helped to convert, at least nine individuals to heretical views and, directly or indirectly, through family and other connections, was instrumental in proselytising more than twenty. Whilst Carder resorted to people's homes to teach them, he also took whatever opportunities came his way to evangelise. For example, before Robert Hilles met with him in his own home about two years before the trials, he had talked with Carder at ale houses, in Carder's own house, in church and in other places always, Hilles claimed, in private and alone. That he travelled about over quite large distances is apparent from Stephen Castelyn's confession that Carder had first taught him to believe against the sacrament of the altar at Maidstone, in about 1508.[85] His infamy was all too apparent to another young convert, Christopher Grebill, who said that,

---

[82] *Kent heresy proceedings*, 18. For Foxe's passionate account of Agnes's trial and fate see AM, 1277. Contrary to Foxe's version of events Agnes does not appear to have recanted during her trial: *Kent heresy proceedings*, 22–5.

[83] *Kent heresy proceedings*, pp. xx, 10–12, 18–22, 52–5, 4–6, 45–8. For a perhaps overly pessimistic account of the limitations on womens' activities and overall lack of status within Lollardy see McSheffrey, *Heresy and gender*, passim and esp. pp. 52–3, 110–12.

[84] *Kent heresy proceedings*, pp. xx–xxi, 20, 1–7; Thomson, *Later Lollards*, 187; Hudson, *Premature Reformation*, 136; C. Cross, 'Great reasoners in Scripture: the activities of women Lollards, 1380–1530', in D. Baker (ed.), *Medieval women* (SCH subsidia, i, 1978), 364.

[85] *Kent heresy proceedings*, 11–12.

Carder hath been the myschief and destruccion of many men by bringyng theym unto the said mysbeleves ayenst the sacrament of thaulter, that it is but oonly brede, and that all other sacraments be not profitable for mannys soule, in bryngyng of [sic] Reignold therto, and also William Baker which William shewed to this deponent that he was brought to the said errors . . . by the said Carder but that it was long er the said Carder coude bring hym to it so to belive.[86]

Carder was wise to persevere in his discipleship of Baker, as not only was the latter literate, but he became a zealous advocate of heresy. Baker admitted to having read from 'a book of Mathewe where yn was conteyned the gospell in Englisshe' to the Bearsted and Maidstone group at Christmas 1509, in Edward Walker's house in Maidstone, and may have taken an important role within this conventicle which involved as many as twelve individuals. Baker also had connections with the circle of suspects comprising the Harwodes of Rolvenden, John Browne of Ashford and Thomas Mannyng of Benenden. He may also have taught heresies to Agnes Reignold of Cranbrook when she was a servant in his household.[87] It is possible that Carder himself taught the Maidstone and Bearsted group, and that it was in this setting that Stephen Castelyn first learned his heresy. It is established that Carder taught Robert Hilles of Tenterden, and that he probably also converted William Riche of Benenden and Robert Reignold of Cranbrook (and possibly formerly of Tenterden) who had all, from time to time, met with the Maidstone group.[88] Finally, Agnes Ive told how her husband John Ive, a heretic since the late 1470s or early 1480s, had always declared that Carder was his 'techer and reder'.[89]

In contrast to R. G. Davies's assessment of the Lollards of the Chiltern Hills, teachers prepared to travel considerable distances between relatively localised pockets of closely linked Lollard groups and households ensured that geography did not hamper the spread of heresy in Kent and that close locality did not define its influence.[90] Thirty-two of the fifty-eight suspects investigated in the trials or presented to the visitation of 1511 were interconnected by either family or through heretical meetings, albeit often distantly in individual cases. But this web of interconnected groups and households

---

[86] Ibid. 13.

[87] Ibid. 75.

[88] Ibid. 11, 52–6, 12. Carder's own curious account of a meeting he had with Robert Reignold is as follows: 'Robert Reignold of Tenterden the friday of the first weke in Lent last past came and dyned at this deponents house and there redde in a booke a sermon of Seynt Austyn spekyng ageynst the sacrament of baptisme, and aftir that he had redde it he askid of this deponent how say ye nowe of the opinion of heretik what avayleth to cristen a childe in colde water, and this deponent aunswered agayn ye be full of questyons, beleve ye as ye will. I well beleve as a cristen man shuld doo' (p. 10).

[89] Ibid. 12.

[90] Davies, 'Lollardy and locality', 206–7.

cannot be termed 'a gathered Church', as Derek Plumb has attempted to define (not altogether successfully) the early sixteenth-century Chiltern Lollards.[91] Most of the Kentish suspects do appear, however, to have formed a fairly loose community that traded in a common currency of heretical ideas, and came together in small groups for teaching, reading, discussion and affirmation. Whilst, as McSheffrey has pointed out, 'the thread that bound a community together was contact with its leaders', if it were possible to uncover them in their fullness, pre-existing ties of real and fictive kinship might take on equal significance.[92] The evolution of Kentish Lollardy fits very well with the more general pattern of change described by Hudson as a shift 'from dominance of the individual, peripatetic preacher to the centrality of the community as a whole', made up of a 'host of lesser figures, men and women, who in the course of their everyday activities proselytised, encouraged and upbraided the wavering, and fostered the faithful'.[93]

Carder's sphere of influence appears to have been restricted to Kent, and the community had no apparent active links with other heretical groups outside the county by the early sixteenth century. There are a number of reasons for seeing Tenterden as the paramount centre of heresy: the largest number of suspects from any one place in 1511 lived in the town; most of the interconnections between the geographically isolated groups were through individuals from there or neighbouring Benenden; Carder used Tenterden as his base; four of the six persons who were sentenced to imprisonment in 1511, and so were probably considered to be especially dangerous, came from the parish, namely Stephen Castelyn, Robert Franke, William Pellond and Juliana Hilles.[94] The migration of Carder's family from Lincolnshire to Tenterden in the 1460s, or perhaps earlier, has been mentioned. Perhaps they were attracted to the town because it remained a Lollard stronghold throughout the middle decades of the fifteenth century. Carder's success as a Lollard evangelist in Kent may have depended on an existing network of safe heretical households, coupled with a general receptivity to his teachings among elements of the local population.

The heretics tried in 1511–12 do not appear to have been ostracised by their neighbours, nor did they withdraw from everyday life. Some of them were relatively prominent members of their local communities. Similar integration of the Lollards of the Chiltern Hills has led Derek Plumb to claim that their beliefs 'must have been known to their orthodox neighbours', and

---

91 Plumb, 'A gathered church?', passim; *Kent heresy proceedings*, p. xxii. On the vagueness and inapplicability of this term see Collinson, 'Critical conclusion', 395–6, and Rex, *Lollards*, 81.

92 McSheffrey, *Gender and heresy*, 15–16; Calhoun, 'Community', 105–29. On the importance of kinship in the creation of Lollard communities see Plumb, 'A gathered Church?', passim; Davies, 'Lollardy and locality', 195, 212; and Spufford, 'The importance of religion', 13.

93 Hudson, *Premature Reformation*, 449–50.

94 *Kent heresy proceedings*, 106–11, 113–15.

to infer that they were not very vigilant in hiding them. In Kent, on the other hand, there is every indication that Lollards were very careful not to reveal their heresy to strangers or the unsympathetic. Admittedly, this does not mean that their activities or views always remained hidden from outsiders.[95] To begin with, there was the pact made between the Grebills not to confess their errors, presumably, that is, to the unsympathetic, as they were in regular contact with other fellow dissenters.[96] In all their meetings together, which were sometimes outside in public places, including alehouses and even a church, deponents stressed how they 'wold never make any body privey nor of counseill when they went aboute suche maters', and meetings in the privacy of suspects' homes as well as other places were seen as occasions 'whan they mought mete togider secretly without suspicion'.[97] Most recorded meetings seem to have taken place at major festivals and saints' days, perhaps because these were the normal times to make social visits, not to mention pilgrimages, and so heretically inspired journeys and meetings might go unnoticed. Perhaps these occasions also offered ideal opportunities to subvert the orthodox practice of honouring saints.[98]

One episode, in particular, illustrates the care taken to hide heretical opinions from threatening quarters. At Christmas 1510 Robert Bright, John Bampton, Richard Bampton, Thomas Feld, William Baker, Stephen Castelyn and William Riche met together in John Bampton's house in Bearsted, whence all but Castelyn travelled the two miles or so to Edward Walker's house at Maidstone by night. There, with Walker and his wife they agreed together against the sacrament of the altar

> and as they were so commynyng [sic] the wif of ye said Walker said, sires it is not good that ye talke moche here of thies maters for the Jaylours will take hede to you uf ye comme huder, and also beware for some folkis will commyn hider anon, and therupon furthwith came yn the Jaylors wife, and they cessed of their communicacion.[99]

According to William Riche, when the jailer's wife arrived, 'Edward Walker beying aferde to be suspectid and espied spake to that other iij saying, Sirs drynke ye and make ye mery and high you from hens agayne and so they

---

95 Plumb, 'A gathered Church?', 132–3, and 'Social and economic status', passim. For the view that Lollards generally maintained a veil of secrecy over their activities see Davies, 'Lollardy and locality', 203, and Hudson, *Premature Reformation*, 142–3.

96 *Kent heresy proceedings*, 18–22. Hudson interprets this as meaning confession to anyone and that it was Agnes who broke the vow 'in her efforts at proselytisation'. Agnes was formally charged with communicating heresies to the orthodox: *Premature Reformation*, 143; *Kent heresy proceedings*, 18–21.

97 *Kent heresy proceedings*, 11.

98 Ibid. 1–24, 43–60. See M. Aston 'Corpus Christi and Corpus Regni: heresy and the Peasants' Revolt', *P&P* cxliii (1994), 3–47, which examines connections between revolt and religious dissent in the context of the Feast of *Corpus Christi*.

99 *Kent heresy proceedings*, 55.

departid agayn'. These efforts at secrecy notwithstanding, some suspects withdrew from certain aspects of orthodox religion, or may even have actively opposed them. John Grebill senior deposed that 'from hir first belive' his wife Agnes 'never dide offer to seynts Images nor yet wold goo to pilgremages' and she was charged with reprimanding pilgrims by telling them they committed idolatry. They had also, on a number of occasions as a family, brought the consecrated bread home from church and ate it as if it were like any other – a dangerous symbolic act of nullification and defiance.[100] The very fact that the Lollard groups were making converts in the late fifteenth and early sixteenth centuries means that they could not have remained entirely closed.[101]

There is little evidence that Lollards in Tenterden or elsewhere in the county withdrew from normal church attendance. In this they appear to have conformed to wider patterns of Lollard behaviour which meant, as recently argued by Patrick Collinson, that Wycliffite heretics should neither be described as separatists nor, indeed, as a sect. At most they were 'semi-sectarian', practising 'occasional conformity and occasional nonconformity', behaviour very similar to that of many post-Reformation Catholics as well as some Protestant Nonconformist groups.[102] Foxe mentions that William Everden of Tenterden, who fled to East Anglia shortly before 1428, had 'wrought' with a man called William Taylor for a month and had refused to be like 'a scribe or a pharisee' by going to church one Sunday, but 'did sit all day upon the table at work'.[103] However, judging by the above account, the Grebills must have attended mass and, according to Robert Hilles, William Carder had talked about heresy in church. Whereas Anne Hudson describes this sort of behaviour as a 'superficial conformity to the normal practices of orthodoxy', it is probable that it accorded with the Wycliffite idea of the visible and invisible Church and that they did not see their activities when gathered in pairs or small groups in each other's homes as constituting an alternative congregation.[104] While passively opposing the cult of saints and ignoring prohibitions to work on holidays and rules about fasting it appears that, on the whole, they continued to attend church services, make annual confession and receive the eucharist. Although they rejected transubstantiation, the Kentish Lollards seem to have retained a belief in the value of the congregation of the parish and the sacrament of the altar as a commemorative service. As J. A. F. Thomson argues, 'they could easily attend mass and receive communion devoutly, believing that it was of spiritual benefit to them, while having mental reservations about the official doctrine'.[105]

[Handwritten margin note: Lollardy was a movement but not separatist]

---

[100] Ibid. 56, 19–20.
[101] Thomson, *Later Lollards*, 190.
[102] Collinson, 'Night schools', 209–35 at pp. 223–4.
[103] AM, 665.
[104] Collinson, 'Night schools', 223–4.
[105] Hudson, *Premature Reformation*, 451; Thomson, *Later Lollards*, 247; Hope, 'Lollardy', 14.

The visitation presentments of September 1511 and, in particular, the fascinating case of John Franke discussed at the beginning of this book, suggest that at Tenterden non-attendance was not generally a Lollard trait and that heresy, or perhaps wider religious discontent, manifested itself rather differently: 'Johan Frank with diverse other eville disposid persones use in the tyme of divine service to be in the churcheyard comenyng & talkyng and many other use to sitt stille in the churche atte processione tyme.'[106] Franke had abjured heretical opinions that August, but he is not connected in the depositions with any other suspect, although he may have been related to Robert Franke of Tenterden who was imprisoned for his errors and activities.[107] Were Lollards in Tenterden going so far as to gather in the churchyard during mass in some sort of oppositional open-air conventicle, or were these merely malcontents? Who were the people who sat still in the church at the procession, perhaps in passive protest? If these were Lollards, then they had adopted a most publicly engaged form of dissent, which is not incompatible with concealment of heretical beliefs and activities, but which would not have been possible in a climate of fear and incrimination.[108] While there may have been Wycliffites among these resolute parishioners, it is entirely possible that many of them would not have thought of themselves in these terms.

In all the places from which Lollards came in Kent, including Tenterden, it seems that the orthodox were reluctant to incriminate their heterodox neighbours. This is suggested by the fact that all the witnesses mentioned in the trials belonged to heretical groups or households of heretics. The authorities appear to have had to rely heavily upon inside informers who, although unnamed, can be guessed at.[109] At Tenterden, although the parishioners presented three individuals to the visitation of September 1511 as heretics, all three were women and one of these was deceased, while John Franke was not labelled a heretic.[110] None of the major Lollard figures mentioned in the trial proceedings were indicted in the visitation, and neither are there any references to heresy in the Tenterden returns for fourteen separate years between 1498 and 1523.[111] There were very few presentments of heretics in

---

106 *Kentish visitations*, 207–10.

107 *Kent heresy proceedings*, 90–1, 110–11.

108 See Collinson, 'Night schools', 222–3, for the less ambiguous contempt shown by powerful Amersham Lollards at the elevation of the host in their parish church.

109 A likely candidate is Christopher Grebill, who was quick to name a number of other suspects, and whose abjuration is entered first in the record of proceedings in Warham's register, even though he did not abjure until 2 May, a few days after the first trials: *Kent heresy proceedings*, 27–8.

110 Alice Raynold and Kateryne Cardar were named as unexamined heretics and another, Agnes Roche, 'commenly knowene as heretike', was said to be buried in the churchyard: *Kentish visitations*, 207–10.

111 CCA, X.8.2, pt 2, fo. 13r; Z.3.1, fo. 41r; Z.3.37, fo. 83r; Z.3.2, fos 4r, 136v, 4v, 25v, 55r, 9r, 82v; Z.3.3, fos 15v, 51v, 83v; Z.3.4, fos 20r, 48v, 68r, 94v, 108r.

1511–12 in other parishes within the archdeaconry of Canterbury in which it is established that Lollards lived.[112] It is almost forty years since J. A. F. Thomson stated with regard to Tenterden that 'even although there is nothing to show that the Lollards were anything other than a minority, the majority does not appear to have been vindictive towards them'.[113] Thomson's hunch that this may have had something to do with sympathetic churchwardens appears to be correct. Sympathy, or even active pressure, from town or parochial leaders provided some protection,[114] but the major underlying question of why sympathy and susceptibility to heresy was an enduring characteristic of Tenterden and the Weald of Kent, occupies the remainder of this chapter.

Heresy in context

Until relatively recently Wycliffite heresy after Oldcastle's revolt in 1414 was seen as the preserve of the socially and economically insignificant.[115] A number of studies and, in particular, the work of Derek Plumb on the Chiltern Hundreds, have now demonstrated that Lollardy was spread throughout all strata of rural society, and had a tendency to be better represented among its wealthier members, including a limited number drawn from the gentry. This work shows that many Lollards were fully integrated into the political and social life of the parish, village or town, being 'dominant members of their society, with contacts throughout the region, and with substantial estates'. Accepted as such by their more orthodox neighbours, it is argued that this local influence was vital to the ongoing survival and geographical stability of Lollard families and groups in certain districts.[116] It is

---

[112] Apart from the case of John Bayly of Rolvenden, the only other reference relates to the parish of St George, Canterbury, where John Hale was indicted for burying the heretic John Ive in the churchyard: *Kentish visitations*, 211, 72; cf. Collinson, 'Night schools', 223.

[113] Thomson, *Later Lollards*, 191.

[114] Plumb, 'Social and economic status', passim; Hope, 'Lollardy', 3–6; McSheffrey, *Gender and heresy*, 44–5, 125–8.

[115] See, for example, C. Haigh, 'The English reformation: a premature birth, a difficult labour and a sickly child', *Historical Journal* xxxiii (1990), 449–59; M. Bowker, *The Henrician Reformation: the diocese of Lincoln under John Longland, 1521–1547*, Cambridge 1981, 38; MacCulloch, *Suffolk and the Tudors*, 150 (but cf. his *The later Reformation in England, 1547–1603*, Basingstoke 1990, 68–9, 126, 154–5, and Plumb, 'Social and economic status', 109 n. 26); Davis, 'Lollard survival', 191–201; and Clark, *English provincial society*, 31.

[116] See, for example, Plumb, 'Social and economic status', 103–31, and 'The social and economic spread of rural Lollardy: a reappraisal', in W. J. Sheils and D. Wood (eds), *Voluntary religion* (SCH xxiii, 1986), 111–29; Spufford, 'The importance of religion', 12–13, 63–4; I. Luxton, 'The Lichfield court book; a postscript', *BIHR* xliv (1971), 120–5; Hudson, *Premature Reformation*, 128–34, 466–7; A. Hope, 'The lady and the bailiff: Lollardy among the gentry in Yorkist and early Tudor England', in M. Aston and C. Richmond (eds),

paradoxical, therefore, that in their efforts to counter any suggestion that these findings indicate that religious dissent was in any way economically or socially determined, Plumb and Margaret Spufford somewhat overstate the breadth of Lollardy's social appeal, in particular to the poorest members of society. The assessments of personal wealth in the subsidy rolls, which underpin their arguments, are not an altogether reliable index of economic and social standing, particularly at the lower end of valuations and the lay subsidy materials have not always been used with proper attention to local variations in social structure and distribution of wealth.[117] In response to this work, Patrick Collinson comments, 'Gone are those contradictory notions, with their shallow polemical and ideological roots, which on the one hand connected Nonconformity with the lowest of the low and on the other made it the possession of a burgeoning bourgeoisie, a monopoly of the industrious and thriving sort of people.'[118] Let us hope he is right, but not because there is no longer any need to consider the social profile of dissent for what it can reveal about its appeal to particular social groups. If the evidence from Kent is anything to go by heresy had a socially specific appeal, but not exclusively, to reasonably wealthy middle-ranking families with some influence in local politics and parish life.

One of the problems with many of the attempts to categorise Lollardy socially is the use of ambiguous and ill-defined terms. Chief among these is 'artisan', which is employed all too often as a means to slide from descriptions of craft and trade activity to blanket classifications of class with all their ramifications of rigid social stratification and, in some conceptualisations, economic marginality.[119] If the term artisan is to be used, then it should be in the correct sense, as a description of engagement in craft or trade activity, or of 'skilled manufacturers, processing goods for sale' by those ranging from wealthy and powerful urban craftsmen with their own workshops to those who were paid a wage or piece-rate.[120] Because of its connotations it is better

---

Lollardy and the gentry in the later Middle Ages, Stroud 1997, 250–77; and Rex, *Lollards*, 101–4.

[117] Aston, 'Iconoclasm at Rickmansworth', 542–3; Plumb, 'Social and economic status', passim and esp. pp. 110–14, tables 3, 4; Spufford, 'The importance of religion', 13. Especially questionable is Plumb's assessment that 'individuals in the middling and upper social levels were *just a little better* represented among Lollards than their economic peers in society in general' (my italics). On the basis of all possible Lollards investigated by Plumb, 18% of them paid on £10 or more of valued wealth in 1524–5, compared to 13% of all taxpayers. When restricted to definitely identified Lollards only, as opposed to all those investigated however, 29% of them – more than twice the proportion of all taxpayers – were assessed in this top wealth bracket. At the other end of the scale, whereas about a fifth of known Lollards paid on 30s. and under, almost two-fifths of all taxpayers did so.

[118] Collinson, 'Critical conclusion', 390.

[119] Davis, 'Lollard survival', passim; M. Lambert, *Medieval heresy: popular movements from Gregorian reform to the Reformation*, 3rd edn, Oxford 2002, 291, 294–300; Clark, *English provincial society*, 30–1, 42.

[120] H. Swanson, *Medieval artisans: an urban class in late medieval England*, Oxford 1989, 2;

to avoid the term altogether, and to employ an alternative such as crafts- or tradesperson.

A handful of references allow for some tentative judgements about the activities and status of early heretics in the Tenterden area. Henry Esteghe of Tenterden, who was apprehended in May 1428 with Peter Attewyde (also of the town), may have been the Henry Esteagh who made his will in October 1461. If so, his bequests show nothing of any previous heresy, as they were enthusiastically orthodox by Tenterden's standards, but they do reveal reasonably substantial resources. He left 6s. 8d. to each of the rectors of High Halden and Woodchurch, devoted a total of 66s. 8d. to obsequies, left 10 marks for a year's temporary chantry before the altar of the Virgin Mary in St Mildred's and gave twelve pieces of his best timber to the building of the new bell tower. He held lands and tenements in Tenterden, High Halden, Woodchurch and elsewhere in Kent. Making no mention of immediate family, he devised lands, woodland and buildings in Tenterden to the heirs of Thomas Austyn and sixteen pieces of land to William Preston and his wife, Preston being his executor. Two things in this will suggest that he had been involved in Lollardy in the 1420s: one of his feoffees was Thomas Harry of Redyng (Reading Street in the parish of Ebony) who may have been either one of the two men of the same name of Tenterden and High Halden, who were arrested after the 1438 disturbances, and he left 10 marks to a John Browne, who may have been the John Browne of Ashford tried for heresy in 1511, although this seems less likely.[121] Also among the 1428 group was Stephen Robyn of Tenterden, who belonged to the family mentioned in at least twenty-five Tenterden wills between 1476 and 1535, often as feoffees, executors and witnesses, as well as legatees. In 1453–4 a Thomas Robyn was among a group of men (including Thomas Kaxton, town clerk of Tenterden, and possibly brother to the printer William Caxton), who travelled to Rye to settle disputes between the two towns. The will of Thomas Robyn (perhaps the same man), made in 1513, is the only one for the family in this period that has survived. It indicates considerable agricultural wealth including land and livestock. Robyn's sole religious bequest was of 16d. every year for four years to 'the masse', possibly the Jesus Mass that had just been established. Robyn served as a churchwarden in 1498 and had connections with the Sorells one of whom, namely John Sorell, was indicted for missing church services in 1511.[122]

B. Sharp, *In contempt of all authority: rural artisans and riot in the west of England, 1586–1660*, Berkeley–London 1980, 1–7; S. H. Rigby, *English society in the later Middle Ages: class, status and gender*, Houndmills–London 1995, 18–19, 40, 152–5, 191, 274–5, 154 n. 8.

[121] PRC 17/1/271.

[122] CCA, X.8.2, pt 2, fo. 13r; Thomson, *Later Lollards*, 191; Riley, 'MSS of the corporation of Rye', 491; PRC 17/12/218; *Kentish visitations*, 207, 210. Perhaps also of significance is the fact that Thomas Hicks's sister Agnes had married into the Robyn family. Hicks made his will in 1522, pointedly leaving his 'body to be buried where it pleasith God', money for the purchase of images of SS Crispine and Crispinianus for St Mildred's and 10s. to a niece,

John Pette was involved in the 1438 rebellion, and belonged to the family, already mentioned, which maintained its considerable status throughout the period. Thomas Pette, who was possibly John's brother, was also involved in disturbances some time before 7 July 1471, receiving a royal pardon for 'rebellion and offences' in December of that year. This did not stop him from becoming the first member of the family to serve as bailiff, in 1472–3, 1482–3 and 1487–8. What appears to be John Pette's will is dated 1489, in which he is described as 'pannarius' (clothier). As well as mentioning two servants and providing for his daughter's education, he left £20 for John Bregghar's children, at the discretion of John Hychecoke, vicar of Tenterden. The dedicatory clause of this will is unusually brief: 'lego animam meam deo omnipotenti corpusque meum sepeliendum in cimiterio sancti Mildrede', and his religious gifts comprised 3s. 4d. to the fabric of the parish church and his best cow to the support of the chaplain of the fraternity of the Blessed Virgin Mary, neither of which rule out adherence to Wycliffite views.[123] The Pettes were one of the more religiously moderate and influential families in Tenterden. References to the descendants or kin of another participant in the 1438 rising, namely John Elnoth, also suggest middling social status and craft activity. Edward Elnoth, 'fuller', of Tenterden was indicted for failing to answer an alderman of London regarding a debt of 40s. in 1467 and Thomas Elnoth, also a fuller, rented Sir John Guldeford's fulling mill in the late fifteenth century, and had a house and garden at West Cross, later occupied by John Pette, clothier.[124] Notwithstanding the fragmentary nature of the evidence, at least some of the early Kentish heretics and agitators belonged to what were, by the standards of local society, substantial, politically active and enduring families, and may have had connections with other dissenters and sympathisers. In at least two cases, possible surviving wills indicate that their makers adhered to an atypical and restrained piety and perhaps even a dissenting disposition to the end of their lives.

McSheffrey claims that because 'little can be discovered about the social status of Lollards' in Kent 'it was probably low'.[125] This is undermined by the few individuals identified so far, as well as those in the early sixteenth century

---

which were in the hands of Robert Castlyn of Lydd, possibly a relative of the Castelyns of Tenterden: PRC 17/15/228.

123 *CPR, 1467–77*, 302; Te/C1, fos 140r–v; PRC 17/5/152; Aston, 'Iconoclasm at Rickmansworth', 542; McSheffrey, *Gender and heresy*, 44–5; Peters, *Patterns of piety*, 212–18.

124 Roberts, *Tenterden*, 30, 94; CCR, 1435–41, 117–18.

125 This judgement is based on what appears to be only a cursory investigation of the local and central government evidence of Lollardy in Kent and, in one case, a misconception of this evidence. McSheffrey apparently interprets the list of freemen contained in the Tenterden custumal as representing the whole franchise in 1529. However, it is in fact a record of admissions to the franchise from 1529 until c. 1558 when the custumal was first drawn up and the list was copied into it: Te/C1, fos 116r–117v. It is not surprising, therefore, that only one name on the list matches that of a suspect involved in the 1511 trials, a

who will be examined later in this chapter. Although it is usually the case that low-status individuals leave few traces in historical sources, it does not follow that those of higher status will always leave enough for us to appreciate their material achievements. The Grebills, for example, have left no extant wills, and very few other indications of their wealth and social position. Nevertheless, the indications are that they were reasonably well-heeled. They may have taken their name from Gribble Wood and Gribble Bridge on the north-west border of the parish of Tenterden, adjacent to Biddenden, suggesting that the family had an old and substantial pedigree in the area. In 1391 a John Grybell of Tenterden, yeoman, was pardoned of outlawry over a trespass and the Thomas Grevill and his son, mentioned in a chamberlain's account book of Rye in 1460–1, may have belonged to the same family. They had visited the mayor of Rye in an attempt to settle Tenterden's yearly payment to the Cinque Port and 'seeing that the same Thomas was great with them of Tenterden', Rye's civic leaders had pinned their hopes on him as an effective power broker.[126] More pertinent still is an early chancery case of 1514–15 that details a dispute between the future Lord Chancellor Sir Thomas More on the one hand, and Richard Babbe of Benenden and John Grebill junior of the Lollard family so thoroughly decimated in 1511, on the other. The case concerned the ownership of a house and fifty acres of land, pasture and wood, which had been in the possession of John Grebill senior. He had seized a number of feoffees in this property around Michaelmas 1511, to the use of the prior of the monastery of St Nicholas in Leeds, near Maidstone, presumably shortly before he was imprisoned for his heretical activities in September of that year in order to try and protect his family estate. John Grebill senior probably intended that his son buy back the house and lands from the prior, which is exactly what John junior claimed to have been in the process of doing, with his associate Babbe. More claimed that he had entered into purchasing the property and that money had changed hands long before John Grebill junior ever approached the prior, a claim which Grebill and Babbe denied. Whatever the rights or wrongs of this case, John Grebill senior's estate placed him at the top end of the social stratum comprising the more substantial farmer-tradesmen, middling craftsmen, and lesser yeomen, what Cornwall calls the 'substantial middle class' of the small town in the early sixteenth century. The property may have been in the family for some time, Grebill claiming that he had offered to purchase it 'for asmuch as hit had long tyme conteynid in his auncestours'.[127]

fact which McSheffrey sees as indicative of the generally low status of suspects in Tenterden: *Gender and heresy*, 125.

[126] Roberts, *Tenterden*, 30; Riley, 'MSS of the corporation of Rye', 493. 'Grevill' may be a mistranscription of 'Grebill': see, for example, Hudson, *Premature Reformation*, 136.

[127] I am indebted to Andrew Hope for bringing this case to my attention: PRO, C1/336, 24–7; *Kent heresy proceedings*, 98–9. Compare with the Hunne affair: Dickens, *English Reformation*, 112–18; Cornwall, 'English country towns', 63.

The important heretical teacher William Carder has left a number of traces in the local records. He was bequeathed goods by Thomasina Piers in 1508, acted as witness to Thomas Fynch senior's will in 1504, and was one of the feoffees seized in a house and lands in Tenterden which had belonged to Thomas Elnode and was passed by will in 1495 to Elnode's son. Thomasina Piers also left household stuff to 'widow Reynolde' who may have been related to the Lollard family of that name of Tenterden and Cranbrook, and Thomas Elnode may have been a descendant of John Elnoth who took part in the 1438 rising.[128] The name Reignold or Raynold appears in the 1523–5 lay subsidy assessments in most of the hundreds around Tenterden, and those encompassing Cranbrook. None of the individuals listed appear to have been very wealthy, but the Raynolds of Tenterden seem to have been of higher status.[129] Confirming the Piers family's links with the Raynolds, John Piers, butcher, mentioned his servant John Reynold in his will of 1461. Another wealthy and influential family with ties to the Raynolds, in this case at the religiously generous end of the pious spectrum, were the Prestons of Tenterden. William Preston senior left John Raynold 6s. 8d. in 1493 and in 1497 William Preston junior's sister, Joan Raynold, was remembered in his testament. Interestingly, the Prestons also had affinal ties with the Selers who were in turn joined by marriage to the Castelyns, a family discussed below.[130] John Raynold was a jurat of Tenterden in 1507, Edward Reynolde became a freeman around 1529 and Richard Raynold served as a taxor in 1539 and 1542.[131]

None of the three possible entries for William Baker of Cranbrook in the 1523–5 lay subsidy suggests more than average wealth.[132] He appears to have made his will in 1530, declining to make any religious bequests. The mention of looms and other equipment confirms him in the same craft as his Lollard teacher William Carder, and John Raynold was one of his witnesses.[133] Robert and Juliana Hilles and their daughter, Alice Hilles, of Tenterden, have left no trace in the records. This is surprising given that they may have been related to the Hylleses, who were prolific will-makers. The latter followed a testamentary strategy comprising sparse or moderate religious bequests and, in one case, patronage of the Jesus Mass.[134] Juliana Hilles was among the few suspects imprisoned for their beliefs and activities, probably because they were unsuccessful in attempting to purge themselves. Robert Franke was another and he and John Franke of Tenterden are a little more visible. There are a number of indications that they lived at Small Hythe.

128 PRC 17/12/73, 17/9/49; BL, Add. Ch. 16330.
129 PRO, E 179, 125/324.
130 PRC 17/1/269, 17/6/10, 17/7/50.
131 *Calendar of the white and black books*, 139; Te/C1, fo. 117r; Te/S1, fos 19r, 39r.
132 PRO, E 179, 125/324.
133 PRC 17/19/152.
134 See p. 48 above.

Thomas Franke, who was possibly Robert and John's father, wrote his will in 1464. He mentioned Richard Colyn who owed him 6s. 8d., which Franke ordained was to be given to the image of the Virgin Mary at Ebony. This suggests a link between the Frankes and Joan Colyn of Tenterden, who abjured errors in 1511.[135]

John and Vincent Lynche of Tenterden and High Halden, respectively, seem to have been brothers and belonged to a large extended family that stretched across a number of Wealden parishes, and which in Cranbrook reached dizzy heights in wealth through the cloth industry.[136] In High Halden the Lynches were styling themselves as yeomen by the 1550s and, in 1523–5, Vincent Lynche's wealth was valued at £4 in lands *per annum* and Thomas Lynche, listed next to him in the subsidy roll, paid on £24 in goods. Vincent was therefore probably one of the lower middling people whose agricultural and industrial activities typified the Wealden economy.[137] John and Vincent Lynche abjured almost identical errors, that is against the eucharist, pilgrimages and images.[138] Fortunately, both of their wills survive, John's, dated 1524–5, and Vincent's 1527.[139] Neither is unorthodox, John's bequests beginning with 12d. to be distributed to poor people, followed by 3s. 4d. to be bestowed upon his burial and month's day for the health of his soul and all Christian souls. John Lynche's testament indicates modest wealth, being largely taken up with gifts of clothing. He did bequeath 12d. to his maid, however, and forgave Thomas Weldisshe 10s. owing on the farm of a house, actions which suggest he was not poor. Vincent's testamentary bequests show a greater engagement with orthodox devotion and, unusually, he requested that his body be buried in the belfry of the parish church of High Halden, bequeathing 20d. to that end, with the proviso: 'if the parishe wilbe content withall or else my body to be leid yn the Churcheyard ther'. He gave 12d. to the lady light and 12d. to the rood light, and devoted 13s. 4d. to his burial, 20s. to his month's mind and 6s. 8d. to his year's mind. In the last will he devised three pieces of land to his son. Vincent had been thoroughly integrated into parish life before the 1511–12 trials, serving as a churchwarden or *parochianus* in 1501, and as *parochianus* in 1506. He does not appear again after the trials but in 1514 a Thomas Lynche was churchwarden in High Halden.[140] As long as the full weight of ecclesiastical authority was withheld,

[135] PRC 17/5/310; U442/T99; PRC 17/1/97; *Kent heresy proceedings*, 38–9. Robert Franke appears to have died in 1522: PRC 3/5/33.

[136] PRO, E 179, 125/324; Zell, *Industry in the countryside*, 190–1, 195, 197, 220, 222.

[137] Thomas Lynche yeoman, High Halden: 1557, PRC 17/30/289; PRO, E 179, 125/324. On the whole, these were smaller farmer-tradesmen and craftspeople who, if they possessed land, held between 10 and around 25 acres, with small numbers of livestock: Zell, *Industry in the countryside*, 10–44, 88–152; Cornwall, 'English country towns', 63–7; McIntosh, *Autonomy and community*, 233.

[138] *Kent heresy proceedings*, 83, 87.

[139] PRC 17/16/152, 17/17/294.

[140] CCA, Z.3.2, fos 105v, 26r; Z.3.3, fo. 16r.

it was this sort of local power that may have afforded Lollardy a certain degree of protection. Finally, the Lynches of Great Chart appear to have been connected by marriage to Gerves Hendley of Cranbrook, with whom the Lollard Agnes Reignold had been in service in 1511.[141]

Stephen Castelyn of Tenterden held heretical opinions from around 1507 or 1508, when he would have been about nineteen, having been convinced by William Carder at Maidstone to 'belive ayenst the sacrament of thaulter'. On 15 May 1511 he abjured this and other errors concerning pilgrimage, images, confession and absolution and, as a result, was sentenced to various penances.[142] On September 11 in the same year he was sentenced again, this time to perpetual imprisonment at the Augustinian priory at Leeds. He may have failed to keep to his penitential regime or perhaps the authorities considered him too dangerous a heretic to be left at large. Castelyn's relation-ship with Carder may have been the bridge to his involvement in heretical meetings hosted by Edward Walker of Maidstone, which Castelyn had attended on at least four occasions between May 1509 at the latest and Christmas 1510. Significantly, John Bampton could not remember whether Castelyn or William Baker had read from a book at one of these meetings and, although Baker himself confessed to being the reader, Bampton's confu-sion suggests that Castelyn had read at other times.[143]

The tenor of the Castelyn family's testamentary piety was explored in detail in chapter 4 and it is possible to place Stephen accurately in his wider family. Stephen's brother, William Castelyn (for whom there is unfortunately no surviving will), died towards the end of 1510 (see figure 2) and the will of his widow Katherine (Stephen's sister-in-law) contains what may be the only direct reference to him outside the heresy trial proceedings. Katherine died shortly after William at the beginning of 1511 and Stephen was an executor and witness to her will. Katherine left him 'half of my husband's remaining steel and a hundred weight of iron', indicating that the brothers may have practised the same or at least similar trades, Stephen being described as a cutler in the trials.[144] He appears to have been named after his father (Stephen Castelyn senior), who was, most probably, one of the two sons of Robert Castelyn junior who died in 1487, who was in turn one of the three sons of Robert Castelyn senior who died in 1473.

To summarise briefly, the Castelyns had a hand in various craft and commercial enterprises as well as agriculture, and were one of Tenterden's more enduring and increasingly important families in this period. Until the 1520s their testamentary piety was conspicuously parsimonious, and Stephen

[handwritten marginal note: Link between Lollardy and Parsimonious-ness]

---

141 The will of Robert Lynche of Canterbury, 1530, formerly of Great Chart, mentions his mother Joan Hendley and Gerves Hendley his 'uncle': PRC 17/19/134. See also Gerveas Hendley, 1534: PRO, PCC 14 Hogen.

142 *Kent heresy proceedings*, 12, 52, 63.

143 Ibid. 62–4, 106–7, 52–4.

144 PRC 3/3/77, 17/11/183.

Castelyn's grandfather, and his father before him, made wills which were devoid of explicitly religious bequests. By the early sixteenth century the family's middling-to-upper wealth and status was confirmed by increasing local political involvement and power. This rise in fortune toward the heights reached later in the century appears to have brought with it the closer engagement with orthodox religious devotion seen in the wills made by Stephen's uncle (Richard) and cousin (Christopher), expressed in more unsparing bequests, but by no means embracing all aspects of orthodoxy such as the cult of saints and chantry foundation that continued to form part of the piety of some other influential families. In particular, they displayed a keen adherence to the Jesus Mass. In 1505, 1506 and 1515 Richard Castelyn served among Tenterden's *parochiani* in ecclesiastical visitations, and Christopher was churchwarden in 1521 and 1522.[145] Connections like these may have helped to protect Tenterden's heretics prior to 1511, and the Castelyns' seemingly uninterrupted rise in parochial government after the trials suggests that any stigma arising from Stephen's involvement in heresy did not result in their social or political marginalisation.

We know much less about William Pellond's involvement in Lollardy, but the familial context of his divergence into heresy is strikingly similar to Stephen Castelyn's. Only the record of Pellond's sentence survives, dated 17 December 1511, which confined him to within two miles of the monastery of Boxley for the rest of his life, providing always that the archbishop might relax his sentence.[146] The Pellonds were also a long-established family in Tenterden, with a hand in trade and craft activities, and considerable wealth by the late fifteenth century which by the early sixteenth, coupled with professional skills, placed them firmly within the middling stratum of local society and ensured them a share in minor office-holding.[147] Before the second decade of the century, like the Castelyns, their testamentary piety was frugal or, at most, modest in its religious arrangements. Significantly, William's father and grandfather made the most religiously sparse wills of all among their kinsfolk. By around the early 1520s they too developed a new approach to will-making which demonstrated a greater generosity of religious giving, but which nevertheless held back from more elaborate orthodox forms and, noticeably, devotion to saints. Again, like the Castelyns, these wills display from possibly as early as 1511 a marked continuity of affiliation to the Jesus Mass. In addition, they contained a strand of charitable and public works. Gifts to the poor typified some wills made by Lollards in other places such as the Chilterns and represented an alternative to offerings to

---

[145] CCA, Z.3.2, fos 4v, 25v; Z.3.3, fo. 51v; Z.3.4, fos 20r, 68r.

[146] *Kent heresy proceedings*, 113–14.

[147] It is unlikely that the William Pellond, who was imprisoned for heresy in 1511, became a freeman of Tenterden around 1529, as McSheffrey proposes: *Gender and heresy*, 125. It was probably his nephew, the son of Moyse Pellond, who died in 1540 (*see* figure 6): PRC 3/3/47.

saints in Lollard thinking, an attitude put into practice by William Baker of Cranbrook.[148]

The close contextualisation of the involvement in Lollardy of Stephen Castelyn and William Pellond not only lends new significance to the tenor of their families' testamentary piety but may also help to explain their excursions into heresy. Attitudes arising from rapid social and economic change, which led to parsimoniousness in testamentary expression, paved the way for these families to embrace what might be described as reformist tendencies within orthodox piety, and had the potential for further divergence into more extreme heretical ideas. These tendencies were encapsulated in the increasing Christocentricism of the Jesus Mass, rather than the cult of saints and, to a lesser extent, in humanitarian charity. There remains much work to be done on the possible radical potential of the Jesus Mass in late medieval England, not least in terms of its appeal to families and groups in urban society that were also attracted to Lollardy. The Castelyn and Pellond wills represent a strand of orthodox piety which contained nothing which was contrary to the Lollard ideas in circulation and perhaps even much in concert with them. The absence of devotion to saints matched the Wealden Lollards' own rejection of saints' cults, and the religious parsimony of the earlier family wills suggests that their writers were distanced from institutions, forms and structures of orthodox devotion. Such a tendency may in part have been inspired by, or may have had the potential to lead to, scepticism of the traditional authority of the clergy in religious life, and so to a rejection of its sacramental basis, an important element within the Wycliffite beliefs investigated in 1511–12.

Larry Poos's work on rural Essex in this period provides a useful comparison to developments in the Weald. He finds signs that among 'the broad middling range of rural people' there existed a scepticism with regard to secular and ecclesiastical authority, which produced a reactionary 'desire for greater involvement in communal life', a growing parochial activism and an essentially conservative concern for the morality of local clergy. This would help to explain the dynamics of Castelyn and Pellond piety and of other families like them. Of equal pertinence is Poos's suggestion that, in Essex, these attitudes were 'reinforced by both theologically orthodox and Lollard-influenced lay piety'.[149] The increasing presence of families like the Castelyns and Pellonds in communal life from the early sixteenth century, heralded a new involvement in structures of authority whose traditional claims had been questioned for some time by adherents to Lollard ideas in and around Tenterden, and which may well have been more openly criticised by the more orthodox. While the likes of Stephen Castelyn and William Pellond were attracted to Lollardy, and so became involved in active dissent,

---

148 Plumb, 'Social and economic spread', 116–17; Jones, 'Lollards and images', 35–6.
149 Poos, *Rural society*, 273.

their kinsmen engaged in a different sort of activism – certainly more orthodox, and probably more integrated into the mainstream of religious life – that was refashioning traditional pieties but shared some of Wealden Lollardy's cultural roots.

The appeal of Lollardy

Historians have offered a number of possible explanations for the continuity of Lollardy and what seems to have been a general susceptibility to religious dissent in areas such as the Weald of Kent. One of the earliest explanations looks to the Wealden cloth industry as having created the networks along which textile middlemen spread Lollard ideas to economically insecure wage-earning artisans, who were the obvious audience for anticlericalism and 'chiliastic prophecies'. The main proponent of this thesis is J. F. Davis who, after A. G. Dickens, argues that the conventicles originating with academics like White and Drayton 'once established . . . were aided by the textile connection in which they had been planted'.[150] This theory has been criticised recently for lacking hard evidence and there are a number of reasons for rejecting the cloth industry as a significant factor in the appeal and survival of Lollard heresy on the Weald.[151] To begin with, there is no evidence that Tenterden was ever a significant broadcloth centre comparable to Cranbrook and its surrounding parishes, and yet it had the stronger tradition of heresy.[152] Any influence that continental ideas had upon religious sentiments in the Weald, through the influx of Flemish weavers into the Cranbrook district in the fourteenth century, seems to have been limited. There are signs of foreign doctrines among the Lollard suspects at Staplehurst, and the extreme sacramentarianism of Kentish Lollardy from the early fifteenth century may have owed something to these influences, but they played no obvious part in early sixteenth-century heresy.[153] It is partly the assumption that cloth-workers were especially mobile that has cast them as the archetypal carriers of Lollard ideas, but recent work on rural mobility in Essex has shown that wage-earning cloth-workers were not as mobile as craftsmen and retailers, although textile middlemen were probably a different matter.[154] Wealden cloth-workers have been portrayed as increasingly economically downtrodden and insecure in this period, with the psychological incentives to be

[150] Davis, 'Lollard survival', 191–201 at p. 197; Dickens, *Lollards and Protestants*, 8–15, 48.
[151] McSheffrey, *Gender and heresy*, 194 n. 201.
[152] See p. 31 above.
[153] Dickens, *Lollards and Protestants*, 14; Davis, 'Lollard survival', 201, and *Heresy and reformation*, 4; Furley, 'Early history of Tenterden', 53; Witney, *Jutish forest*, 146–7. For the possible influence of continental ideas at Staplehurst see p. 154 n. 29 above.
[154] Davis, 'Lollard survival', passim; Dickens, *Lollards and Protestants*, 8–15, 48; Poos, *Rural society*, 280–1; Spufford, 'Importance of religion', 54.

attracted to anticlerical and millenarian doctrines, but there is no evidence of millenarianism in the Tenterden area and good reason to believe that Lollardy was not at all restricted to an artisan under-class as proposed by Davis.[155]

This is not to rule out, however, a connection between religious dissent and occupation in a craft or trade. To some extent, families with the greatest involvement in craft or industrial activity adhered to pious traditions most akin to Lollardy and were more susceptible to conversion to Wycliffite beliefs. The occupational profile of Wealden Lollardy, as in other areas, tends to confirm this.[156] The occupations of nine male suspects in 1511–12 are recorded in Warham's register, namely John Browne, Stephen Castelyn and Edward Walker, all cutlers; William Carder, *textor* (weaver); Robert Bright and William Bukherst, shoemakers/cordwainers; William Riche, glover; John Dodde, fletcher; and Christopher Grebill, tailor. Whether or not the occupations of these men made them more open to heterodoxy, trade connections do appear to have provided some of the weak ties and everyday or occasional relationships which helped to hold the geographically disparate Kentish Lollard groups together, and drew new converts into the more closed circles of the conventicle or household meeting.[157] For example, William Carder had first spoken to John Grebill senior while working at a loom in the latter's house.[158] Stephen Castelyn's more than occasional presence in the Maidstone area, suggests that he may have regularly worked or traded there, away from his home in Tenterden. He was possibly apprenticed to Edward Walker who was also a cutler. John Browne of Ashford also practised this trade and had links, through William Baker of Cranbrook, with the Maidstone group. 'Upon seynt Marks day' 1509, William Ryche of Benenden, glover, had talked about the sacrament of the altar with Robert Harryson of Canterbury at a fair held in Tenterden, a meeting which may have originated out of business activity.[159]

The increasing literacy of crafts- and tradespeople is also seen as a factor in the appeal of an essentially book-centred heresy. There can be no doubt that

155 Davis, 'Lollard survival', 198–200. Lambert hints at the possibility of this sort of attraction to Wycliffite ideas but concludes that there is insufficient evidence to make a firm judgement: *Medieval heresy*, 294.

156 Davis, 'Lollard survival', passim but esp. p. 193; Hudson, *Premature Reformation*, 128–33.

157 McSheffrey, *Gender and heresy*, 47–55, 74–9; M. Granovetter, 'The strength of weak ties', *American Journal of Sociology* lxxviii (1973), 1360–80, and 'The strength of weak ties: a network theory revisited', in P. V. Marsden and N. Lin (eds), *Social structure and network analysis*, Beverley Hills, Ca.–London 1982, 105–30; Hudson, *Premature Reformation*, 130–1; Davies, 'Lollardy and locality', 194–200.

158 *Kent heresy proceedings*, 11.

159 Ibid. 52–5, 45, 5; Spufford, 'Importance of religion', 53; L. A. Clarkson, 'The organization of the English leather industry in the late sixteenth and seventeenth centuries', *EcHR* 2nd ser. xiii (1960–1), 245–56.

Lollardy and literacy 'are entwined with a particular intricacy and resist separation' and the evidence from Kent shows that heretical texts were in circulation and being read in various settings.[160] Sceptical questioning of orthodox doctrine did not, however, rely upon the ability to read and, although exposure to texts may have inspired greater literacy and the formulation of doubts into more clearly articulated beliefs, the depositions suggest that only a minority of suspects actually read them. As long as there were literate individuals with access to texts literacy was not, therefore, a prerequisite for attraction or adherence to heretical ideas, although it undoubtedly helped.[161] There is a conspicuous absence of books in the Tenterden wills made by lay people in this period but this may reveal no more than a general uneasiness about bringing book ownership to the attention of the ecclesiastical authorities given the town's notorious legacy. The slight bias to professional occupations among religiously moderate and frugal families and the fact that the likes of the Castelyns and the Pellonds would have come into greater contact with the manuscript culture of town and parish government as they rose to prominence lends some support to the notion that increasing literacy aided the apprehension and dissemination of heresy. Orthodox devotion may have benefited from this process too, however, and lay education at Tenterden was given a substantial boost with the establishment of a grammar school some time around 1510.[162] This was, of course, shortly before the heresy trials of 1511–12 and the arrival of the Jesus Mass in 1513, and is indicative of the town's importance in wider cultural developments and, not least, a programme of humanist inspired reform. In this sense, growing levels of literacy may have been more important for the way they helped to redefine orthodoxy than for their sustenance of heresy.

Some attempts to explain the attraction of Lollardy to so-called artisans tend to link literacy with what are seen as certain predisposing attitudes to heresy. So, Michael Lambert argues that it was 'Lollardy's appeal to independent judgement', which made it attractive 'to a class in which literacy was incipient, and which included hard-working, independent people anxious to learn and to form judgements for themselves'. He goes on: 'the assumptions and outlook of the craftsman, which made a minority susceptible to the Lollard mission, were what counted'.[163] Similarly, A. G. Dickens claimed that the artisan tended to act and think as an individualist, stemming from 'an old and fiercely independent tradition deriving from medieval

---

[160] A. Hudson, ' "Laicus litteratus": the paradox of Lollardy', in P. Biller and A. Hudson (eds), *Heresy and literacy, 1000–1530*, Cambridge 1994, 235; Lambert, *Medieval heresy*, 277–8, 291–4; McSheffrey, *Gender and heresy*, 143, 148.

[161] R. N. Swanson, 'Literacy, heresy, history and orthodoxy: perspectives and permutations for the later Middle Ages', in Biller and Hudson, *Heresy and literacy*, 279–93.

[162] See p. 193 below.

[163] Lambert, *Medieval heresy*, 278, 291, 294.

town-life'.[164] There is, however, little evidence to suggest that craftsmen were especially individualistic and individualism does not necessarily lead to a greater openness to heresy. If there was any such thing as an 'artisan mentality' in late medieval and early modern England, it has yet to be adequately described or explained.

Others have sought to explain the appeal of religious dissent in terms of the general social, political and economic conditions and dynamics in areas and regions identified as more or less continuous breeding grounds for dissent and Nonconformity. One such type, first highlighted by Professor Everitt, was the forest. Taking Nonconformity in the Weald of Kent in the late seventeenth century as a case study, Everitt suggests that cloth-making and Nonconformity were coincidental symptoms of 'certain local characteristics peculiar to the society and settlement pattern of these areas'.[165] It is now almost taken for granted that the exceptionally large parishes of the Weald and its scattered pattern of settlement hampered regular church attendance and encouraged independent religion. In Tenterden in the late medieval period, it was just these sorts of conditions which led to the establishment of a degree of independence in religious life for the people of Small Hythe, who appear to have developed their own distinctive piety. According to Everitt, the 'comparative weakness of the local manorial structure', the absence of powerful gentry, and the Weald's isolation, which ensured its remoteness from ecclesiastical control, all helped to make it a safe haven for dissenters; a point also made by Christopher Hill in relation to the geographical spread of radical dissent in general.[166] To a certain extent Tenterden fits this model, but its role in the Cinque Ports confederation, domestic and overseas trade links and ancient ties with the great monastic houses of Kent, indicate that the town was far from dislocated from outside influences and religious and secular authorities. Some important county gentry families were thoroughly involved in local affairs and had a significant influence on the course of religion in the area. Andrew Hope may be closer to the truth in his suggestion that 'it was not difficult for the Weald to know what was going on in the outside world, but rather more difficult for the outside world to know what was going on in the Weald'.[167]

A slightly different approach to these problems involves exploring the common social and economic features of industrialising regions for possible explanations of the continuity of heterodoxy.[168] Joan Thirsk's pioneering

---

[164] Dickens, Lollards and Protestants, 8. See also K. Thomas, Religion and the decline of magic, New York 1971, 663.

[165] A. Everitt, 'Nonconformity in country parishes', in J. Thirsk (ed.), Land, Church and people: essays presented to Professor H. P. R. Finberg (AgHR xviii [1970], supplement), 178–99 at p. 189.

[166] Ibid. 191, and Continuity and colonization, 221–2; Hill, 'Lollards to Levellers', passim.

[167] From private correspondence.

[168] For an excellent, although perhaps overly sceptical, discussion see Spufford, 'Importance of religion', 40–64, esp. pp. 41–2 n. 128.

work on 'industries in the countryside', and the endeavours of others after her, have produced a clearer understanding of the nature of the regional economies and societies which were host to handicraft by-industries from the late Middle Ages onwards. It is now established that these regions had a number of things in common – the Weald of Kent being no exception – chiefly, mixed pastoral agriculture of dairying, breeding and fattening, conducted by small farmers with relatively secure tenures; a high density of population; sufficient resources of pasture and/or wood to sustain partible inheritance; and the absence, or weakness, of any manorial or co-operative farming framework.[169] Similarly, Andrew Brown identifies dislocation from ecclesiastical control and certain social, economic and demographic features shared by the cloth towns of the claylands of Berkshire, Wiltshire and Dorset as important factors in creating susceptibility to heresy and dissent in the fifteenth and early sixteenth centuries.[170] Also drawing on evidence from the south-western counties (in this case Wiltshire, Dorset and Somerset) David Underdown argues for the existence of two increasingly polarised regional cultures in the early seventeenth century that underlay geographical patterns of Civil War allegiance. There was much complexity and intermediacy within and between them, but these two different types of region broadly comprised ' "traditional" areas of open-field, sheep-corn husbandry in nucle-ated villages of the chalk downlands' on the one hand, and 'the more individ-ualistic economies and settlement patterns of the . . . cheese and cloth-making country' on the other. The wood-pasture parishes and towns that characterised the cheese and cloth region were more divided than the nucleated, predominantly open-field parishes of the downlands. They were, to begin with, larger and contained more scattered patterns of settlement; due to the influx of poor migrants and growing disparities of wealth between the wealthier parishioners and their less prosperous neighbours they were more divided socially; and they were fragmented also in religion due to the presence of Puritan reformers. Puritanism was particularly attractive to the middling sort who sought a suitable response to problems of disorder and instability arising from overpopulation and landlessness. This was manifested in the moralising assault on traditional festive and communal culture in the decades before the Civil War in the cheese and cloth areas.[171] The attraction of Puritanism to middle-ranking parishioners at a time of increasing social polarisation and dislocation may, in some ways, be analogous to the appeal of moralising, family-centred piety and Lollard heresy to socially mobile middling families in Tenterden and the Weald at a time of similar, if less

---

[169] J. Thirsk, 'Industries in the countryside', in F. J. Fisher (ed.), *Essays in the economic and social history of Tudor and Stuart England*, Cambridge 1961, 70–88; Spufford, 'Importance of religion', 40–64; Zell, *Industry in the countryside*, passim.

[170] Brown, *Popular piety*, 219–22.

[171] D. Underdown, *Revel, riot and rebellion: popular politics and culture in England, 1603–1660*, Oxford 1985, 4–8, 73–105, 206–7, 275–9, quotation at p. 8.

pronounced, economic and social development in parishes with many of the same underlying features.

Coupled with the possible underlying structural and cultural reasons for enduring traditions of dissent in wood-pasture industrialising regions, Margaret Spufford suggests that where there was the time and necessity for by-employments and handicrafts there was also time for reading. Also, areas engaged in sizeable export or import were connected by regular trade to one another and to London and, in turn, they also had strong trade links with Protestant Europe and these factors ensured a steady flow of ideas and a moderate supply of books, both old and new.[172]

This study makes a further contribution to these theories by suggesting some of the specific mechanisms and processes that linked susceptibility to heterodoxy with particular economic, social and cultural dynamics. To begin with, it was not so much craftspeople *per se* who were attracted to Lollardy at Tenterden, as members of upwardly mobile families with some involvement in craft and trade activity, who in some cases advanced from positions of moderate status to dramatically increased levels of wealth and influence by the sixteenth century. These families held attitudes to the disposal and redistribution of family wealth and commercial advance which, coupled with their efforts to fashion distinctive identities for themselves, produced a pious mentality firmly centred on family and kinship. As a consequence they tended to neglect those collective and personal expressions of orthodox religion in their wills which so often involved considerable expenditure. They also appear to have been, at least in the late fifteenth century, somewhat distanced from the religious life of the parish. Underlying the restraints that economic advancement and the careful management of family resources placed upon pious giving were deep-rooted attitudes that were a feature of a region characterised by small and late-enclosed farms where, as Joan Thirsk suggests, the family rather than the hamlet or the village formed the 'cooperative working unit' and was so important in structuring social and religious life.[173] What might be described as a materialistic but no less moral concern for familial continuity and advancement at the expense of involvement in collective religious life appears to have made these families susceptible to both moderate reformist ideas within orthodoxy and more radical Lollard opinions. More work clearly needs to be done on the connections between, on the one hand, the generation of family wealth and upward social mobility and, on the other, continuities of Lollardy and Nonconformity.

---

172 Spufford, 'Importance of religion', 40–64. Peter Clark puts the continuity between Lollardy and Lutheranism on the Weald down to good communication through trade with the rest of the country and abroad, together with 'the absence of effective ecclesiastical policing'. However, he also writes of 'a strong tradition of multi-generational family loyalty to unorthodoxy' in Kent, which was 'to be one of Lollardy's most valuable legacies to Kentish Protestantism': *English provincial society*, 30–1, 42.

173 Thirsk, 'Industries in the countryside', 86.

Equally, very little attention has been given to the links between religious dissent and emergent urban identities, especially in medium-sized towns like Tenterden.[174] As Collinson suggests, 'it seems unlikely that "rural dissent" had a peculiarly rural character'. At Tenterden it seems to have been more urban than rural and it may be no accident that the core of the Spuffordians' work on heresy and Nonconformity in the countryside is centred on a market town and its commercial hinterland.[175]

Political and intellectual influences

Connections between leading Tenterden families and local and county gentry show that the Weald was not politically isolated, that its distance from centres of authority may have been exploited by local gentry, and that their religious leanings may have influenced regional culture as well as helping to provide a degree of protection from ecclesiastical scrutiny. By at least the beginning of the sixteenth century the Castelyn and Pellond families had seemingly strong connections with the Foules, who provided Tenterden with bailiffs on five separate occasions and occupied the ambiguous grey area between yeomen-townsfolk and lesser gentry.[176] They were one of only two of the twenty-three selected families which were religiously generous in their testamentary piety and continued to rise in status and influence after 1500. They were also among those families which patronised the Jesus Mass; a reminder that the devotion had wide appeal.[177] Equally, these links show how leading parish families following quite different pious traditions worked together in both official and unofficial contexts.

Another family with whom the Castelyns, Pellonds and the Foules all had connections were the Haleses.[178] The Haleses held an ambiguous position in their attitudes to reform of the Church. For example, Christopher Hales, elected MP for Canterbury in 1523, appointed attorney-general in 1529 and Master of the Rolls in 1536, was actively involved in the investigation of Elizabeth Barton, the Nun of Kent, and in the 1530s played an important part

[174] Brown, *Popular piety*, 219–22.
[175] Collinson, 'Critical conclusion', 390, and see Margaret Spufford's note on the same page.
[176] All 3 families' wills reveal links and they acted in concert as witnesses and feoffees for others: PRC 17/6/96, 17/11/183, 17/21/58, 17/15/64, 17/19/273, 17/7/250, 17/10/19, 17/12/312, 17/16/269, 17/16/244; BL, Add. Ch. 16330; MS Add. 48022, fos 26r, 27v; Te/S1, fos 43v–44r.
[177] PRC 17/16/64, 17/16/239.
[178] Acting together in a number of probate cases and land-transactions: PRC 17/8/41, 17/7/250, 17/11/188; U410/T21; U455/T88; U455/T87. For example, in 1495 John Hales of Tenterden may have been attorney to the family of the late Thomas Elnode, when lands, in which William Foule had been jointly enfeoffed, were passed to Elnode's son, the deed being witnessed by 'William Pellond senior': BL, Add. Ch. 16330.

in Thomas Cromwell's patronage network in the county. He probably worked with Cromwell in drafting and enacting the early Reformation legislation and benefited greatly in the process from the dissolution of monasteries in Kent. He lacked sympathy for more sweeping reform, however, and in the quarter sessions of 1538 his own group of magistrates took the opportunity to persecute more radical Kentish evangelicals.[179] Sir James Hales was more committed to change. He earned a reputation as a leading evangelical lawyer and, among other things, drafted the Chantries Act of 1547. It was probably not just obstinacy or zeal for the letter of the law that led to his clash with the Marian regime in 1553. His insistence that Catholics be prosecuted for nonconformity at the Kent assizes of that year landed him in prison. Perhaps already unbalanced, the experience of imprisonment and the arguments of a colleague and other men who visited him in the Fleet appear to have driven him to try to take his own life. Shortly after his release in 1554 he was found dead in a stream outside Canterbury. Whether he committed suicide or was murdered remains a mystery.[180] The Haleses represent something of a mixed and essentially human reaction to the changes of the Reformation. Willing to move with the times, especially when there were such great gains to be made in office-holding and seigneurial lordship, before the late 1540s their desire for limited erastian reform was not incompatible with the sort of piety expressed by families like the Castelyns and Pellonds.

The Hales, Foule, Castelyn and Pellond families all had dealings with the Guldefords. For example, in 1524, one William Pellond was named among the men of the Cinque Ports in the retinue of Sir Edward Guldeford.[181] When Sir John Guldeford made his will in 1493 and wished his 'out beryng to be made not pomposely' and that at his year's mind a plain stone with epitaphs rather than a tomb be laid on him, he perhaps left a portent of his family's reformist stance in the future.[182] John's son Richard Guldeford was also intensely pious, making a pilgrimage to Palestine in 1506, having prepared his will the day before his departure. He died in Jerusalem and his travels were recorded by his unnamed chaplain in an account presumably intended to serve as a travel guide for other pilgrims with its matter-of-fact descriptions of journeys and sites alongside references to their various religious significances as recorded in biblical and patristic sources. The text is wholly traditional in its descriptions of legends, shrines and relics but it is impossible to know how much control Sir Richard had over its authorship.[183]

---

179 DNB, s.v. Hales, Christopher; Clark, *English provincial society*, 13, 37, 40–1, 54–7, 62, 63; Roberts, 'Tenterden houses', 296; L&P xv. 942 (61).

180 DNB, s.v. Hales, Sir James (d. 1554); Clark, *English provincial society*, 41, 81.

181 PRC 17/16/269, 17/17/158; U455/T87; L&P iv. 459. Interestingly, in a feoffment of 1475 lands in Tenterden passed from John Guldeford, knight, to John Seler of Reading Street, Katherine Castelyn's father: CKS, U55/T414.

182 PRO, PCC 29 Dogett, fo. 223.

183 *The pylgrymage of Sir Richard Guylforde to the Holy Land A.D. 1506 from a copy believed to be unique, from the press of Richard Pynson*, ed. Sir Henry Ellis (Camden o.s. li, 1851).

There can be no doubt that the Guldefords took time to concern themselves with religious matters. In the late 1520s, when anticlericalism had gathered pace in Kent, they led the attack on church court fees. They were also intellectually important, as Sir Henry Guldeford was a friend and correspondent of Erasmus and the family was instrumental in circulating humanist ideas among the government circle of the county, which may have provided one of the main sources of inspiration for the radical Protestant group centred on Canterbury that emerged over the next decade. At the same time, Lutheranism began to take root on the Weald and in the Medway valley, the areas where the Guldefords held greatest sway.[184] Especially because of their struggles with the religiously conservative Nevilles, the Guldefords may have found it convenient to provide a safe environment for some of their less than orthodox neighbours. In a move that mixed politics with pragmatism, Sir Edward Guldeford wrote to Wolsey in 1528, asking him to release Nicholas Whyte of Winchelsea, who had been arrested on suspicion of heresy, in order for him to attend to sea defences on Walland Marsh.[185] It is possible that the ease with which new converts were made to Lollardy in the early sixteenth century, and the subsequent precocious development of Protestantism in the region, owed something to the Guldeford's political ambitions and patronage networks. They took advantage of the vacuum created by the Weald's isolation from structures of government that worked to shore up traditional religion elsewhere in the county and had a vested interest in keeping things that way. As a result they may have helped to maintain the cohesion of a regional culture that fostered dissenting mentalities.

The Guldefords' interest in humanism suggests a surprising richness and diversity to Wealden culture. Their influence may have exposed townsfolk, already predisposed to intellectual novelty, to further new ideas. It was not the first time that the new learning had had a presence at Tenterden. John Morer, vicar of Tenterden from 1479 to his death in 1489, made an extraordinary last will and testament which reveals his important position within fifteenth-century humanist scholarship.[186] He bequeathed a total of fifty books to friends, including laymen, clergy and religious, to churches, grammar schools and colleges. Many of these were Latin works firmly rooted in medieval traditions of liturgy, pastoral care and theology, but a number were humanistic and some of these were in Greek. Fellow of New College Oxford from 1446, Morer followed the typically humanistic path of supplicating for an advanced degree in medicine instead of theology or canon and

[184] Clark, *English provincial society*, 29–30, 42.

[185] *L&P* iv. 4627; vi. 7 (most probably misdated to 1533). I would like to thank Andrew Hope for kindly bringing this reference to my attention.

[186] PRO, PCC 20 Milles, fos 161v–162v; Taylor, 'Rectors and vicars of St Mildred's', 215–16; H. R. Plomer, 'Books mentioned in wills', *Transactions of the Bibliographical Society* vii (1904), 118–19; J. W. Bennett, 'John Morer's will: Thomas Linacre and prior Sellyng's Greek teaching', *Studies in the Renaissance* xv (1968), 70.

civil law. He probably owed his institution to the vicarage of St Mildred's in 1479 to some previous connection with William Sellyng, prior of Christ Church Canterbury, who held the right of advowson at the time. The vicarage provided a very healthy £24 per annum, to which Morer added the rectory of the London church of St Bennet next Bucklersbury in 1482, the same year that he completed the degree of bachelor of theology.[187]

Morer's carefully deliberate bequests reflect his career path and indicate the compass of his connections. He requested burial in the chancel of St Mildred's, to which he left 23s. 4d. and a number of books, including a Gradual, and a *Pupilla oculi sacerdotis* and commentary on the Gospels, the last two to be chained in the choir. He bequeathed a number of theological books, including the Epistles of St Jerome, which would soon be edited by Erasmus, to the grammar schools of Christ Church and St Augustine's at Canterbury and to Wye and Ashford colleges in the same diocese. He left the master of St Thomas of Acon grammar school in London two books, including St Augustine's *Confessions*, a number of volumes to Magdalen College and to Canterbury College, Oxford, and five books, including St Augustine's Epistles, another text which would be edited by Erasmus, to Eton College where he was a Fellow in the early 1470s. Morer also left five books and £10 to Thomas Linacre who was studying in Florence at the time and would become famous for his Greek scholarship and service as royal physician. Two were unnamed Greek texts, one printed and one in manuscript and it is possible that the former was the Greek grammar of Constantine Lascaris produced in 1476, the first book to be entirely printed in Greek characters. The other three were in Latin, including a printed edition of Thucydides's *History of the Peloponnesian war*, first produced in 1483, and *Tullium in nova rethorica*, both important to the new learning. Morer was some thirty years Linacre's senior and may well have taught him Greek, either at Oxford or Canterbury.[188] From 1509 Linacre acquired the rectory of Merhsam and the incumbency of Hawkhurst, both not far from Tenterden.[189] Other titles, such as the *Confessions* of St Augustine, Cicero's *De officiis* and Vergil's *Aeneid* also attest to Morer's engagement with humanistic studies. The most significant was a work by Laurenzo Valla, most likely to have been the *Elegantiae linguae latinae*, which he gave to Master John Williamson, rector of St George's, Canterbury. It was Erasmus' discovery of another work by Valla, his philological assault on the Vulgate, which provided perhaps the most important building block for the production of his Greek New Testament and represents one of the key intellectual turning points of the sixteenth century.[190]

187 Bennett, 'John Morer's will', 82–6; Taylor, 'Rectors and vicars of St Mildred's', 215–16; Emden, *Biographical register of the University of Oxford to A.D. 1500*, 1309, 1326.
188 Bennett, 'John Morer's will', 70–1, 86–7; Taylor, 'Rectors and vicars of St Mildred's', 215–16.
189 W. Osler, *Thomas Linacre*, Cambridge 1908, 20.
190 J. H. Bentley, *Humanists and holy writ: New Testament scholarship in the Renaissance*, Princeton, NJ 1983, 9, 12, 33–5, 54, 49, 161–2.

While Morer gave to individuals and institutions beyond Kent he used his last will and testament to construct a notion of his local and regional identity. This was focused upon Tenterden and the Weald but encompassed the wider diocese of Canterbury. In addition to the grammar schools mentioned, he remembered the Wealden religious houses of the Carmelites of Lossenham, the Trinitarian Friars of Mottenden and the Friars Minor at nearby Winchelsea. To Sir John Guldeford he bequeathed a book of divers chronicles and histories and may have initiated Guldeford's allegiance to humanism. But it is his bequests of books to fellow parish clergy in the diocese of Canterbury that arguably best delineate the boundaries of his social and ethnic identity. As Josephine Bennett comments on the nature of Morer's will: 'I know of no other document which indicates a similar community of interest among the secular clergy of England' in the fifteenth century.[191] Morer selected volumes to be left to Thomas Copland, rector of Biddenden and Richard Prutt of Sandhurst, both near Tenterden; to Robert Sheffeld, rector of Chartham, near Canterbury; to Master William Page of Maidstone; to John Willyamson, rector of St George's, Canterbury, already mentioned; to a Master John Richardson of Canterbury and Master Richard Stevyns of the parish of St Dunstan, Canterbury; to John Matthew, chaplain; to Master John Carlesse, and Richard Williford, one of his executors, a canon lawyer in the Canterbury archdeaconry courts who held the rectories of Dymchurch and Sevington, both within fifteen miles of Tenterden. The last wills and testaments of four of these men have survived. They date from 1498 to 1521, suggesting that they were all of the same generation and that John Morer, being sixty when he died, was their senior.[192]

All but Robert Sheffeld left books of one sort or another in their wills, to individuals, parish churches and chantries. Richard Stevyns bequeathed a printed Bible in two volumes and an unspecified printed book on the Scriptures (possibly a concordance) to 'le Ropers chantre' in St Dunstan's, Canterbury. It is possible that Richard Stevyns was chantry priest to the Roper foundation and that he and others in this group of clergy were connected with that influential family and shared their preoccupations with education and improving the quality of clerical provision in Kent. Both Richard Stevyns and John Williamson, rector of St George's, Canterbury, named John Roper as one of the executors of their wills. Williamson charged his executors not to sell any of his books (which he rather disappointingly doesn't name or describe) but to give them by their own discretion to such persons and places as they saw convenient 'except suche as they will kepe of theyme to there owne use'. His other executor was John Hales, steward to the Guldefords.[193]

---

[191] Bennett, 'John Morer's will', 87.

[192] Thomas Copland, 1498: PRC 17/7/53; Richard Stevyns, 1500: PRC 32/6/2a; Robert Sheffeld, 1509: PRO, PCC 14 Bennett, 106v–107r; John Williamson, 1521: PRC 17/15/101; Bennett, 'John Morer's will', 87–8.

[193] PRC 32/6/2a, 17/15/101.

In addition to more wide-ranging connections across the diocese, the sense of locality and, specifically, collegiality between neighbouring parish clergy is forcefully expressed in these wills, as is their sense of service to the locality underlined by their gifts to the poor. Morer, like Sheffeld and Copland, requested burial in the chancel of his parish church. The tombstone which can still be seen in the floor on the north side of the high altar, bearing an indent of a figure in priestly vestments, may be his. He left five marks at a rate of 6s. 8d. a year to fund a chantry priest for the fraternity of the Blessed Virgin Mary at Tenterden and his will does not give the impression that he was divorced from the parish. His mention as a witness in one out of the eighteen surviving Tenterden wills made during his ten-year incumbency at least establishes that he was not altogether absent.[194]

John Morer and his influential role in a network of scholarly parish clergy illustrates that Tenterden and the Weald were by no means culturally isolated or backward. St Mildred's was a wealthy living and Tenterden's status as the chief centre of the Kentish Weald and its heretical legacy made it strategically important to the ecclesiastical hierarchy. Seven out of the other ten priests who held the living from the 1440s to the 1540s appear to have been university educated, at a time when something like a third of institutions to benefices in the diocese went to graduates.[195] It is hard to believe that these clergy did not exert influence over religious culture in their parishes through preaching and patronage of grammar schools, religious houses and other foundations across the Weald and East Kent. The circulation of books, some with radical doctrinal potential, between clergy and institutions may have aroused and fed the curiosity of lay people who had an interest in devotional and instructional literature.[196] Local clergy are likely to have associated most closely with the middling to upper strata of local society who enjoyed increasing access to literacy and education, the Ropers, Haleses and Guldefords being cases in point. However, social boundaries were not impermeable. John Morer's connections with a Tenterden man named Moses Pette, who acted as one of his executors and to whom he left his best wet-weather cope, are a case in point. Pette, as mentioned above, belonged to a religiously moderate and influential Tenterden family that had been involved in the Tenterden rebellion of 1438, and in disturbances in 1471. The troubles of 1438 were linked to heresy and Moses Pette's seemingly close relationship with Morer suggests that families drawn to dissenting opinions may also have had the social standing and education to gain access to, or at least an awareness of, more learned discourses.

---

194 PRC 17/5/310.
195 Taylor, 'Rectors and vicars of St Mildred's', 213–19; Emden, *Biographical register of the University of Oxford to A.D. 1500*, 272–3, 975, 1229, and *Biographical register of the University of Oxford A.D. 1501 to 1540*, Oxford 1974, 21, 1500; M. L. Zell, 'The personnel of the clergy in Kent in the Reformation period', EHR lxxxix (1974), 525–6.
196 Swanson, *Catholic England*, 22.

Access to new ideas could involve other types of cultural and social exchange. The Lollards Agnes Ive, sister to Robert Hilles of Tenterden, her late husband John Ive, and Agnes Chetynden all lived in St George's parish, Canterbury, where John Williamson was vicar. It is possible that around the same time as Williamson received the Lorenzo Valla text from Morer, Agnes Ive (and perhaps her husband) came under his pastoral care. Undoubtedly unconnected as these events were, they signify the importance of overlapping networks of cultural transmission, which in terms of the religious changes brought about by the increasing circulation and social penetration of new learning in the early decades of the sixteenth century, may have been more closely related than we yet realise. For example, humanist influences at Tenterden may partly explain the success of the Jesus Mass there. John Colet, dean of St Paul's was, after all, one of the devotion's greatest publicists and patrons.[197]

Morer and the diocesan clergy with whom he was associated appear to have expressed shared religious affiliations, which placed them firmly within the more progressively orthodox strands of pre-Reformation piety. All but one of their testamentary dedicatory clauses are straightforwardly orthodox and Robert Sheffeld emphasised his dependence on the mercy and merits of Christ and the Virgin. All requested memorial services, masses and prayers, usually to be carried out in conjunction with charity to the poor, and two asked for trentals. Three out of four gave to lights and the same number expressed devotion to the Virgin but none of their wills named any other saints' cults or images. This, coupled with their educational preoccupations, suggests that they anticipated and possibly helped to drive forward the sorts of reformist but orthodox sensibilities that were beginning to dominate expressions of lay piety in Tenterden by the early sixteenth century and which may typify a more general dynamic in other parts of East Kent in this period. This has further implications for the crucial position of parish clergy at the social, cultural and intellectual intersections between heresy, heterodoxy and various shades of orthodoxy.

Peter Marshall, bachelor of theology and vicar of Tenterden from 1494 to 1512, may have played an especially significant role in the crucial years in the run-up to the heresy trials of 1511–12. He helped to establish the parish's grammar school around 1510 in concert with the local gentle family of Hayman. The school was attached to the permanent chantry endowed by Marshall and which bore his name and was also substantially supported by his brother William, vicar of nearby Warehorne. William's unusually wealthy will of 1523 named John Hales as one of his executors, Peter Hayman and Christopher Hales among his witnesses, displayed strong links with the Guldefords and left books to Oxford University. In his will of 1518 Peter Marshall bequeathed 20s. to the poor of Tenterden and 10 marks in works of

[197] J. B. Gleason, *John Colet*, Berkeley, Los Angeles–London 1989, 239–40.

charity but curiously failed to mention St Mildred's or the chantry. He appears to have belonged to reformist, and probably humanist, orthodox circles. He resigned as vicar of Tenterden in 1512, no doubt because of the events of the previous year, but his precise relationship to early sixteenth-century Wealden Lollardy remains a mystery and it is possible he was somehow implicated.[198]

The Wycliffite tradition established in Tenterden and its hinterland parishes by the 1420s was sacramentarian, anti-sacerdotal and hostile to the cult of saints. Chichele's and subsequent purges do not appear to have eradicated heresy from the area and there is good reason to believe that heretical opinions were kept alive locally throughout the second half of the fifteenth century. Tenterden remained the most important focus of dissent in Kent, and the network that was uncovered in 1511–12 was well-established and growing, with documented origins in the 1470s, and some possible familial continuities from the 1420s. The evidence suggests that extensive and entrenched sympathy with Lollard calls for reform afforded heretics a degree of protection, and ensured they were not ostracised from town or parish affairs. Convinced Lollards at Tenterden on the whole appear to have attended church and so were not separatists and cannot be described as a sect. They do not appear to have conceived of their activities as constituting an alternative Church and may have exercised considerable influence over parish religion. Most of the fifteenth- and sixteenth-century suspects in the Tenterden area, who can be traced in local sources, appear to have been moderately wealthy themselves or belonged to families that were reasonably well to do by the standards of small town society. Recent reassessments of the social breadth of Lollardy have arguably overemphasised the appeal of heretical ideas to the lowest social levels in order to undermine long-standing theories about the social specificity of English heresy, but it would appear that Lollardy did have a particular social profile at Tenterden, being largely confined to middling to upper-middling, socially mobile and politically influential families.

Reconstruction of the testamentary traditions of these families suggests that an individual's familial piety was an important deciding factor in whether or not he or she diverged into heresy. It also tells us something about the sorts of orthodox pious traditions that were closest to Lollard concerns and attitudes. There may not have been much between the parsimony of the late fifteenth-century wills produced by these families, and the beliefs of convinced heretics. Equally, the more engaged piety of the early sixteenth century, practised by the likes of the Castelyns and the Pellonds, remained aligned with Lollardy in a number of ways, and may have had the effect of

---

198 PRC 32/12/158; PRO, PCC 18 Bodfelde, fos 138v–140r; Taylor, 'Rectors and vicars of St Mildred's', 216, 243; W. K. Jordan, 'Social institutions in Kent, 1480–1660: a study of the changing pattern of social aspiration', AC lxxv (1961), 71–2.

incorporating previously marginalised elements of local religion into the mainstream. First, there was a certain radicalism and doctrinal reformism to their neglect of the cult of saints and adherence to the Jesus Mass; secondly, there was a continuing moderation in expenditure on religious ceremony and display; and, thirdly, an emphasis upon humanitarian charity. Religious dissent was an outgrowth and one of the more extreme expressions of an enduring and entrenched piety shared by a sizeable minority of leading parish families. Family and the multi-generational descent of dissent were undoubtedly important to the survival of Lollardy but so was the familial transmission of orthodox pieties that rendered their adherents susceptible to heterodox ideas. In this sense, the genealogy of certain types of orthodoxy was as important in the formation of heretical continuities in particular localities and regions as the descent of heresy.

This does not mean that heresy and orthodoxy were indistinguishable. Efforts to maintain the secrecy of heretical meetings show that Wycliffites understood that their views were illicit and condemned by the ecclesiastical hierarchy and that they had a clear sense of their own identities as heretics. The events of the 1420s and subsequent prosecutions in the fifteenth century ensured that this was the case. Conversion to heretical opinions appears to have been experienced by some in the form of an intellectual, emotional or psychological moment of passage into heresy but there may have been a substantial proportion of parishioners who held more ambiguous views which lay somewhere on the pious spectrum between convinced Lollardy and more traditional forms of orthodoxy. While many of these families and individuals may have been aware of Lollardy, or even on its fringes, they did not become actively involved and so in that sense remained orthodox, but their orthodoxy appears to have been informed by Wycliffitism as well as broader legitimised reformist influences and initiatives, and typified the tenor of piety at Tenterden by the 1520s. This suggests that the most significant shifts in religious beliefs and practices prior to the Reformation may not have been experienced as conversion from orthodoxy to heresy but as processes or moments of transition and reconstruction for which there was no official vocabulary of articulation.

Epilogue

Late Medieval Piety and the Reformation

Heterodoxy and orthodoxy in pre-Reformation Tenterden

One of the central aims of this book has been to challenge the usefulness of approaches that have been adopted by historians of pious practices. In this sense, the reconstruction of late medieval piety is as much its theme as its aim, with Tenterden providing a test case for a new approach. Due to the nature and survival of the evidence of piety at Tenterden, discussion of method has centred largely on testamentary analysis. Large-scale quantitative approaches and subsequent pessimism toward the value of last wills and testaments have been equally unhelpful in this regard; the merits of using testamentary sources lie in the close and comparative reading of these documents, within appropriate units of analysis, together with detailed linkage to other materials. Comparative analysis to some extent provides access to the relative intensity of testamentary piety, and reveals how considerable commitment sometimes lay in the most seemingly insignificant of acts. The making of a will was, on the whole, a deeply significant and self-consciously symbolic act, firmly rooted within the traditional practice of the moral economy, and a vocabulary by which the individual testator expressed his or her preoccupations. Pious bequests derived their meaning from their relationship to the practices of family, kin and the wider community.

The foregoing reconstruction of piety at Tenterden, underpinned by this approach to probate materials, presents a significant challenge to recent revisionist notions about the vigour, coherence and harmony of traditional orthodoxy before the Reformation. Orthodox piety was clearly not the same thing for all Tenterden's will-making parishioners. It involved markedly different levels of giving to, and engagement with, a range of religious institutions, and entailed contrasting patterns of practice and devotion from one individual to the next. Such differences in individual allegiance to traditional orthodox practices were part, to one extent or another, of definable and traceable traditions in family piety. There were consistent quantitative and qualitative differences between the testamentary pieties of leading families. There was much subtlety to these gradations at the centre of the pious spectrum but a marked contrast between the most sparing and the most lavish will-making practices. Although they provide only a partial picture of involvement in religious life, these variations indicate the existence of significant differences in commitment to the forms of orthodox devotion.

It is difficult to imagine how the differences between contrasting traditions could have remained entirely inconspicuous. Families that endowed chantries, and arranged for trentals and masses at *Scala Coeli* for the health of their souls, remembered the religious orders in their wills, gave to lights and maintained and decorated saints' images, rubbed shoulders and attended church and chapel with those which seem rarely to have engaged in these activities. This suggests that orthodox religious culture at Tenterden may not have been recognisable as a 'single system of belief and practice'[1] but was heterogeneous, multi-layered and subject to significant stresses and divergences. Although differences in piety do not appear to have resulted in schism, the allegation in 1511 that many members of the congregation sat still in church during procession suggests a significant degree of fragmentation of the religious community of the parish. What appears to have been an ostensibly orthodox body of worshippers, disengaged from traditional ceremonial, was not afraid to make its views known.[2] Quite possibly not convinced heretics themselves, the orthodox piety of these parishioners may have been influenced by Lollard ideas that had been in circulation for a number of generations.

It should not be assumed that families that were parsimonious in their testamentary giving were less pious or devout than their more generous counterparts. They do, however, appear to have had misgivings about certain aspects of orthodox practice whilst possessing their own moral imperatives and materialist concerns which contended for resources to the exclusion of religious giving. The cultural differences between their pious practices and those of the more traditionally orthodox arose, to some extent, out of social distinctions and dynamics among relatively established families. The social and cultural gulf between middling crafts- and tradespeople and truly wealthy yeoman farmers was not as great as that between the latter group and the gentry, but it nevertheless seems to have been real and widening and had some part to play in forging divergent pieties. To some extent, generosity and diversity in religious giving were dependent on wealth and relatively high status. However, although the availability of disposable wealth set limits to religious generosity, attitudes varied between families across the testamentary spectrum as to the correct uses of surplus resources and suggest the existence of real cultural distinctions. Additionally, differences in wealth alone do not explain qualitative distinctions between testamentary traditions. For example, the Castelyns and the Pellonds became more generous and diverse as they rose in wealth and status, but they broadened their giving in a selective and deliberate fashion, concentrating on certain aspects of orthodox practice whilst ignoring others.

---

[1] Rex, *Lollards*, 148.
[2] See p. 170 above; cf. A. Ryrie, 'Counting sheep, counting shepherds: the problem of allegiance in the English Reformation', in Marshall and Ryrie, *Beginnings of English Protestantism*, 94, and *Gospel and Henry VIII*, 227.

Generally, the rate of upward social mobility was in inverse relationship to generosity and elaboration in testamentary piety. This was probably because rapid social mobility involved intensive investment in industrial and commercial enterprise and estate-building by households tied together by biological, affinal and fictive kinship. These families were also most involved in fashioning an urban identity, tending to live within the more industrial and commercial sectors of the parish. For them, social mobility involved risk and material insecurity. Coupled with this were the psychological effects of social advancement. These factors may have helped to foster an ideology that emphasised their distinctive identity in relation to other leading families, many of which were more religiously generous. In addition, as a rule, business failure often quickly followed business success, which in some instances may explain the frugal testamentary piety of these families. Their mentality appears to have been materialistic and acquisitive, centred on the family and unsparing in religious giving. It is probable that the process of rapid economic growth and social restructuring that led to Tenterden's exceptional wealth by the mid-sixteenth century began in the late 1300s and that the origins of a materialistic and religiously parsimonious mentality lay in the fourteenth century. This would support Collinson's suggestion that 'anti-catholic and specifically anti-sacramentarian sentiment' in the Kentish Weald 'may have had older, indigenous origins' that pre-dated the arrival of Lollardy in the 1420s.[3]

Despite the heterogeneity of piety at Tenterden, the beliefs and practices of will-making families shared common elements centred on the services of parish church or subparochial chapel. Belief in purgatory appears to have remained important across the pious spectrum evidenced, in particular, by the general popularity of funereal and commemorative ritual. However, adherence to particular forms of intercession for the dead varied, just as charitable and civic giving took divergent paths which further suggests the existence of traditionalist and reformist strands within parochial piety. The most significant devotional development during the period was the growth of Christocentricism, largely in the form of the Jesus Mass. Its polyvalency rendered it attractive to both traditionalists and reformists and thus the devotion represented something of a revivification of officially sponsored orthodoxy. It was established in Tenterden in the immediate aftermath of the heresy trials of 1511–12 and the ecclesiastical hierarchy may have seen its subsequent popularity as a resounding success for orthodoxy in Lollardy's Kentish heartland. However, the wide appeal of the Jesus Mass at Tenterden was not accompanied by a revival in other aspects of devotional practice but, rather, in their sustained decline by the second and third decades of the sixteenth century. In particular, the cult of saints, the religious orders, chantries, other newer intercessory forms and giving to church fabric were all

3   Collinson, 'Cranbrook and the Fletchers', 402.

either absent from wills by the late 1520s or were significantly less important than they had been at the turn of the century. The singular intensity of the Jesus Mass, and Christocentric devotion in general, may have contributed to this cultural shift as well as offering a pious outlet that was in tune with it. The generally restrained, pared down and Christocentric tenor of piety adhered to by Tenterden's leading burgess families by the 1520s, compared to the late fifteenth century, is evidence of a fundamental redefinition of orthodoxy prior to the Reformation that had much in common with the reformist agendas of humanist orthodox evangelicalism. Further study of the dissemination, reception and evolution of the Jesus Mass and other Christocentric devotions, in relation to other orthodox devotional developments at a local level across England, will begin to map variations in what may have been a widespread trend prior to the Reformation.[4]

Tenterden does not fit the model of the late medieval parish, either as an essentially harmonious expression of community, or as a flexible framework for the negotiation of the choices of the individual or group in matters of orthodox religion. The fragmented nature of settlement, the size of the parish and the development of Small Hythe and its chapel ensured that conceptions of the parish were neither uniform nor static. Equally, freedom of choice in parochial religious practice was constrained by pious expectations and conventions that were defined by locality, family and kinship as much as by parish. In a similar way to religious dissent, piety was transmitted within families from one generation to the next. Patrilineage appears to have been the most important route for transmission but, to some extent, this may be an impression resulting from the under-representation of women in probate evidence. However, a large enough number of women's wills survives to show that testamentary piety was distinctively gendered within the constraints of household and family convention. Presumably lifetime belief and practice were similarly patterned.

At Tenterden, the patrilineal family therefore presents itself as the most appropriate unit of analysis of probate and other types of evidence alongside the locality and the parish. This notwithstanding, is there a danger of overemphasising the importance of the family in processes of cultural transmission? This study focuses on a stable core of enduring families, for which enough wills survive to gain an impression of their sensibilities over time. They were exceptional for their stability and longevity but they were also the most socially dominant among non-gentry families, and so their pious traditions probably represent the most influential strands within parochial piety. The beliefs and practices of less stable families are also represented here and did not diverge from the spectrum of practice followed by the more estab-

---

[4] I intend, in due course, to write a national study of the Jesus Mass and Christocentricism that incorporates this sort of close local contextualisation.

lished. Regrettably, due to lack of evidence, we know next to nothing about the piety of the truly economically insecure and transient who survived on wage-labour alone and left very few, if any, wills. This book is not about them, although it is about the formation and evolution of a religious culture in which they, to some extent, partook. The family may have been an especially important social institution in Tenterden and the Weald of Kent while elsewhere the collectivity of the parish or the fraternity may have been more central in shaping pious choices. However, the findings presented here have significant implications for regions and localities that shared a number of the Weald's features, namely, predominantly wood/pasture economies with weak lordship, scattered settlement, partible inheritance and a diversity of agricultural and industrial activities.

Late medieval piety in Tenterden was, in a number of important ways, an extension of social and economic relations and material culture and was linked particularly to the generation and recirculation of wealth within and beyond the family. Saints' cults were appropriated in the recreation of identity by the burgesses of Tenterden town and the residents of Small Hythe and most had a distinctly material basis, emphasising the intimate relationship between the quotidian and religious belief and practice. Small Hythe offers a particularly coherent and vivid illustration of the origins of particular pieties. Commercial and industrial growth and development at an intensely local level, and concentrated estate-building by certain leading families, had a pious dimension within the moral economy. Land, houses, cash and material goods were employed for the provision of local religious services and a new chapel that expressed cultural links that sprang from commercial success and, in its austerity and attention to fashion, a distinctive ethos. These findings have implications for other 'wilderness' foundations in this period, and the types of mentality that developed in such rapidly developing centres. They also raise wider questions regarding the proliferation of England's subparochial chapels and suggest that Rosser's theory that lay desire for greater choice in devotional life was the essential driving force behind the enhancement and diversification of provision does not adequately take into account the relationship of piety to demographic, economic and social developments and their variation across the countryside.[5]

What then is the significance of Lollardy in Tenterden and the Weald? There is no doubting that Tenterden was at the centre of an important tradition of Wycliffite heresy that was probably continuous from the 1420s to the Reformation and that peripatetic figures like William White and William Carder were crucial to its establishment and ongoing survival. Tenterden was aware of its radical history, and long-standing families that met with heretical ideas for the first time in the late fifteenth and early sixteenth centuries would

---

5 Rosser, 'Parochial conformity', 176, 182–3.

have remembered successive attempts to purge heresy from the Weald. Lollards appear to have continued to participate in parish religion and some, or at least their kinsfolk, were involved in parish administration and local government. As appears to have been the case in other areas of long-term continuity in dissent, such as the Chilterns, there was widespread sympathy for, or at least tolerance of, Lollardy in Tenterden and surrounding villages.[6] On the whole, heresy and parsimonious piety seem to have been located in the same social stratum of middling crafts- and tradespeople, and the long-term appeal of heterodoxy in the Weald may have arisen out of a religiously frugal and materialistic mentality. The sacramentarian, anti-sacerdotal and anti-cultic continuities in Lollard doctrines and opinions accord with the general tenor of religious practice seen in the wills of frugal and socially mobile families, and with the significant changes in devotional practice in this period. The general direction in which piety was heading by the early sixteenth century, including the growth of Christocentricism, had much in common with Lollard calls for reform and the families of individuals who became involved in Lollardy became noticeably preoccupied with the Jesus Mass and, to a lesser extent, with humanitarian charity. Despite these similarities, adherence to heretical ideas appears to have remained a distinct position in the broad spectrum of belief. It is likely, however, that Lollardy had a long-term influence on orthodox opinions, pushing them in reformist directions. The boundary between orthodoxy and heterodoxy was neither fixed nor clearly defined over the period but Christocentric devotion was quite different from the definite and dangerous step into heresy. What is suggested is that both of these phenomena were symptomatic of the engage-ment of an entrenched mentality and a particular indigenous form of ortho-doxy with radical, or potentially radical, religious ideas.

Not all these ideas were Wycliffite in origin and some, particularly Christocentricism, stemmed from orthodox evangelicalism. Moderate reformist attitudes to some of the more questioned aspects of traditional orthodoxy may have been inspired, in part, by Erasmian humanism and had more in common with traditional Lollard complaints. Local clergy and noble and gentry families that took an interest in humanism heralded intellectual influences and educational developments that brought a new degree of sophistication to potentially radical shifts in orthodox piety in the Weald. This cultural milieu may have seeped into, and helped to sustain, religious heterodoxy. Equally, regional patronage networks possibly provided the channels for Lollardy and indigenous divergences within orthodoxy to contribute to and mould evangelicalism and Protestantism.

---

6 Rex, *Lollards*, 97–8.

Lollardy, orthodoxy and the Reformation

So what of the reception of radical evangelical ideas and the progress of reform at Tenterden after 1535? It is not possible within the scope of this book to do justice to these questions but some suggestions can be made as to how best to approach them. Given the advances that can be made in the interpretation of probate materials by using the sorts of methods outlined in this study, in particular by comparing continuities in practices between families, the extension of this approach into the remaining decades of the sixteenth century, and particularly the 1540s and 1550s, may well begin to reveal the relationships between early sixteenth-century Catholic pieties and the formation of mid-Tudor Protestant identities. Such an approach may overcome some of the considerable problems of using wills 'to build a systematic representation of the shifts in religious culture' during these years.[7] There is evidence, for example, that families like the Castelyns and the Pellonds, already with a history of divergence into Wycliffite heresy, were quick to embrace reform. In 1549 George Castelyn, the son of Christopher whose testamentary piety is examined in chapter 4, gave evidence against the survival of Small Hythe chapel and shortly afterwards helped to pull down the rood loft in St Mildred's parish church.[8] Examination of the testamentary practices of these families, and their involvement or otherwise in reform, in comparison with other groups in the parish, might help to begin to make sense of the complex processes of cultural change during these years and shed light on the significance of Tenterden's pre-Reformation pieties and tradition of Lollard heresy for the reception of Lutheran and other continental ideas.[9]

To begin with, the social status of Stephen Castelyn and William Pellond goes some way towards bridging the gulf suggested by Peter Clark between Lollard 'small peasant farmers and artisans' on the Weald and converts there to Lutheranism who, in his opinion, 'tended to be substantial men or clergy'.[10] More recently, Richard Rex has also argued for the existence of these sorts of social barriers but if the Castelyns and the Pellonds are anything to go by, then the precise social distinctions between Protestants and Lollards may not have been so very great.[11] The religiously parsimonious in Tenterden were susceptible to radicalism, whether in the form of Wycliffitism or Lutheranism, but the predominant tenor of their piety seems to have been more moderately reformist.[12] Their increasing dominance in town affairs by

---

7 See the very useful summary of these methodological problems and comprehensive references in Ryrie, 'Counting sheep', 86–7 at p. 86.
8 Roberts, *Tenterden*, 73.
9 I intend to write an article that will address these questions in detail.
10 Clark, *English provincial society*, 31.
11 Rex, *Lollards*, 133–9.
12 This may accord with Collinson's notion of 'a kind of religious voluntarism which contrived to remain in some sense and degree within the religious establishment' but which

the late 1520s may have ensured that Tenterden was not slow to embrace the changes of the Reformation. There is reason to believe that the town's leading families were conscientious in investigating resistance to reform in the 1530s and 1540s. The cases that have survived all relate to clergy and it seems that some of Tenterden's parish priests were not sufficiently responsive to the changes demanded by the Henrician regime, or were too outspoken in their opposition to reform, for the religious tastes of a significant element of the townsfolk. However, there were also instances of local clergy being examined for heresy who may have been too radical in a climate of cautious change.

The first instance concerns William Broke, vicar of Tenterden from 1512 to 1539, whose conservatism led him into controversy as early as 1534. In a letter to Cromwell, Sir John Dudley, a local landholder, reported how Broke had 'exhorted his parishioners to stand on their old fashions and fly this new learning, and many other papists' doctrines'. When Broke bade his beads he allegedly indicated his reluctant obedience to reform by declaring 'because it was newly ordered that they should pray first to the King, therefore he would do it'. Dudley had been informed of Broke's behaviour by John Brekynden, Cromwell's young servant and member of the influential Small Hythe family. He finished his letter by stating that he would not have troubled Cromwell with the matter if Broke 'had not been already before you', implying that this was not the first time Tenterden's vicar had been in trouble for his public stance on reform. Broke had died by late 1540 but may have been replaced before then as Tenterden had a new vicar by June 1539.[13]

In 1538 there was a more official denunciation of the conservatism of a local priest. John Fuller appears to have served as the Jesus Mass priest for six months before his outspokenness led to an enquiry before the bailiff and jurats of Tenterden. Richard Hope, an 'innholder' of the town, told how in his dwelling house he heard Fuller say 'that as for looking upon the Bible men should not be the nere before Doomsday'. According to Hope, Stephen Cowper had replied to Fuller, 'ye do naught to discomfort anyman for looking upon the Bible' and Cowper himself stated that he had rebuked Fuller, saying 'The King's Grace has set it out for every man to look upon'. Both deponents told how at this point Fuller denied he had ever said such a thing. Another witness, Christopher Baker, stated that in the parish church Fuller had declared 'well, ye shall see another world shortly'. Baker warned Fuller 'I would advise you to speak no more thereof, for if ye do it will be to your displeasure', to which the priest replied defiantly 'In faith, if I die I care not, for there will be a thousand die more than I'. The bailiff and jurats sent the depositions together with Fuller, Cowper and Baker, to Cromwell to seek his

nevertheless rendered its adherents especially open to new and unorthodox ideas: 'Critical conclusion', 396.
13 *L&P* vii. 1251; Taylor, 'Rectors and vicars of St Mildred's', 216–18.

advice on how to proceed but no record appears to survive of the outcome.[14] In this same year the bailiff and jurats examined another witness who made similar accusations against a priest at Bilsington, about eight miles from Tenterden, called John Bromfyld. James Freeston told how he had overheard a conversation between his then master Robert Sentlyger of Bilsington and an unnamed man who also lived in the village. Freeston stated how the latter told Sentlyger that two or three men of Bilsington claimed that Bromfyld had said to them in confession 'Suffer a while and ye shall see the Pope in as great authority as ever he was.' Freeston claimed that his master wrote these words down 'and said that he would cause the said priest to be brought to a higher promotion then ever he was'.[15] This third-hand deposition suggests that the Corporation of Tenterden was taking a leading role in pursuing these cases within Tenterden itself and across its hinterland.

In 1543, during Archbishop Cranmer's investigations into heresy in Kent, Tenterden's vicar from 1539 to 1545, Peter Baker, was accused of failing to keep pace with required changes in the liturgy. It was reported that 'he hath not put out of the manual which he daily useth the Bishop of Rome's name, his usurped authority and pardon expressed in the rubric and last absolution of extreme unction'.[16] However, two other Tenterden priests were investigated in 1543, whose alleged errors were quite different from Baker's. The first was Humphrey Cotton, a chantry priest who was reported to have said that there were heresies in the Bible and that 'every Christian man being baptised & holpen by the grace of God is in as full state of free will as Adam was before his fall'. Also, he allegedly had a 'book of prophecies', the contents of which are not recorded.[17] Cotton's errors are difficult to place but there is no doubting the evangelical credentials of Hugh Cooper. He had reportedly said 'that God was neither pleased with fasting nor discontent with eating' and preached 'that neither alms deeds, fasting, nor prayer did help the soul, but faith only' and 'that whoever trusted to have help by the prayers of any person that ever god made committed idolatry', opinions which suggest adherence to Lutheranism. Cooper had 'inverted the order of the *Confiteor*, omitting the name of Mary and All Saints' and had preached that God did not regard prayers, but rather the persons who said them. Finally, he had said in the week before Whitsunday Eve, traditionally a time of fasting, that 'you need not to fast except you will'.[18] Cooper, and probably Cotton also, fell foul of the conservative backlash that came to a head in the prebendaries plot against Cranmer in 1543. Cooper's articulation of his ideas was probably too crude even for Cranmer, especially at a time when the outcome of the struggle between evangelicals and conservatives within Church and State

---

14 *L&P* xiii/2, 1015; appendices at p. 1353.
15 *L&P* xiv/1, 1074.
16 *L&P* xviii/3, 296.
17 *L&P* xviii/3, 546, p. 294; xviii/8, 318.
18 *L&P* xviii/7, 546, p. 310; Collinson, 'Night schools', 228.

remained in the balance.[19] It is difficult to judge what the general opinion was among the townsfolk of Tenterden regarding this sort of radical preaching. What we do know is that it continued in the parish but that some were ready to denounce it.

A sense of this climate is provided by a case that arose during the final traditionalist offensive of Henry's reign in 1546. The 'inhabitants' or 'men of Tenterden' are recorded as having reported to the Privy Council that a 'seditious' and 'lewd sermon' had been preached at Tenterden on Easter Wednesday. The culprit appears to have been Richard Blostoke, a curate of Tenterden, who was arrested, imprisoned and examined before the Council. Under examination he declared that there was heresy in the hallowing of holy bread and holy water. Held for further questioning it emerged that he and 'a light priest which he maintained in his parsonage, had brought sundry of his parishioners to light opinions concerning religion'.[20] Did Tenterden provide a platform for radical preaching during the 1530s and 1540s? If so, was there continuity between these radical ideas and Lollardy on the Weald? The main direction of religious change in Tenterden may have been more moderately reformist and in step with erastian evangelicalism but there also appears to have been continued sympathy with radicalism.[21] Alec Ryrie's recent re-examination of the evidence of Kentish evangelicalism from the investigations of 1543 finds that the early Protestant conventicles had strong clerical leadership and were characterised by a particular propensity for iconoclasm that distinguished them from the English evangelical leadership. This 'private face of reformism' was always likely to be more radical than the publicly disseminated views of national leaders but it was accommodated and perhaps even encouraged by Cranmer's party within the ecclesiastical hierarchy in Kent and may have owed something to the influence of Lollardy.[22] Diarmaid MacCulloch has argued that the relatively rapid spread of reform in the diocese of Canterbury was to a large degree due to the dissemination of new evangelical doctrines in Kent by evangelical preachers supported by Cranmer. Following his lead, Richard Rex asserts that the early development of Protestantism in the county should not be taken as proof of a connection between Lollardy and Protestantism, but neither historian pays proper attention to the changing nature of orthodoxy or the broader influence of Lollard heresy upon the types of pieties that may have been susceptible to new doctrines.[23] The precise relationship between Lollardy and Protestantism in

---

[19] D. MacCulloch, *Thomas Cranmer*, New Haven–London 1996, ch. viii; Ryrie, *Gospel and Henry VIII*, passim.

[20] *L&P* xxi. 790, 823, 848, 859, 1232.

[21] On the interaction between what he defines as the three roots of Protestantism in the south-east of England, 'conservative', 'erastian' and more radical 'evangelical' reform see Davis, *Heresy and Reformation*, 1–101.

[22] Ryrie, *Gospel and Henry VIII*, 223–38 at p. 223.

[23] Rex, *Lollards*, 122–3, following D. MacCulloch, *Tudor Church militant: Edward VI and the Protestant Reformation*, London 1999, 112.

Kent is far from clear, and one suspects that there was a variety of interactions and outcomes in terms of personal commitment to ideas both old and new. By the early years of Elizabeth's reign the Weald was host to a significant minority of radical early Puritans who sought to shape local religion and convert the ungodly majority, and at least one of Tenterden's vicars took a leading role in a network of preachers operating across Wealden and Medway parishes. It is possible that Lollardy was absorbed into these more radical networks, but Puritanism and more mainstream Protestantism were far from clearly delineated in the late sixteenth century, and fully-blown separatism does not appear to have emerged before the 1640s in the form of Baptist and Independent chapels and sects. Whether descended from Lollard families or not, the more radical types of late sixteenth-century Wealden dissenter seem to have shared their predilection for measured integration into the social and religious life of the parish.[24]

The readiness of the likes of MacCulloch and Rex to dismiss the wider implications of early Protestantism in Kent rests upon a model of change that fails to take account of local responses to reform as well as reformist traditions that pre-dated the Reformation, such as that found at Tenterden. The icono-clastic views of evangelicals in the 1540s may have owed as much to long-standing orthodox sensibilities regarding saints' images, as they did to the survival of Lollard networks in the county. Whilst it is clear that growing support for reform was, in part, a product of political manipulation by evan-gelicals through a powerful party of opportunists and idealists, a change of perspective reveals the crucial role of local figures below the level of the gentry, largely unknown to us but who were none the less central to the execution of reform within their parishes. In Tenterden and the Weald, Protestant evangelicalism may have been shaped as much by long-standing reformist attitudes as by preaching and patronage; it is probable that the two were mutually dependent. Colin Richmond's characterisation of those who aided religious change within their own communities as 'moles' who acted on behalf of socially superior 'wolves' is untenable in relation to Tenterden.[25] The likes of George Castelyn and his forebears had been shaping their reli-gious worlds to their own pious ideals for generations and appear to have been culturally attuned to important elements of the reformist agenda before the first officially sponsored changes began to have an impact on local reli-

24 Collinson, 'Cranbrook and the Fletchers', passim, and 'Night schools', 225–35; Everitt, 'Nonconformity in country parishes', passim; Spufford, *World of rural dissenters*, passim. Collinson and Everitt question Peter Clark's characterisation of Nonconformity in Kent as overwhelmingly separatist by the late sixteenth century: Clark, *English provincial society*, 77, 177.
25 Clark, *English provincial society*, 34–107; C. Richmond, 'The English gentry and religion, c. 1500', in C. Harper-Bill (ed.), *Religious belief and ecclesiastical careers in late medieval England*, Woodbridge 1991, 149–50.

gious life in the late 1530s. It is unlikely that they would have been dismayed by much of what was to come as they were party already to their own, quieter, less dramatic and perhaps more private reformation.

Implications for Reformation studies

Finally, this book has wider implications for Reformation studies in general and, in particular, the models and methods used to map and explain the progress of reform across the countryside. Since Haigh, Scarisbrick and Duffy, the revisionist position with regard to late medieval piety on the eve of Henrician reform has generally been accepted as the point of departure for research on the English Reformation. Thus, it is now widely assumed that the central elements of traditional orthodox religion were genuinely popular across the country, formed a reasonably coherent system of belief and practice and that local and regional variations in piety had little bearing on receptivity to new doctrinal ideas or, for that matter, the assault on images, cult of saints, fasting, the real presence in the mass, purgatory and the religious houses. As a result, one of the most important questions to dominate Reformation studies in recent years has been what Christopher Marsh refers to as 'the compliance conundrum', the problem of explaining 'majority acquiescence in an unwanted religious transformation'.[26]

Christopher Marsh, for one, presents a less homogeneous and happy picture on the eve of the Reformation than that depicted by the revisionists. Questioning the degree of attachment to traditional ceremonial and belief he, like Christine Peters and Susan Wabuda, identifies continuities between pre- and post-Reformation religious life and beliefs that were not subject to, or survived, the changes imposed by state-sponsored reform. Peters and Wabuda, in particular, identify some of the significant changes in orthodoxy in the generation preceding Henrician reform that contributed to the formation of a new religious culture, but there is much more work to be done to map variations and contradictions in practice at a local and regional level and to compare these to responses to the Reformation.[27] Margaret Aston and Peter Marshall have alerted us to pre-Reformation debates concerning the veneration of images and the doctrine of purgatory and intercession for the dead, and highlight the reformist critiques of these central pillars of traditional religion that may have met with significant support across the countryside. Marshall, for example, demonstrates how the vagueness of the doctrine

---

[26] See, for example, P. Collinson, 'England' in R. W. Scribner, R. Porter and M. Teich (eds), *The Reformation in national context*, Cambridge 1994, 88–9, and *Reformation*, 106–9; Ryrie, 'Counting sheep', 84; Shagan, *Popular politics*, 5, 164, 272; and Marsh, *Popular religion*, 197–219 at pp. 197–8.
[27] Marsh, *Popular religion*, 197–9, 209–11, 215–16, and references therein; Peters, *Patterns of piety*, chs iii–ix; Wabuda, *Preaching*, passim.

of purgatory and its lack of authoritative coherence 'presaged a fundamental pregnability' to evangelical attack.[28] Yet those who seek for late medieval contributory factors to the progress of reform, such as Marshall, Rex and Ryrie, look largely to the hotly debated contribution of Lollardy, rather than to continuities between orthodox pieties and early Protestantisms.[29] Although taking very different approaches, Rex's work on the significant role that the friars had to play in the early Reformation and Wabuda's and Peters's important contributions in the areas of attitudes to women, the development of preaching and transitional Christocentric pieties do indeed pay attention to the importance of late medieval Catholicism in the shaping of Protestantism. While Rex tends to focus upon the individual dramatic conversion of intensely 'devout' Catholics, who were on the whole priests or members of the religious orders, through contact with the doctrine of justification by faith, Wabuda and Peters have begun sensitively to identify gradual pre-Reformation shifts in lay religious practice and belief that, consciously or not, anticipated reform.[30] The experience of some sort of conversion does appear to have been one of the defining features of early Protestantism in the 1520s and 1530s and it is clear that solifidian theology was the common element in bringing this about. However, although there is no doubting that individuals understood themselves to have undergone dramatic moments of transformation, their arrival at that point was preceded by a process shaped by transitions in orthodox religious culture.[31] What we do not yet know in any systematic way, aside from the anecdotal self-conscious accounts of the conversion of leading Protestant figures, is whether particular aspects of orthodox culture may have rendered their adherents susceptible to evangelical beliefs. To describe someone as 'devout' and 'Catholic' in 1525 does not tell us very much about their piety.

Both Marsh and Ryrie have alerted us to the possibility that the appeal of new evangelical ideas may have had much to do with the sense of liberty to be gained from acceptance of the doctrine of justification by faith; in particular, the lifting of the burden of purgatory and all that that complex of beliefs entailed.[32] What this present study implies is that there may already have been changes in orthodox devotion prior to the arrival of outright solifidianism that were lessening the centrality of purgatory and the saints,

---

28 Aston, *Iconoclasts*, 23–158; Marshall, *Beliefs and the dead*, 12–46 at p. 12.

29 Rex, *Lollards*, 14–15, 115–42; P. Marshall and A. Ryrie, 'Protestantisms and their beginnings', in Marshall and Ryrie, *Beginnings of English Protestantism*, 8.

30 Rex, 'Friars', passim and *Lollards*, 119, 133–7; Marshall and Ryrie, Protestantisms', 9; S. Wabuda, 'Sanctified by the believing spouse: women, men and the marital yoke in the early Reformation', in Marshall and Ryrie, *Beginnings of English Protestantism*, 111–28, and *Preaching*, passim; Peters, *Patterns of piety*, passim.

31 P. Marshall, 'Evangelical conversion in the reign of Henry VIII', in Marshall and Ryrie, *Beginnings of English Protestantism*, 14–37, esp. pp. 36–7; Marshall and Ryrie, 'Protestantisms', 9.

32 Marsh, *Popular religion*, 198–201; Ryrie, 'Counting sheep', 101–5.

and reducing some of the more burdensome elements of religious observance. Equally, the 'reformist penumbra', a significant minority of reformist sympathisers identifiable throughout England by the 1550s (as opposed to converted new types of evangelicals), might actually be identifiable at a parochial level before the 1530s, their pre-Reformation pieties an important factor in their reaction to novel doctrines.[33]

Two aspects of pre-Reformation piety that have been mentioned several times in preceding chapters, in terms of their contribution to the transformation of devotional culture from the late fifteenth century onwards, are beginning to attract greater attention from a number of historians, in particular Wabuda and Peters but others also. The first is the influence of humanism (particularly in its Erasmian forms), which has long been posited as a rather shaky bridge between Catholicism and Protestantism but almost wholly restricted to clerical, gentry and noble circles. Closely linked to this is the growth of Christocentricism and orthodox evangelicalism.[34] These important cultural trends enjoyed widespread influence in pre-Reformation England and appear to have had a considerable impact on the piety of Tenterden's townsfolk by the early sixteenth century. It might well be possible to trace the progress of reform at a local level from the 1530s through identification of continuities between parsimonious and moderate Christocentric piety and later Protestantism using the sort of approach adopted here.

One of the, as yet, untested implications of this book is, then, that late medieval piety should be rewritten into explanations of the Reformation. This is suggested with an acute awareness that some accounts of reform focus not on the processes of religious persuasion and conversion or on the complex encounters and negotiations between belief, doctrine and polemic within the social realm, but on what were essentially political mechanisms and arenas. Both Marsh and Shagan, for example, argue that the majority of people remained relatively neutral and noncommittal compared to the few staunch traditionalists on the one hand, and a minority of fiery Protestants on the other. For Marsh their beliefs can best be classified as a sort of syncretic pragmatism informed by a desire to maintain social harmony. For Shagan, responses to reform were, on the whole, all about negotiating a satisfactory political position in relation to the perplexing twists and turns of governmental policy and local and county allegiance.[35] Leaving aside the debate about the significance of Lollardy, the dominant model of religious change at a local level remains that of 'gradual "inculturation" ' by evangelical clerical preachers, bishops and their patrons within the nobility, gentry

[33] Ryrie, 'Counting sheep', 98–105 at p. 105.
[34] Wabuda, *Preaching*, 64–106, 148, 168–9; Peters, *Patterns of piety*, passim. See also, for example, Rex, *Lollards*, 119, 133–7; Marshall, 'Evangelical conversion', 16–17, 30; Brown, *Popular piety*, 248; and Marsh, *Popular religion*, 208.
[35] Shagan, *Popular politics*, passim; Marsh, *Popular religion*, 212–14. See also Whiting, *Blind devotion*, 187, 268.

and central government.[36] What is required is a more sophisticated model that can accommodate consideration of processes of interaction and engagement between indigenous orthodox religious cultures and evangelical preaching, and variations in these dynamics across the country. Taking Shagan's study as a case in point, even when the influence of local evangelicals who actually belonged to the communities they were attempting to transform is considered, unless they appear to have been died-in-the-wool Protestants, they do not tend to be taken seriously as religiously inspired agents of change. Similarly, if Catholics, or at least those who cannot be termed convinced Protestants, were divided in their opposition to reform, it was not because of differences in piety of the sort identified in Tenterden, but because of political divisions with regard to the royal supremacy, the English Church's relationship with Rome, anticlericalism or a complex web of political allegiances at a local and regional level. Shagan is right to seek to develop a model of religious change that transcends the constraints of confessional polemic and places less emphasis on conversion than many historians of the Reformation but, in so doing, he fails to acknowledge the more subtle, but no less significant, shifts in piety which contributed to the progress of reform and the richly heterogeneous depths of sixteenth-century religiosity.[37]

Due attention to the multiplicity of late medieval piety, and the transformative reconstruction of pre-Reformation religious culture described in the above chapters, widens the 'compliance conundrum' beyond the various factors and strategies that encouraged obedience to reform, and the ability of the Tudor state and a hierarchical society to police and enforce change.[38] In particular, it calls for consideration of the interaction between various layers of long- and short-term cultural transformation conducted by a wide range of agents. It is hoped that this study will provoke further enquiries that question the now widely held assumption that, for the vast majority of the orthodox population, the series of changes beginning with the closure of the monasteries in 1535 were simply unimaginable before they occurred. The evidence of religious reconstruction in Tenterden before the 1530s suggests that at least some elements of reform were anticipated by the orthodox and that this was only partly due to the influence of heresy.

[36] Marshall and Ryrie, 'Protestantisms', 3 n. 5. See also, for example, Rex, *Lollards*, 119–32, and Ryrie, 'Counting sheep', 98–110.
[37] Shagan, *Popular politics*, passim.
[38] Marsh, *Popular religion*, 201–3, 205–8; S. Brigden, *London and the Reformation*, Oxford 1989, 403; Collinson, 'England', 88; Ryrie, 'Counting sheep', 107–8.

Bibliography

Unpublished primary sources

Canterbury, Canterbury Cathedral Archive
Visitation books
Z.3.1–4, 37
X.8.2

Rentals
Dcc/C Christchurch Priory register

Kew, The National Archives

PRO
C1/336 early chancery proceedings

Prerogative court of Canterbury wills
Prob. 11/4 (21 Stokton); 11/5 (25 Godyn); 11/8 (20 Milles); 11/9 (29 Dogett); 11/14 (39 Holgrave); 11/16 (14 Bennett); 11/21 (18 Bodfelde); 11/22 (17 Porche); 11/23 (20 Jankyn); 11/25 (14 Hogen)

Subsidy rolls
E 179, 125/324; 230/182; 231/228; 234/7

Court of Augmentations: certificates of colleges, chantries and similar foundations
E 301/29

Court of Augmentations and Predecessors and Successors: miscellaneous books
E 315/114

London, British Library
Property deeds and charters
Add. Charter 16319, 16320, 16322, 16324, 16326, 16328–31, 41799, 56976–7, 56979–85, 58708
MS Add. 48022
MS Stowe 850

London, Lambeth Palace Library
Register of Archbishop William Warham, i

Maidstone, Centre for Kentish Studies
Probate records

Wills archdeaconry and consistory
PRC 16/1–3 Canterbury archdeaconry court office copies
PRC 17/1–22 Canterbury archdeaconry court probate registers

211

PRC 32/2–16 Canterbury consistory court probate registers
DRb/Pwr 2 Rochester consistory court probate register

Archdeaconry act books
PRC 3/3–8

Tenterden borough records
Te/C1 Tenterden custumal
Te/S1 Tenterden Corporation minute book

Property deeds
U36/T1453–4 British Record Association
U55/T414 Knocker collection
U455/T84–8/T90 Tufton MSS
U410/T12/T21/T178–9 Roberts MSS
U442/T99 Gordon Ward collection
U1044/F1 Hendle MSS, family book

Published primary sources

The Brut, ed. F. W. Brie (EETS, 1906–8)
Calendar of close rolls, London 1902–
Calendar of patent rolls, London 1901–
A calendar of the white and black books of the cinque ports, 1432–1955, ed. F. Hull
    (KR xix, 1966)
Councils and synods with other documents relating to the English Church, II: *A.D.*
    1205–1313, ed. F. M. Powicke and C. R. Cheney, Oxford 1964
Dives and pauper, ed. P. H. Barnum (EETS cclxxx, 1980)
Fasciculi zizaniorum Magistri Johannis Wyclif cum tritico, ed. W. W. Shirley (Rolls
    Series, 1858)
Foxe, John, *Actes and monuments of these latter and perilous dayes*, London 1583
The golden legend or lives of the saints as Englished by William Caxton, ed. F. S. Ellis,
    London 1900
Heresy trials in the diocese of Norwich, 1428–31, ed. N. P. Tanner (Camden 4th ser.
    xx, 1977)
Hoskins, E., *Horae beatae Mariae virginis, or Sarum and York primers*, London 1901
Jeaffreson, J. C., 'MSS of the *custos rotolorum* and justices of the peace of the
    county of Essex, at the Shire-Hall, Chelmsford, Essex', in HMC, *Tenth report*,
    appendix, pt iv (1885), 466–513
Kent chantries, ed. A. Hussey (KR xii, 1932)
Kent heresy proceedings, 1511–12, ed. N. P. Tanner (KR xxvi, 1997)
Kent obit and lamp rents, ed. A. Hussey (KR xiv, 1936)
Kentish visitations of Archbishop William Warham and his deputies, 1511–12, ed.
    K. L. Wood-Legh (KR xxiv, 1984)
Letters and papers, foreign and domestic, of the reign of Henry VIII, 1509–47, ed. J. S.
    Brewer and others, London 1862–1932
Lincoln wills, 1271–1530, ed. C. W. Foster (Lincoln Record Society x, 1918)
Mirk's festial: a collection of homilies by Johannes Mirkus, ed. T. Erbe (EETS e.s.
    xcvi, 1905)

Missale ad usum insignis ecclesiae eboracensis, ed. W. G. Henderson (Surtees Society lx, 1874)

Missale ad usum insignis et praeclarae ecclesiae Sarum, ed. F. H. Dickinson, Burntisland 1861–83

Naval accounts and inventories of the reign of Henry VII, 1485–8 and 1495–7, ed. M. Oppenheim (Publications of the Navy Records Society viii, 1896)

The prymer in Englyshe and Latyn wyth the Epystles and Gospelles of euery sonday & holyedaye in the yere, and also the exposycion upon miserere mei deus wyth many other prayers, London 1542 (RSTC, 16026)

The pylgrymage of Sir Richard Guylforde to the Holy Land A.D. 1506 from a copy believed to be unique, from the press of Richard Pynson, ed. Sir Henry Ellis (Camden o.s. li, 1851)

Register of Henry Chichele, ed. E. F. Jacob (Canterbury and York Society xlii, xlv–xlvii, 1938–47)

Registrum statutorum et consuetudinum Ecclesiae Cathedralis Sancti Pauli Londensis, ed. W. Sparrow Simpson, London 1873

Riley, H. T., 'MSS of the corporation of Rye', in *HMC, Fifth report*, appendix (1876), 488–516

—— 'The corporation of Tenterden', in *HMC, Sixth Report*, appendix (1877), 569–72

Testamenta cantiana: East Kent, ed. A. Hussey, London 1907

Testamenta cantiana: West Kent, ed. L. L. Duncan, London 1906

Woodruff, C. E., 'An archidiaconal visitation of 1502', AC xlvii (1935), 13–54

Secondary sources

Aers, D., 'Altars of power: reflections on Eamon Duffy's *The stripping of the altars: traditional religion in England, 1400–1580*', *Literature & History* 3rd ser. iii (1994), 90–105

Alsop, J. D., 'Religious preambles in early modern English wills as formulae', *JEH* xl (1989), 19–27

Anderson, M., *Approaches to the history of the western family, 1500–1914*, Basingstoke–London 1980

Ariès, P., *Western attitudes toward death from the Middle Ages to the present*, London 1976

—— *The hour of our death*, London 1981

Aston, M., 'Lollardy and sedition, 1381–1431', *P&P* xvii (1960), 1–44, repr. in *Lollards and reformers*, 1–47

—— 'William White's Lollard followers', *Catholic Historical Review* lxviii (1982), 469–97, repr. in *Lollards and reformers*, 71–100

—— *Lollards and reformers: images and literacy in late medieval religion*, London 1984

—— *England's iconoclasts, I: Laws against images*, Oxford 1988

—— 'Iconoclasm at Rickmansworth, 1522: troubles of churchwardens', *JEH* xl (1989), 524–52

—— 'Corpus Christi and Corpus Regni: heresy and the Peasants' Revolt', *P&P* cxliii (1994), 3–47

Atchley, E. G. C. F., 'Jesus Mass and anthem', *Transactions of the St Paul's Ecclesiological Society* v (1905), 163–9

Barnard, A. and A. Good, *Research practices in the study of kinship*, London 1984

Barron, C. M., 'The parish fraternities of medieval London', in C. M. Barron and C. Harper-Bill (eds), *The Church in pre-Reformation society: essays in honour of F. R. H. Du Boulay*, Woodbridge 1985, 13–37

Bennett, J. M., 'The ties that bind: peasant marriages and families in late medieval England', *Journal of Interdisciplinary History* xv (1984), 111–29

Bennett, J. W., 'John Morer's will: Thomas Linacre and prior Sellyng's Greek teaching', *Studies in the Renaissance* xv (1968), 70–91

Bentley, J. H., *Humanists and holy writ: New Testament scholarship in the Renaissance*, Princeton, NJ 1983

Beresford, M., 'Journey along boundaries', in M. Beresford, *History on the ground: six studies in maps and landscapes*, London 1957, 26–52

Bestard-Camps, J., *What's in a relative? Household and family in Formentera*, New York–Oxford 1991

Biller, P. and A. Hudson (eds), *Heresy and literacy, 1000–1530*, Cambridge 1994

Blanchard, I., 'Industrial employment and the rural land market, 1380–1520', in Smith, *Land, kinship, and life cycle*, 227–75

Bloch, M., 'The long term and the short term: the economic and political significance of the morality of kinship', in J. Goody (ed.), *The character of kinship*, Cambridge 1973, 75–87

Bonney, D., 'Early boundaries in Wessex', in P. J. Fowler (ed.), *Archaeology and the landscape: essays for L. V. Grinsell*, London 1972, 168–86

Bossy, J., 'Blood and baptism: kinship, community and Christianity in western Europe from the fourteenth to the seventeenth centuries', in D. Baker (ed.), *Sanctity and secularity: the Church and the world* (SCH x, 1973), 129–43

—— 'The mass as a social institution, 1200–1700', *P&P* c (1983), 29–61

—— *Christianity in the west, 1400–1700*, Oxford 1985

Boulard, F., *An introduction to religious sociology: pioneer work in France*, London 1960

Bourdieu, P., *The logic of practice*, Cambridge 1990

Bowker, M., *The Henrician Reformation: the diocese of Lincoln under John Longland, 1521–1547*, Cambridge 1981

Boyer, P. and S. Nissenbaum, *Salem possessed: the social origins of witchcraft*, Cambridge, Mass. 1974

Brigden, S., 'Religion and social obligation in early sixteenth-century London', *P&P* ciii (1984), 67–112

—— *London and the Reformation*, Oxford 1989

Brown, A. D., *Popular piety in late medieval England: the diocese of Salisbury, 1250–1550*, Oxford 1995

Burgess, C., ' "For the increase of divine service": chantries in the parish in late medieval Bristol', *JEH* xxxvi (1985), 46–65

—— ' "By quick and by dead": wills and pious provision in late medieval Bristol', *EHR* ccccv (1987), 837–58

—— 'A service for the dead: the form and function of the anniversary in late medieval Bristol', *Transactions of the Bristol and Gloucestershire Archaeological Society* cv (1987), 183–211

—— 'Late medieval wills and pious convention: testamentary evidence reconsidered', in M. Hicks (ed.), *Profit, piety and the professions in later medieval England*, Gloucester 1990, 14–33

────── and B. A. Kümin, 'Penitential bequests and parish regimes in late medieval England', *JEH* xliv (1993), 610–30

Burke, P., *History and social theory*, Cambridge 1992

Calhoun, C. J., 'Community: toward a variable conceptualization for comparative research', *Social History* v (1980), 105–29

Campbell, B., 'The population of early Tudor England: a re-evaluation of the 1522 muster returns and the 1524 and 1525 lay subsidies', *Journal of Historical Geography* vii (1981), 145–54

Carlson, E., 'The origins, function, and status of the office of churchwarden, with particular reference to the diocese of Ely', in Spufford, *World of rural dissenters*, 164–207

Carpenter, C., 'The religion of the gentry of fifteenth century England', in D. Williams (ed.), *England in the fifteenth century*, Woodbridge 1987, 53–74

Carsten, J., (ed.), *Cultures of relatedness: new approaches to the study of kinship*, Cambridge 2000

The Catholic encyclopedia, ed. C. G. Herbermann, E. A. Pace and others, New York 1912

Chaytor, M., 'Household and kinship: Ryton in the late sixteenth and the early seventeenth centuries', *HWJ* x (1980), 25–60

Clark, J. G., 'The religious orders in pre-Reformation England', in Clark, *Religious orders*, 3–33

────── (ed.) *The religious orders in pre-Reformation England*, Woodbridge 2002

Clark, P., *English provincial society from the Reformation to the Revolution: religion, politics and society in Kent, 1500–1640*, Hassocks 1977

Clarkson, L. A., 'The organization of the English leather industry in the late sixteenth and seventeenth centuries', *EcHR* 2nd ser. xiii (1960–1), 245–56

Cohen, A. P., *The symbolic construction of community*, Chichester 1985

Collinson, P., 'Cranbrook and the Fletchers: popular and unpopular religion in the Kentish Weald', in P. Collinson, *Godly people: essays in Protestantism and Puritanism*, London 1983, 399–428

────── 'England', in R. W. Scribner, R. Porter and M. Teich (eds), *The Reformation in national context*, Cambridge 1994, 80–94

────── 'Critical conclusion', in Spufford, *World of rural dissenters*, 388–96

────── 'Night schools, conventicles and churches', in Marshall and Ryrie, *Beginnings of English Protestantism*, 209–35

────── *The Reformation*, London 2003

Coppel, S., 'Will-making and the deathbed', *Local Population Studies*, no. xl (Spring 1988), 37–45

Cornwall, J., 'English country towns in the fifteen twenties', *EcHR* 2nd ser. xv (1962–3), 54–69

────── 'English population in the early sixteenth century', *EcHR* xxiii (1970), 32–44

────── *Wealth and society in early sixteenth-century England*, London 1988

Cotton, C., 'St Austin's Abbey, Canterbury, treasurers' accounts, 1468–9, and others', *AC* li (1940), 66–107

Cox, J. C., *The English parish church*, London 1914

Cox Hales, Revd R., 'Brief notes on the Hales family', *AC* xiv (1882), 61–84

Craig, J. and C. Litzenberger, 'Wills as religious propaganda: the testament of William Tracy', *JEH* xliv (1993), 415–31

Cressy, D., 'Kinship and kin interaction in early modern England', *P&P* cxii (1986), 38–69

Cross, C., *Church and people, 1450–1660: the triumph of the English Church*, Hassocks 1976

—— 'Great reasoners in Scripture: the activities of women Lollards, 1380–1530', in D. Baker (ed.), *Medieval women* (SCH subsidia i, 1978), 359–80

—— 'The development of Protestantism in Leeds and Hull, 1520–1640: the evidence from wills', *Northern History* xviii (1982), 230–8

Cullum, P. H., ' "And hir name was charite": charitable giving by and for women in late medieval Yorkshire', in Goldberg, *Woman is a worthy wight*, 182–211

Davies, K. M., 'Continuity and change in literary advice on marriage', in R. B. Outhwaite (ed.), *Marriage and society: studies in the social history of marriage*, London 1981, 58–80

Davies, R. G., 'Lollardy and locality', *TRHS* 6th ser. i (1991), 191–212

Davis, J. F., 'Lollard survival and the textile industry in the south-east of England', in G. J. Cuming (ed.), (SCH iii, 1966), 191–201

—— *Heresy and Reformation in the south-east of England, 1520–1559*, London 1983

Davis, N. Z., 'Some tasks and themes in the study of popular religion', in C. Trinkhaus and H. Oberman, (eds), *The pursuit of holiness*, Leiden 1974, 307–36

—— 'The sacred and the body social in sixteenth-century Lyon', *P&P* xc (1981), 40–70

Dewindt, E. B., *Land and people in Holywell-cum-Needingworth*, Toronto 1972

Dickens, A. G., *Lollards and Protestants in the diocese of York, 1509–1558*, Oxford 1959

—— *The English Reformation*, London–Glasgow 1964, 2nd edn, London 1989

Dinn, R. B., 'Baptism, spiritual kinship, and popular religion in late medieval Bury St Edmunds', *Bulletin of the John Rylands Library* lxxii (1990), 93–106

—— ' "Monuments answerable to mens' worth": burial patterns, social status and gender in late medieval Bury St Edmunds', *JEH* xxxxvi (1995), 237–55

Dobson, R. B., 'The foundation of perpetual chantries by the citizens of York', in G. J. Cuming (ed.), *The province of York* (SCH iv, 1967), 22–38

Draper, G., 'Romney Marsh and its towns and villages, c. 800–1500', in T. Lawson and D. Killingray (eds), *An historical atlas of Kent*, Philimore 2004, 56–7

Du Boulay, F. R. H., 'Dens, droving and danger', *AC* lxxvi (1961), 75–87

—— *An age of ambition: English society in the late Middle Ages*, London 1970

Duby, G., 'The diffusion of cultural patterns in feudal society', *P&P* xxxix (1968), 3–10

Duffy, E., 'Holy maydens, holy wyfes: the cult of women saints in fifteenth and sixteenth century England', in W. J. Sheils and D. Wood (eds), *Women in the Church* (SCH xxvii, 1990), 175–96

—— *The stripping of the altars: traditional religion in England, 1400–1580*, New Haven–London 1992

—— *The voices of Morebath: reformation and rebellion in an English village*, New Haven–London 2001

Duncan, L. L., 'Notes on Cranbrook church', AC xxxvii (1925), 21–31

Dyer, C., *Lords and peasants in a changing society: the estates of the bishopric of Worcester, 680–1540*, Cambridge 1980

—— 'Changes in the size of peasant holdings in some west midland villages, 1400–1540', in Smith, *Land, kinship, and life cycle*, 277–94

—— 'The rising of 1381 in Suffolk: its origins and participants', *Proceedings of the Suffolk Institute of Archaeology and History* xxxvi (1988), 274–87

—— *Standards of living in the later Middle Ages*, Cambridge 1989

Eco, U. and T. A. Sebeok (eds), *The sign of three: Dupin, Holmes, Pierce*, Bloomington, Indiana 1983

Eddison, J., 'Developments in the lower Rother valleys up to 1600', AC cii (1986), 95–108

—— 'Drowned lands: changes in the course of the Rother and its estuary and associated drainage problems', in J. Eddison and C. Green (eds), *Romney Marsh: evolution, occupation, reclamation*, Oxford 1988, 142–61

Elvey, E. M., *The courts of the archdeaconry of Buckingham, 1483–1523* (Buckingham Record Society xix, 1975)

Emden, A. B., *Biographical register of the University of Oxford to A.D. 1500*, Oxford 1957–8

—— *Biographical register of the University of Oxford A.D. 1501 to 1540*, Oxford 1974

Evans, N., 'The descent of dissenters in the Chiltern Hundreds', in Spufford, *World of rural dissenters*, 288–308

Everitt, A., 'Nonconformity in country parishes', in J. Thirsk (ed.), *Land, Church and people: essays presented to Professor H. P. R. Finberg* (AgHR xviii [1970], supplement), 178–99

—— *Continuity and colonization: the evolution of Kentish settlement*, Leicester 1986

Faith, R. J., 'Peasant families and inheritance customs in medieval England', AgHR xiv (1966), 77–95

Fann, K. T., *Pierce's theory of abduction*, The Hague 1970

Fleming, P. W., 'Charity, faith and the gentry of Kent, 1442–1529', in A. J. Pollard (ed.), *Property and politics: essays in later medieval English history*, Gloucester 1984, 36–58

French, K. L., *The people of the parish: community life in a late medieval English diocese*, Philadelphia 2001

Furley, R., *A history of the Weald of Kent*, Ashford–London 1874

—— 'The early history of Tenterden', AC xiv (1882), 37–60

Galpern, A. N., *The religions of the people in sixteenth-century Champagne*, Cambridge, Mass.–London 1976

Gasquet, F. A., *Parish life in medieval England*, London 1906

Geertz, C., 'Religion as a cultural system', in C. Geertz, *The interpretation of cultures* (1973), London 1993, 87–125

Ginzburg, C., 'The inquisitor as anthropologist', in C. Ginzburg, *Clues, myths and the historical method*, Baltimore 1989, 156–64

Gittings, C., *Death, burial and the individual in early modern England*, London 1988

Gleason, J. B., *John Colet*, Berkeley, Los Angeles–London 1989

Goldberg, P. J. P., 'Female labour, service and marriage in the late medieval urban north', *Northern History* xxii (1986), 18–38

────── 'Marriage, migration, servanthood and life-cycle in Yorkshire towns of the later Middle Ages: some York cause paper evidence', *C&C* i (1986), 141–69

────── ' "For better, for worse": marriage and economic opportunity for women in town and country', in Goldberg, *Woman is a worthy wight*, 108–25

────── *Women, work, and life cycle in a medieval economy: women in York and Yorkshire, c. 1300–1520*, Oxford 1992

────── (ed.), *Woman is a worthy wight: women in English society c. 1200–1500*, Stroud 1992

Gottfried, R. S., *Epidemic disease in fifteenth century England*, Leicester 1978

────── *Bury St Edmunds and the urban crisis: 1290–1539*, Princeton, NJ 1982

Granovetter, Mark, 'The strength of weak ties', *American Journal of Sociology* lxxviii (1973), 1360–80

────── 'The strength of weak ties: a network theory revisited', in P. V. Marsden and N. Lin (eds), *Social structure and network analysis*, Beverley Hills, Ca.–London 1982, 105–30

Haigh, C., *Reformation and resistance in Tudor Lancashire*, Cambridge 1975

────── 'The English reformation: a premature birth, a difficult labour and a sickly child', *Historical Journal* xxxiii (1990), 449–59

────── *English reformations: religion, politics, and society under the Tudors*, Oxford 1993

Harris, J., *The history of Kent in five parts*, London 1719

Harris, O., 'Households and their boundaries', *HWJ* xiii (1982), 143–52

Harvey, I. M. W., *Jack Cade's rebellion of 1450*, Oxford 1991

Hasted, E., *The history and topographical survey of the county of Kent, 1797–1801*, Wakefield 1972

Hatcher, J., 'Mortality in the fifteenth century: some new evidence', *EcHR* 2nd ser. xxxix (1980), 19–38

Heath, P., *The English parish clergy on the eve of the Reformation*, London 1969

────── 'Urban piety in the later Middle Ages: the evidence of Hull wills', in R. B. Dobson (ed.), *The Church, politics and patronage in the fifteenth century*, Gloucester 1984, 209–34

Hill, C., 'From Lollards to Levellers', in *Collected essays of Christopher Hill, II: Religion and politics in seventeenth-century England*, Brighton 1986, 89–116

Hill, R., ' "A chaunterie for soules": London chantries in the reign of Richard II', in F. R. H. Du Boulay and C. M. Barron (eds), *The reign of Richard II*, London 1971, 242–55

Hilton, R. H., 'R. S. Gottfried, Bury St Edmunds and the urban crisis, 1290–1539', review article, *Urban History Yearbook* (1983), 185

Hope, A., 'Lollardy: the stone the builders rejected?', in P. Lake and M. Dowling (eds), *Protestantism and the national Church in sixteenth century England*, London 1987, 1–35

────── 'The lady and the bailiff: Lollardy among the gentry in Yorkist and early Tudor England', in M. Aston and C. Richmond (eds), *Lollardy and the gentry in the later Middle Ages*, Stroud 1997, 250–77

Horrox, R., 'The urban gentry in the fifteenth century', in Thomson, *Towns and townspeople*, 22–44

Houlbrooke, R. A., *Church courts and the people during the English Reformation*, Oxford 1979

———— *The English family, 1450–1700*, Harlow 1984

———— 'Womens' social life and common action in England from the fifteenth century to the eve of the civil war', *C&C* i (1986), 171–89

Houston, R. and R. M. Smith, 'A new approach to family history?', *HWJ* xiv (1982), 120–31

Howell, C., *Land, family and inheritance in transition: Kibworth Harcourt, 1280–1700*, Cambridge 1983

Hudson, A., 'The examination of Lollards', *BIHR* xlvi (1973), 145–59

———— *The premature Reformation: Wycliffite texts and Lollard history*, Oxford 1988

———— ' "Laicus litteratus": the paradox of Lollardy', in Biller and Hudson, *Heresy and literacy*, 222–36

Hughes, J., *Pastors and visionaries: religion and secular life in late medieval Yorkshire*, Woodbridge 1988

Huizinga, J., *The waning of the Middle Ages*, Harmondsworth 1968

Hutton, R., 'The local impact of the Tudor reformations', in C. Haigh (ed.), *The English Reformation revised*, Cambridge 1987, 114–38

———— *The rise and fall of merry England*, Oxford 1994

H. V. R., *The parish church of St Mildred Tenterden*, St Ives n.d.

Illustrated catalogue of the exhibition of English medieval alabaster work, London 1913

Jenkins, R. C., 'The family of Guldeford', *AC* xiv (1882), 1–17

Johnson, F., 'The chapel of St Clement at Brundall', *Norfolk Archaeology* xxii (1924–5), 194–205

Jones, N., *The English Reformation: religion and cultural adaptation*, Oxford 2002

Jones, W. R., 'Lollards and images: the defense of religious art in later medieval England', *Journal of the History of Ideas* xxxiv (1973), 27–50

Jordan, W. K., *Philanthropy in England, 1480–1640: a study of the changing pattern of English social aspirations*, London 1959

———— 'Social institutions in Kent, 1480–1660: a study of the changing pattern of social aspiration', *AC* lxxv (1961), 1–172

Kermode, J. I., 'The merchants of three northern English towns', in C. H. Clough (ed.), *Profession, vocation and culture in later medieval England*, Liverpool 1982, 7–50

Kilburne, R., *A topographie or survey of Kent, with some chronological, historical, and other matters touching the same and the several parishes and places therein*, London 1659

Kitching, C., 'Church and chapelry in sixteenth century England', in D. Baker (ed.), *The Church in town and countryside* (SCH xvi, 1979), 279–90

Kreider, A., *English chantries: the road to dissolution*, Cambridge, Mass.–London 1979

Kümin, B. A., *The shaping of a community: the rise and reformation of the English parish, c. 1400–1560*, Aldershot 1996

Lambert, M., *Medieval heresy: popular movements from Gregorian reform to the Reformation*, 3rd edn, Oxford 2002

Lander, J. R., *Government and community: England, 1450–1509*, London 1980

Lee, P., *Nunneries, learning and spirituality in late medieval English society: the Dominican priory of Dartford*, Woodbridge 2001

Levi, G., 'On microhistory', in P. Burke (ed.), *New perspectives on historical writing*, Cambridge 1991, 93–113

Lewis, K. J., *The cult of St Katherine of Alexandria in late medieval England*, Woodbridge 2000

Lightfoot, W. J. (ed.), 'Notes from the records of Hawkhurst church', *AC* v (1863), 79–84

Lutgens, C., 'The case of Waghen vs. Sutton: conflict over burial rights in late medieval England', *Medieval Studies* xxxviii (1976), 145–84

Lutton, R., 'Godparenthood, kinship and piety in Tenterden, England, 1449–1537', in I. Davis, M. Muller and S. Rees Jones (eds), *Love, marriage and family ties in the Middle Ages*, Turnhout 2003, 217–34

Luxton, I., 'The Lichfield court book; a postscript', *BIHR* xliv (1971), 120–5

MacCulloch, D., *Suffolk and the Tudors: politics and religion in an English county, 1500–1600*, Oxford 1986

—— *The later Reformation in England, 1547–1603*, Basingstoke 1990

—— *Thomas Cranmer*, New Haven–London 1996

—— *Tudor Church militant: Edward VI and the Protestant Reformation*, London 1999

MacFarlane, A., *The origins of English individualism*, Oxford 1978

McFarlane, K. B., *Lancastrian kings and Lollard knights*, Oxford 1972

McIntosh, M. K., *Autonomy and community: the royal manor of Havering, 1200–1500*, Cambridge 1986

—— 'Local change and community control in England, 1465–1500', *Huntington Library Quarterly* xlix (1986), 219–42

—— *A community transformed: the manor and liberty of Havering, 1500–1620*, Cambridge 1991

McSheffrey, S., *Gender and heresy: women and men in Lollard communities, 1420–1530*, Philadelphia 1995

Mace, J. E., *Notes on old Tenterden*, Tenterden 1902

Manning, B. L., *The people's faith in the time of Wyclif*, Cambridge 1919

Marsh, C., *Popular religion in sixteenth-century England*, Basingstoke–London 1998

—— 'In the name of God? Will-making and faith in early modern England', in G. H. Martin and P. Spufford (eds), *The records of the nation: the Public Record Office, 1838–1988: the British Record Society, 1888–1988*, Woodbridge 1990, 215–49

—— *The Family of Love in English society, 1550–1630*, Cambridge 1994

Marshall, P., *Beliefs and the dead in Reformation England*, Oxford 2002

—— 'Evangelical conversion in the reign of Henry VIII', in Marshall and Ryrie, *Beginnings of English Protestantism*, 14–37

—— and A. Ryrie, 'Protestantisms and their beginnings', in Marshall and Ryrie, *Beginnings of English Protestantism*, 1–13

—— and A. Ryrie (eds), *The beginnings of English Protestantism*, Cambridge 2002

Mason, E., 'The role of the English parishioner, 1100–1500', *JEH* xxvii (1976), 17–29

Mate, M. E., 'The East Sussex land market and agrarian class structure in the late Middle Ages', *P&P* cxxxix (1993), 46–65

Mayhew, G. J., 'The progress of the Reformation in East Sussex, 1530–1539: the evidence from wills', *Southern History* v (1983), 38–67

—— *Tudor Rye*, Brighton 1987

Mertes, R. G. K. A., 'The household as a religious community', in J. Rosenthal and C. Richmond (eds), *People, politics and community in the later Middle Ages*, Gloucester 1987, 123–39

Morris, R., *Churches in the landscape*, London 1989

Muir, E., 'Introduction: observing trifles', in E. Muir and G. Ruggiero (eds), *Microhistory and the lost peoples of Europe*, Baltimore–London 1991, pp. vii–xviii

Neame, A., *The holy maid of Kent: the life of Elizabeth Barton, 1506–1534*, London 1971

Needham, R., 'Polythetic classification', *Man* x (1975), 349–69

A new English dictionary on historical principles, ed. J. A. H. Murray, Oxford 1843

Newman, J., *West Kent and the Weald: the buildings of England*, London 1980

O'Day, R., *The debate on the English Reformation*, London–New York 1986

O'Hara, D., ' "Ruled by my friends": aspects of marriage in the diocese of Canterbury, c. 1540–1570', *C&C* vi (1991), 9–41

—— *Courtship and constraint: rethinking the making of marriage in Tudor England*, Manchester 2000

Orme, N., 'Church and chapel in medieval England', *TRHS* 6th ser. vi (1996), 75–102

Osler, W., *Thomas Linacre*, Cambridge 1908

Outhwaite, R. B., *Inflation in Tudor and early Stuart England*, London–Melbourne–Toronto 1969

Owen, D. M., *Church and society in medieval Lincolnshire* (Society for Lincolnshire History and Archaeology, History of Lincolnshire v, 1971)

—— 'Medieval chapels in Lincolnshire', *Lincolnshire History and Archaeology* x (1975), 15–22

Palliser, D. M., 'Popular reactions to the Reformation during the years of uncertainty, 1530–1570', in F. Heal and R. O'Day (eds), *Church and society in England: Henry VIII to James I*, London 1977, 35–56

—— 'Introduction: the parish in perspective', in Wright, *Parish, Church and people*, 5–25

Pantin, W. A., *The English Church in the fourteenth century*, Cambridge 1955

Pearson, S., *The medieval houses of Kent: an historical analysis*, London 1994

Penny, D. A., 'Family matters and Foxe's *Acts and monuments*', *Historical Journal* xxxix (1996), 599–618

Peters, C., *Patterns of piety: women, gender and religion in late medieval and Reformation England*, Cambridge 2003

Pfaff, R. W., *New liturgical feasts in later medieval England*, Oxford 1970

—— 'The English devotion of St Gregory's Trental', *Speculum* xlix (1974), 75–90

Phythian-Adams, C., 'Ceremony and the citizen: the communal year at Coventry, 1450–1550', in P. Clark and P. Slack (eds), *Crisis and order in English towns, 1500–1700*, London 1972, 57–85

—— *Desolation of a city: Coventry and the urban crisis of the late Middle Ages*, Cambridge 1979

Plomer, H. R., 'Books mentioned in wills', *Transactions of the Bibliographical Society* vii (1904), 99–121

Plumb, D., 'The social and economic spread of rural Lollardy: a reappraisal', in W. J. Sheils and D. Wood (eds), *Voluntary religion* (SCH xxiii, 1986), 111–29

——— 'A gathered Church? Lollards and their society', in Spufford, *World of rural dissenters*, 132–63

——— 'The social and economic status of the later Lollards', in Spufford, *World of rural dissenters*, 103–31

Po-chia Hsia, R., 'Civic wills as sources for the study of piety in Muenster, 1530–1618', *Sixteenth Century Journal* xiv (1983), 321–48

Poos, L. R., *A rural society after the Black Death, Essex, 1350–1525*, Cambridge 1991

Prior, E. S., 'The sculpture of alabaster tables', *Illustrated catalogue*, 16–50

Quiney, A., *English domestic architecture: Kent houses*, Woodbridge 1993

Raftis, J. A., *Warboys: two hundred years in the life of an English mediaeval village*, Toronto 1974

Razi, Z., 'The myth of the immutable English family', *P&P* cxl (1993), 3–44

Rex, R., 'The friars in the English Reformation', in Marshall and Ryrie, *Beginnings of English Protestantism*, 38–59

——— *The Lollards*, Basingstoke–New York 2002

Reynolds, S., *Kingdoms and communities in western Europe, 900–1300*, Oxford 1984

Richmond, C., 'The English gentry and religion, c. 1500', in C. Harper-Bill (ed.), *Religious belief and ecclesiastical careers in late medieval England*, Woodbridge 1991, 127–50

Riddy, F., 'Mother knows best: reading social change in a courtesy text', *Speculum* lxxi (1996), 66–86

Rigby, S. H., *English society in the later Middle Ages: class, status and gender*, Houndmills–London 1995

Roberts, H., *Tenterden: the first thousand years*, York 1995

Robertson, Canon S., 'On Kentish rood-screens', AC xiv (1882), 370–3

Rollason, D. W., *The Mildrith legend: a study in early medieval hagiography in England*, Leicester 1982

Rosser, G., *Medieval Westminster, 1200–1540*, Oxford 1989

——— 'Communities of parish and guild in the late Middle Ages', in Wright, *Parish, Church and people*, 29–55

——— 'Parochial conformity and voluntary religion in late-medieval England', TRHS 6th ser. i (1991), 173–9

——— 'Going to the fraternity feast: commensality and social relations in late medieval England', *Journal of British Studies* xxxiii (1994), 430–46

Rubin, M., *Charity and community in medieval Cambridge*, Cambridge 1987

——— *Corpus Christi*, Cambridge 1991

——— 'Small groups: identity and solidarity in the late Middle Ages', in J. Kermode (ed.), *Enterprise and individuals in fifteenth-century England*, Stroud 1991, 132–50

Ryrie, A., 'Counting sheep, counting shepherds: the problem of allegiance in the English Reformation', in Marshall and Ryrie, *Beginnings of English Protestantism*, 84–110

——— *The Gospel and Henry VIII: evangelicals in the early English Reformation*, Cambridge 2003

St John Hope, W. H., 'On the early working of alabaster in England', *Illustrated catalogue*, 1–15

Scammel, G., 'Shipowning in England, c. 1450–1550', *TRHS* 5th ser. xii (1962), 105–22

Scarisbrick, J. J., *The Reformation and the English people*, Oxford 1984

Schweitzer, P. P. (ed.), *Dividends of kinship: meanings and uses of social relatedness*, London–New York 2000

Searle, E., *Lordship and community: Battle abbey and its banlieu, 1066–1538*, Toronto 1974

Shagan, E. H., *Popular politics and the English Reformation*, Cambridge 2003

Sharp, B., *In contempt of all authority: rural artisans and riot in the west of England, 1586–1660*, Berkeley, Ca.–London 1980

Sheils, W. J., 'Catholics and their neighbours in a rural community: Egton Chapelry, 1590–1780', *Northern History* xxxiv (1998), 109–33

————— 'Household, age and gender among Jacobean Yorkshire recusants', in M. B. Rowlands (ed.), *English Catholics of parish and town, 1558–1778*, London 1999, 131–52

————— and S. Sheils, 'Textiles and reform: Halifax and its hinterland', in P. Collinson and J. Craig (eds), *The Reformation in English towns, 1500–1640*, Basingstoke 1998, 130–43

Slavin, A. J., 'Upstairs, downstairs: or the roots of reformation', *Huntington Library Quarterly* xxxxix (1986), 243–60

Smith, R. M., 'Kin and neighbours in a thirteenth century Suffolk community', *Journal of Family History* iv (1979), 219–56

————— 'Some issues concerning families and their property in rural England, 1250–1800', in Smith, *Land, kinship, and life cycle*, 1–86

————— (ed.), *Land, kinship, and life cycle*, Cambridge 1984

Smith, T. P., 'The Roper gateway, St Dunstan's street, Canterbury', *AC* cviii (1991), 163–82

Spufford, M., *Contrasting communities: English villagers in the sixteenth and seventeenth centuries*, Cambridge 1974

————— 'The importance of religion in the sixteenth and seventeenth centuries', in Spufford, *World of rural dissenters*, 1–102

————— (ed.), *The world of rural dissenters, 1520–1725*, Cambridge 1995

Spufford, P., 'The comparative mobility and immobility of Lollard descendants in early modern England', in Spufford, *World of rural dissenters*, 309–31

Summers, W. H., *The Lollards of the Chiltern hills: glimpses of English dissent in the Middle Ages*, London 1906

Swanson, H., *Medieval artisans: an urban class in late medieval England*, Oxford 1989

Swanson, R. N., *Church and society in late medieval England*, Oxford 1989

————— *Catholic England: faith, religion and observance before the Reformation*, Manchester 1993

————— 'Literacy, heresy, history and orthodoxy: perspectives and permutations for the later Middle Ages', in Biller and Hudson, *Heresy and literacy*, 279–93

————— (ed.), *Religion and devotion in Europe, c. 1215–c. 1515*, Cambridge 1995

Sweetinburgh, S., *The role of the hospital in medieval England: gift-giving and the spiritual economy*, Dublin 2004

Tanner, N. P., *The Church in late medieval Norwich*, Toronto 1984

——— 'The Reformation and regionalism: further reflections on the Church in late medieval Norwich', in Thomson, *Towns and townspeople*, 129–47

Taylor, A. H., 'The chapel of St John the Baptist, Small Hythe', AC xxx (1914), 133–92

——— 'The rectors and vicars of St Mildred's, Tenterden', AC xxxi (1915), 207–20

——— 'The municipal records of Tenterden, part i', AC xxxii (1917), 283–97, 300–2

——— 'The municipal records of Tenterden: part ii', AC xxxiii (1918), 108–11

——— 'The will of a medieval Kentish parson', AC xliii (1931), 123–32

——— 'The clergy of St John the Baptist, Smallhythe', AC lv (1943), 26–8

Thirsk, J., 'Industries in the countryside', in F. J. Fisher (ed.), *Essays in the economic and social history of Tudor and Stuart England*, Cambridge 1961, 70–88

Thomas, K., *Religion and the decline of magic*, New York 1971

Thompson, A. H., *The English clergy and their organization in the later Middle Ages*, Oxford 1947

Thompson, B., 'Monasteries, society and reform in late medieval England', in Clark, *Religious orders*, 165–95

Thompson, E. P., *Customs in common* (1991), London 1993

Thomson, J. A. F., 'Tithe disputes in later medieval London', EHR lxxviii (1963), 1–17

——— 'A Lollard rising in Kent: 1431 or 1438?', BIHR xxxvii (1964), 100–2

——— *The later Lollards, 1414–1520*, Oxford 1965

——— 'Piety and charity in late medieval London', JEH xvi (1965), 178–95

——— *The early Tudor Church and society, 1485–1529*, London 1993

——— (ed.), *Towns and townspeople in the fifteenth century*, Gloucester 1987

Thrupp, S., *The merchant class of medieval London, 1300–1500*, Chicago 1948

Toussaert, J., *Le Sentiment religieux en Flandre à la fin du moyen âge*, Paris 1960

Tupling, G. H., 'The pre-Reformation parishes and chapelries of Lancashire', *Transactions of the Lancashire and Cheshire Antiquarian Society* lxvii (1957), 1–16

Tyrrell-Green, E., *Parish church architecture*, London 1924

Underdown, D., *Revel, riot and rebellion: popular politics and culture in England, 1603–1660*, Oxford 1985

Vale, M. G. A., *Piety, charity and literacy among the Yorkshire gentry, 1370–1480* (Borthwick Papers l, 1976)

Victoria history of the county of Kent, ii, ed. W. Page, London 1926

Vovelle, M., *Piété baroque et déchristianisation: les attitudes devant le mort en Provence au XVIII siècle*, Paris 1973

——— *Ideologies and mentalities*, Cambridge 1990

Wabuda, S., *Preaching during the English Reformation*, Cambridge 2002

——— 'Sanctified by the believing spouse: women, men and the marital yoke in the early Reformation', in Marshall and Ryrie, *Beginnings of English Protestantism*, 111–28

Wall, R., 'Household and kinship', HWJ xii (1981), 199

Wallenberg, J. K., *Kentish place-names*, Uppsala 1931

——— *The place-names of Kent*, Uppsala 1934

Ward, G., 'Saxon records of Tenterden', AC xlix (1938) 229–46

Whiting, R., *The blind devotion of the people: popular religion and the English Reformation*, Cambridge 1989

Winnifrith, J., 'The 'priest' house at Smallhythe: a false identification', AC xcvi (1980), 363–6

—— 'The medieval church of St Mary, Ebony, and its successors', AC c (1985), 157–63

Witney, K. P., *The Jutish forest: a study of the Weald of Kent from 450 to 1380 A.D.*, London 1976

Wood-Legh, K. L., *Perpetual chantries in Britain*, Cambridge 1965

Wright, S. J. (ed.), *Parish, Church and people: local studies in lay religion, 1350–1750*, London 1988

Wrightson, K., 'Household and kinship in sixteenth century England', HWJ xii (1981), 151–8

—— 'Kinship in an English village: Terling, Essex, 1500–1700', in Smith, *Land, kinship, and life cycle*, 313–22

—— and D. Levine, *Poverty and piety in an English village: Terling, 1525–1700*, New York–San Francisco–London 1979

Zell, M. L., 'The personnel of the clergy in Kent in the Reformation period', EHR lxxxix (1974), 513–33

—— 'The use of religious preambles as a measure of religious belief in the sixteenth century', BIHR i (1977), 246–9

—— 'Population and family structure in the sixteenth-century Weald', AC c (1984), 231–57

—— 'A wood-pasture agrarian regime: the Kentish Weald in the sixteenth century', SH vii (1985), 69–93

—— *Industry in the countryside: Wealden society in the sixteenth century*, Cambridge 1994

Unpublished theses and papers

Dinn, R. B., 'Popular religion in late medieval Bury St Edmunds', unpubl. PhD diss. Manchester 1990

Draper, G., G. Hornby, J. Hosking, C. Richardson and A. Wiggins, 'The fitting of the altars: gender and popular piety in east Kent', paper given at the Summer Conference of the Ecclesiastical History Society, University of Kent at Canterbury 1996, held by the Templeman Library, University of Kent

Higgs, L. M. A., 'Lay piety in the borough of Colchester, 1485–1558', unpubl. PhD diss. Michigan 1983

Lee, P., 'Monastic and secular religion and devotional reading in late medieval Dartford and West Kent', unpubl. PhD diss. Kent 1998

Roberts, J., 'Tenterden houses: a study of the domestic buildings of a Kent parish in their social and economic environment', unpubl. PhD diss. Nottingham 1990

Index

227

Felip, Edward, churchwarden of St
    Mildred's, Tenterden, 121
Felip, George, bailiff of Tenterden, 125
Felip, Stephen, 98
festivals: Relics Sunday, 161. See also
    Lollardy; saints
Fletcher, John, 94
Foche, Robert, 125
Fordman, Thomas, parochianus of St
    Mildred's, Tenterden, 123
Foule, family: bailiffs, service as, 41, 187;
    churchwardens, service as, 42; freemen
    among, 41; gentry, links with, 187–8;
    industrial activity of, 43; jurats, service
    as, 41; kinship of, 144; land market
    activity of, 40–1; property of, 43;
    taxable wealth of, 40; testamentary
    piety of, 48, 144, 187
Foule, Bartholomew, 43
Foule, Elizabeth, 43
Foule, John, generosus and bailiff of
    Tenterden, 41, 43, 126, 127
Foule, Katherine, 53, 99
Foule, William, 43, 53, 99
Fowlyn, John, 151–2
Franke, John, 162, 170, 176–7
Franke, Robert, 162, 167, 170, 176–7
Franke, Thomas, 177
Freeston, James, servant, 204
friars, see religious orders. See also religious
    houses
Frittenden (Kent), 153, 156
Fuller, John, priest, 203–4
funerals, see obsequies
funeral doles, see obsequies

gender, see testamentary piety. See also
    Lollardy
Gervese, family: agricultural activity of,
    45; bailiffs, service as, 41, 42;
    churchwardens, service as, 42; freemen
    among, 41; industrial activity of, 45;
    land market activity of, 41; taxable
    wealth of, 40; testamentary piety of,
    48–9
Gervese, William, 41, 45
Gibbon, family: testamentary piety of,
    48–9
Gibbon, Thomas, 54
gilds, see fraternities
Gillingham (Kent), 150
Glover, John, 152, 153
Glover, Thomas, 152
Godmersham (Kent), 154, 155, 156

godparenthood, see kinship
Great Chart (Kent), 154
Grebill, family, 157, 160, 163–5, 168, 169;
    household of, 165; property of, 175. See
    also Grevill, Thomas
Grebill, Agnes, 155, 156, 159, 163–5,
    169
Grebill, Christopher, tailor, 157, 159, 160,
    163–4, 165, 170, 182
Grebill, John, jun., 157, 163–4, 175
Grebill, John, sen., 155–6, 160, 163–4,
    169, 175
Grenestede, Thomas, 'alleged chaplain',
    151–2
Grevill, Thomas, 175
Gryme, Thomas, Sir, priest, 109
Guldeford, family, 193: and Cinque Ports,
    47, 188; and heresy, 189; humanism,
    interest in, 189, 191; piety of, 47;
    property of, 47; and reform, 126,
    188–9; Tenterden families, links with,
    188–9
Guldeford, Edward, Sir, 47, 188, 189
Guldeford, Henry, Sir, 189
Guldeford, John, Sir, 58, 66, 89, 98, 191;
    fulling mill of, Tenterden, 174; piety of,
    188
Guldeford, Richard, Sir, 109; piety of, 188;
    pilgrimage of, 188

Hale, John, 171 n. 112
Hales, family: and chapel of St John the
    Baptist, Small Hythe, 126; legal careers
    of, 47; property of, 47, 188; and
    Reformation, 47, 187–8
Hales, Christopher, MP for Canterbury
    and Master of the Rolls, 187–8, 193
Hales, Edward, bailiff of Tenterden, 47
Hales, Henry, 46
Hales, James, Sir, 126, 188
Hales, John, MP for Canterbury and
    second baron of the exchequer, 46–7,
    191, 193
Harry, Thomas, of High Halden, 153
Harry, Thomas, 'labourer', 153
Harry, Thomas, 'of Redyng', 173
Harryson, George, 111, 117
Harryson, Robert, 155, 160, 165, 182
Harwode, family, 166
Harwode, Joan, 156
Harwode, Philip, 156, 163
Harwode, Thomas, 155, 156
Harynden, William, bailiff of Tenterden,
    135